Naturalistic Realism and the Antirealist Challenge

Representation and Mind

Hilary Putnam and Ned Block, editors

Representation and Reality Hilary Putnam

Explaining Behavior: Reasons in a World of Causes Fred Dretske

The Metaphysics of Meaning Jerrold J. Katz

A Theory of Content and Other Essays Jerry A. Fodor

The Realistic Spirit: Wittgenstein, Philosophy, and the Mind Cora Diamond

The Unity of the Self Stephen L. White

The Imagery Debate Michael Tye

A Study of Concepts Christopher Peacocke

The Rediscovery of the Mind John R. Searle

Past, Space, and Self John Campbell

Mental Reality Galen Strawson

Ten Problems of Consciousness: A Representational Theory of the Phenomenal Mind Michael Tye

Representations, Targets, and Attitudes Robert Cummins

Starmaking: Realism, Anti-Realism, and Irrealism Peter J. McCormick (ed.)

A Logical Journey: From Gödel to Philosophy Hao Wang

Brainchildren: Essays on Designing Minds Daniel C. Dennett

Realistic Rationalism Jerrold J. Katz

The Paradox of Self-Consciousness José Luis Bermúdez

In Critical Condition: Polemical Essays on Cognitive Science and the Philosophy of Mind Jerry Fodor

Mind in a Physical World: An Essay on the Mind-Body Problem and Mental Causation Jaegwon Kim

The Mind Doesn't Work That Way Jerry Fodor

New Essays on Semantic Externalism and Self-Knowledge Susana Nuccetelli

Consciousness and Persons: Unity and Identity Michael Tye

Naturalistic Realism and the Antirealist Challenge Drew Khlentzos

Naturalistic Realism and the Antirealist Challenge

Drew Khlentzos

A Bradford Book
The MIT Press
Cambridge, Massachusetts
London, England

First MIT Press paperback edition, 2005

© 2004 Massachusetts Institute of Technology

All rights reserved. No part of this book may be reproduced in any form by any electronic or mechanical means (including photocopying, recording, or information storage and retrieval) without permission in writing from the publisher.

This book was set in New Baskerville on 3B2 by Asco Typesetters, Hong Kong.

Library of Congress Cataloging-in-Publication Data

Khlentzos, Drew.
  Naturalistic realism and the antirealist challenge / Drew Khlentzos.
    p. cm. — (Representation and mind)
  "A Bradford book."
  Includes bibliographical references and index.
  ISBN 978-0-262-11285-7 (hc : alk. paper), 978-0-262-61209-8 (pb)
  1. Realism. 2. Naturalism. I. Title. II. Series.
  B835.K49   2004
  149′.2—dc22
                                                    2003059679

Contents

Preface vii

Introduction: Naturalistic Realism and Antirealism 1

I
Metaphysical Realism and Truth 11

1
Contesting Realism 13

II
Dummett's Antirealism 45

2
The Antirealist Arguments 47

3
Realist Replies to Antirealism 75

4
Intuitionistic Foundations of Antirealism 117

III
Putnam's Internalism 185

5
The Internalist Critique of Realism 187

6
Models, Representation, and Reality   225

7
Internalism, Pluralism, and Antirepresentationalism   247

IV
Prospects for Naturalistic Realism   279

8
Realism, Facts, and Truth   281

Notes   355
References   391
Index   401

Preface

Metaphysical realism is a little like religion. It has its zealots who accept the doctrines uncritically; it has its thoughtful apologists, its agnostics and apostates too. Metaphysical realism *is* the religion of some. I wrote this book for the reason most philosophers write books: I was curious. I was curious to see whether metaphysical realism could withstand the innovative attacks on it due to Michael Dummett and Hilary Putnam. What I wanted to find out was whether the form of realism I find most appealing—a naturalistic form—could answer the antirealist challenge. In the pages that follow the reader will find my answer to that question.

It is an affirmative answer, although a qualified affirmative. One thing that emerged from my investigations was that neither realists nor their antirealist opponents seem to have grasped fully what the antirealist's semantic challenge to realism actually *was*. When this is set out, it emerges that although there is strong evidence *that* metaphysical realism is true, we have no positive account at all of *how* this can be.

Although I expect no conversions to my way of seeing things, I hope that realists who read this book will realize, if they have not done so already, that antirealist arguments cannot be easily dismissed. To the contrary, these arguments raise fundamental questions to which *no one* has good answers. Antirealists who read this book will, I think, find much with which they can agree, although I do not expect them to be fully persuaded either. The most I can hope is that they will be stimulated to think some more about these issues.

This book is primarily for those who are undecided about the issues and who genuinely want to understand what motivates either side in the dispute between realism and antirealism. I place a high value on philosophical fairness. Partisan presentations only damage the credibility of the presenter. So I hope that my exegesis of antirealism is accurate and comprehensive.

Early versions of some of the ideas in chapters 2 and 3 appeared in chapters 1 and 2 of my *Realism, Rationality, and Truth*, REFIA Moscow, 2001. Section 3.3 is based on my 1989 *Dialectica* article, "Anti-Realism Under Mind?" My thanks to the editor of REFIA Press and to the editor of *Dialectica* for permission to make use of this material here.

I have many people to thank for many sorts of support. My greatest intellectual debt is to my former dissertation advisor, Dr. Peter Röper—fifteen years on, I still owe him more than I can ever hope to repay. My thanks also to those who have read and commented on various parts of the book. I cannot hope to mention all but a list must include William Grey, Michaelis Michael, Barry Taylor, and Neil Tennant, as well as my colleagues at the University of New England—in particular, Arcady Blinov and Tony Lynch. I am especially grateful to my colleague Peter Forrest for the many conversations we've enjoyed over the years about matters related to realism. I am very grateful to Lindsay Rowlands for his work in preparing the manuscript for publication.

My greatest debt is to my family—to my four children Alexander, David, Stephen, and Georgina, and above all to my wife Philippa to whom in love and gratitude this book is dedicated.

Introduction: Naturalistic Realism and Antirealism

A Historical Conundrum

When the conversation turns to metaphysical realism, anyone who believes what I believe apparently has an awful lot of explaining to do—at least, if current wisdom is anything to go by. I hold that metaphysical realism is a thesis about the nature of the world and what it contains, and as such it has nothing to do with how humans represent that world in thought and word. Yet I also hold that this very thesis is vulnerable to a semantic challenge that asks precisely how humans represent the world in thought and word.

In fact, there is no great mystery here. The connection is simple and direct. If metaphysical realism is true, its critics aver, there *can be no* explanation of how humans mentally represent the world. The real mystery is not how semantics and metaphysics are thus connected but why both sides in the now notorious realist–antirealist dispute failed to make this connection explicit. What went wrong? In section 1.2 of chapter 1, under the heading "A Sorry History of Misunderstandings," I set out some of the false starts and dialectical anomalies that have dogged the dispute between realism and antirealism from the beginning, and which partially explain why today this dispute is regarded by many either as a dead one or else as one that we must transcend. After faltering attempts to characterize each others' views, mutual incomprehension predictably led to polarization and entrenchment. One had only to look at the controversy surrounding the status of Putnam's model-theoretic argument to get the feeling that there could be no metaphysically neutral standpoint from which one could assess who was right with regard to this issue. It was as if reporting on the skirmish was impossible without joining one or other of the warring armies.

Things need not have gone that way, however, and it is, in my view, a great pity that they did. It led to a comfortable consensus among those attracted to the most fashionable form of metaphysical realism today, naturalistic realism, that their metaphysics had nothing at all to fear from antirealist attacks, which they saw as based on a confusion of semantics with metaphysics. If this is your view and you do not wish to forsake this comforting illusion, my suggestion is blunt: do not read on! Take Hume's advice and consign this book to the flames, for in it, I argue that it is precisely this metaphysical view—naturalistic realism— that is most vulnerable to the antirealist challenge. In the remainder of this introduction, though, I set out what I take realism to be, what I take the antirealist challenge to consist in, and what theses I shall defend in this book.

1 What Is Realism?

Realism[1] is the thesis that the objects, properties, and relations the world contains exist independently of our thoughts about them or our perceptions of them. *Naturalistic realism* holds in addition that the world's constituents are those posited by our best overall theory of nature. Antirealists either doubt or deny the *existence* of the entities the realist believes in or else doubt or deny their *independence* from our conceptions of them. As a sample of current realist–antirealist debates concerning the *existence* of particular sorts of entities or properties: Are there moral values? What of abstract objects like numbers or spaces or symphonies? Are there selves or minds? What of afterimages, pains, and other sensations? Is the past in some sense real? What of the future? Are fictional characters in some sense real? Do muons and quarks and other theoretical entities exist?

Similar questions could be and have been raised about the *mind-independence* of the disputed entities or properties. For example, many think that colors are mind-dependent. That is, although they do not dispute the existence of things that are red, green, or blue, they think that if no sentient creatures had ever evolved nothing would have been colored. If not in the eye of the perceiver, the tomato's redness is nonexistent. Others deem moral values mind-dependent. Once more, they do not doubt the existence of moral values but instead question their independence from the mind, believing them instead to be psychological or social constructs of some sort or other. Neither Dummett nor Putnam is concerned with such local realist–antirealist skirmishes. They both purport to find metaphysical realism incoherent. The world cannot be as it is independently of what human conceivers take it to be. Their antirealism is thus systematic or global. However, their common opposition to metaphysical realism springs from very different metaphysical commitments, to such an extent that it is not really appropriate to call Putnam's own metaphysical position antirealist. Putnam has never fully endorsed the verificationism Dummett has consistently argued for. Neither has he been prepared to follow Dummett in contesting certain fixed points in commonsense thinking about the world.

An obvious problem with the above characterization of realism in terms of mind-independent existence is that it seems to make antirealism about minds or experience obligatory, for the existence of minds is surely "mind-dependent." To be sure, but *the world's containing minds* is not. This is a mind-independent fact if there are minds at all, according to the metaphysical realist.

Note that naturalistic realists are *not* compelled to adopt scientific realism simply because they see science as the final arbiter of truth. They may be agnostic in the end as to the ultimate constituents of reality. They are naturalistic realists, though, to the extent that they regard this question as the sort of question that only our total theory of nature can decide, but which, in the absence of any conclusive decision from that quarter, still has an answer not constrained by human perception and conception. *Scientific realism and metaphysical realism are distinct.*

2 Realism and Factualism

It is often claimed that realism is a thesis about discourses or theories—that the sentences in some discourse or theory are to be construed literally as fact-stating ones. Call this view *factualism*. It is often added that what these sentences state is largely true. This is a mistake. The antirealist views of Michael Dummett and Hilary Putnam are factualist about the discourses describing certain contentious domains. What they contest is that the entities in these domains can exist mind-independently. Realism about a given class of entities may entail that discourse about them is factual, but it certainly does not entail that most of our assertions concerning them are true. To the contrary, all our claims about the relevant domain could be mistaken. Consider medieval discourse about the cosmos. The medievals surely did believe that the cosmos was as it was, independently of what anyone thought about it. They were realists about the cosmos. Yet most of their beliefs were false, not true.

3 The Problem of Representation

Realism is a metaphysical thesis about what the world is like, what it contains. It is not a semantic thesis concerned with how humans represent the world in thought or language. *How, then, can it be vulnerable to a semantic challenge?*

Quite simply: If the world is as resolutely mind-independent as the realist makes out, there is a problem about how we get to know about it in the first place. On what grounds can we trust our theories if they could all be radically mistaken? Wouldn't a truly mind-independent world make any representation of it in thought or language unreliable or even impossible? These are precisely the questions antirealists urge in their various semantic challenges to realism. Realists do think, in the main, that we are able to represent the world reliably. Scientific realists think science is the best representation we have of what the world is like and that its representations correspond pretty closely to the way things actually are. Yet it is crucial to their position that even our best scientific theories—general relativity, quantum theory, the theory of evolution—could be radically mistaken. For the scientist's representations of the world to be reliable, there must be a correlation between these representations and the states of affairs they portray. So the cosmologist who utters the statement "The entropy of the big bang was remarkably low" has uttered a truth if and only if the entropy of the big bang was remarkably low. Thus a natural question to ask is how the correlation between the statement and the mind-independent state of affairs that makes it true is supposed to be set up. How does it come about that the word "entropy" refers to the amount of disorder in a system, that the descriptive name "the big bang" refers to the event with which the universe began? The only plausible answer is that it is something about the way we use our words or deploy our mental symbols in thought and action that effects this correlation between mental symbol and worldly referent. Suppose this is not so. Assume instead that God or nature has solved this problem for us. God or nature has set up just the right connections between our mental symbols and the bits of the world we take ourselves to be referring to in thought. Still we face the problem of finding evidence that this has occurred. Yet it seems the relevant evidence will be just what it was if God or nature had not been so obliging—linguistically, it will be the use speakers make of their words, the statements they endorse and the statements they dissent from, the rationalizations they provide for their actions, their defense and explanations of their views and criticisms of opposing views, and so on; cognitively, it will be the functional role of mental symbols in thought, perception, language learning, and so on.

A main contention of this book is that realism is vulnerable to antirealist attack precisely because the representation problem remains unsolved. We have, I will argue, strong evidence *that* we are able to represent mind-independent states of affairs, but we have no believable extant account of *how* this is possible.

4 Overview of the Antirealist Challenges to Realism

Manifestation

The first antirealist challenge we consider derives from Michael Dummett and focuses on the use we make of our words and sentences. The challenge is simply this: What aspect of our linguistic use could provide the necessary evidence for the realist's correlation between sentences and mind-independent states of affairs? Which aspects of our semantic behavior, linguistic or cognitive, manifest our grasp of these correlations, assuming they do hold? When we look at how speakers actually use their sentences, antirealists claim, we see them responding not to states of affairs that they cannot in general detect but rather to agreed on conditions for asserting these sentences. Scientists assert "The entropy of the big bang was remarkably low" because they all concur that the conditions justifying this assertion have been met. What prompts us to use our sentences in the ways we do are the public justification conditions associated with those sentences, justification conditions forged in linguistic practices that imbue these sentences with meaning. The realist believes we are able mentally to represent mind-independent states of affairs. But what of cases where everything that we know about the world leaves it unsettled whether the relevant state of affairs obtains? Did Socrates sneeze in his sleep the night before he took the hemlock or did he not? How could we possibly find out? Yet realists hold that the sentence "Socrates sneezed in his sleep the night before he took the hemlock" is true if Socrates did sneeze then and false if he did not, and that this is a significant semantic fact.

The manifestation challenge to realism is to isolate some feature of the use agents make of their words or their mental symbols that effects the link between mind-independent states of affairs and the thoughts and sentences that represent them. Nothing in the thinker's linguistic behaviour, according to the antirealist, provides evidence that this link has been forged since linguistic use is keyed to public assertibility conditions, not undetectable truth conditions. In those cases, such as that of Socrates, where we cannot find out whether or not the truth condition is satisfied, it is simply gratuitous to believe that there is anything we can think or say or do that could provide evidence that the link has been set up in the first place. So the antirealist claims. Dummett's manifestation argument forms the focus of chapter 2 and is laid out after some essential stage-setting in section 2.3. Dummett's views are subtle and systematic. Partly because of this, they are notoriously difficult to comprehend. This is why much of chapter 2 and some of chapter 3 is exegetical. Chapter 3 is concerned to use the resources of naturalistic realism to rebuff the manifestation challenge.

Language Acquisition

An antirealist challenge related to the manifestation challenge concerns our acquisition of language. Suppose God had linked our mental representations to just the right states of affairs in the way required by the realist. If so, this is a semantically significant fact. Anyone learning his native language would have to grasp these correspondences between sentences and states of affairs. But how can one do this if even the competent speakers one seeks to emulate cannot detect when these correspondences hold? In short, competence in one's language would be impossible to acquire if realism were true.

Brains in a Vat?

States of affairs that are truly mind-independent go hand in glove with radical skepticism. The skeptic contends that for all we can tell we could be brains in a vat—brains kept alive in a bath of nutrients by mad alien scientists. All our thoughts, all our experience, all that passed for science would be systematically mistaken if we were. We'd have no bodies although we thought we did; the world would contain no physical objects, yet it would seem to us that it did; there'd be no Earth, no Sun, no vast universe, only the brain's deluded representations of such. At least this could be the case if our representations derived even part of their content from links with mind-independent objects and states of affairs. According to antirealists, since realism implies such an absurd possibility could hold without our being able to detect it, it has to be rejected. A much stronger antirealist argument due to Hilary Putnam, examined in section 5.3, proceeds by claiming that *if we were brains in a vat we could not possibly have the thought that we were.* If we were so envatted, we could not possibly mean by "brain" and "vat" what unenvatted folk mean by these words, since our words would be connected only to neural impulses or images in our brains whereas the unenvatteds' words are connected to real-life brains and real-life vats. Similarly, the thought we pondered whenever we posed the question "Am I a brain in a vat?" could not possibly be the thought unenvatted folk pose when they ask themselves the same-sounding question in English. But realism entails that we could indeed be brains in a vat. As we have just shown that were we to be so, we could not even entertain this as a possibility, realism is incoherent.

Conceptual Relativity

Antirealists follow Kant in rejecting any notion of a mind-independent reality as that to which we have cognitive access. The mind has access to reality only through the mediation of a conceptual scheme for representing that reality. Realists think there is a unitary sense of "object," "property," and so on for which the question "What objects and properties does the world contain?" makes sense.

Antirealists who follow Putnam's lead reject this claim. For them, terms like "object" and "property" shift their senses as we move from one conceptual scheme to another. There cannot be a totality of all the objects the world contains since the notion of "object" is indefinitely extensible, and so, trivially, there cannot be a privileged description of any such totality.

How does the antirealist defend conceptual relativity? Putnam does so by arguing that there can be two complete theories of the world that are *descriptively equivalent yet logically incompatible from the realist's point of view*. For example, theories of space-time can be formulated in one of two mathematically equivalent ways: either with an ontology of points, where spatiotemporal regions are defined as sets of points, or with an ontology of regions, where points are defined as convergent sets of regions. Such theories are descriptively equivalent since they are mathematically equivalent and yet logically incompatible from the realist's point of view, antirealists contend. The issue of conceptual relativity is examined in chapter 5, section 5.4.

The Model-theoretic Argument

The model-theoretic argument, again due to Hilary Putnam, is the most technical of the antirealist arguments. It also, in my view, presents the most formidable of all the antirealist challenges to realism. The argument purports to show that the problem of representation introduced earlier is insoluble for realists. That problem, recall, was to explain how our mental symbols and words get "hooked up" to mind-independent objects, and how our sentences and thoughts target mind-independent states of affairs.

According to the model-theoretic argument, *there are simply too many ways in which our mental symbols can be mapped onto items in the world*. A consequence of this is that realists must either accept massive indeterminacy in what our symbols refer to or insist dogmatically that even an ideal theory, whose terms and predicates can be demonstrably mapped onto objects and properties of some sort in the world so as to make that theory's theses come out true might still be false, that is, that such a mapping might not be the *right* one, the one "intended." Neither alternative can be defended, according to antirealists. Massive indeterminacy in perfectly determinate terms is absurd, and for realists to contend that even an ideal theory could be false is to resort to dogmatism, since on their own admission we cannot tell which mapping the world has set up for us. Such dogmatism leaves the realist with no answer to a skepticism that undermines any capacity to reliably represent the world, antirealists maintain. The model-theoretic argument proceeds thus:

We imagine that we have an ideal theory T that passes every observational and theoretical test we can conceive of. Assume we can formalize T in first-order logic. Assume also that the world is infinite in size and that our formal theory T is consistent. Then, by the completeness theorem for first-order logic, T will have a model M of the same size as the world (since by that theorem T will have models of every infinite size). Match up the objects in the model M one to one with the objects the world contains and use this mapping to define the relations of M directly in the world. We now have a correspondence between the expressions of the language L in which T is expressed and (sets of) objects in the world. T will then be true if "true" just means "true-in-M." If T is not guaranteed true by this procedure it can only be because M is not the *intended model*. Yet all our observation sentences come out true according to M, and the theoretical constraints must be satisfied because T's theses all come out true in M also. So the realist owes us an explanation of what constraints a model has to satisfy for it to be "intended" over and above its satisfying every observational and theoretical constraint we can conceive of. Suppose, on the other hand, that the realist is able to somehow specify the intended model. Call this model M^*. Then nothing the realist can do can possibly distinguish M^* as intended from a permuted variant P that, for example, switches every concrete object, identified by the spatiotemporal region it occupies, with, say, one that is one meter to the left of it.

5   Metaphysical and Semantic Theses to Be Defended

The metaphysical position I defend is naturalistic realism. However, it is my conviction that any replies to the antirealist's challenges must remain both incomplete and inconclusive until we can describe a credible mechanism for linking mental representations to mind-independent states of affairs. For the naturalistic realist, the representation problem is particularly acute: *how can a world of fields and forces give rise to anything so strange as creatures able to represent that very world by virtue of being in certain electrochemical states?* My view is that we have not even a glimmer of a credible answer to this question, that current answers in the form of teleosemantic, indicator semantic, indeed any "externalist" semantics positing natural content-fixing mechanisms are palpably inadequate. Nonetheless, I do defend a correspondence theory of truth to the extent that I believe that facts, in some sense of "make," make our statements and beliefs true. However, I reject current theories of both "truthmaking" and facts and argue for an alternative view of both. To my reckoning, facts are properties of the world as a whole, and truths are not made true by being entailed by objects.

This view about facts and the correspondence theory is susceptible to attack from pragmatists who hold that our linguistic and other cognitive practices stand in no need of external justification: in particular, no correspondence with the world is required—truth is to be identified with that which is instrumentally best to believe. In chapter 8, section 8.2, I present a case for believing that truth *cannot* be identified with what is best, all things considered, to believe. This attack on pragmatist models of truth and acceptability should be taken in tandem with the attack in chapter 4, section 4.5, on antirealist attempts to provide a credible notion of truth by generalizing intuitionistic provability, and the discussion in section 7.2 of Crispin Wright's moderate internalism. Together, these three sections comprise an attempt to demonstrate that *truth cannot be epistemically constrained.* If my arguments are sound, truth cannot be identified with either what is instrumentally or epistemically best to believe. Moreover, unless this is so, realism is flatly indefensible.

I argue for truth-conditional semantics throughout the book, especially in chapter 4, sections 4.4 and 4.5. That sets me against deflationary views of truth. Deflationary theories of truth are all very well, but they are philosophically uninteresting unless formulated within the context of a general deflationary attitude to semantics. To be a deflationist about truth while taking content as primitive is a little like not letting one's left hand know what one's right hand is doing. Moreover, it is flatly inconsistent with naturalism.

Acquiescing in the vague Wittgensteinian formulation that *use fixes meaning* is a remarkably effective way of forestalling serious questions surrounding mental representation—somehow, in ways we do not understand, what we do with our mental symbols fixes what we mean. Indeed; but that is a statement of the representation problem, not a solution to it. Going beyond this by adverting to specific features of our practices, recurrent normative elements in our social interactions and so on, is of use only if we do not help ourselves to unexplained content in the process.

Specific models of assertibility-based semantics are few and far between. Dummett has provided the most comprehensive one. Chapter 4 is devoted to an examination of it, and my conclusion is that it is found wanting. In addition, section 8.3 examines the semantic irrealism of Saul Kripke's Wittgenstein, based on a different sort of assertibility-based semantics than that of Dummett's.

Nothing in this book proves that our intuitive conception of truth is so much as coherent. Indeed, there cannot possibly be any such demonstration without a full examination of semantic paradox. That, unfortunately, lies outside the scope of this present work.

I
Metaphysical Realism and Truth

1
Contesting Realism

1.1 Realism and Metaphysical Determinacy

It is possible to characterize the crucial difference between metaphysical realism and antirealism, as Michael Dummett sees it, in terms of differing answers to a "truthmaker" question.

Consider the sentence:

(S) Socrates sneezed in his sleep the night before he took the hemlock.

Everyone agrees that there is no evidence one way or the other as to whether this sentence is true. Everyone also agrees that we have no way of obtaining any such evidence and that it is utterly improbable any relevant evidence will turn up. In Dummett's terminology, (S) is paradigmatically "evidence-transcendent."

Now ask yourself "What could make (S) true?" If your answer is "Some fact about the distant past concerning Socrates that we have no prospect of discovering, but which obtains or not independently of our ability to discover it," then, in Dummett's eyes, you are a metaphysical realist. If you answer "Some piece of confirming evidence for Socrates' nocturnal sneezings that night in Athens 399 B.C.," you are, in Dummett's eyes, an antirealist.

Dummett thus diagnoses the fundamental divide between metaphysical realists and their antirealist opponents as deriving from differences in their respective understandings of what makes truth-evaluable or truth-apt sentences such as (S) true. Where metaphysical realists take these sentences to describe *states of the world that either obtain or not independently of our ability to find out which,* antirealists understand them to be *rendered true or false by the types of evidence we recognize as confirming or disconfirming them.* Absent such evidence, we have no grounds for thinking these sentences *are* either true or false, Dummett's antirealist contends.

Dummett often calls sentences such as (S) "verification-transcendent," "evidence-transcendent," or "undecidable," the last because we lack any effective means of determining their truth-value. The term "undecidable" is more restrictive than "evidence-transcendent" or "verification-transcendent," for there are any number of sentences for which there exists weak or even good evidence of a sort that is not sufficient to decide their truth value. Indeed, if confirmational holism is correct, then just about every empirical sentence falls into this category—"undecidable" but not evidence-transcendent—since these are deemed confirmable or disconfirmable in the light of empirical evidence, albeit not individually so.

Dummett has not always been as clear as he might have been about who the "we" who grasp these undecidable sentences actually refers to —humanity in general, people individually, twenty-first-century humans, who? It is implicit in all his arguments, though, that he is distinguishing linguistic communities in different epochs. Sentences decidable for one linguistic community in a previous epoch might now be undecidable for twenty-first-century humans. Perhaps Xanthippe awoke that fateful night to Socrates' sneezing, thus making it determinate for fourth-century B.C. Athenians that Socrates did indeed sneeze in his sleep the night before he took his own life, thereby rendering (S) true. (S) is not decidable for twenty-first-century humans, though. This issue will be explained in a little more detail in section 2.2 of chapter 2.

Since Dummett's own formulations of realism are complicated and in many respects misleading, it is useful to have this rough characterization of the essential difference between metaphysical realism and antirealism in mind in thinking about his arguments against realism. For Dummett, the issue boils down to *the determinacy of states of affairs for which there is no and never feasibly will be any evidence.* Metaphysical realists are precisely those who subscribe to a belief in the metaphysical determinacy of such states of affairs. To the extent that you think such states of affairs can hold independently of our best efforts to determine whether they do, you must, Dummett argues, be thinking of them in the way a metaphysical realist does.

Dummett's antirealist then sets out to attack the metaphysical realist's assumption of the metaphysical determinacy of verification-transcendent states of affairs, such as those described in (S). His arguments, the most important of which is the *manifestation argument*, are all designed to show that to believe in metaphysical determinacy is to fall victim to a type of semantic illusion—it is to engage in a form of metaphysical credulism since, according to both Dummett and Putnam, it is simply inconsistent with any plausible account of how semantic content is determined that we be able to set up links between the uses of our words and states of affairs we cannot possibly detect.

It is this latter problem of *how mental representation of a mind-independent world is possible* that I mean to refer to when I talk of the antirealist challenge to realism. I call it the representation problem. If the representation problem was first raised by Dummett, it received its definitive formulation in a variety of ingenious arguments put forward by Hilary Putnam: the argument from conceptual relativity, the brains in a vat argument, and, most significantly, in my view, the model-theoretic argument.

In fact, neither Dummett nor Putnam explicitly put the problem they found with metaphysical realism in quite these terms. Neither said in so many words that metaphysical realism was untenable *because* it is impossible to explain how mental representation of a mind-independent world is possible, although Putnam came closest to doing so. Had they done so, it would have been clear what metaphysical realists had to do to meet the antirealist challenge, namely, give an account of mental representation compatible with their own strictures on mind-independence. It would also have been clear that the metaphysical realists least able to shirk the antirealist challenge were naturalistic ones committed to an explanation of mental representation in terms of physical mechanisms of some sort. Anyone conversant with the history of the realist–antirealist debate will know that this is the exact opposite of what actually happened. The realists most vulnerable to the antirealist challenge, naturalistic realists, were the first to dismiss it. Dispute centered and then largely stalled on a relatively minor issue, namely, how exactly metaphysical realism ought to be characterized. In particular, naturalistic realists questioned whether metaphysical realism presupposed a correspondence (or otherwise robust) theory of truth. Since both Dummett and Putnam seemed to ascribe just such a robust theory to their realist opponents and since many naturalistic realists saw their realism as a metaphysical thesis logically independent of any semantic theses, these naturalistic realists concluded that whatever it was that Dummett and Putnam had in mind by "realism," it was not the honest-to-goodness metaphysical realism that they subscribed to. They concluded they had nothing at all to fear from antirealist arguments.

How this situation came about and how far some influential current protagonists in the realist/antirealist debate actually are from appreciating the significance of the antirealist challenge to realism is the subject of the rest of this chapter. Section 1.2 recounts the sorry history of mutual misunderstanding that has dogged the debate, while section 1.3 shows how some currently influential proposals about how to understand and resolve the dispute are based on misunderstandings. To forestall confusion on this matter, I should point out that none of the antirealists arguments to be reviewed in this book contains explicit formulations of the representation problem, although, as indicated, the model-theoretic argument comes pretty close. Nonetheless, the representation problem underlies them all in the following sense: Whereas naturalistic realists do indeed have some plausible initial responses to the antirealist arguments put forward by Dummett, Putnam, and Wright, as we shall see in the pages ahead, these responses all presuppose that there exists some natural mechanism in virtue of which our mental symbols are able to target just the right mind-independent objects. But *how* this is possible is never explained, and *that* it is possible is precisely what antirealists doubts insofar as they reject the notion of "mind-independence" as incoherent.

1.2 Realism and Antirealism: A Sorry History of Misunderstandings

There is a widespread impression among realists of a naturalistic frame of mind that semantic challenges to their metaphysics posed by antirealists can be quickly and uniformly dismissed. All that one need do to disarm the antirealist's challenge is show that the metaphysical issue of realism has nothing at all to do with disputes about the nature of truth. This disarms all such challenges since all of these saddle realism with a belief in a correspondence theory of truth, a semantic doctrine wholly independent of the metaphysical question of which entities and structures exist in the world. Even if a truth predicate is needed to frame the debates between realists and their opponents in various domains, these debates are not about truth or reference or indeed anything semantic. They are about the furniture of the world. As to the significance of the issues raised by Michael Dummett's antirealism: it is but "a storm in a British teacup."[1] The view Dummett and Putnam attack has nothing at all to do with the naturalistic metaphysical realism to which such realists subscribe; it is, rather, a "semantic realism" completely orthogonal to their metaphysics and epistemology. Thus is one of the most powerful attacks on realist metaphysics and epistemology allegedly defused.

Realists are not alone in endorsing this deflation of the significance of antirealism. Pragmatists such as Richard Rorty and, albeit problematically,[2] Donald Davidson also believe that there is something deeply wrong with antirealism, but this is because they believe that there is something deeply wrong with the whole debate between realists and antirealists. So, for the pragmatist, *both* parties to the realist–antirealist dispute are in error; both sides err, according to Rorty, in seeking truthmakers for our beliefs and statements. Realists err in thinking that such truthmakers could only be mind-independent states of affairs of some sort, whose obtaining or not need not fall within the compass of our recognitional capacities. This makes it inexplicable why we should value truth in the first place if we cannot reliably detect it whenever it obtains. Antirealists err in taking truthmakers to be some mind-dependent ersatz. Their mistake is to respond to the gratuitous demand for mind-independent truthmakers by supplying epistemically sanitized mind-dependent surrogates.

Against both sides we can note that there need be nothing in the world or our minds or our linguistic practices that *makes* our statements true. Our practices do not need the type of externalist or internalist justification that the realist and the antirealist respectively seek to provide in the first place. Truth is not the important property both sides evidently take it to be.

I believe that all these views are bluntly mistaken in their assessment of the significance of antirealism. Take the naturalistic realist's quick dismissal first. Those who oppose metaphysical realism do so because they see it as a form of metaphysical credulism. Metaphysical realists of a naturalistic bent can thus no more afford to ignore the challenges to their view posed by Michael Dummett's antirealism than they can afford to ignore the challenges posed by Hilary Putnam's internal realism. Moreover, the neglect of the antirealist challenge to naturalistic realism has seen dogma and rigidity replace argument and openness in realist's defense of their metaphysics.

As to the pragmatists' "deconstruction," this backfires for precisely the reason that naturalistic realists cite in defense of their neglect of antirealism: naturalistic realists need not be committed to a correspondence theory of truth in the first place. So the realist–antirealist dispute is not about truthmakers at all. It is not about truth; nor is it about Truth. So what *is* it about?

I want to explain how the above (and other) misunderstandings occurred in the complex evolution of the realist–antirealist debate. I will explain what the antirealist challenge to realism *is* and why no realist of any stripe can afford to ignore it. It will emerge that it is crucial to distinguish the sometimes wild characterization of realism antirealists have often provided from the legitimate challenge to realism that their own view presents. I focus on naturalistic realism not only because it is that version of realism which is today most prominent but also because it is naturalistic realists who are most susceptible to the delusion that they can dismiss attacks on their metaphysics and epistemology. I will deal with influential misunderstandings of the nature of the realist–antirealist dispute due to Crispin Wright, Michael Devitt, William Alston, Donald Davidson, and Richard Rorty.

Given the high degree of confusion surrounding these issues, it is unsurprising that the dialectical situation realists and their opponents find themselves in is often one of deadlock. There is no clearer illustration of this than the debate over Hilary Putnam's model-theoretic argument (MTA). Surveying the recent literature on this leaves one with the impression that there is an impassable chasm between realist and antirealist. One either holds it to be a genuine question whether an ideal theory passes all conceivable constraints or claims that passing these constraints is a matter of "just more theory." But in actual fact what one says about this issue in the MTA will largely be determined by one's theory of truth. In particular, it will be determined by whether one holds with the realist that truth is radically nonepistemic or sides with antirealists like Dummett or internal realists like Putnam in believing it to be an epistemic notion. Because he sides with the antirealists on this matter, Putnam holds[3] that for an ideal theory to pass all the constraints *is* in the end just more theory. For any theory *T* to pass every conceivable constraint just is, for Putnam's "internal realist," for an ideal theory to assert that *T* does pass every conceivable constraint.

It is not hard to justify a decision to take seriously Putnam's challenge to what he calls metaphysical realism. To the contrary, it would appear remiss of any naturalistic realist to *shirk* that challenge, given that Putnam aims his principal attack fairly and squarely at *naturalistic* versions of metaphysical realism. Michael Dummett's arguments, on the other hand, can seem, on first acquaintance, to engage a doctrine that he calls "realism" but which has more to do with semantics than with the metaphysical question of realism. Indeed, to many a card-carrying realist Dummett's a priori meaning-theoretic arguments against realism represent precisely the sort of misguided transcendentalism that it is the purpose of naturalism to oppose. So what profit can there be in responding to his arguments?

A sticking point has been whether the so-called metaphysical issue of realism has anything at all to do with disputes about the nature of truth. Correspondingly, an appearance of incommensurability between realist and antirealist arguments has been fostered with the metaphysical purists (realists) campaigning to extrude from the realist–antirealist debate those very "semantic" issues that some antirealists take to lie at its heart. As a result, the dispute threatens to become *dialectically intractable*, with no neutral standpoint from which the claims of each disputant can be impartially assessed. Small wonder, then, that many despair of progress.

There is, in fact, a simple way around this apparent deadlock. It is for the antirealist to *agree* with the realist's own characterization of realism as a metaphysical issue. Indeed, let both parties just accept ab initio that realism is a purely metaphysical view, say, the view that the objects and structures that comprise the furniture of the universe exist mind-independently. Well and good. Precisely how to characterize realism is not terribly important from the antirealist's viewpoint, for surely, as good fallibilists, we should acknowledge that our initial intuitions—even about what realism is—may and typically will need revision as enquiry progresses. Moreover, there surely is something *right* about this characterization, as difficult as it may prove to explicate "mind-independent existence." The point then is that even if, as realists, we take realism to be a metaphysical issue, wholly uncontaminated by semantics, we can still find ourselves obliged to defend realism from "semantic" attacks.

This point should be obvious, but I fear that it has been ignored in the confusion engendered by the characterization debate. So let me illustrate it by a historical parallel: Most of us take David Hume to have presented a fairly powerful case against the rationality of belief in miracles. Faced with the prospect of attempting to establish the negative existential claim that miracles cannot occur, Hume chose instead to try to establish something simpler—that even if miracles did or could occur it would never be rational to believe any report attesting to their occurrence. This is a methodology the naturalist understands and endorses. The antirealist or internal realist response to realism *qua* the thesis that objects exist mind-independently exactly parallels Hume's response to the believer in miracles: *"Even if such mind-independent objects exist, one could never have any rational ground for believing that they do!"*

Thus the antirealist attack on realism, as I see it, is just a version of Hume's strategy against the credulist. Let us call this strategy the Hume–Kant gambit (since Kant surely deserves equal billing for arguing that mind-independent objects were singularly inappropriate objects of knowledge). Dummett's version of the Hume–Kant gambit is this: Even if the mind-independent states of affairs the realist believes in exist, it would never be possible for an agent to recognize that they did, so that an ascription of a grasp of such states of affairs to any such agent is completely unwarranted. Putnam's version is similar: We could never succeed in *referring* to objects so wholly divorced from our cognitive capacities.

Admittedly, the realist might retort to Putnam or Dummett, "Even if your grounds for skepticism about the possibility of our cognizance of or reference to mind-independent objects are sound, you still haven't shown that tables and rocks do *not* exist mind-independently!" Quite so. In just the same way, the credulist might respond to Hume: "Even if your grounds for skepticism about reports of miracles are cogent, you still haven't shown that miracles cannot occur!" The Hume–Kant–Dummett–Putnam response is, then (in unison): *"No. But we have established that nothing could compel belief in such things!"*

But *why* does the antirealist think that belief in mind-independent entities constitutes an indefensible metaphysical credulism? Hume's reason for dismissing the belief in miracles as metaphysical credulism was, as everybody knows, that they violated the laws of nature, which all our experience attested to, where by "laws" he meant those observable regularities in our experience with which we are most familiar. Dummett's and Putnam's reasons for dismissing belief in mind-independent entities as metaphysical credulism are similar. For Dummett, since there is no way of detecting such entities where and when they exist, there is nothing in what we say and believe about the world that could justify construal in terms of commitment to their existence; for Putnam, similarly, any reference to such entities is impossible.

Presumably, the realist does not want a Pyrrhic victory that accords his mind-independent real world the same status as that which the naturalist accords to miracles. That is why the naturalistic realist is *obliged* to square up to the challenges posed by Dummett and Putnam rather than ignore them by rigidly legislating their irrelevance.

Since Dummett's views have caused the most confusion, let me try to clear up some exegetical points concerning them and show in a little more detail why his attack on realism ought to be taken seriously by naturalistic realists. Dummett is fond of arguing for the foundational status of the theory of meaning in philosophy, suggesting at various points that metaphysical disputes *just are* at bottom disputes about the correct model of meaning for certain classes of statements. If we interpret Dummett as making an *epistemological* point we will be forced, on naturalistic grounds, to reject this claim. That the theory of meaning (or any other part of total science) should enjoy some privileged a priori epistemic status in relation to the rest of the corpus of knowledge is flatly inconsistent with the naturalist's epistemological holism.

However, I do not believe that this epistemological reading is how Dummett means to be interpreted. I take him to be advancing a *semantic* rather than an epistemological thesis, namely, that once we examine the content of the realist's and antirealist's respective claims, we will see that the dispute arises because each party tacitly adopts incompatible interpretations of the same sentences. The theory of meaning is foundational for Dummett, then, not in the sense that it secures *epistemic* foundations for the metaphysician's erstwhile faltering edifices, but in the sense that it clarifies what the metaphysician is trying to say. The foundations are *logico-semantic* rather than epistemic, then, just as Frege's foundations for arithmetic were intended to be. Far from being inimical to naturalism, the thesis that metaphysical disputes just are at bottom disputes about the truth conditions of various statements is entirely compatible with it—indeed, it affords us a plausible naturalistic explanation of why such disputes arise in the first place.

It is a sad commentary on the contemporary debate that Dummett's fascinating, bold, and original conjecture about the nature of metaphysical disputes has been caricatured in the ways that it has—as a *confusion* of semantic with metaphysical issues or as representing a naturalistically unacceptable plea for the privileged epistemic status of the theory of meaning. Of course, the realist is not obliged to agree with Dummett's assessment of the nature and causes of metaphysical disputes. Dummett may or may not be right about this. However, Dummett's challenge to the realist to explain our grasp of verification-transcendent truth conditions is entirely independent of his being right about the nature of metaphysics, as should be obvious. What the realist *cannot* afford to do with this conjecture is ignore the reasons Dummett has for advancing it. Tractable philosophical debates between disputants who hold radically different beliefs are possible only if both parties strive to understand the reasons offered in support of those divergent beliefs.

Although not obliged to take a stand on whether metaphysical disputes are reducible to meaning-theoretic ones, the realist *is* obliged to defend his professed belief in objective mind-independent states of affairs. Since such states of affairs simply *comprise*, on his account, the conditions under which certain sentences of the language are true, it follows that such a realist is obliged to answer Dummett's challenge to explain how we could become aware that such states of affairs obtain if and when they do, or if, per impossibile, we are somehow capable of doing so, how we could then *communicate* such knowledge to our fellows. Dummett's arguments focus largely on the impossibility of a speaker's *communicating* a grasp of verification-transcendent truth conditions to fellow language-users, but it is clear that this putative inability to communicate such an understanding stems, in Dummett's estimation at least, from the fact that such an understanding is impossible to come by in the first place. Accordingly, realist attempts to answer Dummett ought to correct for Dummett's own skewing of the debate along an axis of communication. If there is any substance to the complaint that Dummett's concern with meaning-theoretic issues distorts the real metaphysical issues, it is surely this and nothing more.

The realist has to explain how we are able to grasp the meaning of sentences with verification-transcendent truth conditions. Or, better, he has to explain what justifies a belief in the *existence* of such states of affairs in the first place. If that can be done, explaining how we acquire *a grasp* of sentences correlated with such states of affairs as their truth conditions might not be too difficult, and an account of how we manage to *communicate* our understanding of such truth conditions might be less difficult again. Expressing things this way around might make it look as if it is Dummett's so-called language acquisition argument (LAA) that presents the central challenge to the realist. However, recalling the analogy with Hume, we can see that the manifestation argument (MA) presents, if anything, a purer version of the Hume–Kant gambit than the former one. In fact, even if we ignore the analogy, the direction of dependence goes from the LAA to the MA rather than conversely, since it is the task of the latter to establish that nothing in our linguistic behavior *could* warrant an ascription of a grasp of realist truth conditions to us; given that we have a notion of truth at all, it must be a nonrealist one. The LAA then proceeds to argue that relative to our acquisition of such a nonrealist conception of truth, the use of distinctively classical modes of reasoning cannot be justified and therefore ought to be revised. In other words, the antirealist holds an error theory about our ordinary "realist" notion of truth—those features of our linguistic practice that attest to the existence of a shared conception of truth transcending any ability to recognize it simply attest to the pervasiveness of a shared illusion.

It is crucial to realize that Dummett's challenge to the realist still stands even if meaning is *not* constituted by truth conditions. One might be skeptical about meaning or adopt a non-truth-conditional account of meaning. But so long as one holds that a given class of sentences has verification-transcendent truth conditions at all, one is obliged to answer the antirealist's challenge. Moreover, how, compatibly with realism, can one afford to *relinquish* such an assumption? One is a realist, we have agreed, just to the extent that one believes in the existence of mind-independent entities and structures involving those entities. Verification-transcendent states of affairs arise through mind-independent entities being mind-independently structured in just those ways suggested by our theory of nature. Such states of affairs, we have seen, constitute the truth conditions for the sentences of total theory. To the extent that one believes the theory, one believes that the truth conditions for its constituent sentences obtain. To the extent that one believes that the theory may nonetheless be mistaken, one believes that the truth conditions for its sentences are not *guaranteed* to obtain.

More controversially, I contend that both Dummett's and Putnam's challenges to realism still stand even if truth is deflationary rather than substantial. Much of the contemporary debate over realism has, I suspect, actually been marred by worrying about the difference it would make to the overall configuration of the metaphysical issues if truth *were* deflationary or, as I will henceforth term it, "minimal." *In actual fact, the answer is simple: "None."*[4] The intuition to the contrary goes like this: Suppose one believes that "is true" is a purely disquotational predicate, or suppose one is a Horwich-styled minimalist or a Grover- or Brandom-styled prosententialist about truth. Then why should one take any interest at all in the meaning-theoretic attacks of Dummett or Putnam, which apparently build substantial content into the notions of truth and reference, burdening the realist unnecessarily with commitments to a substantial correspondence relation of truth or a substantial causal or information-theoretic account of reference?

If the dispute between realist and antirealist really *were* about the semantics of "true" or the explanatory power of truth, if it were concerned with whether truth is a correspondence relation or reducible to physicalistically specifiable causal or information-theoretic relations between appropriate bits of reality and linguistic expressions, the minimalists would have a point. But it is about *none* of these things. It is, to repeat, about the *metaphysics* of realism: about what the world contains. To be sure, Putnam has some powerful arguments against reductive physicalist accounts of reference, which he hopes to deploy to overturn metaphysical realism. By themselves, however, they are powerless to do this, a fact that Putnam now acknowledges. The reason is simple: it is consistent to believe in a mind-independent reality while rejecting particular accounts of the way our minds make epistemic and semantic contact with that reality. Even if the reference relation *were* some relation between agents and the world (which disquotationalists and prosententialists precisely deny), that relation could hold inscrutably without impugning the mind-independent status of that world.

Thus the minimalist can lay claim to believing consistently in both a mind-independent reality and in minimal truth. It is commitment to the former that both Dummett and Putnam seek to undermine—Dummett by arguing that it is impossible to communicate, let alone acquire in the first instance, knowledge of such a reality, and Putnam by arguing that the supporter of the mind-independence of reality is committed to defend, incoherently in Putnam's view, the thesis that even an ideal theory might be false and that, for all we could tell, even in principle, we may yet be brains in a vat.

One cannot evade the antirealist's challenge merely by subscribing to a realist metaphysics and to a minimalist view of truth, then. The challenge is to justify belief in those mind-independent states of affairs that comprise the *truth conditions* of the sentences of a mature theory of nature; it is *not* to justify the claim that *truth* is a substantial property. Naturalistic realists who are minimalists about truth will want to say that one should no more think that one is predicating a substantial property—a property that can feature in bona fide naturalistic explanations of phenomena—of the sentences "$2 + 2 = 4$" and "Napoleon was exiled to Elba" by calling both true than one would be by predicating the property "either summing to 4 when added to itself or being exiled to Elba" of both Napoleon and the sole even prime. Truth's dissentients as well as its true believers can still be metaphysical credulists—or so the antirealist maintains.[5] The task now is to come up with a formulation of realism that is acceptable to naturalistic realists and antirealists alike. Even though the formulations proferred will be rough, they suffice to provide a characterization of realism that allows debate between realists and antirealists to proceed with the prospect of some intelligible resolution.

What Is "Metaphysical Realism"?

Realists and antirealists need to agree about the characterization of realism if any progress is to be made in the dispute between them. Since it is naturalistic versions of realism on which I wish to focus, and naturalistic realists may be minimalists about truth, I suggest that we accept the following formulation as our working characterization of metaphysical realism:

(MR)   The objects and structures that comprise the furniture of the universe exist mind-independently.

In fact, I think this formulation is substantially correct and can be defended against semantic construals.

The *metaphysical* dispute about realism underwent a wholesale *semantic* transformation in Dummett's hands, becoming a dispute about the right explanatory concept to use in the theory of meaning. For one who thinks that metaphysical theses just are disguised meaning-theoretical claims, this is, of course, completely unexceptionable. Dummett's problem is that virtually no one else agrees with him on this. This was precisely why naturalistic realists thought they could and still think they can just dismiss Dummett's arguments. What they typically fail to see, though, is that Dummett's arguments present a legitimate challenge to their views even if his formulation of those views goes a little awry.

However, on the opposing side, the puzzle is that antirealists have been equally insistent that realism is intimately concerned with truth, with the unfortunate result that meaningful debate simply stalled. One side, the naturalistic realists, insisted that realism was a metaphysical issue completely independent of semantics and that no progress could be made in the dispute with antirealists until they recognized this; and their opponents replied that realism is in actual fact an alethic matter and that no progress could be made until realists recognized this.

Why did antirealists make this reply when they didn't need to? Couldn't they have predicted that realists would respond in the way they did, as indeed would anyone have whose favored characterization of their own views was not being taken seriously? It is hard to avoid the conclusion that antirealists did so because they were not entirely clear about *what it was* that they really objected to in metaphysical realism.

Case Study 1: Wright on the Realist–Antirealist Debate
In the light of the above, we should not be surprised that little progress is to be made in the realist–antirealist debate by searching for a "lowest common denominator" conception of truth that even the most die-hard physicalistic realist and the most extreme idealistic antirealist can agree

on. Yet this is precisely the tack taken by Crispin Wright in his *Truth and Objectivity*. As this book has proved highly influential and presents a challenge to the views expressed above on truth and realism, I think I should take some time explaining why I believe its suggested reconfiguration of the realist–antirealist dispute is unpromising. Wright's project might have some real chance of success if the relevant lowest common denominator were argued to be *disquotational* truth, for this would be to acknowledge the point made above about the logical independence of debates about the nature of reality from those to do with the nature of truth, a point Michael Devitt has most forcefully made.[6] Truth would be discussed only to be set aside, so to speak—a useful ploy given the problems that differing conceptions of truth pose for their partisans when attempting to communicate with one another about *any* philosophical matter.

But Wright will have none of this strategy. Deflationary conceptions of truth are fatally flawed, he believes. The argument he takes to constitute a "fundamental and decisive objection to deflationism as classically conceived," however, rests on a misconception of deflationism about truth. Wright's argument can be represented as follows:

(1) A deflationary conception of truth is one that is committed to two theses:

(T1) The predicate "true" functions purely as a device for endorsing assertions, beliefs and so on and therefore registers no norm distinct from justified assertibility.

(T2) The disquotational schema (DS), "p" is true if and only if p, constitutes a complete explanation of the meaning of "true."

(2) Consider now a sentence we can neither verify nor refute, for example, Goldbach's conjecture (GC) that every even number is the sum of two primes. We aim to show that T1 combined with T2 for this case yields an absurdity, for (DS) implies:

(i) "It is not the case that p" is true iff it is not the case that p.

But (i) in combination with:

(ii) It is not the case that p iff it is not the case that "p" is true

yields:

(iii) "It is not the case that p" is true iff it is not the case that "p" is true.

So far we have the standard Tarskian recursion clause for negation. But how does this represent any *problem* for the deflationist?

Although Wright never fully explains what he means by his claim in (T1) that the predicate "true" "registers no norm distinct from justified endorsability—that is, assertibility," it seems that it is meant to imply at least that extensionally different predicates cannot "register the same norm." But for the GC case, although "Every even number is the sum of two primes" is not assertible, neither is "It is not the case that every even number is the sum of two primes." Thus the extension of "true" cannot coincide with that of "assertible," since substitution of "assertible" for "true" in the extensional context of (iii) implies that we should now assert the negation of GC since GC is not currently assertible. Thus (T1) in conjunction with (T2) yields an absurdity for undecidable statements like GC, the absurdity that "while 'is true' and 'is warrantedly assertible' are normatively coincident, satisfaction of the one norm does not entail satisfaction of the other."[7]

I think there is a legitimate objection to *something* lurking behind Wright's argument. But that something certainly is not deflationism "as classically conceived." The theorist who *ought* to be embarassed by the problem undecidable statements like GC present for attempts to satisfy Tarski's material adequacy condition is not the deflationist but the proponent of an *epistemic* view of truth—one who wishes to define or at least explicate truth in terms of some epistemic notion such as warranted assertibility. This is typically an antirealist such as (a previous stage of) Wright himself.

The deflationist, however, is no such theorist. Truth is to be neither defined nor explained in terms of assertibility or of any other epistemic notion for the deflationist. *Nor is there any general requirement that the extension of "is true" should coincide with the extension of "is assertible."* Indeed, were only the latter to hold, the Tarskian definition of truth could be recast in terms of assertibility, thereby belying the deflationist's insistence that truth is nonepistemic. All such epistemic explications would have the effect of reinstating precisely what the deflationist is at pains to deny—that truth is some sort of substantial notion. Moreover, disquotationalism—the view that the primary function of the truth predicate in terms of which all its other functions are ultimately to be explained is the disquotation of the quoted sentences of one's own language—is surely a deflationist view par excellence. Wright therefore owes us an explanation as to why belief in this (paradigmatic) version of deflationism automatically commits one to holding that there can be no fact to the matter as to whether every even number is the sum of two primes. Holding that there *is* such a fact to the matter is, apparently, tantamount to denying that "true" and "assertible" are "normatively coincident," something no deflationist can afford to deny by the lights of (T1).

But how *could* this be right? How could the mere relegation of the little word "true" to the menial role of quotation-mark-stripper possibly carry any metaphysical implications at all? Disquotation is simply a syntactic operation that undoes the effects of quotation. So is it the minimality clause in the disquotationalist's theory that has this effect—the claim that *all there is* to the notion of truth is what is implicit in the logical behavior of the truth predicate, namely its foundational use in disquotation and supervenient roles of generalization over sentences and the formation of infinitary conjunctions?

Why should such a (deflationary) assessment of the expressive role of a single predicate foreclose on the metaphysical possibilities that *the rest of one's predicates* can be used to express? To the contrary, it would appear straightforward for the disquotationalist to contemplate the possibility that "Every even number is the sum of two primes" is true—for this is just the possibility that every even number is the sum of two primes. The extent to which this represents a nonfactual or fictive possibility for the disquotationalist is the extent to which he is already a mathematical antirealist; it is no consequence at all of his deflationary attitude to truth. It is, as deflationists themselves rightly insist, logically independent of the latter. Wright seems to have ignored or forgotten the deflationist's insistence that the truth predicate cannot be used to arbitrate metaphysical and epistemic disputes. Hence (T1), as Wright intends it to be interpreted, would be rejected *in principle* by most deflationists. The deflationary conception of truth as exemplified in disquotationalism, prosententialism, and Horwich-styled minimalism, at least, stands as implacably opposed to epistemic theories of truth as to correspondence theories. On paradigmatically deflationary theories, then, the truth predicate is a logico-syntactic device that earns its keep by permitting us to disquote sentences or propositions or to refer anaphorically to a speaker's statements or utterances. Yet neither in disquoting sentences (or propositions) nor in generalizing over them, nor even in anaphorically referring to statements or utterances, does a predicate function to *endorse* "assertions, beliefs, and so on" in such a way that it "registers no norm distinct from justified assertibility."

Endorsement is thus irrelevant except in the trivial sense explicitly allowed for by disquotationalism—that *if I believe p then I will also believe* "*p*" is true (provided I understand the disquotational use of "*true*"), where "*p*" represents a sentence of my own language. The only "norms" that "true" registers for the disquotationalist are those already registered by the sentences it serves to disquote—which is to say all and any, or, more soberly, none at all. Endorsement, justified assertibility, and so on are all epistemic functions that no mere quotation-stripper can possibly discharge.

Moreover, what exactly is "justified assertibility" supposed to come to? This strikes me as a fairly urgent question for Wright's deflationist to ask, given that "is true" is supposed to have the same extension as this predicate. One well-understood alternative explication of "justified assertibility" goes by way of the notion of degrees of belief, where through a Dutch book argument[8] these are taken to obey the rules of the probability calculus. One should assert *p* if one's degree of credence in *p* is sufficiently high, that is, if one assigns a high subjective probability to *p*. In such theories little interest is shown in the source of such prior probabilities, the whole focus being on the dynamics of belief revision via conditionalization on the receipt of new evidence. The important point for our purposes is that even though many have essayed to identify the extension of "justifiedly assertible" with "highly probable," *no one* would dream of identifying the extension of "true" with the extension of "highly probable." For one thing, truth is probability of 1, whereas probability remains high for values somewhat less than that. For another, truth is a monotonic property, whereas probability is not. Moreover, probabilities, as David Lewis has reminded us, are probabilities of truth.

Wright's deflationist apparently can no more afford to explicate justified assertibility in Bayesian terms, say, than he can afford to believe it a factual question whether every even number is the sum of two primes. Many would take this to be an abrogation of the theory of rationality along with any theory of a mind-independent world. Some even see these two theories as intimately connected. In fact, the only deflationary theory of truth I can think of that might assent to something like (T1) is Strawson's "amen" theory of truth. The problems facing that theory are well documented and are, in my estimation, crippling.

So why does Wright believe that any defensible version of deflationism should be committed to (T1)? My guess is that it is because he cannot see how truth could be anything other than something constructed out of assertibility, because he is, at heart, still wedded to an epistemic theory of truth.

Case Study 2: Devitt on Realism and Truth

Whereas Wright thinks that progress in the realism–antirealism dispute is contingent on both sides adopting a common notion of truth, Michael Devitt holds that truth has nothing at all to do with realism.[9] I think there is something true and important in Devitt's view, as I've already indicated. Realism is a metaphysical issue, whatever else it may be. Realists about moral values or numbers or electrons hold that the relevant entities exist mind-independently, and metaphysical realists hold that *whatever* objects the world contains, they exist independently of our perceptions and conceptions of them.

There is nothing in such metaphysical existence claims that involves reference to human beings or their cognitive powers at all. In response to questions about what it means for such entities to exist *mind-independently*, reference to minds or products thereof such as scientific or ethical theories might be needed by way of clarification of the original bald theses, but the theses themselves can be stated without reference to truth.

It may subsequently transpire that a disquotational truth predicate is needed to explicate various sorts of realisms—indeed I think it is. But this by itself need represent no concession at all to the Wright-styled view that the metaphysical issue of realism is intimately connected with the nature of truth, for disquotational truth is eliminable in favor of infinitary conjunction or primitive substitutional quantification. Admittedly there are good reasons for believing that neither of these latter devices can be understood without a notion of truth, but all that that need establish is the explanatory priority of disquotational truth in the circle of three notions of truth, infinitary conjunction, and substitutional quantification. Such an explanatory priority might be reversed for creatures with different cognitive makeups from our own.

The point, then, is that realism is rightly conceived, in my view as in Devitt's, as a thesis about what the world contains, one that says nothing at all about how human or other inquirers are cognitively related to that world. Realist theses posit domains of entities without venturing any opinion about how humans are semantically or epistemically related to those entities. Yet it is precisely this fact that antirealists see as the fundamental weakness of realism. Not only does the realist not venture any opinion about how human enquirers can know about or refer to numbers or moral values or electrons, no plausible realist account *can* be given of our abilities here at all.

What is puzzling about Devitt's approach is that he seems to see this apparent weakness of realism as one of its strengths, as if he is exalting in the following argument from ignorance:

> Realism per se has nothing at all to say about such epistemic or semantic matters, so any attack on realism on these grounds must be based on a confusion about what the real issues are.

When pressed, Devitt simply assumes that some plausible naturalistic story can be told about how humans can succeed in referring to mind-independent entities or in detecting verification-transcendent states of affairs. The problem is that he neither tells it nor provides any evidence that it can be told. But this is precisely what is at issue. In the next section we will see precisely how Devitt has misinterpreted Dummett's antirealist challenge, and we shall also see how other influential responses to Dummett's challenge first from William Alston and then from Richard Rorty and Donald Davidson also seriously misconstrue its nature.

1.3 Antirealism Misconstrued

1.3.1 Devitt's Response to Dummett

Dummett invests much energy in attacking the verification-transcendent notion of truth. This is of concern to the naturalistic realist, for whatever else he is uncommitted to semantically, he is committed to the claim that those statements he interprets realistically at all can be true or false independently of whether we can verify which they are.

Yet Devitt surprisingly denies this commitment. He thinks that any semantic issue is simply irrelevant to the metaphysical issue of realism. Disquotationalists about truth characteristically claim that appending the predicate "is true" to the name of a sentence s results in a sentence that says the same thing as, or is cognitively equivalent to, the named sentence s. So consider the sentence "The entropy of the big bang was very low." Devitt is a scientific realist. So he believes in the reality of those entities that our best scientific theories posit. The event known as the big bang is surely among them. Presumably he also believes in bona fide physical properties such as entropy and so will believe the sentence "The entropy of the big bang was very low," which is implied by our best current physical theory. Moreover, as a good scientific realist Devitt will want to insist that even if no human had been clever enough to discover this fact about the origins of our universe or even if, universally dazzled by the brilliance of postmodernist arguments, we all come to believe this sentence represents nothing more than a raw grab for power on the part of the scientific establishment, a sentence not even evaluable for truth or falsehood, it would still be the case that the entropy of the big bang was very low. But then, using disquotationalist precepts, since "The entropy of the big bang was very low" is cognitively equivalent to "'The entropy of the big bang was very low' is true," the claim that the sentence "The entropy of the big bang was very low" could be true even if no one recognized that it was *just is* the distinctive scientific realist claim above that the entropy of the big bang could have been very low even if no one had recognized that it was. There is *no cognitive difference*, in other words, for the disquotationalist, between claiming that a certain state of affairs posited by our best scientific theory could have obtained independently of whether humans were capable of ascertaining that it did and claiming that the sentence for which that state of affairs comprises the disquotational truth condition could have been true independently of our capacity to verify it.

If there are verification-transcendent states of affairs, there are verification-transcendent truth conditions for the sentences our language correlates with those states of affairs. Of course, the fact that the big bang had very low entropy is not verification-transcendent. But it might have been, as in the imagined counterfactual circumstances, and there are any number of sentences that do have verification-transcendent truth conditions. One such sentence is this: "Julius Caesar's systolic blood pressure rose by 30 mmHg the moment before he crossed the Rubicon." Contrary to what he maintains, then, Devitt is committed to verification-transcendent truth conditions at least to the extent that he is committed to disquotational truth and to scientific realism. Devitt might respond that he is not committed to verification-transcendent correspondence truth, as he terms it. This is true but irrelevant; Dummett's and Putnam's challenges to realism require no favored theory of truth on the part of the realist. What has caused confusion is that both Dummett and Putnam *frame* the realism issue in terms of a substantial theory of truth.

With these preliminaries in mind, let us see what Devitt has to say about Dummett's antirealism. Devitt ascribes the following 3 premises to Dummett in an effort to reconstruct his argument for antirealism:

A. The realism dispute is a dispute about whether statements have realist (evidence-transcendent) truth conditions or only verificationist truth conditions.

B. This dispute is in turn a dispute about whether a competent speaker's understanding is realist (evidence-transcendent) or only verificationist.

C. Competent speakers' understanding is only verificationist.

Devitt notes that Dummett seems to invest all his energies in establishing premise (C) without really attending to premises (A) or (B), which he takes to be crucial to Dummett's case. As a consequence, Devitt invests most of his energies in arguing against (A) and (B). Unfortunately for Devitt, (A) and (B) not only are *not* crucial to Dummett's case against realism, they are not even clearly part of it—which is why he spends little time defending them.

To be sure, Dummett has a favored way of framing the realism dispute, a rather recherché way, in which something like (A) and (B) do figure. But Dummett's case against metaphysical realism, even of the naturalistic sort favoured by Devitt, can be formulated, as below, in a way that makes no use of premises (A) and (B). To repeat, it is not crucial to Dummett's case against metaphysical realism (or Putnam's, for that matter) that he get the characterization of metaphysical realism exactly right. He could and should defer to the realist on this. A better way to formulate Dummett's argument might be this:

I. Realism implies that certain statements have realist (evidence-transcendent) truth conditions.

II. If such statements have realist truth conditions it must be possible for speakers to detect when such conditions are satisfied.

III. Speakers are capable of detecting only when verificationist truth conditions are satisfied.

This formulation is itself far from perfect, but it is an improvement over Devitt's ABC formulation. Dummett does not have to show that realism *just is* the thesis that statements have realist truth conditions, even if as a matter of fact he believes this. All he need show is that realism *implies* this thesis, which, as I argued above, it clearly does. Devitt commits a rather revealing error in discussing his premise (A), which I think explains his otherwise mystifying insistence that realism does *not* imply that certain sentences have evidence-transcendent truth conditions. The error is this: *Devitt glosses premise (A) as "realism is correspondence truth." This is mistaken. Evidence-transcendent truth conditions are not the sole province of correspondence theorists of truth.*

Disquotationalists who deny that truth has any hidden nature waiting to be uncovered (whether through naturalistic reduction to causally specified reference relations between words and things in the way Devitt favors or through anything else) are still obliged to acknowledge evidence-transcendent truth conditions wherever they acknowledge evidence-transcendent states of affairs. It is a common error to suppose that disquotationalism denies word-world connections. It doesn't. Indeed, versions of disquotationalism that define truth via disquotational reference can specify their reference relation *only* by making use of such connections.

Unfortunately for his case against Dummett, Devitt's critique is based on this misunderstanding. Devitt tells us on page 260 of his *Realism and Truth*, when elaborating on premise (A), "So, for Dummett, abbreviating, Realism is Correspondence Truth," where correspondence truth for sentences of type *x* is explicated as follows:

Sentences of type *x* are true or false in virtue of: (1) their structure; (2) the referential relations between their parts and reality; and (3) the objective and mind-independent nature of that reality.

What makes Devitt's misattribution even more extraordinary is that Dummett takes Donald Davidson to be his paradigmatic "realist" yet Davidson explicitly rejects the correspondence theory of truth. The evidence-transcendent truth conditions of Devitt's premise A need not be Devitt's correspondence truth conditions. They might be disquotational truth conditions instead. Evidence-transcendence, rather than correspondence, is all that Dummett's argument against realism needs.

When this error is unmasked, Devitt's critique of Dummett's antirealism collapses. It consists mainly in the attempt to show that realism is independent of correspondence truth, a proposition Dummett need not contest and has independently argued for. Correlatively, because he is confident that Dummett has so thoroughly confounded the metaphysical question of realism with the semantic question of correspondence truth, Devitt does not even bother to respond to Dummett's crucial challenge to the realist—to say how unreflective speakers can detect evidence-transcendent truth conditions when they are in place, or why reflective truth theorists should believe such denizens of Plato's heaven exist to start with. Devitt effectively ignores the challenge, or brushes it aside impatiently when he does recognize it: "Verificationist arguments to show speakers do not know realist truth-conditions are irrelevant to Correspondence Truth," he tells us at page 261. Ironically, it is Devitt's correspondence truth that is irrelevant to Dummett's verificationist arguments. These target realist truth conditions in general.

1.3.2 Alston on Dummett

William Alston has recently advanced a different response to Dummett's arguments, but one that, like Devitt's, fails to take the antirealist challenge seriously. Alston sets out to show that Dummett's manifestation and language acquisition arguments are flawed and that the verificationist semantics that Dummett advocates is quite compatible with realist truth.

Alston's Critique of Verificationism In his assessment of Dummett's verificationism, Alston adduces a consideration he takes to be fatal to it.[10] This is that: "... with the possible exception of sentences usable for making observational or introspective reports ... no empirical sentence can be empirically verified or confirmed unless we assume the truth of various other sentences."[11] Why should such a simple consideration sink Dummett's program? The reason Alston gives is that "Dummett thinks in terms of assigning meanings one by one to sentences in terms of what would (conclusively or inconclusively) verify the sentence."[12] Alston provides a sample sentence to show that this thesis cannot be sustained—that any empirical verification of the sentence "Jim is insecure" must depend on a "mini-theory of insecurity"; an extensive background theory and cannot depend just on the meaning of this sentence alone. Let us refer to this form of verificationism that Alston ascribes to Dummett as holophrastic verificationism (HV), since it apparently takes sentences to be discrete isolable units of significance, to be paired holophrastically with verification conditions.

Unfortunately, Alston provides no evidence at all that Dummett accepts HV. This is not surprising since Dummett himself provides ample evidence that he would reject it in principle. Dummett insists that our understanding of the sentences of our language has an interesting structure to it—it is partially, or at least quasi, ordered.[13] "Jim is insecure" does indeed require a grasp of the verification conditions of sentences in those strata below the stratum containing the target sentence. Alston has apparently mistaken Dummett's insistence on molecular theories of meaning and his animadversions against holism as evidence for a belief in holophrastic verificationism. This is a simple exegetical mistake.

Alston tries to undercut the verificationist reply that the meaning of a sentence is determined also by the contribution it makes to various complexes in which it may feature (observing, rightly, that this requires to be worked out) by producing a sentence whose meaning can be grasped even though it has no verification conditions. His example is "Matter is composed of tiny, invisible, indivisible particles" as uttered by Leucippus, who, we can reasonably suppose, lacked any means for verifying this.

The problem here is again partly exegetical. Dummett's thesis is *not* that the meaning of such a sentence for Leucippus (or any of the Ancients who considered and disputed it) is given by the extant evidence for it, but rather that it is given by what would verify it. The relevant question is therefore not whether Leucippus or his cohorts could themselves verify this sentence, but whether they would recognize a verification of it if presented with one.

Naturally, since our current reason for believing that matter is composed of tiny particles, albeit ones that need not be indivisible (fundamental particles may be divisible "all the way down") involves concepts Leucippus was not privy to, this type of verification is unacceptable. So we need to ask what what would have verified, relative to the concepts Leucippus actually possessed, the (possibly false) sentence "Matter is composed of tiny, indivisible particles." Given that Leucippus had a grasp of a process of divisibility that could be carried on beyond the limits of human visual acuity and an argument for the thesis that any process of physical division must come to an end that he, along with the other Greek atomists, took to be convincing, there is no special problem at all in understanding why Leucippus considered himself justified in asserting the sentence "Matter is composed of tiny, indivisible, invisible particles"; neither is there any problem in understanding what its content might have been for him. The argument that convinced atomists such as Leucippus, Democritus, and Epicurus that matter could not be infinitely divisible was Zeno's, according to Aristotle in his *Physics* 139, 24–140, 26:

1. If an object (or a magnitude such as a line or temporal period) were infinitely divisible, no contradiction should arise from the supposition that it has been divided "exhaustively."

2. But any such exhaustive division would resolve the object (or magnitude) into elements of zero extension, which is clearly impossible, since:

3. No extensive magnitude could consist of extensionless elements.

This is perhaps the most famous argument in all antiquity against plurality. Aristotle's own refutation of it in the *Physics*, 316b 19ff, made no impression whatsoever on the atomists. Thus Epicurus was so persuaded by Zeno's argument that he asserted with utter confidence that if matter were infinitely divisible, Being, that which truly exists, would be reducible to Nonbeing.

Alston's Critique of Dummett's Manifestation and Acquisition Arguments
Alston's attack on Dummett's two central arguments for antirealism are, unfortunately, predicated on the mistaken attribution to him of holophrastic verificationism. Thus, he rejects the language acquisition argument on the basis of considerations that have to do with compositionality. Alston complains on page 113 that we do not acquire the use of sentences "one by one ... attaching verification and falsification conditions to each one," but instead use our understanding of the components of a sentence to construct indefinitely many novel and complex sentences.

It is puzzling that Alston takes this to be a criticism of Dummett since, as he later recognizes, Dummett himself stresses the compositional character of our semantic competence.[14] Leaving that to one side, though, he cites the aforementioned sentence, "Matter is composed of tiny, indivisible, invisible particles," and claims that if we understand the terms "particle," "composed of," "divisible," and so on, we'd understand the sentence without understanding any verification conditions.[15] But this conclusion is a non sequitur. Subsentential expressions, on Dummett's model of semantic competence, are to be understood in terms of the contribution they make to the recognizable truth conditions, that is, verification conditions, of sentences in which they occur. With holophrastic verificationism firmly entrenched as his (mistaken) exegesis of Dummett's verificationism, Alston confidently asserts that "The 'Manifestation Argument' can be dismissed on the same grounds. Since our understanding of sentences is not, in general, a matter of knowing their verification conditions, we cannot expect a 'manifestation' of that understanding to amount, in general, to showing that we know under what conditions they are verified or falsified."[16]

In summary, much more work needs to be done to "dismiss" Dummett's manifestation argument than to saddle him with a version of verificationism he explicitly rejects. It is Alston's exegesis that should be rejected, not Dummett's legitimate challenge to realism.

Alston's Critique of Verificationism (II)—"Realist" Truth and Verificationist Semantics Alston makes a further attempt to rebut Dummett, arguing that Dummett's own verificationism is quite compatible with realist truth. This is a rather strking claim on the face of it. Dummett's view is that truth is epistemically constrained by human recognitional capacities and that the semantic contents of the sentences of a language are given by their recognizable truth conditions. How can this position possibly be squared with the view that truth is epistemically unconstrained?

The appearance of conflict quickly dissipates, however, once one discovers that by "realist truth" Alston does not mean what Dummett or most philosophers mean, namely, evidence-transcendent truth. At least, Alston cannot assume that his "realist truth" coincides with this more familiar understanding. Alston tells us that the following truth schema for propositions (which he takes to be the basic truth-bearers) completely characterizes truth:

(T) Πp. The proposition that p is true if and only if p.

This sounds like a straightforward version of minimalism about truth, in the manner of Paul Horwich. Minimalists claim that truth is merely a logical property, as opposed to a substantive one, such as having a mass, being a genotype, suffering from an attentional deficit, and so on. Such views stand opposed to traditional theories of truth such as correspondence or coherence theories. Nonetheless, Alston believes that his theory of truth will, on closer inspection, reveal itself to be a covertly realist one, since (T) is actually equivalent, he argues, to an "overtly realist" schema:

(TSp) Πp. The proposition that p is true if and only if it is a fact that p.

The problem with Alston's view, and the reason that Dummett's theory of truth poses a challenge to it, is that there is nothing "overtly realist" about (TSp) at all. Merely appending the operator "it is a fact that" to the right hand side of the biconditional in (T) does not a realist theory of truth make—not unless antirealists can make no sense of the notion of a fact, which they clearly can. Why does Alston think otherwise?

He tells us that his version of truth is a "minimalist correspondence" theory of truth. This sounds like an oxymoron, but let us pursue his ideas. Minimalist correspondence theories of truth are to be distinguished from robust correspondence theories, he informs us, in that the latter, unlike the former, make truth a matter of a certain sort of structural fit between propositions and nonlinguistic facts. In contrast, minimalist correspondence theories leave propositions and facts unanalyzed. Furthermore, robust theories try to explicate the fact–proposition relation on which truth supervenes, whereas minimalist theories treat the relation as one of content identity between fact and proposition.

Two comments. First, there is nothing in any of this to distinguish Alston's view from Horwich's. Deflationists generally will read Alston's (TSp) as little more than a platitude—"it is a fact that *p*" is simply an alternative way of saying "it is true that *p*," for them. So they can endorse (TSp) while claiming that, *pace* Alston, the direction of explanation goes from (TSp) to (T) rather than conversely. Perhaps Alston thinks that deflationists in general and minimalists in particular must eschew the correspondences between true propositions and those states of affairs they describe in rejecting the correspondence theory of truth, but if so, this is an error. Witness Horwich:

The correspondence conception of truth involves two claims:

(a) that truths correspond to reality; and

(b) that such correspondence is what truth essentially is.

And the minimalist response ... is to concede the first of these theses but to deny the second.[17]

Minimalists also agree with Alston that the fact-proposition relation is one of content identity—"the fact that snow is white" has exactly the same content as "the proposition that snow is white is true," that content simply being: *snow is white.*

Second, not all correspondence theories of truth make the relation between their favored truthbearers and the corresponding facts a matter of "structural fit." Such a view of the correspondence relation, most clearly attributable to Wittgenstein of the *Tractatus*, has comparatively few supporters today largely because many think that the "picturing relation" between propositions and facts is simply too mysterious. Naturalistic-minded philosophers attracted to the correspondence theory are more likely to follow the lead of (the early) Hartry Field and Michael Devitt in seeing correspondence as a relation between subsentential expressions such as singular terms and objects, predicates and properties of objects, and so on. If objects together with their properties and relations are conceived of as *components* of facts, then this "referentialist" theory is clearly still a version of the correspondence theory of truth.

In recent years, an alternative understanding of the correspondence theory has been gathering momentum wherein true propositions do not require unique correspondents to make them true. "Truthmaker theory" holds that for every truth p there is a truthmaker, where by "*truthmaker*" is simply meant *any entity whose existence entails p*. So it may be that the mere existence of Hersch the kelpie makes it true that dogs exist and also makes it true that unless dogs exist the big pet food manufacturers have an awful lot of explaining to do. Indeed, it may even be that Hersch's existence makes it true that thirteen is a prime number if in making true some contingent truth Hersch's existence a fortiori makes true all necessary truths. This theory has considerable independent interest and is discussed in the final chapter where I develop my own version of the correspondence theory, distinct from both the truthmaker and referentialist versions alluded to above.

Plainly, if Alston's theory of truth is to be distinguished as a genuine version of the correspondence theory, he has to tell us something more about the relation between facts and propositions. As the quotation from Horwich indicates, Alston has to at least show how positing a relation of correspondence between facts and propositions *explains* why those propositions are true. Content identity is too weak to discharge this explanatory task, since minimalists and other deflationists who reject the correspondence theory independently advance the "content identity" account of the relation between true propositions and facts precisely because they wish to demonstrate the explanatory *vacuity* of that theory.

To return now to Alston's critique of Dummett. Suppose that one understands propositions in the manner of Frege as encapsulations of truth conditions and that, along with Dummett's antirealist, one can make no sense of the idea that truth can outrun human recognitional capacities. Then both facts and propositions, if one accepts Alston's minimalist correspondence theory of truth, become epistemically circumscribed since their contents are identical. In this way one would be led to endorse an epistemic theory of truth, which is flatly inconsistent with a realist theory in the sense in which we have been using the term "realist."

Alston does not think his own minimalism about truth *excludes* verificationist theories of content. Indeed, his position is just the opposite: One can subscribe to a verificationist theory of content, he argues, while accepting minimalist correspondence truth. Yet although Alston takes this to be a criticism of Dummett's verificationism—establishing that there is no passage from verificationist content to verificationist truth—in actual fact the alleged incompatibility between the two rebounds on him.

We have just seen that if content is determined by recognizable truth conditions, as Dummett maintains, truth is epistemically constrained. If content is not so determined, then, of course, there need be no passage from the nature of content to the nature of truth. But on Alston's view, minimalist correspondence truth is silent about content, treating it as unanalyzed. It is therefore an open question how it is to be best analyzed. So, since on one analysis, Dummett's, we are led from verificationist content to verificationist truth and verificationist content is compatible with minimalist correspondence truth, Alston has not said enough about truth to rule out (Dummett's brand of) verificationist truth as a species of minimal correspondence truth. The result is that Alston's claim that the schema (T) *completely* characterizes his theory of truth must be wrong. The schema patently admits as one of its instances a type of truth that Alston is at pains to reject—verificationist truth.

Alston would undoubtedly reject this criticism of his views since he has an argument to show that Dummett can maintain his verificationist semantics only "at the price of rendering his concept of truth gratuitous."[18] His argument goes like this. There are two possible ways in which verificationist semantics can be distinguished from realist semantics:

(I) by adopting a verificationist account of propositional content; or

(II) by adopting a verificationist account of truth, leaving propositional content alone.

Alston interprets Dummett as proceeding by way of (II) even though he has "already made it verificationist in the first way."[19] He then contends in the same passage that "although Dummett says that his view is distinctively verificationist in the second way, he has already made it verificationist in the first way. That being the case, he is unwarranted in claiming that ... verificationism requires the second way—adopting a different understanding of truth." From this he infers: "The reductionist theory of content cuts the ground from under the demand for a nonrealist theory of truth."[20]

What are we to make of this argument? Alston tells us that he does not believe (I) and (II) are incompatible, but he then adds: "My point is only that the verificationist semantics does not provide a basis for the verificationist account of truth."[21] If Alston simply wishes to make the general point that one can be a verificationist about content while holding a nonverificationist view about truth, or conversely that one can believe in verificationist truth but give some nonverificationist account of content, then this point is perfectly true but entirely orthogonal to Dummett's position, which is that propositional content must needs be truth-conditional. Once this is appreciated, it no longer appears gratuitous that Dummett should argue from the nature of content to the nature of truth, since content is to be understood in terms of recognizable truth conditions, and Alston's forced choice between (I) and (II) becomes a false dichotomy.

The answer to Alston's charge on page 124 that "Dummett cannot take the second way instead of the first without abandoning the verificationist account of sentence meaning, thus rendering his position unrecognizable" is therefore quite simple: Dummett neither intends nor is forced to choose between an account of content and an account of truth, since his position *just is* that content is truth-conditional.

1.3.3 Rorty and Davidson on Transcending the Realist–Antirealist Debate

Richard Rorty and Donald Davidson think that instead of siding either with realists or with their opponents, we should transcend the whole realist–antirealist debate. For Davidson, this is because both sides assume a scheme–content division that would allow us a neutral vantage point from which we could examine our beliefs or statements and see what items (either in the world or in minds or linguistic practices) could make those beliefs or statements true, a division he believes to be senseless. Rorty, for his part, likewise rejects any conception of our beliefs or conceptual schemes or languages as mirroring the world.

Perhaps Davidson and Rorty are right. Perhaps representationalism, the view that we construct representations of the world that are true or false according to how the world is or is not, ought to be rejected.

Does granting this imply that the realist–antirealist debate has been spirited away? No. Not unless granting this also implies that no sense can be made *either* of the idea of certain objects such as electrons or numbers or values *existing* mind-independently or of their *not existing* mind-independently. One serious problem arises with the attempt to deny sense to both the notion of mind-independent existence and its complement, non-mind-independent existence, without denying sense to the notion of existence altogether. Even assuming this can be done, perhaps because the whole idea of "mind-independence" involves some pernicious confusion, how is the resultant view to be distinguished from antirealism? If one claims that the concept of mind-independent existence is *incoherent*, one has a reason, perhaps the best of reasons, for opposing the realist's thesis that mental states or moral values or inaccessible cardinals exist independently of the mind. Once we reject the illusion of a distinction between a conceptual scheme or a system of practices and a reality to which the conceptual scheme or system of practices is answerable, the realist's credo is revealed as simply incoherent. This is an even more serious failure than garden-variety falsity, one might have thought. However one assesses it, though, this is a ground, perhaps the strongest possible ground, for antirealism.

Despite their protestations, then, both Rorty and Davidson, to the extent that they wish to really reject a conceptual scheme–world distinction, are antirealists. There has been no "going beyond" the realist–antirealist debate, only a failure to appreciate which side of the fence they're really on. In fact, I believe that it is possible to show that the pragmatist conception of truth that Rorty, at any rate, endorses is flatly mistaken. I undertake that task in the final chapter at section 8.2.

Summary

I have argued that naturalistic realists cannot afford to ignore the charge of metaphysical credulism that antirealists level against them. I have tried to show that the debate between realists and antirealists has stalled largely because of a worry about how precisely to formulate the commitments of realism. But characterization is a minor issue. Indeed, the whole characterization problem is a blind alley. I have argued that pervasive confusions and false starts have obfuscated the real issue between antirealists and realists. Last, I have tried to show that there is no "going beyond" the realist–antirealist debate in the manner of Rorty or Davidson—the logical space they wish to occupy has already been occupied by antirealism. Antirealism is simply any type of principled opposition to realism, an opposition ultimately motivated by the suspicion that realism is an indefensible form of metaphysical credulism.

II
Dummett's Antirealism

2

The Antirealist Arguments

2.1 Semantic Competence

Frege believed that the semantic significance of a sentence derived from its being true or false. The semantic significance of subsentential parts consisted in the contribution they made to the sentence's having one or the other truth value. The *sense* of an expression was that feature of its meaning that contributed to the truth conditions of the sentence. A sentence that expressed *a thought* was said to be *complete*. The sense of the complete sentence was the thought expressed. A speaker who asked "Did Fermat prove his last theorem?" and one who asserted "Fermat proved his last theorem," were, according to Frege, expressing different attitudes toward the same *thought*: The first speaker was questioning whether the thought that Fermat proved his last theorem was true; the second speaker was asserting that that selfsame thought was true.

Frege was insistent that psychologistic theories of meaning that construed the meanings of words as ideas or mental images characteristically associated with those words were totally mistaken. Such theories portrayed the meanings of sentences as derivative on antecedently given word meanings—complex ideas composed of the simple ideas associated with their constituent words. In contrast, Frege described his own position thus:

My particular conception of logic can be characterised first by the fact that I rank the word "true" at the highest point and next by the fact that I immediately follow this with the thought as that with respect to which the question of truth can be raised. Thus I do not start with concepts and build thoughts or judgements out of them but rather I arrive at the parts of the thought through an analysis of the thought.[1]

None of these general considerations lends support to an unrestricted version of Frege's *Grundlagen* claim that words have a meaning *only* in the context of a sentence. Yet Dummett has sought to give the context principle a wholly general application.

According to Dummett, the truth contained within this principle is this: "In the order of explanation the sense of a sentence is primary, but in the order of recognition the sense of a word is primary."[2] Dummett is not forced, therefore, to deny the obvious fact that we understand new sentences by recognizing familiar component words—indeed, it is a fundamental tenet of his antirealism that our understanding of sentences is *compositional:*

> To say that the sense of a sentence is composed out of the senses of its constituent words is to say, not merely that, by knowing the senses of the words, we can determine the sense of the sentence, but that we can grasp that sense only as the sense of a complex which is composed out of parts in exactly that way, only a sentence which had exactly that structure, and whose primitive constituents corresponded in sense pointwise with those of the original sentence, could possibly express the same sense.[3]

According to Dummett, then, Frege's point about the primacy of sentence sense is that the only way we can understand the notion of sense in its application to subsentential expressions is through the contribution the expression makes to determining the sentence as true or false, depending on the state of the world. The only justification for invoking the notion of a complex predicate is to explain the truth conditions of sentences containing certain expressions of generality; the only justification for attributing sense to complex expressions that are not sentences is that the sense of a sentence is constructed in stages in which at some point the complex expression's sense features.

Given that the sense of a word is derivative "in the order of explanation," it is mandatory to explain the sense of a sentence other than by means of the senses of its constituent words. Frege sought to do this by associating a truth condition with each sentence that expressed a determinate thought: To understand a sentence was to "grasp" its truth-condition. Dummett does not believe that Frege's realist model of the senses of sentences can ultimately be sustained. Still, he thinks that we can make progress in deciding the issue only by working within a Fregean conception of a theory of meaning. Fundamental to that conception are two related theses:

(1) Words have a meaning only in the context of a sentence.

(2) Sense is a cognitive notion.

Quine's suggestion that we try to make scientifically acceptable sense of meaning in terms of synonymy between expressions is declared inadequate by Dummett because "It is impossible to explain in general what is meant by 'knowing (or learning) the meaning of a word' in terms only of the relation of synonymy."[4] To understand Dummett's conception of sense more fully, we need to examine his conception of a theory of meaning within which the theory of sense plays a crucial role. Dummett sets exceedingly high standards of adequacy for theories of meaning to satisfy. A theory of meaning must account for what a speaker knows in understanding the expressions and sentences of his language in such a way as to show "not only how it (the language) does what it does but what it is that it does."[5]

In doing so, the theory must not employ any concepts that presuppose the notion of linguistic understanding or of being able to use a language at all. Only when we have constructed such a theory of meaning will we be able to command a clear view of what our highly complex linguistic ability consists in, Dummett contends. At pages 413–420 of *Frege*, Dummett sets out his ideas on the form an acceptable theory of meaning should take. These ideas are later modified and refined in "What Is a Theory of Meaning?" and "What Is a Theory of Meaning? (II)". The conception of sense undergoes a transformation in the process:

A theory of meaning should make clear the roles played by the notions of truth and falsity in the language. Just as the rules of a game take for granted the significance of classifying certain states of play as "winning" or "losing" ones, a semantic theory for a language assumes the notions of truth and falsity as they feature in the systematic assignment it makes to the sentences of that language are likewise understood.[6]

When the language in question is a formal one and our interest is in logical notions such as those of soundness and completeness, this assumption does no harm. But when we are trying to understand the workings of a natural language, the mere assignment of truth conditions to sentences is uninformative so long as we are uncertain as to how these truth conditions are connected with the actual *use* to which their respective sentences are put in the practice of speaking the language.

Thus, a Russellian language in which the predicate "false" is applied to sentences with vacuous names and a "Strawsonian" language in which such sentences are classified as "neither true nor false" would reflect a difference in the meanings assigned to sentences containing proper names (rather than a slight divergence in the meanings of the predicates translated as "true" and "false") only if we could point to some difference in the use made of such sentences over and above the differing truth values assigned to them: "Until a connection is made between the truth-value of a sentence and the linguistic activities of asserting, questioning, etc., which can be accomplished by its utterance, we are in the dark as to what truth and falsity are, what is the difference between them, or what is the significance of ascribing them to sentences."[7]

Sentences have a sense or express thoughts only in virtue of the practices of using them to make assertions, ask questions, and so on, according to Dummett. Dummett follows Frege in holding (as against Wittgenstein) that it is legitimate to separate the sense of an utterance from its force but claims that this is warranted only if it is possible to give a uniform description of the linguistic act that is effected by uttering an arbitrary sentence whose sense is presumed known with just that force.

Given that such a separation is justifiable, we can regard the theory of meaning as containing a pragmatic part—the theory of force—and a semantic part. The concept of truth will be relevant to *both* parts of the total theory: The semantic theory will provide a recursive truth definition for the sentences of the language by specifying in its base clauses the semantic values of the primitive expressions of the language and rules for determining the semantic value of any complex expression from that of its parts; the theory of force will explicate the defined concept by locating it against the background of interests, activities, and attitudes that linguistic practice subserves.

So far, Dummett's view of the form a theory of meaning should take parallels Davidson's view, on which within a context of radical interpretation a recursive truth theory specifies the truth conditions of sentences and a theory of force specifies the mode or type of linguistic act an utterance should be construed as comprising. The only difference is that Dummett calls that part of the bipartite Davidsonian theory which specifies the contents of utterances the theory of *reference* rather than the theory of *sense*. There is a reason for this differing terminology: Dummett believes that a theory of sense properly called is a theory of what the competent speaker of a language knows.

So, alongside the inductive truth definition, there will, on Dummett's picture, be a theory of (Dummettian) sense—call it a theory of sense$_D$—which will *supply an account of the cognitive aspects of an expression's use*. The theory of reference will act as input to the theory of sense$_D$, specifying the reference of each expression, and the theory of sense$_D$ will then say what a speaker grasps in grasping that reference. Dummett sums up his views in this way: "The semantic part of the theory specifies the application of the notions of truth and falsity to sentences of the language (while the cognitive part shows how we recognise the application): the pragmatic part provides the point of so classifying sentences as true or false, by describing the use that can be made of any given sentence in terms of its truth-conditions."[8] Now, although "sense can be taken only as a cognitive notion,"[9] Dummett is clear that "an account of sense does not aim to uncover an actual psychic mechanism."[10] Rather, the account the theorist gives of sense "must be a theoretical model the test of which is its agreement with observable linguistic behaviour."[11] The theory of sense$_D$ is thus to be construed as a model of what the speaker knows in grasping the reference of an expression of any complexity.

Dummett allows at page 381 of *Frege* that a theorist might conceive of certain notions employed in the model (in particular those of truth and falsity) as "theoretical notions, which cannot be correlated directly with linguistic behaviour, the model being judged correct or incorrect, according to its agreement with linguistic practice only as a whole." In "What Is a theory of meaning? (II)" however, Dummett is far less willing to make this concession. Here, the structure of and constraints on acceptable theories of meaning are spelled out in finer detail. The competent speaker of a language obviously possesses the practical knowledge of how to speak the language: "but this is no objection to its representation as propositional knowledge; mastery of a procedure, of a conventional practice, can always be so represented.... what we seek is *a theoretical representation of a practical ability.*"[12]

The meaning theory will represent the practical ability as consisting in a grasp of a system of deductively connected propositions. As before, the semantic portion of the theory will center around an inductive specification of the semantic values of each expression in the theory of reference. But now, surrounding this "core" as a "shell," the theory of sense "will lay down in what a speaker's knowledge of any part of the theory of reference is to be taken to consist, *by correlating specific practical abilities of the speaker to certain propositions of the theory.*"[13] So, whereas before Dummett was content to regard a theory of sense$_D$ with Frege as whatever it is the speaker knows in knowing the theory of reference, he now requires the theory of sense$_D$ to *correlate known propositions of the theory of reference with practical linguistic abilities.* This additional requirement is incurred, Dummett thinks, whenever we think of a theoretical model of a certain practical capacity as an item of implicit knowledge for the person whose capacity it models.

But isn't it highly implausible to attribute an implicit knowledge of a theory of meaning for his language to the average competent speaker? Since no one supposes a competent speaker of a language to be able to explicitly formulate a theory of meaning for his language, it is clear that we should ascribe *at most* an implicit knowledge of the theory to the speaker. But why ascribe such knowledge at all?

It is the burden of Dummett's case in "What Is a Theory of Meaning? (II)" that the ascription to the speaker of a knowledge of the *classical* truth conditions of a sentence is indeed vacuous. The reason Dummett gives, to oversimplify, is that the clearest test for the possession of such tacit knowledge—the speaker's recognizing that the sentence is true when and only when its truth condition is fulfilled—fails in the case of sentences that are *not effectively decidable*, that is, whose truth value is not determinable (even in principle) in finite time; and the only other models for what knowledge of a possibly recognition-transcendent truth might amount to also fail to generalize to the non-effective case.

Dummett goes on to argue that a theory of meaning that takes verifiability or falsifiability (rather than classical truth) as its central explanatory concept can pass the test above, since a speaker can be accredited an ability to recognize states of affairs that verify or falsify a sentence when they obtain. We've yet to be convinced, however, that we need to ascribe implicit knowledge to begin with.

Dummett's preferred model for a theory of meaning is a *molecular* one—one that pairs practical capacities with the theorems of the theory of reference. Against this model, it might be claimed that there is simply no prospect of pairing anything less than the whole theory of reference with the practical ability to speak the language—that there is a problem in principle with compartmentalizing this ability. So why can't the meaning theorist abstain from the task of pairing theorems with practical abilities, leaving this to the psycholinguist? He can do so, Dummett argues, only if he is prepared to relinquish the claim that competent speakers of a language *implicitly know* the theorems of a theory of meaning for their language—such as that "Der Schnee ist weiss" means that snow is white. It is a general methodological principle, according to Dummett, that ascriptions of implicit knowledge must, if they are not to be vacuous, specify not only what the ascribee is held to know, but also how this knowledge is evidenced in her behavior. Thus expressed, this methodological principle seems highly plausible—there is nothing intrinsically antirealist about such a maxim. It is a sound means of controlling the ascription of content to putative tacit cognitive states. What plausible psychological theory could possibly violate it?

In fact, *cognitivist* psychological theories may violate it. Chomsky argues that speakers tacitly know the grammar of their language. They may not, and almost certainly will not, acknowledge the grammarian's description of their syntactic competence as correct, but their ability to learn the complex grammatical rules they do on the basis of meager evidence bespeaks an innate module in the mind–brain dedicated to just this task. Tacit knowledge of grammar is only indirectly connected to behavioral dispositions for Chomsky. For a start, flawed behavioral performance is only a rough guide to underlying grammatical competence. Further, because it is "hard-wired," it is not accessible to awareness. The module is *encapsulated*, in Fodor's terminology. So there will be no simple way of pairing the tacit knowledge encapsulated in the grammar module with discrete practical abilities.[14]

What of *holistic* theories such as Davidson's? Do they really fail this condition? Doesn't Charles distinctively manifest his linguistic ability whenever Elsie addresses him in English by being able to redescribe her actions as utterances of a specified kind with a specified meaning? At this stage, we are in no position to decide this issue; at the very least, we require a clarification of semantic holism and Dummett's precise objections to it.[15]

Dummett claims that a nonclassical molecular theory of meaning *does* warrant the attribution of implicit knowledge of a sentence's verification (or falsification) conditions to a competent speaker. His argument for this claim is this:

It is not necessary that we should have any means of deciding the truth or falsity of the statement, only that we should be capable of recognising when its truth has been established. The advantage of this conception is that the condition for a statement's being verified, unlike the condition for its truth under the assumption of bivalence, is one which we must be credited with the capacity for effectively recognising when it obtains; *hence there is no difficulty in stating what an implicit knowledge of such a condition consists in—once again, it is directly displayed by our linguistic practice.*[16]

We have so far left the notion of implicit knowledge unanalyzed, and it might well transpire that it breaks down under analysis into a less clearly cognitive one—that of a skill, say (albeit a very intricate one). If so, the assumption that the ordinary speaker had at some deep level internalized the propositions of an abstruse theoretical model of his semantic competence would appear dangerously misleading.[17]

Dummett addresses this worry in "What Do I Know When I Know a Language?"[18] He asks whether the practical knowledge attributed to the speaker explains the practical ability or whether the practical ability is all there is to the practical knowledge.[19] Someone sympathetic to the latter will want to assimilate the case of language-learning to the learning of any other technique or skill—as Dummett puts it, for such a person "'to know' in these cases means 'to have learned.'"[20]

Yet there is a contrast between knowing how to speak Spanish and knowing how to swim, Dummett contends: Although it is conceivable that a person could just swim naturally without any previous training, it is not conceivable that a person could just find themselves able to speak Spanish on first arriving in a Spanish-speaking country. If a person were miraculously to find themselves uttering words that Spanish speakers recognized as Spanish, this would not amount to a knowledge of Spanish. As long as there was a doubt in that person's mind as to whether they had interpreted a sentence at all (rather than whether they had interpreted it correctly), he could not be ascribed a knowledge of Spanish. Unlike skills such as swimming, there can be no gap between knowing what it is to speak Spanish and knowing how to do so.

Clearly there are degrees of conscious involvement in the performance of different skills. So a fairer comparison, Dummett notes, would be between speaking a language and playing a game requiring reflective judgment, such as chess. Dummett thinks that it would be possible for someone to learn to play chess by simply being corrected whenever he made an illegal move without ever being told the rules of the game. In that case, we should say that he had acquired a knowledge of the rules of chess, Dummett decides, rather than describe his new state as one in which he had merely acquired a technique: "it would be unthinkable that, having learned to obey the rules of chess, he should not then be able and willing to acknowledge those rules as correct when they were put to him.... Someone who had learned the game in this way could properly be said to know the rules *implicitly* ... he does not merely follow the rules, without knowing what he is doing: he is *guided* by them."[21]

Dummett gives us a tolerably clear guide to the application of "implicit knowledge," namely: "knowledge which shows itself partly by the manifestation of the practical ability, and partly by a readiness to acknowledge as correct a formulation of that which is known when it is presented."[22] He then goes on to argue for the disputed thesis about knowledge of a theory of meaning: "A speaker's mastery of his language consists, on this view, in his knowing a theory of meaning for it: it is this that confers on his utterances the senses they bear, and it is because two speakers take the language as governed by the same, or nearly the same theory of meaning that they can communicate with one another by means of that language."[23] I am not convinced by this argument of Dummett's. We can certainly agree that language-mastery implicates an agent in epistemic states otherwise unavailable to him, but the question is whether knowledge of the propositions of a meaning theory plays any role in the speaker's semantic competence, and I do not see how Dummett's test for distinguishing between practical abilities is supposed to help us decide this issue.

Davidson disagrees with Dummett here. Spanish speakers know the consequences of a truth theory for Spanish, that is, they know the propositions expressed by the T-sentences of a homophonic truth theory for Spanish, although this is a highly misleading way to put it, given the holistic character of their knowledge. A radical interpreter R can acquire this knowledge if he constructs from the evidence of Spanish speakers' behavior an interpretative truth theory for their language. But his arcane way of acquiring this knowledge need not bear (and surely won't bear) any psychological relation to the way native Spanish speakers themselves acquire their linguistic ability, even if both routes to mastery involve radical interpretation. Thus:

Kurt utters the words "Es regnet" and ... we know that he has said that it is raining.... we are able to ... interpret his words.... What could we know that would enable us to do this? How could we come to know it? The first of these questions is not the same as the question what we *do* know that enables us to interpret the words of others. For there may easily be something we could know and don't, knowledge of which would suffice for interpretation, while on the other hand it is not altogether obvious that there is anything we actually know which plays an essential role in interpretation. The second question, how we could come to have knowledge that would serve to yield interpretations, does not, of course, concern the actual history of langauge acquisition. It is thus a doubly hypothetical question: given a theory that would make interpretation possible, what evidence plausibly available to a potential interpreter would support the theory to a reasonable degree?[24]

I think Davidson's way of seeing the relation between *theories* of the practical ability and the ability itself is by far the more attractive one. The theory of sense$_D$ plays a governing role in the total theory of meaning for Dummett. His favored theories of meaning are molecular ones in which the theory of sense$_D$ specifies what a speaker's knowledge of the T-sentences for each object-language sentence consists in by pairing these theorems with practical capacities to recognize the sentence's truth conditions as obtaining whenever they do. The theory of sense$_D$ thus constrains acceptable theories of reference to segment the practical ability to speak the language into such component abilities.

The theory of reference can be thought of as stating *what* a speaker knows, the theory of sense$_D$ as stating *how* this knowledge is manifested in behavior. Hence Dummett seeks to explain the significance of language in terms of a speaker's knowledge of his language. Earlier I said that Dummett's methodological principle governing the attribution of implicit knowledge ought to be acceptable to anyone. Yet Dummett insists on something much stronger than behavioral evidence for an ascription of tacit semantic knowledge; he insists that this knowledge should be *exhaustively manifest in use*, a demand that converts an acceptable methodological principle into a quasi-behaviorist one. What is Dummett's justification for this stronger requirement?

Dummett's justification is that meaning is *essentially communicable* and that for meaning to have the nature it has, it is necessary that what a speaker means by any expression be exhaustively recoverable just from the use that he makes of it. This is Dummett's manifestation constraint, and, as we shall see, it plays a pivotal role in his argument against realism. Dummett's clearest justification of this demand occurs in "The Philosophical Basis of Intuitionistic Logic," pages 216–217:

> The meaning of a mathematical statement determines and is exhaustively determined by its use. The meaning of such a statement cannot be, or contain as an ingredient, anything which is not manifest in the use made of it, lying solely in the mind of the individual who apprehends that meaning: if two individuals agree completely about the use to be made of the statement, then they agree about its meaning. The reason is that the meaning of a statement consists solely in its role as an instrument of communication between individuals, just as the powers of a chess-piece consist solely in its role in the game according to the rules. An individual cannot communicate what he cannot be observed to communicate: if one individual associated with a mathematical symbol or formula some mental content, where the association did not lie in the use made of the symbol or formula, then he could not convey that content by means of the symbol or formula, for his audience would be unaware of the association and would have no means of becoming aware of it.

The argument is meant to apply to all sorts of statements, not just mathematical statements—indeed, Dummett's thesis is that the most plausible ground for repudiating classical reasoning in mathematics for intuitionistic reasoning is the wholly general version of the meaning-theoretic argument above. I simply record it at this stage in order to expound Dummett's position accurately.

Let us assume for now that Dummett is right about the central concept of a theory of meaning having to be one that a speaker can recognize as obtaining whenever it does. Let us also assume, as seems undeniable, that a speaker comprehends the truth conditions of a sentence by understanding the component senses of subsentential parts. How, according to Dummett, does the speaker derive his understanding of the sentence's truth conditions from an understanding of its parts? Dummett offers the realist the following model as an initially plausible one that might meet his strictures, deriving it from Frege's writings on sense:

Since the central concept of the meaning theory has to be a recognizable one, the sense of a sentence is to be thought of as a method for determining the truth value of that sentence. Moreover, if the speaker's understanding of any sentence of his language is to be, as it must be, compositional, he must acquire an understanding of this method for determining the truth value of the sentence from his understanding of the sentence's constituents. Taking the simplest case of an atomic sentence first, a sentence of the form Fa, the sense of the singular term a is comprised of some method of identifying an object as the referent of that term; the sense of the predicate F consists in some means of determining whether a given object satisfies F. Having applied the two procedures, the speaker is in a position to determine the truth value of the sentence.

Clearly this model will not generalize, because there are many sentences for which we lack any method of determining their truth value but which we understand perfectly clearly—the model only fits a decidable language. Yet our language is rife with undecidable sentences. On the naive realist model being mooted, we therefore appeal, in such cases, to the recognitional capacities of a superhuman being for whom undecidable statements would become decidable.

Dummett finds such an appeal incredible, as tantamount to an admission that we, with our finite recognitional capacities, systematically misunderstand at least the undecidable sentences of our own language. But instead of dropping the requirement that a theory of meaning explicate the meanings of sentences of a language by means of a recognizable concept, he recommends that we drop the assumption of bivalence—that is, that every statement must possess one or the other of two truth values. Having given up bivalence, the model of understanding above now becomes defensible. He writes:

Thus, for the naive Realist, the connection between that which renders a statement true and our knowledge of its truth is an intimate one, just as it is for the Anti-Realist: from what it like to know it to be true, we see just what it is for it to be true. Only they draw opposite conclusions. The Anti-Realist draws the conclusion that the statement cannot be true unless we know it to be true, at least indirectly, or unless we have the means to arrive at such knowledge, or at least unless there exists that which, if we were aware of it, would yield such knowledge. The naive Realist believes that the statement must be determinately true or false, regardless of whether we are able in the particular case, to perceive that which renders it true or false; but it is our capacity, in favourable circumstances, to perceive directly that which renders true or false other statements of the same type that constitutes our understanding of what it is for the given statement to be true or to be false.[25]

2.2 Decidability and Truth

There is no dispute between the realist and the antirealist over the decidable fragment of a language, according to Dummett. The dispute arises solely over sentences for which we lack any actual deciding evidence or any procedure for deciding their truth value in finite time. I shall refer to such sentences as "non–effectively decidable sentences" ("non-ED" sentences, for short). I will assume there *are* decidable empirical statements—statements whose truth value can be definitely ascertained within a finite stretch of time.

What statements in a natural language could reasonably be thought of as non-ED? Crispin Wright replies: "multifarious types of sentence are in this situation: unrestricted spatial or temporal generalisations, many subjunctive conditionals, descriptions of the remote past, hypotheses about the mental life of others or of animals."[26] Such statements, though *presently undecidable*, might at some time be *decided*—it is just that we lack an effective way of bringing into being any deciding information. Unlike the realist, the antirealist denies that there are any intelligible absolutely undecidable statements—statements about the properties of inaccessible ordinals, for example, are regarded as incoherent. J. J. C. Smart's fantasy of a five-dimensional universe consisting of two causally isolated four-dimensional subuniverses would also be thought of as unintelligible—since we could in principle have no means of determining whether the truth conditions of "The universe is five-dimensional" obtained, the antirealist denies that we have a coherent grasp of its truth conditions. Presumably the antirealist would tender the same evaluation for the many-worlds interpretation of quantum theory in which "the" universe is in reality a multiverse—every time the universe is faced with a choice at the quantum level, it splits into as many copies of itself as are required to realize each possible option.

There is a principled basis for the rejection of such examples, at least if the antirealism in question deploys an intuitionistic logic: Such cases lead to the assertion of a contradiction. If we have grounds for asserting that it is logically impossible that p should be verified, we thereby have grounds for asserting $\neg p$, and similarly, if we have grounds for asserting that it is logically impossible that $\neg p$ should be verified, we thereby have grounds for asserting $\neg\neg p$; hence we have grounds for asserting a contradiction, to wit $\neg p$ & $\neg\neg p$ (which is intuitionistically equivalent to the denial of the law of the excluded middle). Thus the supposition that such cases represent coherent possibilities has to be rejected.

In fact, Dummett's notion of undecidability has been widely misunderstood. So it is best to explicate it as clearly as possible. Recall our Socrates sentence:

(S) Socrates sneezed in his sleep the night before he took the hemlock.

Recall from section 1.1 that it was precisely the assumption of *metaphysical determinacy*—that the world determinately either contains Socrates' sneezing, σ_s, or Socrates' not sneezing, $\sigma_{\neg s}$, irrespective of whether we twenty-first-century humans have any evidence as to which—that Dummett identified as definitive of metaphysical realism.

Dummett has not been entirely clear in his writings as to how he means the notion of undecidability to be understood. But it is implicit in all he has said on the topic that undecidability is a notion that applies first to speakers within a linguistic community. As Dummett understands it, undecidability is indexed to linguistic communities, relative to the evidence at their disposal and the conceptual resources they collectively possess, as well as more obvious things such as their position in space and time.

When Dummett says that there are undecidable sentences, then, what he means is:

At any time t and for any given linguistic community C there will be sentences p that all competent speakers s in C can then understand but for which no decision procedure Π_p exists such that if implemented at any time t' subsequent to t will either yield the verdict p or the verdict $\neg p$.

In symbols:

$$\forall t. \forall s_C. \exists p [U spt \ \& \ \neg \exists \Pi_p \exists t' \{t' \geq t \ \& \ Is\Pi_p t' \rightarrow (\Pi_p \Vdash_{t'} p \vee \Pi_p \Vdash_{t'} \neg p)\}]$$

"Undecidable" sentences are thus undecidable for speakers of C at t relative to their conceptual resources Ψ, their means of detection Δ, their total state of information Σ, and other possible parameters such as their location λ in space. Likewise, "verification-transcendent" or "evidence-transcendent" sentences need only be so for C at t relative to Ψ, Δ, and Σ.

How, then, do we understand undecidable statements, according to the antirealist? *By understanding their canonical verification conditions.* We understand the meaning of "Parmenides first walked on his first birthday" because we know what it would be to be in receipt of evidence conclusively attesting to this fact.[27] The antirealist claims that our understanding of sentences is both *compositional* and *molecular*: we associate sentences with sets of assertibility conditions that confer an individual sense on them, and we recognize the meaning of sentences through familiarity with the meaning of their parts and structure. Thus the antirealist need not insist implausibly with the positivists of yore that we understand a sentence only if we can conduct some test to verify or falsify it.[28]

Antirealists contend that truth cannot outrun our capacities to determine truth and so recommend replacing truth with some nontranscendent concept, such as verification or falsification (or possibly both) as the central explanatory concept(s) of a theory of meaning. *Is it necessary, though, for the antirealist to allot any explanatory role to truth at all?* Dummett has urged that it is: Truth will no longer be the central concept in terms of which other semantic notions are to be explained, but it will play a fundamental role in the theory of meaning. The most important function it will fulfill is in giving an account of the valid inferences in the language, for there is no other way, ultimately, of characterizing a valid inference than as one that preserves truth from premises to conclusion.[29]

Another possible reason for requiring truth to play an explanatory role in an antirealist theory of meaning is this:

In a theory of meaning in which truth plays the central role, the content of any assertion is fully determined by the condition that the sentence uttered be true.... There is, however, no a priori reason why the truth condition of a complex sentence should depend only on the truth-conditions of its constituent sentences.... likewise, the general conception of a theory of meaning in terms of the conditions for the verification and falsification of a sentence carries no presumption that the meanings of the sentential operators will be explained in the comparatively simple way that they are in intuitionistic logic.[30]

Although it does not follow from this observation alone that the notion of truth will be *required* to account for the meanings of the sentential operators, there are certain semantic intuitions that support this thought. For example, my belief that a certain judge influenced the natural course of justice is more plausibly construed as a belief that the corresponding content sentence is *true* rather than warrantedly assertible; similarly, the antecedents of conditionals seem to be hypotheses of truth rather than warranted assertibility, which explains the strong intuitive connection between truth and conditional statements that Dummett has so often emphasized. It will follow from these considerations that "the doubt is exactly whether a systematic antirealist theory of meaning is possible"[31] *only if* we can demonstrate that the concept of truth is unavailable to the antirealist. Contrapositively, an acceptable antirealist meaning-theory ought, it seems, to include an account of truth.[32] Such a concept of truth would have to be one that speakers could in principle recognize as obtaining whenever it was held to obtain. It would not be necessary for truth to be effectively decidable—"recognizable 'in principle'" is a notion weaker than effective decidability, allowing for cases of recognition of truth being prevented by contingent misfortune or lack of ingenuity.

2.3 Dummett's Manifestation Argument against Metaphysical Realism

The task now is to outline Dummett's case against metaphysical realism. This case needs some redescribing, because for Dummett, realism is an explicitly semantic thesis, defined over classes of sentences. It is the view that:

The meanings of sentences in a given class can be explicated by a classical two-valued semantics together with a truth-conditional theory of meaning based on that semantics.

Opposed to that thesis stand a variety of antirealisms:

(I) The most radical, anti-objectivism, denies that a truth-conditional account of meaning can be given at all.

(II) The least radical, antireferentialism, denies that reference (qua word–world relations) plays any role in an explanation of truth or falsity.

(III) The denial that Bivalence is generally warranted, antibivalence, lies somewhere between the two extremes (I) and (II).

Dummett has most explicitly opposed version (III) to realism, though his arguments easily generalize to the other variants. Antirealism, as Dummett envisages it, is thus first and foremost a negative doctrine. It is (most typically) *the denial that classical truth and falsity (truth subject to bivalence) can be the central explanatory concepts in the theory of meaning*. It carries no positive commitments at all—in particular, it ought not to be identified with the claim that some other non-verification-transcendent notion of truth such as intuitionistic truth should play that role.[33] Stated thus, there is little in this doctrine to worry proponents of an austere metaphysical realism who conceive of realism as the pure metaphysical thesis that some realm of objects exists independently of the mind. Opposition to the use of truth and falsity in the theory of meaning often comes, after all, from within the ranks of such realists—those who believe that wide semantic concepts such as truth or reference are powerless to explain cognitive behavior posit narrow ersatzes to fill that role.

Thus conceptual or computational role, notional worlds, subjective probability, and, indeed, verification and falsification have all been mooted as suitable explanantia for narrow content. By Dummett's lights, then, such avowedly realist philosophers as Hartry Field, Jerry Fodor, and Michael Devitt all turn out to be antirealists. This couldn't be right. It highlights once more the inadequacy of Dummett's understanding of realism, already found wanting. However, even if Dummett's characterization of metaphysical realism is inadequate, which it is, and even if his argument against realism makes some highly contentious assumptions, which, we will shortly see, it does, there is a challenge to realism contained therein that no realist can afffford to duck: *the Humean challenge to justify belief in the existence of mind-independent objects and states of affairs.*

The antirealist's Humean claim is that *it would never be rational to believe in such things*. The argument against realism, if successful, would therefore reveal belief in these entities to be a form of metaphysical credulism. How is this Humean challenge to be motivated against a naturalistic realist who may be a thoroughgoing semantic deflationist? Instead of casting antirealism as the denial that classical truth and falsity (truth subject to bivalence) can be the central explanatory concepts in the theory of meaning (which a deflationist realist would also deny), we should cast it as *the denial that mental representation of mind-independent states of affairs and objects is possible.* So, even if the naturalistic realist is a semantic deflationist, he must still hold that we are somehow able mentally to represent those states of affairs we mean to represent when we use words or mental symbols in the way we do. This is so even if our mental representations are subject to a large amount of (unsuspected) semantic indeterminacy. This means that the deflationist realist still believes that sentences such as our "Socrates sneezed in his sleep the night before he took the hemlock" are true or false independently of whether we are able to ascertain which. This is all Dummett's manifestation argument needs.

2.3.1 Dummett's Manifestation Argument

I shall proceed by setting out Dummett's manifestation argument, noting contentious assumptions as they occur and indicating possible realist rejoinders where appropriate. We now need only to review Dummett's conception of the structure of a theory of meaning before presenting his case against realism:

(1) The "core" of a theory of meaning is the theory of reference, which consists of a finitely axiomatized Tarskian truth theory assigning references to the semantic primitives of the object language and recursively specifying the truth conditions of its sentences.

(2) This core provides a theoretical representation of the content of the competent speaker's knowledge of her language.

(3) Surrounding the core as a shell is the theory of sense. This provides a model of what the speaker's knowledge of any part of the theory of reference consists in by correlating certain practical linguistic abilities with known propositions of the theory of reference.

(4) Finally, the theory of force will provide an account of the conventional significance of an utterance of a sentence in a given mood—it will demonstrate the kind of linguistic act typically performed by an utterance of a sentence in a designated mood.

The theory of sense is pivotal in Dummett's case against realism, for it will rule out as unacceptable *any meaning theory that does not permit a mapping of implicitly known propositions of the theory onto recognitional abilities manifesting that knowledge.*

There are three sorts of ways this mapping might, in principle, be achieved—in an atomic, molecular, or holistic fashion:

(A) An atomic theory of meaning will correlate recognitional abilities with the axioms of the truth theory.

(B) A molecular theory will correlate these abilities with the theorems of that theory.

(C) A holistic theory will attempt *no partitioning* of the theory but will instead take the whole theory to provide a model of the *undifferentiated* practical ability.

The "shell" that is the theory of sense thus provides a theoretical representation of the manner in which the speaker's semantic knowledge is made manifest in linguistic practice. Dummett argues for a molecular theory against the restrictiveness of an atomic one. He also argues against the acceptability of a holistic theory, as we shall see later.

It is important to see that Dummett's model for the structure of a theory of meaning can be generalized to apply to the meanings of expressions in a language of thought (LOT), as repugnant as he would find the notion of a LOT, or even a more "maplike" system of representation. It might prove necessary to lift some restrictions in ways that Dummett might not approve of—for example, to replace "recognitional abilities" in (A) above with more general cognitive abilities, or to allow for a more radically Chomskian reading of "implicit knowledge" than Dummett would ever endorse. Finally, to accommodate semantic deflationists we might replace "theory of meaning" with "theory of mental representation." The result would be something like this:

(A*) An atomic theory of mental representation will correlate specific cognitive abilities with the axioms of the theory.

(B*) A molecular theory will correlate these abilities with the theorems of that theory.

(C*) A holistic theory will attempt *no partitioning* of the theory but will instead take the whole theory to provide a model of *undifferentiated* cognitive ability.

We can now set out Dummett's argument against realism. Dummett specifies three constraints on acceptable theories of meaning:

(C_1) The meaning of any statement (or expression) is exhaustively determined by and exhaustively determines the use of that statement (expression).

(C_2) Semantic competence is the practical ability to use the expressions of a language in appropriate circumstances. Although practical, the ability is nonetheless cognitive and represents a form of implicit knowledge.

(C_3) Since it is implicit knowledge, semantic competence must make an observable difference to the behavior of the person who possesses it.

Dummett's reason for (C_1) is that language is essentially a vehicle for communication. To suppose that meaning could somehow transcend use is to make meaning ineffable, according to him. As for (C_2), Dummett's idea is that on pain of regress or circularity the knowledge required to be able to speak a language cannot generally be explicit, so it must be implicit. As the case against realism is easier to grasp with those background constraints in mind, I shall summarize these as:

(C_1) Meaning is use.

(C_2) Semantic knowledge is implicit.

(C_3) Implicit knowledge must be manifestable in behavior.

Once again, a more liberal version of these constraints can be fashioned so as to accommodate the semantic deflationists among our target realists:

(C_{1*}) The state of affairs (object) any LOT sentence (or expression) represents is exhaustively determined by the functional role of that LOT sentence (expression).

(C_{2*}) Cognitive competence is the practical ability to use the expressions of one's LOT in appropriate circumstances. Although practical, the ability is nonetheless cognitive and represents a form of implicit knowledge.

(C_{3*}) Since it is implicit knowledge, cognitive competence must make an observable difference to the behavior of the person who possesses it.

To summarize:

(C_1) Mental representation is a matter of functional role.

(C_2) Cognitive competence deploys implicit knowledge of LOT symbol-object links.

(C_3) Implicit knowledge must be manifestable in behavior.

Now consider the realist's suggestion that the meaning of a sentence (or the state of affairs it represents) is either determined by or else determines its truth condition. By the constraints above, this theory of meaning (mental representation) will be acceptable only if speakers' knowledge of truth conditions is largely implicit. Dummett's argument against realism then proceeds:

(1) For effectively decidable sentences, the ascription to a speaker of implicit knowledge of their truth conditions can be justified if the speaker can recognize whether or not those conditions are satisfied within a finite time.

(2) For non-ED sentences this type of test cannot apply, since the truth conditions may hold or fail to hold without the speaker's recognizing this fact.

(3) So no practical ability on the part of the speaker can be involved that manifests a grasp of the truth conditions of non-ED sentences.

(4) Thus the attribution of implicit knowledge of these conditions is wholly vacuous.

(5) The only type of knowledge that a speaker can have of the truth conditions of non-ED sentences is thus explicit, verbalizable knowledge, which is useless here.[34]

(6) But we clearly do understand the various types of non-ED statements speakers utter on occasions, since we know the types of circumstances in which their assertion is warranted.

(7) Realism, however, makes the attribution of such knowledge to speakers indefensible.

(8) Hence, as speakers undoubtedly do possess such knowledge, realism is false.

Suppose we try to respect, for the time being, the constraints (C_1), (C_2), and (C_3) above. What should we make of premises (1) to (7)? Premise (5) might seem dubious; it is not by any means *obvious* that explicit knowledge of non-ED sentences is useless.

Premises (2) and (3) also look questionable. Why should the practical abilities that manifest a grasp of truth conditions be concerned *solely* with the recognition of the fulfillment of those truth conditions? Why isn't a language-user's ability to interpret another speaker's utterances *practical ability enough*, irrespective of whether the speaker's statements have verification-transcendent truth conditions?[35] Premise (2) seems to assume without justification that a sufficient condition for the ascription of implicit knowledge in (1) is a necessary condition as well, and realists naturally deny that this is so.[36]

We clearly need to look more closely at the support Dummett provides for his premises. Dummett thinks that there are just two models for a speaker's knowledge of the truth conditions of a sentence:

(A) explicit verbalizable knowledge; and

(B) the capacity to observe whether the truth condition holds or not.[37]

The reason for restricting knowledge to types (A) and (B) has partly to do with how he thinks application of the concept of truth to sentences is determined. Dummett contends in "What Is a Theory of Meaning? (II)" that two principles control its application:

(1) Principle C: If a sentence is true there must be something in virtue of which it is true.

(2) Principle K: If a sentence is true, it must be possible in principle to know that it is.

Dummett then connects the two principles thus: *If it were impossible to know the truth of a given sentence, then there could be nothing that made that sentence true.*[38]

Dummett clearly does not believe that these principles tell us the *whole* truth about truth; however, I doubt they tell us *nothing but* the truth, either. What does Dummett mean by principle C? Clearly it is a truthmaker principle of sorts. Yet Dummett surely doesn't intend it as an explication of the correspondence theory of truth, as those who propose such a principle do, since he believes the correspondence theory to be false.[39] His idea seems to be that the attribution of the predicate "true" to a statement must be *justifiable* on some ground or other, rather than that there must be some state of affairs in the world whose obtaining "makes" a given sentence true. To the extent that he holds this doctrine, though, he has already inscribed a distinctively antirealist understanding of truthmakers into his prescriptions for truth.[40]

I find it hard to grasp this talk of "making true" under its usual interpretations. I am happy to admit such relations of correspondence—indeed, as a realist I insist on them—but I balk at the suggestion that they can by themselves *explain* what the truth of a true statement consists in. Dummett, by way of contrast, seems to balk at the correspondences while agreeing that we need some truth-maker or other. These issues are taken up in the final chapter. The crucial point for our purposes here is this: Naturalistic realists can be minimalists about truth, as we've seen. Yet minimalists reject the notion of truth-making. So do those who, like Donald Davidson, take truth to be primitive. Davidson puts the point thus: "Nothing, however, no thing, makes sentences or theories true: not experience, not surface irritations, not the world, can make a sentence true."[41] This quotation expresses a point minimalists also insist on.

Why does Dummett think we need truthmakers? I suspect it is because he believes that unless there were some explanation as to what the truth of a true statement consists in, our practice of applying the concept of truth must really be incoherent. Minimalists and those who take truth as primitive would both contest this—minimalists on the grounds that there is no hidden nature of truth to explain, "primitivists" on the grounds that there is no feasible naturalistic (or other) reduction of truth to other concepts or relations. Again, these matters are pursued in chapter 8.

We can sum up the import of principles C and K as follows:

For a sentence to be true, it is necessary that there be some knowable ground for its truth.

Dummett's problem is that no realist will accept this thesis as it stands. Since this is what grounds his restriction of the acceptable manifestions of linguistic understanding to verbal and recognitional abilities, realists are unlikely to accept those restrictions either.

2.3.2 Bare Truths

Dummett calls a sentence p *barely true* if it is true and there is no reductive class of sentences for any class of sentences containing p. The truth of barely true sentences, in other words, supervenes on the truth of no other sentences. A sentence p that cannot be barely true has some reductive class R of sentences such that p can be true only if all the sentences in some subset of R are true.

Dummett maintains that there is no problem in ascribing to a speaker a knowledge of a *non–barely true* sentence—either the *theory of reference* will provide a "nontrivial" T-theorem for it, articulating the way in which its truth depends on the prior truth of some subset of sentences in its reductive class, or, because of some problem in translating the sentence into the metalanguage, the T-theorem will be of a "trivial" form (e.g., "snow is white" is true iff snow is white) and it will then be the task of the *theory of sense* to describe the relationship between the sentence and its reductive class.[42]

It is *barely true* sentences that cause the problem. With a barely true sentence, the corresponding T-sentence must be trivial, and so the whole burden of explaining what it is to grasp the meaning of such a sentence falls on the theory of sense. However, the only plausible model for a speaker's understanding of a barely true sentence, Dummett contends, is an observation report.[43] Yet however generously we extend the notion of a sentence whose truth can be settled by observation, we cannot include within its compass sentences quantifying over infinite or unsurveyable domains, counterfactual conditionals, sentences referring to inaccessible regions of space or time or any other non-ED sentence. Hence, if the realist permits certain non-ED statements to be barely true, she will be bereft of a model that could justify the attribution of implicit knowledge of their truth conditions to a speaker.

2.3.3 Bare Truths Assessed

Dummett's notion of bare truths, as we might call them, is an interesting one, and I think it *is* responsive to some of our intuitions regarding truth. But which ones? It is scarcely credible to believe that we accept or reject some of the sentences from the classes mentioned above for no reason at all. We accept "The entropy of the big bang was surprisingly low" because we accept a sophisticated theory about the origins of the universe. It is in the very nature of the case that it not be directly susceptible to confirmation by observation. Dummett presumably exempts such highly confirmed sentences from his criticisms. His point must rather be that there are other sorts of sentences in this class not even weakly confirmable/disconfirmable for which realists still hold there to be a fact to the matter as to whether they are true or false.

To take a different sort of example, although it seems plausible to reject "If Oswald had not killed Kennedy someone else would have," it seems implausible to either accept or reject "If the next pope were to be an Englishman, he'd probably be called Adrian." For sentences like this, with no visible means of support in total theory, bivalence looks to be inappropriate, and someone who insists on it really must think that such hypothetical modal sentences can be barely true in Dummett's sense. Such a person would be hard-pressed to explain *how* the rest of what we know about the world dictates that this sentence must either be true or false. Allegiance to bivalence in this case does seem to flow from a thesis about (the completeness of) truth, and one who believed this thesis would be holding a clearly realist attitude to the truth of arbitrary modal sentences. Much the same could be said of someone who insisted that "Harry is tall" is either true or false when he is a borderline 180 cm.

Counterfactual or hypothetical modal sentences are anomalous enough for the naturalistic realist to dismiss, as are vague statements. Things look different for certain past-tense claims. Take this one: "Julius Caesar's heart skipped a beat just before he crossed the Rubicon." Realists about the past think that this is either true or false. But is it *barely* true or false? Is there *no* class of sentences on which its truth value supervenes? To the contrary, there seem to be any number of sentences one would have to stubbornly ignore to maintain that there is simply no ground for believing this sentence to be either true or false—"Julius Caesar really existed, he was a real human being, not a creature of myth," "Every human has a heart," "Human hearts have determinate histories beating at determinate rates for only a finite time," "Julius Caesar really did cross the Rubicon," and so on. There is, in other words, a rich subvenience or reductive class of sentences for this sample sentence.

Moreover, it is implausible in the extreme to construe our willingness to assert bivalence for it as deriving from a prior commitment to the completeness of truth for past-tense claims. Our adherence to bivalence in this instance arises from a well-grounded conviction that Julius Caesar was a real human being who did cross the Rubicon river. One could believe this and be completely agnostic as to whether bivalence holds generally for past-tense claims.

The contrast between the temporal case and the modal (or vague) case thus couldn't be sharper. In the latter, our theory of the world has nothing (or little) to say on whether an English pope would most likely be called Adrian; in the former it has everything to say on whether or not at any given time a human heart experiences ectopic beats. And what it does say is mute on the nature of truth. Realism about truth is thus strictly irrelevant to our grounds for believing in the factuality of this sentence. I think Dummett simply has to admit this. If the antirealist has any general problem with past-tense claims it had better not be a problem shared by "Julius Caesar's heart skipped a beat just before he crossed the Rubicon." This sentence is patently not barely true (false) in the sense that Dummett gives to that expression, the sense in which "If the next pope were to be an Englishman he'd probably be called Adrian" is barely true, if true at all. Antirealists thus do their cause a disservice when they adopt an overly restrictive notion of "undecidable" in "undecidable sentence."

2.3.4 Holism and Bare Truths

The discussion of bare truths might lead the naturalistic realist to suspect that there are no interesting bare truths that naturalistic realism need defend. Rather, since any sentence with genuine naturalistic content must somehow be related to total theory there will be a subvenience base for any contentful sentence—namely, the whole theory, although certain sentences might have a more compact reductive class in some subset of the whole set. This, it might be held, is a simple consequence of confirmational holism.

So, if there need be no barely true non-ED sentences for the naturalistic realist, why doesn't Dummett's manifestation argument simply collapse? The problem of manifestation was supposed to be a problem for only barely true non-ED sentences, so it seems to disappear if there aren't any such sentences.

This is a "wise monkey" response—the response of a monkey who sees no problem. Unfortunately, there *is* a problem, and the monkey has confused myopia for wisdom. The problem lies with the reductive class, which is supposed to shoulder the burden of meeting the manifestation demand. This class will either itself directly contain non-ED sentences (which, of course, it will if it is the whole theory), or, where it is some finite subset of the whole set of sentences, its sentential elements will still be inferentially connected to non-ED sentences in other, possibly quite remote, regions of the total theory. This is an inevitable result of the very holism that was supposed to *undercut* the manifestation argument.

It is irrelevant for the confirmational holist to protest against this point that confirmational holism does not entail semantic holism. The philosophers who insist on such a divide, such as Jerry Fodor and Michael Devitt, are clear that, *pace* Dummett, a theory of meaning is precisely *not* a theory of semantic competence.[44] And for good reason. The *meaning* of "The big bang had extremely low entropy" may be semantically isolable from the theory that implies it, but the *evidence* that supports it is most assuredly not.

It is the supporting theory that "faces the tribunal of experience," to use Quine's lovely metaphor, not the sentence by itself. Since understanding this sentence is among other things a matter of knowing what evidence supports it, what the implications of its truth or falsity would be for other sentences and so on, the above point holds good. Confirmational holism simply inflates the problem of sentence-specific manifestation to a problem for the whole theory.

This confusion may help explain an otherwise anomalous feature of Dummett's assessment of the various ways semantic knowledge may be manifested. Normally we do credit speakers with an understanding of a statement if they evince a sensitivity to the types of evidence that would confirm it and to the network of implications that the statement sustains and, conversely, refuse to so credit them unless they can do this. The connections between ascriptions of understanding and demonstrable evidential or inferential sensitivity are thus pretty tight. So why doesn't Dummett include these crucial abilities as manifesting a grasp of a sentence's truth conditions? The short answer is that he does. But what makes the attribution of understanding defensible in these instances is, he would argue, our tacit conviction that the speaker would recognize the truth conditions as obtaining whenever they did (or that the speaker can relate these truth conditions to other recognizable truth conditions of sentences in some *suitable* reductive class). Dummett plainly regards a speaker's evidential evaluations as derivative upon her grasp of the sentence's meaning: "... the principles which govern what counts as evidence for the truth of a sentence must be systematically derivable from its meaning."[45] So, although Dummett could agree that evidential and inferential abilities on the part of the speaker do give us reason to ascribe (and withhold) a grasp of a sentence's meaning to a speaker, these abilities are derivative upon a verbal or observational grasp of truth conditions—they are part of what a theory of meaning has to *explain*.[46] Note that for the purposes at hand, it does not matter that the holist may disagree with Dummett about whether evidence for a sentence is determined by its meaning.

The question, then, is how a grasp of recognition-transcendent truth conditions can determine that certain evidence is good evidence for the truth of a given statement and how mere reasoning in accord with classical logical principles can answer the antirealist challenge to show that the ascription of implicit knowledge of recognition-transcendent truth conditions to a speaker is not vacuous. The holist's attempt to evade the manifestation argument thus fails. All the naturalistic realist's invocation of holism does is map the demand for manifestation of understanding for any particular non-ED sentence onto all the other sentences of total theory. It *intensifies* the problem rather than evades it.

Summary

Let us review the course of Dummett's manifestation argument against realism:

(1) Dummett lays down three constraints on any acceptable theory of meaning:

(C_1) Meaning is exhaustively determined by and determines use.

(C_2) Semantic knowledge is implicit knowledge.

(C_3) Implicit knowledge must be manifestable in behavior.

(2) In accord with these constraints, an acceptable realist theory of meaning must show how a speaker's implicit knowledge of the truth conditions of a sentence both determines the use she makes of that sentence and is manifest in behavior.

(3) The argument then proceeded:

(P_1) Ascription of an implicit knowledge of an ED sentence's truth conditions is unproblematic because the speaker can recognize these truth conditions as obtaining whenever they do.

(P_2) But for non-ED sentences, such attributions are vacuous just because the speaker cannot recognize their truth conditions as obtaining whenever they do and such recognitional ability is the only practical ability that would demonstrate such a grasp.

(P_3) Ascribing explicit knowledge is equally useless.

(P_4) But we clearly do understand the assertibility conditions of non-ED sentences.

(C) Realism must therefore be false.

(4) We saw that (P_2) and (P_3) look questionable. In particular, (P_2) seems to treat what was acknowledged as a sufficient condition for the ascription of implicit knowledge as a necessary condition also.

(5) We then noted that Dummett's principles C and K afford some reason for identifying understanding with a recognitional ability—for according to those constraints, if a sentence is true at all there must be some knowable ground for its truth. This requirement is unacceptable to realists, however.

(6) The request for such a knowable ground led to the narrowing of acceptable models for understanding to just two—a verbal model for sentences whose truth depended on the prior truth of sentences in some reductive class and an observational model for barely true sentences.

(7) It was then seen to be a moot question whether these models were exhaustive of our conception of semantic knowledge, the realist objecting that evidential and inferential abilities should also be included.

Of the assumptions, (C_1) and (C_2) seem to be ones that the realist might well take issue with. (C_3) is the entirely reasonable requirement that ascriptions of implicit knowledge (whether of meaning or of anything else) be borne out by behavior. It is Dummett's quasi-behaviorist interpretation of (C_1), that such knowledge be exhaustively manifest in use, that the realist could and I believe should contest.

3
Realist Replies to Antirealism

3.1 Warranted Assertibility and Truth

Antirealists contend that realist truth is an incoherent concept. This is the thrust of Dummett's manifestation argument against realism. In effect, antirealists hold an error theory with respect to realist truth. Since they agree that many, perhaps most, speakers unreflectively take truth to be verification-transcendent, it is incumbent on them to explain how we come by the notion of realist truth and what genuine notion it is a distortion of.

3.1.1 Dummett on Assertion

Dummett's project is to exhibit truth as a construct out of the primitive notion of correct assertibility. Realist truth will emerge as a distortion of the notion of truth that we actually acquire when we learn our native language. In *Frege*, Dummett claims that it "belongs to the essence of language" that "assertions are understood as governed by the convention that the speaker is aiming at uttering those whose truth condition is fulfilled" (p. 3). Yet if the concept of truth derives from the primitive notion of an assertion's being correct (or incorrect), the claim above appears to be a truistic one since the convention is then just to utter those statements it would be correct to assert. For this reason, it seems unlikely that Dummett intends to characterize assertoric force by means of a convention to utter true sentences.

So what does Dummett take assertoric force to be? Dummett considers and dismisses the general possibility that illocutionary forces are individuated by the intentions of speakers: intention cannot bear the weight of the distinctions, since the relevant intentions can arise only against the background of a general convention endowing certain utterances with a certain significance.[1] Instead of starting with utterances as an undifferentiated class and attempting to specify which constitute assertions, which questions, and so on, by reference to the intentions of the speaker, "the correct approach is to consider utterances as conventionally demarcated into types, by means of the form of linguistic expressions employed, and enquire into the conventions governing the use of the various types of utterance."[2]

Convention is thus invoked to characterize the illocutionary force of the linguistic act of assertion. Each distinguishable type of illocutionary act is governed by a distinctive sort of convention—by those conventions, we can correlate illocutionary acts with distinctive purposes on the part of the speaker, pairing assertions with intentions to utter truths, commands with intentions to get hearers to realize truths, questions with intentions to find out about truths, and so on; the intentions in question being those that the speaker is conventionally taken to have via his issuing utterances with the appropriate force. As to what signals that an utterance has one rather than another type of force, convention is again invoked to provide the explanation—Dummett thinks it "roughly correct" that the indicative mood carries assertoric force, and similarly for the relation between other moods and forces.[3]

Dummett does not think it *arbitrary* that the person who asserts that *p* is thereby taken to have the intention to utter a truth. In fact he clearly thinks there is a *conceptual* connection between the assertion and the relevant intention. He dismisses as "spurious" the possibility that speakers could have adopted the convention to utter falsehoods in issuing statements with assertoric force, acknowledging Wittgenstein as making a "cognate point" in the *Tractatus,* 4.062.[4] Wittgenstein's argument there was that if a speaker uttered "It is raining" and meant by it that it was *not* raining, then since truth depends on meaning we should say that what he said was *true,* not false, if in fact it were not raining—"if by '*p*' we mean '$\neg p$' and things are as we mean them, then '*p*' is on the new interpretation true and not false." So it must be strictly incorrect on Dummett's view to say that the intention to utter a truth is *conventionally* related to an assertion, given that an alternative regularity to utter falsehoods (which seems just as useful) is "spurious."

Dummett cannot therefore be wanting to characterize the convention governing assertion primarily in terms of the speaker's being imputed a certain intention or belief. Very crudely, there are two ways in which assertoric force could be characterized:

(1) by means of the beliefs or intentions on the part of the speaker; or

(2) by means of the commitments that a speaker makes in asserting a sentence.

In accord with (2), there is at least one well-defined commitment that the assertor makes to her audience, namely, to withdraw her assertion that *p* if she cannot, when challenged, supply adequate grounds for *p*.

3.1.2 Dummett's Rejection of Psychologism

I think it is important to grasp why Dummett is so opposed to relying on mental states to characterize assertoric (or other) force. Explaining this goes a long way toward explaining his insistence on the manifestability of semantic understanding. What lies behind this idea of manifestability is the idea that the *contents of thoughts* are themselves *essentially public and communicable*. Thus he shares Frege's distrust of all psychological incursions into the theory of meaning:

> The procedure we have agreed on, however, is to give an account of these exterior linguistic acts *directly*, by describing the conventions governing the use of the various forms of expression: the alternative procedure, of describing first the nature of the various interior acts, and then explaining the various types of utterance as being conventionally used to express the occurrence of these mental acts, we have rejected as leading to the confusion of psychology with logic.[5]

On Dummett's view, this latter confusion leads to the mistaken picture of *assertion as the manifestation of a mental act*.[6] After adverting to Russell's attempts to distinguish a logical from a psychological sense of "assertion" and to the early Wittgenstein's counter that "assertion is merely psychological," Dummett remarks: "This supposed 'psychological' kind of assertion which appears in Russell and Wittgenstein is a phantasm produced by the mistake of interpreting assertion as the manifestation of an internal mental attitude adopted toward the proposition; *in fact, there is nothing any more psychological about assertion than about the sense expressed by a sentence.*"[7]

3.1.3 Response to Dummett on Assertion

The natural response to Dummett's views is that if assertion is not some sort of psychological act, it is hard to see what else it could be. But Dummett's attack is directed against *psychologism*—the view that *an inner process of assent to a proposition must precede the public act of assertion, which merely exteriorizes it*. This view depends on a model of language as a *code* for our preexistent and perfectly determinate thoughts. Again, this point is crucial for understanding the manifestation constraint. The only alternative Dummett can see to meaning or content that is fully manifestable is that meaning is a code for preexistent thought.

I agree that the psychologistic code model is of dubious coherence, but I do not think that we need accept it in order to make out the connection between assertion and belief. Here is an alternative view loosely based on Davidson's theory of intentional action: We can agree with Dummett that there *need* have been no event that was the speaker's judging that p temporally distinct from the event of her asserting that p, though some such judgment *could* have preceded her giving expression to it through assertion. Whether there will be one event or two, a distinct mental judgment as well as the assertion, will depend largely on the reflectiveness of the speaker, the nature of the judgment and associated assertion as well as the context in which it is made.

So Dummett is right to oppose the psychologistic model on which assertion is *generally* to be understood as an encoding of an already determinate and temporally prior judgment, which is in all cases to be construed as the cause of the agent's assertion at any given time. But it does not follow from this that there are *no* mental causes of an agent's assertion or that judgment has to be viewed behavioristically as the "interiorization" of assertion (saying in one's heart).

According to Davidson's theory, assertion is the expression or communication of a judgment that may, but need not, be a causal factor in the agent's production of the assertion. What is always the main causal determinant in acts of asserting that p is the agent's beliefs (or judgments) from which, in conjunction with all her other concurrent attitudes and evidence, she reasons to p, a belief (or judgment) she gives expression to in asserting that p.

Dummett thinks that we have only two choices—to describe the conventions governing assertion directly or to accept psychologism. Having rejected psychologism, we must explain what it is to judge a thought to be true as "the interiorisation of the act of assertion":[8]

We have opposed throughout the view of assertion as the expression of an interior act of judgement; judgement, rather, is the interiorisation of the external act of assertion. The reason for viewing the two this way round is that a conventional act can be described, without circularity, as the expression of a mental state or act only if there exist non-conventional ways of expressing it.[9]

It is opaque to me how one *could* "interiorize" the act of assertion in the first place—there is no clear analogue to attempting to persuade in the mental case, so the primary point of assertion would be lost, one might have thought, on oneself. But be that as it may, Dummett presents us with a stark dichotomy between conventions and intentions without himself providing any analysis of what a convention might be. Yet there is at least one highly plausible analysis of the notion of convention that rejects such a dichotomy: David Lewis's theory of convention.[10] On Lewis's theory, a behavioral regularity R arises as a solution to a coordination problem and persists as a convention among a populace P when the preference of members of P is to perform R, conditional on their expectation that all or most other members of P will perform R. The convention will persist in P only if members of P are mutually *aware* of each others intentions, Lewis argues. Lewis's analysis is unavailable to Dummett. As we have seen, on Dummett's theory an intention to utter true sentences cannot itself be used to demarcate assertoric force; this has to be done by "describing the conventions directly." But if Lewis is right, as I believe him to be, we will be able to *explain* why a convention to utter true sentences should persist in a populace at all only by appeal to the intentions and beliefs of speakers—although it might be preferable to characterize assertoric force by means of the commitments a speaker incurs in the course of dialogue, the explanation of what those commitments consist in will have to advert to the fact that one who utters p assertorically seeks thereby to convey his judgment that p to his audience.

3.1.4 *Truth and Assertibility*
The realist believes that there is a simple relation between truth and assertibility: a sentence is assertible just in case there are good grounds for believing it to be true, where the relevant notion of truth is classical truth. For the antirealist, the relation is less straightforward: truth, if it is a coherent concept at all, can only be some construct from the more primitive notion of correct assertibility.

Dummett argues that assertion is an act that can be evaluated only as correct or as incorrect. There is no third possibility—that is, no assertion can be neither correct nor incorrect (a principle he calls Tertium Non Datur [TND]).

Let me interpose some remarks about this claim, for as it stands it may seem to spell trouble for Dummett's rejection of bivalence if truth is to be constructed out of assertibility. It might also seem inconsistent with the existence of non-ED sentences. For Dummett, non-ED sentences are ones whose truth value we cannot presently decide. An example is Goldbach's conjecture (GC) that every even number greater than two is the sum of two primes, which we can currently neither prove nor disprove. Someone who asserted (denied) GC would have no basis for this assertion (denial). This assertion (denial) would be incorrect relative to what we now know. However, to maintain that GC is neither true nor false would, for the antirealist, be tantamount to holding that we know in our present state of information that we will never be able to prove or disprove it, which, intuitionistically, leads to contradiction, as we've seen. These matters will, I trust, become clearer when discussed more fully in connection with intuitionism in chapter 4.

So to return to Dummett. He accepts TND. Whatever notions of truth and falsity we might think we can give substance to, they must have their origins in our primitive and foundational practice of evaluating assertions as correct and incorrect, on pain of their failing to connect with that practice at all, according to him. In so evaluating assertions, we learn to distinguish the *grounds* a speaker has for making an assertion from the objectively agreed *truth value* of what she states. Thus we arrive at the concept of truth as *correspondence with reality* by learning to make and answer criticisms to do with the grounds a speaker has for her assertions given criticisms to do with the truth value of the content of that assertion. Hence we could identify p's being *true* with its being *objectively correct*. So, true to the error-theoretic analysis of realist truth, we are being provided with a genetic account of truth's origin.

Thus far there is nothing in our practice of issuing and criticizing assertions to justify the notion of truth as an *epistemically unconstrained* correspondence between our assertions and reality, one that may obtain *independently of whether we can recognize it or not*. So to the extent that we think of the sense of a sentence as the content of its assertion, Dummett argues, there can be no justification for allowing our declarative sentences to take any value other than truth (objective correctness) and falsity (objective incorrectness). Yet, to give a systematic account of the use of more complex sentences, we might well be forced to introduce more than two truth values or possibly even truth-value gaps. But then we would be obliged to show how these assignments mesh with the primitive evaluations of assertions as correct and incorrect. This would involve allowing that there are different ways in which an assertion can be correct or incorrect. Dummett gives several examples of how this might work: for instance, if we wished to preserve the semantic principle that *a sentence is false if its negation is true*, we might have to allow that an atomic sentence, p, containing a vacuous singular term take a truth value other than truth or falsity, call it U ("undecided"). We could then give a truth-functional account of the "¬" operator. But the mere knowledge that p took the value "true" in A-type (assertible) circumstances, the value "false" in D-type (deniable) circumstances, and the value "undecided" in N-type circumstances would not suffice to impart a knowledge of the sense of p. To understand the content of an assertion of p, we would have to at least know "which states of affairs are understood to be ruled out by making such an assertion; if none of those states of affairs obtains, then the assertion is correct."[11] If we do this for the case of a sentence containing a vacuous singular term, we will see that the speaker who asserts "St. Thomas More's eldest son became a Protestant" must be ruling out the possibility that More had no sons and would retract it if he discovered that he in fact had none; if he had meant to allow for this possibility, he would have said "If St. Thomas More had any sons, the eldest became a protestant."[12]

So, we must regard the value U as registering another way for the assertion of an atomic sentence p to be incorrect. Adherence to the negation principle (NP) that p is false just when $\neg p$ is true gives us a justification for calling atomic sentences with vacuous names "undecided" or "neither true nor false"—namely, that we can then construe other sentences as their negations.[13]

Dummett concludes:

> ... the linguistic act of assertion makes ... no intrinsic provision for the introduction of a gap between two types of consequence which the making of an assertion might be supposed to have.... the rationale ... for the introduction of a gap ... always relates, not to the use of the sentence by itself to make an assertion, but to its use as a constituent of complex sentences, in particular, of sentences formed by the application to it of a negation operator.[14]

I am not sure that Dummett is right about this. Isn't the liar sentence, "This sentence is false," sufficiently puzzling by itself to warrant serious consideraton of truth-value gaps, à la Kripke or Martin and Woodruff? How this sentence embeds in complex sentences is a further and in fact complicating issue. Rather than providing the rationale for truth-value gaps, compounding the liar sentence with other sentences raises some rather notorious problems associated with that approach. Still, Dummett's point may hold good for sentences that are not semantically pathological.

So Dummett believes that nothing in the practice of assertion justifies attributing to speakers a *classical* notion of truth—that none of the evidence so far adduced forces us to depart from the equation of *truth* with *correct assertibility*. We may have to distinguish different ways in which an assertion might be true (correct) or false (incorrect) to give a satisfactory description of our uses of sentential operators, but this just forces us to operate with a more sophisticated notion of correctness.

Likewise, the distinction between the *grounds* a speaker has for her assertions and the objectively agreed *truth value* of what she says, although it might provide some impetus for thinking of truth as a correspondence between a statement and reality, does not justify the notion of that correspondence being epistemically unconstrained—of *its being possible that p might be true even though no one could in principle determine its truth*.

3.1.5 The Genesis of Realist Truth

Dummett thinks the realist notion of truth arises as a consequence of the semantic behavior of sentences as antecedents of indicative conditionals and of tenses and moods within the scope of sentential operators. Thus he writes:

> The notion of *truth*, as opposed to *justifiablility*, that may be induced by the use of a sentence as the antecedent of a conditional, or as modified by a tense-operator, *remains one for which the law of bivalence strictly holds*: these considerations ... merely allow us to distinguish between having a good reason for saying something and being right in saying it. In the absence of such a distinction, however, we become uncertain how to apply the notion of truth at all: it is precisely because indicative conditionals of natural language can neither be negated nor appear as antecedents of more complex conditionals that philosophers have floundered over the application to them of the notions of truth and falsity. It is, in fact, from the distinction between truth and justification that the realistic conception takes its rise.... One reason why such a conception appears so plausible is that the notion of truth is born in the first place ... from the necessity to distinguish between it and the epistemic notion of justifiability: and this necessity is in turn imposed by the requirements for understanding certain kinds of compound sentence.[15]

How precisely do the constructions mentioned above give rise to the classical conception of truth? Dummett surmises:

> If future-tense sentences could not come within the scope of sentential operators, there would be no place for such a distinction between justification and truth. We should, for example, have no basis for distinguishing between an expression of intention and a statement of intention, that is, between the forms "I am going to marry Jane" and "I intend to marry Jane," which differ, not in respect of the circumstances in which their utterance is justified, but solely in their truth-conditions. This distinction has to do solely with the different behaviour of the two forms as constituents of more complex sentences, and, particularly, as antecedents of conditionals.[16]

Following Robert Brandom, let us call the compounding devices that Dummett claims induce a separation between assertibility and truth, truth-inducing sentential contexts (TISCs).[17] Our question is whether the *classical* conception of truth is forced on us by acknowledging the existence of TISCs. Dummett in *Frege* seems to think it is, for, as we saw, he wrote that "The notion of truth, as opposed to justifiability, that may be induced by the use of a sentence as the antecedent of a conditional, or as modified by a tense-operator, *remains one for which the law of bivalence strictly holds.*" Certainly, if truth must be opposed to justifiability in such TISCs, a classical conception alone seems able to fulfill the role of the auxiliary semantic concept required to explicate the assertibility conditions of the resultant compound sentences. But it is by no means obvious that this is so.[18]

3.1.6 Truth, Assertibility, and Tense
Let us examine then whether tense operators induce any distinction between assertibility and truth. Dummett takes this question up in *Frege*, pages 389–400. There he examines a variety of semantic systems adequate for the formalization of tensed statements in which the basic semantic notion is not truth at a time t, but truth at t under a possible total course C of world history. Each of these semantic systems has a treelike structure, the branches of the tree representing differing total courses of world history possible at the origin of the universe.

If we call a sentence without temporal operators a *radical*, we stipulate that each radical is determinately *true or false at a node*, where a *node* is to be thought of as representing a state of affairs on a particular day, under a total course of world history. Tensed sentences are represented as comprising a token-reflexive temporal operator and a sentence-radical. Letting the unit of time be a day, we write "It was the case n days ago that ..." as "Pn"; "It will be the case in n days ..." as "Fn."

A semantics that validates all the laws of classical logic will have such clauses as:

(6) A is true (false) under C iff it is true (false) at every time t under C.

(7) FnA is true (false) at t under C iff A is true (false) at $t + n$ under C.

(8) PnA is true (false) at t under C iff A is true (false) at $t - n$ under C.

For someone who believes the future is *essentially indeterminate*, this semantics has two drawbacks, according to Dummett:

Since it validates all the laws of classical logic, it is impossible to refute the argument for fatalism by rejecting certain of those laws, as applied to statements about the future.... Secondly, although no one future course of world history is taken to be the actual one, the understanding of the future tense (or of temporal operators relating to times later than the the present) depends essentially upon the conception of a possible total future course of history.[19]

Dummett then suggests an alternative *nonclassical* semantics in which truth is defined in terms of *assertibility*. He introduces the notion of the coincidence of two total courses of history and uses this to define *assertibility at a time t*:

(a) We say that C *coincides with* C' up to t^* just when for every radical A and every $t^* < t$, A is true at t^* under C iff A is true at t^* under C'.

(b) A is *assertible at t* under C iff for every C' that coincides with C up to t, A is true at t under C'.

If we then *identify* truth with assertibility thus defined, we obtain a nonclassical semantics in which:

(9) "FnA" is true at t under C iff, for every C' that coincides with C up to t, A is true at $t+n$ under C'.

(10) "PnA" is true at t under C iff, for every C' that coincides with C up to t, A is true at $t-n$ under C'.

This "Aristotelian" semantics differs sharply from the classical one in that A may be true at t under C though FnA is false at $t-n$ under C. As a result, although $Fn(PnA)$ is always equivalent to A, A does not imply $Pn(FnA)$ since A might be true at t under C while $Pn(FnA)$ is false since for some C' coinciding with C only up to $t-n$ but not t, A is false at t under C'.

Dummett comments that this failure of equivalence between A and $Pn(FnA)$ might be considered "a weakness of the system."[20] He seeks to secure this equivalence in the following way: Suppose that there is no distinction between the *assertibility* conditions of future-tensed statements and their *truth* conditions—that is, that an assertion of a future-tensed sentence is correct just in case the future event described does in fact take place at the appropriate later time. Then we can construct a *nonclassical* semantics validating the equivalence of A and $Pn(FnA)$ using the previous nonclassical semantics if we but relativize the truth of a tensed sentence not only to its *time of utterance* but also to its *time of assessment*. We would then have:

(11) "A," uttered at t, is true at t^* under C iff for every C' that coincides with C up to t^*, A is true at t under C'.

(12) "FnA," uttered at t, is true at t^* under C iff, for every C' that coincides with C up to t^*, A is true at $t+n$ under C'.

(13) "PnA," uttered at t, is true at t^* under C iff, for every C' that coincides with C up to t^*, A is true at $t-n$ under C'.

Dummett notes that the desired equivalence between A and $Pn(FnA)$ is now restored. The equivalence failed before because it was possible for the courses of world history C and C' to diverge up to the time of assessment. But this possibility is ruled out in this new semantics.

Thus if we were *now* to evaluate the truth of a Greek soldier's present-tensed claim "A sea battle is being fought off the shores of Pylos now" as uttered in 234 B.C. and compare it with a Greek historian's endorsement of the Delphic Oracle's prediction in 334 B.C. that this very battle would take place one hundred years on, as expressed by the historian's response to the soldier "It was the case one hundred years ago that a sea battle would take place off the shores of Pylos now," we can use our clauses to show that the soldier's and historian's statements have the same truth conditions. By clauses (12) and (13), "It was the case one hundred years ago that a sea battle would take place off the shores of Pylos now" is true now in 2002 in the actual course of world history just when, for every C' coinciding with the actual course of history up to now, had "A sea battle is being fought off the shores of Pylos now" been uttered, it would have been true 2236 years ago in C'. But these are precisely the same truth conditions for "It was the case one hundred years ago that a sea battle would take place off the shores of Pylos now" uttered and evaluated in the same situation as "A sea battle is being fought off the shores of Pylos now." Dummett writes:

> ... we should have no need of the distinction between the genuine future tense, yielding a statement true or false according to what later happens, and the future tense expressing present tendencies, as occurring in, e.g., "The wedding announced between ... and ... will not now take place." The difference between the two uses of the future tense is registered only in compound sentences, such as a conditional whose antecedent is a future-tense sentence, or one involving a compound tense like "was going to ..."[21]

I think that Dummett means to be saying that we grasp the distinction between statements that, though future-tensed, record only present dispositions and statements that really are about the future (such as the

Delphic Oracle's prediction above) by being taught to regard certain future-tensed statements uttered in the past as equivalent to certain present-tensed statements (e.g., as in the example above, "It was the case one hundred years ago that a sea battle would take place off the shores of Pylos now" and "A sea battle is being fought off the shores of Pylos now"). We are taught that this is a mark of the distinction between statements *really about* the future and those that are merely future-tensed dispositional statements.

But on an antirealist semantics for tensed statements such as the one given by (12) and (13), there will be *no* distinction between truth and assertibility—a future-tensed statement is *both correctly assertible* and *true* just when the future event it describes does occur at the appropriate later date. So we can explain how we could have arrived at a bogus notion of truth transcending all possibility of verification by means of a mistaken construal of our linguistic practices with tensed statements, at the same time correctly construing those features of our practice (such as the semantics of conditionals and tensed statements) that gave rise to this misconception.

3.1.7 Evaluation of Dummett's Argument

If the above *is* Dummett's argument, it is an ingenious one indeed. It provides just the sort of genetic account of the origin of the (antirealistically) bogus conception of realist truth required by a defensible error theory. The parallels with J. L. Mackie's original error theory for moral values are evident. Mackie held that our ordinary moral judgments and beliefs presupposed a belief in an objective, rationally compelling property of "to-be-doneness" inhering within certain acts. Yet since we lacked any means for detecting this property it was gratuitous to ascribe it to those judgments. Dummett similarly holds that our ordinary semantic judgments presuppose belief in an objective determinate reality to which our statements correspond. There is thought to be a rationally compelling property of "matching reality" inhering within certain judgments, and it is this that explains why they are true when they are. Again for Dummett just as for Mackie, we lack any means of detecting this property. So the puzzle (for both philosophers) is how we come to believe in it in the first place. Dummett attempts to explain this with his story about misconstruing our linguistic practices with tensed statements.

Naturally, the realist will and indeed *must* contest this analysis. Even if Dummett and Brandom were right about the origin of the notion of truth in the behavior of certain sentential operators, TISCs, particularly temporal contexts, the mere project of explicating the assertibility conditions of compound sentences with the aid of truth conditions oughtn't to worry the realist. To pose any threat to realism, the antirealist must show *not* that the assertibility conditions of complex sentences depend not just on the assertibility conditions of their sentential constituents, but that the *truth* conditions of those compounds depend not just on the *truth* conditions of their constituent sentences. If the truth of a complex sentence depends not just on the truth of its atomic sentential parts, the semantic value of a sentence cannot be its truth value and the way a sentence is determined as true cannot be constitutive of its meaning, which is precisely the claim of antirealist semantic theorists. This crucial claim still awaits vindication.

3.2 Holism

As we saw in section 2.3, Dummett's manifestation argument rules out meanings that are not manifest in use. According to this argument, we can justifiably ascribe implicit knowledge of sentence p's truth condition to a speaker in either one of two disjoint circumstances:

(A) When p is not barely true and the speaker patently understands the relevant subset of sentences in p's reductive class, or

(B) When p is barely true and the speaker can observe it to be true.

Any realist position that denies that non-ED statements can be barely true will constitute a defensible response to the manifestation argument *provided that* it can produce for each type of non-ED sentence a reductive class of statements whose truth conditions a speaker can unproblematically be credited with grasping.

In section 2.3 we noted that holistic theories of meaning do in fact deny that there can be barely true non-ED statements, since they deny that *any* statement can be barely true. Dummett is thus concerned to establish that such theories of meaning are untenable. I don't see Dummett really does need to establish this. The reader may recall the "wise monkey" of section 2.3 who saw no problem with the holist's response to the manifestation demand. In the end, this turned out to be a problem for the monkey's eyesight, not a solution to (or, as really intended, a dissolution of) the manifestation demand. This was because holism simply inflated the demand for manifestation of understanding for a particular non-ED sentence into a global demand for manifestation of understanding of every other sentence in total theory.

Why bother looking at Dummett on holism if it is unnecessary for the success of his case against realism, then? Because the philosophical problems Dummett raises for holists are difficult and important ones. If he is right, there may be internal reasons why naturalistic realism cannot be sustained, reasons other than the familiar antirealist ones. Naturalistic realists need to know about these. I shall commence by outlining Quine's version of holism and then Davidson's version. After that we shall be in a position to set out Dummett's objections to these views.

Quine's Holism

Donald Davidson builds his theory of radical interpretation on the overt behavioral evidence of the sentences a native holds and prefers true. Because he thinks there are no psychophysical laws, Davidson believes that neurophysiological facts or facts about functional organization are of no use to his interpreter. Quine is even more insistent that Dummett's manifestation constraint be met: "Language is a social art which we all acquire on the evidence solely of other people's overt behaviour under publicly recognisable circumstances."[22] Whatever the shortcomings of Davidson's and Quine's versions of holism, then, violation of the manifestation constraint does not appear to be among them.

What makes Quine's theory of meaning *holistic* is its adherence to *Duhem's thesis*: theoretical sentences have their meaning and evidence only when taken together; they face the tribunal of experience collectively. Duhem's thesis is a claim about the theoretical sentences of a scientific theory and their relation to experience; Quine extends the thesis to the sentences of a natural language that are in the main theoretical by his reckoning. So, to understand Quine's holism, we first need to see why he assimilates languages to theories. In "The Nature of Natural Knowledge," page 68, Quine asserts: "Our only source of information about the external world is through the impact of light rays and molecules on our sensory surfaces."[23]

Quine believes a theory of meaning must observe the crucial consequence he draws from this fact, namely, that *science is the sole arbiter of truth and meaning*. Indeed, there are two cardinal tenets of empiricism that Quine finds "unassailable": "whatever evidence there is for science is sensory evidence; the other that all inculcation of meanings of words must rest ultimately on sensory evidence."[24] It is through their connection with sensory evidence that the sentences both of natural language and of science ultimately derive whatever objectivity and factuality they possess. The acquisition of a language and the acquisition of a theory of the world are, Quine contends, inseparable—"we're working up our science from infancy on."[25]

Certain linguistic expressions—occasion sentences—are directly linked to nonlinguistic reality via simple conditioning; a subclass of occasion sentences—observation sentences—are expressions we've learned to associate holophrastically with publicly observable concurrent circumstances. It is "through these expressions that language and science imbibe their empirical content."[26] The language learner has successfully mastered the use of an observation sentence when he knows when to expect a veteran speaker to approve his utterance of it. For Quine, deeply influenced by Skinner, this is simply a matter of conditioning. The success of such conditioning depends on the existence of *shared standards of similarity*—a fact attested to by the common pattern of expectations evinced by veteran and novice. Quine admits that: "direct conditioning or simple induction does not suffice for the acquisition of language generally."[27] The use of more complex grammatical constructions such as those involving tenses or modality, the use of metaphors, and the use of theoretical terms all elude instruction by this method. Quine simply claims for such cases that "the superstructure is cantilevered outward from that foundation by imitation and analogy, by trial and error."[28] *Sensory stimuli* thus form the common base from which our language and our science develop. But even where an observation sentence is firmly conditioned to sensory stimuli, Quine maintains, there is no way of telling whether the language learner has acquired this sentence by direct conditioning to the relevant stimuli or by indirect conditioning through the transitivity of the conditoning of old connections of sentences with sentences. Hence *the nontheoretical empirical content of the speaker's language cannot be isolated.*

If we now go along with Quine in regarding "a man's theory on a given subject ... as the class of all the sentences ... that he believes true,"[29] it becomes clear that no distinction can usefully be drawn between those sentences the speaker holds true because of their logical and semantic relations to other sentences (indirect conditioning) from those he holds true because they are confirmed by specific types of sensory stimuli (direct conditioning). In this manner, Quine is led to a holistic theory of meaning for the sentences of a language *generally* and not just for its scientific subpart—these have their evidence and meaning only when taken together just as the theoretical statements of physics do and for just the same reason: There can be no isolating the empirical content of either. As Quine himself puts it, "the evidence relation and the semantic relation of observation to theory are coextensive."[30]

Dummett on Quine's Holism

Dummett thinks that this holistic theory precludes the possibility of a systematic theory of meaning. He finds "useful and licit" the Quinean metaphor of language as an articulated web of inferentially connected sentences with experience impinging only on its periphery, and he wholeheartedly supports the verificationism Quine subscribes to. His worry is that Quine's holism ultimately subverts both of these insights.

Dummett's objection is to Quine's generalization of Duhem's thesis—the suggestion that some sentences of our language have no independently ascertainable assertibility conditions, "no fund of experiential implications they can call their own."[31] *Semantic holism* is often identified with a network model of meaning whereby a sentence's meaning is identified with its location within the inferential network. Dummett has no objection to the network per se—indeed, he insists both that natural languages do form such structures and that these structures are or approximate to partial orderings.[32] What he objects to is *the Quinean account of how this network relates to experience.* As a result of that he cannot agree that the meaning of a sentence is *constituted by* its inferential connections. What transforms the network metaphor into a holistic theory are the related theses that:

(I) No experience compels the rejection of any sentence, and

(II) No sentence is immune from revision.[33]

Dummett draws several unwelcome consequences from these theses:

(i) That they destroy the internal structure of the network, obliterating the distinction between periphery and interior and generally making it unclear what constitutes the totality of our linguistic practices.[34]

(ii) That there is something arbitrary and unwarranted in the representation of a speaker's linguistic dispositions by a constant theory of meaning—there is no way of discriminating between one sentence being held true according to the reasons S had for accepting it and any other sentence's being accepted as true: no possible behavioral manifestation could reveal this.[35]

(iii) That a holistic theory of meaning is tantamount to a denial of the possibility of a theory of meaning for a language since "no model can be given of the individual contents of sentences."[36]

Claim (iii) seems question-begging since a holistic theory of meaning such as Davidson's *does* deny precisely that sentences have "individual contents" yet purports nonetheless to provide a theoretical representation of a speaker's linguistic capacity. Objections (i) and (ii) are more serious. Dummett argues that Quine's theory has these consequences in *Frege*, page 596:

Quine's thesis involves that the principles governing deductive connections themselves form part of total theory.... But in that case there is nothing for the inferential links between sentences to consist in. They cannot be replaced by super-inferential links compelling us, if we accept certain logical principles, to accept also the consequences under those principles of other sentences we accept for any such super-logical laws could in turn be formulated and considered as sentences no more immune to revision than any other.

Dummett's claim, in other words, is that no sense can be made of empirical pressure forcing readjustment in the truth values of the sentences a speaker holds true in his language-cum-theory if the inferential relations between those sentences are *themselves* revisable. To attempt to meet this problem by replacing those inferential rules by super-inferential rules brings us no closer to understanding the content of these new rules, since these too are subject to Duhem's thesis according to Quine. We are thus precluded from understanding the inferential relations between sentences in a given language on Quine's theory and thereby prevented from theorizing about meaning at all.

Dummett's argument is a powerful one to bring against the global application of Duhem's thesis to a language. Still, Quine has some sort of answer to it. It is true that Duhem's thesis cannot make clear the contents of the logical constants and thus of the contents of theoretical sentences (since these consist in their inferential relations with other sentences). But I take it that Quine would contend that it is not meant to—this is the task of a naturalized epistemology instead. Quine undertakes this task in "The Nature of Natural Knowledge" and more fully in *The Roots of Reference*. In "The Nature of Natural Knowledge," for instance, Quine tells "in outline and crude conjecture" a psychologistic story about "how one might start at the observational edge of language and work one's way into the discursive interior where scientific theory can begin to be expressed."[37] Thus the child might learn conjunction by noticing that the adult assents to "p and q" in just those circumstances in which he assents to "p" and also to "q." The route to learning the use of other truth-functions is a little more involved, and the route to mastery of the apparatus of objective reference and of variables still more so.[38]

Will this psychologistic story suffice as an answer to Dummett? Dummett was after a specification of the contents of inference rules, rules that are meant to tell us how we *ought* to reason; nothing in the above account explains why modus ponens is a *good* inference rule or why affirming the consequent is a *bad* way to reason. The naturalized epistemologist simply tells us how we all end up more or less converging in our inferential habits. Dummett would complain (and this is one of his principal objections to holism) that *this psychologistic account fails to show how or why the inferential rules we use are justified.*

Quine's probable reply to this criticism would be that the only measure of rationality we possess is that provided by science. We justify our scientific practices generally and our inferential practices in particular only by using the techniques and doctrines of science itself, for it is successful practice alone that justifies science. Scientific theories can be expressed in classical first-order logic,[39] an idiom that both is simple and makes ontological commitments manifest; our classical inference rules are therefore justified as part of a revisable but generally successful theory of the world.

I cannot hope to resolve this dispute between Quine and Dummett here, but we should note in passing that although psychologistic theories by themselves invariably look implausible, Quine's advocacy of them is well motivated by his desire to uncover the empirical foundation of our language and theory.[40] A holist less skeptical about semantics than Quine and more critical of psychologistic accounts of the meanings of the logical constants might object to Dummett's claim that no sense can be made of empirical pressure forcing revisions in total theory if the inferential links between sentences are themselves revisable on the following grounds: Each inferential rule is revisable individually; perhaps even clusters of them are revisable. What is *not* conceivable, however, is that all should simultaneously be revised in the face of some recalcitrant sequence of experiences, for this would be effectively to abrogate one's capacity to theorize. We can repair each inferential plank of our boat at sea. But try uprooting them all simultaneously and you'll sink.

It may well be that Dummett's objection trades on an extreme interpretation of confirmational holism in which it is deemed conceivable that some sequence of experiences could lead us to revise all our inferential laws in one fell swoop. If so, it is spurious. This question bears further investigation and is of obvious concern for naturalistic realism. To return to Quine, however: Quine's empiricist philosophy of language and epistemology are fashioned around the concept of *empirical content*—the meanings of all sentences depend on their conditioning to observation sentences that are directly keyed to stimulatory patterns, and it is the task of the empirical psychologist to discern these pathways of conditioning from sensory content to assent.

Davidson's Holism

In "A Coherence Theory of Truth and Knowledge,"[41] Davidson explicitly disavows Quine's "unassailable" tenets of empiricism: the relation between sensations and beliefs cannot be one of justification, Davidson claims, but is rather a *causal* one; all that can justify a belief is a further belief; and meaning and knowledge are *causally* dependent on sensory stimuli. Duhem's thesis is also unavailable to Davidson insofar as it depends on the notion of a confrontation between our beliefs and experience. Davidson finds the idea of such a confrontation absurd, since "we cannot get outside our skins to find out what's causing the internal happenings of which we're aware."[42] We should look elsewhere than Duhem's thesis for the source of Davidson's holism. Dummett cites the following claim of Davidson's as a "characteristic expression" of holism in *Truth and Other Enigmas*, p. 134: "To give up the analytic-synthetic distinction as basic to the understanding of language is to give up the idea that we can clearly distinguish between theory and language. Meaning, as we might loosely use the word, is contaminated by theory, by what is held to be true."[43] These words could just as well have been uttered by Quine, and Dummett goes on to discuss this passage "in terms of Quine's ideas."[44]

Quine and Davidson both agree that language and theory (or meaning and belief) are inextricable but for rather different reasons. For Quine, the *inextricability thesis* amounts to this: Because the empirical evidence supports only sets of sentences without supporting any one individual sentence and because science is simply a refinement of our ordinary talk, the empirical content of both ordinary language and science is inextricably confounded. The radical translator looking for the stimulus conditions that uniquely prompt assent to a given queried sentence will be thwarted overall. Quine's inextricability thesis thus depends on two notions Davidson rejects: empirical content (at least on Quine's construal of that notion) and Duhem's thesis.

Inextricability has a far more straightforward sense for Davidson—whether a native holds a sentence true will depend jointly on his propositional attitudes and on what the sentence means. So one cannot without circularity use the subject's meanings as evidence for his attitudes or conversely use his attitudes as evidence for his meanings.

Dummett on Davidson's Holism

Dummett distinguishes holism "in respect of evidence" from a "holistic view of language"[45]—the latter relates to how a speaker's implicit knowledge of a theory of meaning for his language determines the use he makes of its expressions. Dummett attempts to articulate what he takes to be Davidson's form of holism in the following way:

(i) We start with the class of sentences the native holds true, call it {T}.

(ii) We define a preferred assignment as that which maximizes the number of sentences in {T} that are actually true.

(iii) We then simultaneously assign references to singular terms and extensions to predicates such that the referent of t is that object assigned to t under the preferred assignment, and similarly for predicates.

What makes this theory *holistic* is that *the same piece of knowledge* is required to grasp the senses of all names and predicates, namely, the make-up of {T}. Dummett claims that it is beyond human capacities to determine simultaneously the references of all singular terms and predicates in this manner. It is no help to be told that the referent of t is that individual of whom the majority of predicates derived from sentences containing it are true if one does not already understand what it is for any one such predicate to be true of any individual.[46] Thus, on this version of holism as well, a systematic theory of meaning is impossible.

Evaluation of Dummett on Davidson

I agree with Dummett that the theory above lacks any plausibility for just the reasons he adduces, but I think that this could not be what Davidson's holism consists in. Davidson has never held the *stochastic* version of the *principle of charity* that Dummett saddles him with. The spirit of that principle is to *optimize* truth, not statistically maximize it.[47]

What are the sources of Davidson's holism? First, the methodology for constructing and testing a truth theory itself is holistic—the interpreter cannot do other than pair sentences the native holds true with sentences she herself holds true under like circumstances, and it is only at the end of this process, when the theory has shown that it can pass the relevant formal and empirical constraints, that the interpreter can have any confidence that the metalinguistic sentences used on the right-hand side of the T-sentences translate or give the truth conditions of the object language sentences mentioned on the left-hand side. The constraints are constraints on the theory *as a whole.*

There is a further crucial source of holism for Davidson: meaning is itself treated holistically. Davidson is a semantic holist. Dummett is naturally aware of this further element (a "holistic view of language") and is I think right to see this as surviving a separation of meaning from belief ("holism in respect of evidence"), but I do not believe he correctly perceives its nature. To give content to it he proposes the stochastic version of the principle of charity, which misconstrues its import. Davidson is chary of talking of meanings at all and hopes to achieve a means of interpreting the speech of a native by articulating just the truth conditions of his sentences together with their logical form in a truth theory for his whole language.

What makes this theory holistic is the thesis that the inferential connections between sentences can be justified only by a systematic theory of truth for the language, showing that they lead from true sentences to true sentences in every case. Ascriptions of logical form can be justified only in the context of a truth theory for the entire language, the resultant logical relations between sentences affording the only genuine criterion of when a language commits us to the existence of entities. It is true that on this holistic theory, the meaning of a statement "simply consists in the place which it occupies in the complicated network which constitutes the totality of our linguistic practices."[48] But without some explanation of the crucial connection between the enterprises of articulating logical form and of discerning ontological commitments that the construction of a truth theory for a language forges, this metaphor lacks clear motivation. Moreover, it is essential to realize that for Davidson, sentences still have objective truth conditions of their own, unlike Quine's picture, in which most sentences lack individual verification conditions and truth is merely a disquotational property. Indeed, for Davidson, were it not for the fact that sentences are lawfully connected with states of affairs in the world, interpretation could not even begin.

Because he rejects the notion that we understand a sentence by testing its truth either singly or in concert with other sentences (as in Duhem's Thesis) against reality, experience, sensory stimuli or any uninterpreted empirical content, Davidson eschews "confrontationist" models of our grasp of a statement's truth conditions. Rather, we understand the truth conditions of a given sentence when we discern the logical form of that sentence and thereby appreciate the inferential relations between that sentence and others of the language in a truth theory for the language as a whole. Davidson subscribes to three holistic theses, in effect:

(1) Sentences derive their contents from their place in a truth-theoretic inferential network.

(2) Beliefs similarly derive the content they have from their inferential and evidential relations with other beliefs in a system of beliefs.

(3) Our ascriptions of beliefs and meanings to speakers are inextricably interlocked.

Dummett's central objections to holism are these:

(1) Holism precludes the possibility of a systematic theory of meaning since:

(a) The inferential relations between sentences cannot be made out on such a theory.[49]

(b) The appearance of structure is a sham in a holistic theory as there is no distinctive behavioral manifestation of the grasp of any propositions of the truth theory.[50]

(c) A meaning theory based on a holistic view can give no content to the notion of a speaker's being mistaken about the meaning of an expression.[51]

(2) Holism cannot account for the usefulness of deductive reasoning, nor can it even consider how such reasoning might be justified.[52]

(3) Holism cannot account for the progressive acquisition of a language.[53]

I have already queried Dummett's claim that Quine cannot answer (1a), and one of the apparent strengths of Davidson's position is that it precisely does explicate the inferential relations between sentences of a language by means of a truth theory for that language. Claim (1b) has already been encountered in section 2.1.

It seems to me that both (1a) and (1b) do present serious challenges to the realist proponent of a holistic theory of meaning, such as our naturalistic realist. So too does (1c), the charge that a holistic theory can give no content to the notion of a speaker's being mistaken about the meaning of an expression. A holist might be tempted to regard this with equanimity as a natural consequence of the inextricability of belief and meaning, but I think it is a highly undesirable consequence.[54] When we settle for Davidson's "bootstraps" methodology, of attributing coarse-grained attitudes to the native that we seek to continuously refine in the light of further evidence, but take a more realistic attitude to the mental life of the native than Davidson does, allowing that, under certain unusual conditions, the native could be massively in error in his general beliefs about the world, we have, I contend, made room on a holistic theory of meaning for the possibility of error and ignorance on the part of those whose speech we seek to interpret.[55]

Dummett's second main criticism of holism—that it cannot account for the usefulness of or provide a justification for deduction—is difficult to assess until we know what sort of "justification" is being envisaged. Inference rules are the blood vessels of theory. Inferences of the deductive and probabilistic sort receive their justification as integral and essential parts of overall theory. What further justification is required?

As to Dummett's third criticism—that holism cannot account for a child's piecemeal acquisition of language since it cannot make sense of the child's knowing part of a language—I wonder whether Dummett's description of the child's language-learning situation is not tendentious from the holist's point of view. Presumably, the holist will see the child at any stage of the language-learning process as possessing a complete, albeit primitive, language that may be a proper subpart of "our" language, but which will most probably only approximate to such. Language-learning involves the (surprisingly swift) acquisition and abandoning of a series of progressively less primitive languages, each stage growing out of its predecessor by an evolutionary process involving revisions, "paradigm changes," and so on with respect to that predecessor.

We might choose to describe this process as the child's knowing at any one time only part of English, say, but this is misleading inasmuch as it suggests that what is really going on is that the child possesses, at any stage, only a partial language. At some stage he will have mastered English, to the extent that we are willing to attribute such mastery to any person, "without it ever being accurate to say he has mastered part of it first."[56]

Holism—Moderate and Immoderate

I cannot leave the topic of holism without briefly outlining the form I find most appealing. I shall call it moderate holism and contrast it with an immoderate holism that holds with Quine that the meaning of each sentence depends on its place in total theory. Moderate holism, by way of contrast, makes no grandiose presumption that there even could be, let alone actually is, such a thing as "total theory." There isn't even a "final theory" of physics, let alone of anything else. Moreover, even if there were completed theories of all the sciences, including neurophysiology and, *pace* Quine, psychology and linguistics, the question of reduction, supervenience, and so on between each science would still, in my view, remain desperately unclear.

Where immoderate holists maintain that there is a theory Θ such that for each sentence p, p's meaning is determined by its place in that theory, $\exists \Theta \forall p \; \Re(\Theta, p)$, where $\Re$ is the relation of "meaning-determination," moderate holism eschews such worries. The moderate holist's thesis is instead given symbolically as $\forall p \exists \Theta \; \Re(\Theta, p)$: For each sentence p of a given language, some theory Θ can be found within which the meaning of p is determined.

3.3 The Problem of Other Minds

In this section I argue that there is a class of barely true non-ED sentences for which only a truth-conditional rather than an assertibility-conditional theory of meaning looks feasible. These have to do with the first-person avowals of others about their sensations.

3.3.1 The Problem for Antirealism

The antirealist's challenge to the realist is to explain how an understanding of a verification-transcendent state of affairs could be acquired or manifested. Strawson has replied on behalf of the realist that there are two domains for which we *do* possess such a conception: that of the past and of other minds.[57] Dummett and Wright have not been persuaded by Strawson's claim.[58] Dummett has concentrated on the problem of the past[59] whereas Wright has sought to explicate our grasp of statements about the mental states of others without appealing to any verification-transcendent notions.[60]

Strawson had claimed:

> It is part of what it is now regrettably fashionable to call our general theory of the world that we regard other people as subject to roughly the same range of sensations as we are.... And it is in no way contrary to reason to regard ourselves, as in any case we cannot help doing, as justified in certain circumstances in ascribing to John a particular state of feeling *which we cannot in the very*

nature of the case experience ourselves and his being in which is therefore ... necessarily verification-transcendent.[61]

Commenting on this passage, Crispin Wright wrote:

The assumption is that to oppose Realism is to call into question these aspects of our "general theory of the world." But it is open to an Anti-Realist to seek to interpret them. Thus, the susceptibility of others to the same range of sensations as we ourselves may be viewed as an expression of the existence of a communal vocabulary of sensation, any element of which is applicable to any of us on the basis of communally acknowledged criteria and the inaccessibility of others' states of feeling may be viewed as an expression of the essential defeasibility of other-ascriptions of sensation, the fact that any state of information which warrants such an ascription can always coherently be envisaged as being added to in such a way that the resulting state of information no longer does so. By contrast, the "privileged access" we are traditionally thought to have to our own sensations may be viewed as an expression of the fact that our grammar of sensation provides for the possibility of discovering that one did not know what one was saying in making a particular self-ascription, but *not* for the possibility that one understood it and was mistaken.[62]

It seems to me that both Wright and Dummett have simply failed to appreciate the *particular* problem for antirealism posed by other minds. Ironically, it was the later Wittgenstein, whose views both Dummett[63] and Wright[64] take themselves to be closely approximating, who best articulated the problem Strawson raises: "If one has to imagine someone else's pain on the model of one's own, this is none too easy a thing to do: for I have to imagine pain which *I do not feel* on the model of the pain which I *do feel*.... For I am not to imagine that I feel pain in some region of his body."[65] Someone who utters "I am in pain," if sincere, will characteristically be experiencing some painful sensation but not, or not usually, be perceiving a person writhing or grimacing. An onlooker reporting this event as "Jones is in pain" sees a person, whom he identifies as Jones, writhing or grimacing, but he does not experience his sensation. Truistic though these facts be, they are sufficient to generate a problem that is particularly vexing for the antirealist.

Let us call the mode of epistemic access Jones has to his own pain an "internal" mode of presentation (MOP) of pain and the mode of access others apart from Jones have to Jones's pain, an "external" mode of presentation of pain. An internal MOP of pain derives from an experience of pain; an external MOP of pain derives from the observation of the behavioral manifestations of pain. The *problem* in the "problem of other minds" derives from the fact that there is an *epistemic assymetry* between Jones and everyone else with respect to Jones's pain: Jones has both an internal and an external MOP of his own pain, whereas everyone else has only an external MOP.[66] The conditions for justifiably asserting "I am in pain" in the case of Jones and "Jones is in pain" in the case of anyone else differ accordingly.

There now arises a problem for the antirealist: If the meaning of a statement is given by its canonical assertibility conditions, the antirealist must show how "I am in pain" uttered by Jones and "Jones is in pain" uttered by me could possibly mean the same or, at the very least, report the same state of affairs.[67] The canonical assertibility condition for the former is that Jones experience, or at the very least believe himself to be experiencing, a pain; the canonical assertibility condition for the latter, that the person satisfy the criteria of identity for Jones and that he evince a reliable behavioral manifestation of pain—for example, that he wince or moan or sincerely claim that he is in pain.[68] *Since canonical assertibility conditions differ, the meanings of the two statements must also differ.*

Two problems thus face the antirealist: First, he must show that the predicate "pain" has a unitary sense even though its canonical criteria of application differ so starkly in first- and third-person exemplifications. Antirealistically, the presumption must surely be that "pain" in these separate exemplifications differs in sense. Let us call the internally presented instance *pain* and the externally presented instance *pain**, the former a sensation, the latter a cluster of behavioral criteria. I shall call it the problem of *semantic variance* that "pain" is equivocal as between pain and pain*. Second, he must allay the suspicion that it is belief in the verification-transcendent state of affairs of Jones's pain that ultimately warrants the assertion of "Jones is in pain."

How then should the antirealist best respond to the problems above? Semantic variance suggests that when Jones says "I am in pain," by "pain" he means *pain*, and that when I report this as "Jones is in pain," by "pain" I mean *pain**. Trivially, I cannot then be reporting the same event as Jones is reporting. Unless he is to somehow show that, contrary to all appearances, it is innocuous, the antirealist must somehow block semantic variance.[69] The obvious move is to deny that Jones has an internal MOP available only to him. We were wrong in thinking that "pain" was the name of a certain sensation. This seems to have been Wittgenstein's position. Let us index the "I" in Jones's utterance "I am in pain" as "I_j." Then we wish to know how to assign assertibility conditions to "I_j am in pain."

Wittgenstein's position looks like behaviorism. Dummett claims that it is not—that both behaviorism and realism arise only when we illicitly assume that our understanding of pain-ascriptions is a truth-conditional one.[70] "The thrust of the argument," Dummett tells us, "is ... first, that we cannot employ the notion of reference to explain how expressions for inner sensations function ('if we construe the grammar of the expression of sensation on the model of "object and name," the object drops out of consideration as irrelevant'—*Philosophical Investigations* §293) and, secondly, that an understanding of ascriptions of inner sensation cannot be explained as consisting in a knowledge of the condition for them to be true."[71]

Insofar as I grasp this Wittgensteinian point at all, it seems to be that the truth of "*x* is in pain" does not involve the identification of any *object*, namely, the referent of "pain." To the question "what does 'pain' refer to?" we can give only a trivial reply: "'pain' refers to pain," just as we can provide only a trivial axiom in response to the request for the truth conditions of "Jones is in pain"—namely, "'Jones is in pain' is true iff Jones is in pain." So, it is wrong to expect an understanding of "*x* is in pain" to be obtained by knowing its satisfaction conditions. How then *do* we come to understand it, according to Dummett?

> To understand statements like "John is in pain," we must know how they are *used*. That involves knowing that pain-behaviour, or the presence of an ordinarily painful stimulus, is normally a sufficient ground for an ascription of pain, but one that can be rebutted, in the former case by the clues that betray the shammer or by subsequent disclaimer; learning the symptoms of inhibiting the natural manifestation of pain, and the limits beyond which this is impossible; knowing the usual connection between pain and bodily conditions, and the sort of cases in which the connection may be broken; and so on. To know these and similar things, on Wittgenstein's account, just is to know what "John is in pain" means; and, for one who knows this, there need be no more informative answer to the question what makes that statement true than, "John's being in pain." We looked for an informative answer, midway between those of the realist and the behaviourist, when no informative answer was to be had.[72]

There are several things to note about this passage. First and foremost, the account of the assertibility conditions of "John is in pain" is simply incoherent *unless* "pain" is taken to refer to the sensation of pain. To see this, suppose we try to use the account to inform a Putnamesque super-Spartan, who successfully inhibits the behavioral manifestation of his sensations, moods, and emotions, of what the word "pain" means. When the super-Spartan is in pain, the red light on his C-fiber monitor lights up; when he is afraid, the D-fiber monitor lights; when happy, the E-fiber monitor lights.[73] Dummett's account works just as well as an account of the assertibility conditions of "John is afraid" or "John is happy." How is our Spartan friend to know whether "pain" means happy or afraid rather than pain? Until he advances the hypothesis that *"pain" refers to a sensation similar to the one he experiences when his C-fiber monitor lights*, he will surely be completely lost as to both the meaning of "pain" and the *explanation* of the motley of wincings, curses, moans, and so on he observes in connection with its use. Contrary to Dummett, then, we *must* employ the notion of reference, to explain how sensation terms function, as his own theory demonstrates.[74]

Second, given that "pain" does refer to the sensation of pain as it must for the above account to be coherent, Dummett's explanation of the assertibility conditions of "Jones is in pain" is precisely the type of explanation a *realist* would give of that statement's assertibility conditions. Realism is emphatically *not* the (absurd) thesis that a grasp of assertibility conditions plays no part in a model of a speaker's competence with a given range of sentences; on the contrary, it will be crucial to an understanding of the meaning of "Jones is in pain" that a speaker knows what would constitute good grounds for believing it to be true. Since, for a realist, a sentence is assertible just when there are good grounds for believing it to be true, not to know what constitutes such grounds would result in a failure to know when one could legitimately assert the sentence.[75]

Doubts about the internal coherence of Dummett's theory aside, how does it deal with the problem of semantic variance? It doesn't: It simply ignores it. We are left completely in the dark as to what the assertibility conditions of "I_j am in pain" are[76] and as to whether or not these are the *same* as "Jones is in pain." The fact that "pain" is not the name of a sensation seems to prevent "I am in pain" from being assertible just when I experience a certain sensation, although even this is unclear. If so, how are we to communicate to super-Spartan Jones the assertibility conditions of "I_j am in pain"? Nothing observable is of any use here unless one accepts a behaviorist reduction of the meaning of the statement.

One suggestion, consistent with Dummett's theory and again inspired by some of Wittgenstein's remarks, is that "I am in pain" is simply a more sophisticated way of saying "Ouch!" The sentence *expresses* pain, it does not *describe* it. It is a semantically unstructured or "holophrastic" phrase (à la Quine's observation sentences). Then, "I_j am in pain" and "Jones is in pain" do *not* have the same assertibility conditions; we are thus to acquiesce in semantic variance. Call this the *holophrastic thesis*. Then this seems to be a straightforwardly behavioristic thesis and thus to suffer from all the problems behaviorism suffers from. If accepted, it would mean that our mental language would have to be extensively revised. Existential generalization and universal instantiation would no longer apply to "I am in pain."

This result has some rather bizarre consequences: Suppose amnesic Jones lies groaning in agony in a hospital bed. A doctor breezing by remarks to the nurse who accompanies him, "There is one and only one person in pain in this ward"; "Yes," the nurse responds, "Jones is in pain"; Jones, upon hearing this snatch of conversation, says out loud "Well I am in pain, so I must be Jones!" If the holophrastic thesis were correct, it would follow that Jones is *mistaken* in inferring thus; that, supposing the doctor's and nurse's remarks to be true, he would have acquired knowledge of who he was by *illicit* means; that the doctor and the nurse could not have conspired to truly *inform* him of his identity in this way—for the meaning of "pain" differs in Jones's mouth from its meaning in the mouths of the doctor and the nurse.

The antirealist might seek to avoid the problem of semantic variance by denying that pain and pain* are independent properties—it is just that one's own experience of pain includes an element incommunicable to any one other than the sufferer: the pain qualia. But since it also includes communicable manifestations—behavioral or verbal—there is no equivocation: The states of affairs under which "I_j am in pain" is assertible are just those states of affairs in which "Jones is in pain" is assertible. So although "I_j am in pain" assuredly has a richer cognitive content than "Jones is in pain" for Jones, the semantic information conveyed in both cases to an onlooker is identical.

This position would be tenable only if there were entailments between "I_j am in pain" and behavioral manifestations of some sort, but there need not be any such manifestations at all, outside of the verbal report—we cannot accept the verbal report itself as such evidence unless we know what it means, and the question is precisely what is the assertibility condition of the statement, and hence its meaning. Moreover, even if we were to grant that, per impossibile, nonverbal behavioral manifestations could in principle be observed for any utterance of "I_j am in pain," it still would not follow that the circumstances in which this statement can justifiably be uttered invariably constitute the circumstances in which "Jones is in pain" could be asserted, at least so far as Jones is concerned. Consider amnesic Jones again and imagine that the doctor is a deranged sadist who has completely refashioned Jones's body while he was comatose (perhaps he transformed it into a body that is externally that of a woman's); then noncomatose Jones, who asserts "I$_j$ am in pain," will, on learning once more of his name and seeing his own female body contorted in pain, deny "Jones is in pain," on the evidence of the writhing body he sees. Even after the grisly truth is revealed to him, it still might remain that Jones is never inclined to assert, in point of fact he might be still inclined to deny, "I$_j$ am in pain" on the basis of an external MOP available to others.[77]

As far as I can see, the antirealist simply has to admit the existence of semantic variance between "I$_j$ am in pain" and "Jones is in pain." The thing to do then is to try to play down its importance. It would be quite unconvincing to attempt to argue that the class of mental phenomena that have internal MOPs is too small to worry about—it is surely no smaller than the whole range of moods, feelings, sensations, and so on that agents consciously experience. He could contend along Paul Churchland's lines[78] that the language we use to report not only our sensations but also our conscious experiences at large is just incoherent at heart—that our scientifically astute successors would revise on neurophysiological grounds our folk-experiential vocabulary. Then both "I$_j$ am in pain" uttered by Jones and "Jones is in pain" uttered by anyone else would be assertible just when the red light on Jones's C-fiber monitor lit up. Until such times as neurophysiology develops, we are left with semantic paradoxes in our attempts to systematize the assertibility conditions of psychological statements.[79]

There may be other, more plausible responses an antirealist can make to the problem of semantic variance but I cannot see how he can avoid it.[80] So the question still remains: How is the antirealist to assign assertibility conditions to the first-person psychological utterances of others? My conjecture is that antirealism cannot provide *any* plausible model of the conscious experiences of others. For these reasons, I am inclined to think that the fact that we manifestly *do* understand the first-person utterances of others provides a counterexample to the global antirealist's claim that our understanding of any sort of statement is given by our grasp of its assertibility (or deniability) conditions. Rather, as Strawson originally claimed, it is given by a grasp of their *truth* conditions.

3.4 Realist Responses to the Manifestation Argument

Let's get straight to the point. The only way for a realist to answer the antirealist's challenge is to come up with some class of non-ED sentences speakers patently do understand that could have only evidence-transcendent truth conditions. This is no trivial task. However, I argued in the previous section that the first-person avowals of others plausibly constitute just such a class.

In this section I first review some tempting alternative answers to Dummett. The first two are, in my view, instructively mistaken. The third I believe is not so much wrong as incomplete. The reader favorably disposed to realism may well disagree with my assessment and wish to further develop one or other of these responses. I then focus on the manifestation demand, presenting some cognitivist reasons for ultimately rejecting it in the strong form in which Dummett presents it.

3.4.1 Some Mistaken Responses

Colin McGinn on Dummett In "Truth and Use" and in "Realist semantics and content ascription," Colin McGinn has attempted to contruct counterexamples to the theory of content ascription implicit in Dummett's writings. In his earlier article, McGinn imagines a community of intelligent immobile creatures living on the north side of a mountain for whom sentences about what is happening on the south side of the mountain are undecidable in principle. If certain recurrent features of their experience—such as the appearance and disappearance of sheep traveling from one side of the mountain to the other—could most reasonably be explained by postulating the existence of a south side to the mountain, what is to stop these creatures from so doing? Only an objectionable reductionist dogma of empiricism: "the dogma ... that our conceptual scheme cannot transcend our experience,"[81] McGinn replies. Moreover, this realist conception could be manifested by the tendency of these creatures to interpret the relevant assertions of fellow speakers "as expressions of the very realist beliefs we have seen no good reason to deny them."[82] This suffices to answer Dummett's challenge, which should apply to this language if it applies at all, McGinn claims.

I am not convinced that this example has even been properly described. All McGinn tells us is that his mountain dwellers are like humans in their observational powers except that they are rooted to the spot. We are then supposed to just accept that they have a language with an undecidable fragment involving sentences about the south side of the mountain, which they interpret realistically. Yet even if a realist were to acquiesce in these stipulations without demanding some account of how the mountain dwellers' sentences were to be interpreted in the absence of their possessing any clear analogue of agency and intention, it is certain that the antirealist would not do so. The fact is that these creatures' *recognitional capacities* are *not* the same as our own: Sentences we would find decidable are undecidable *in principle* for them. Hence, if meaning is determined by recognitional capacity, as the antirealist asserts, it follows that their sentences *do not* and *cannot* mean the same as ours. We are therefore debarred from deciding whether their "undecidable" sentences should be interpreted realistically or not.[83]

Apart from the issue of intelligibility, McGinn's diagnosis of and answer to the antirealist's challenge are, I think, inadequate. It is question-begging to claim that the mountain dwellers' conceptual scheme can transcend their experience: This is precisely the point at issue between the realist and the antirealist. McGinn's suggestion as to how such a realist conception could be manifest in behavior is also unacceptable as it stands—how does a mere propensity to interpret one another's assertions about the south side of the mountain as expressive of a realist belief about an inaccessible part of reality manifest an *understanding* of the relevant truth conditions for those assertions?

One moral we can draw here is this: A realist cannot just point to the prevalence of certain realist-inspired practices in his attempt to meet the manifestation challenge. Since no one doubts that we often give expression to incoherent beliefs, the realist has to show that realism is not among these. Recall the antirealist holds an error theory about realist truth.

Thus the antirealist has two replies to McGinn's attempt to meet the manifestation challenge. The first reply is that the beliefs the mountain dwellers form and impute to each other are incoherent. They have, like us, wrongly assimilated the assertibility conditions and inferential relations of undecidable sentences to those of decidable sentences wherein assertibility conditions and truth conditions coincide. They have been misled, as we have, by the twin indefensible notions of truth as correspondence to reality and meaning as truth conditions.[84] The second reply is that even if, per impossibile, these beliefs were coherent, the mountain dwellers would have no more chance of communicating them to each other than we have of communicating our beliefs about verification-transcendent states of affairs to one another. All either they or we actually communicate is the assertibility conditions of undecidable sentences.

Reductivist Realism Consider a scientific realist strongly attracted to supervenience theses. In the extreme, imagine she holds that *all* theoretical statements supervene on some set of observational ones. So for every theoretical sentence p of a given scientific theory Θ, some reductive class R_o of observational sentences can be found containing only observational vocabulary. Assume we are talking about scientific theories that have been formalized with their vocabularies divided into a theoretical part T and an observational part O. Assume further that the reductive class R_o for each theoretical p is some subset of the set of observational consequences of O and that R_o has only observational terms. Then we know from Craig's theorem that O can be derived from a subtheory Θ_o of Θ, which contains no theoretical term from T whatsoever. So it is plausible in the light of Craig's theorem, our reductive realist might claim, to regard any arbitrary non-ED theoretical sentence p as being supported entirely by ED observational sentences, so that the sentences in its reductive class R_o do not covertly rely for their intelligibility on that of any non-ED theoretical sentences.

If these views were the case quite generally, then wouldn't we have shown even for the non-ED theoretical sentences of our scientific theories that ascribing a grasp of their realist truth conditions to a speaker is quite unproblematic? No. Decidability would *fail* to be preserved in any case where the non-ED theoretical sentence p has a reductive class with an infinite number of decidable observational sentences as its members. Although p would then not be barely true and although every member of the R-class is decidable, statements quantifying over such an infinite totality *would be* non-ED (of the same type as statements quantifying over an infinite domain of natural numbers). Clearly, many if not most theoretical sentences in science fall into this category, having an infinite number of decidable observational consequences.

Classical Inferential Practices This realist response takes issue with Dummett on the status of a speaker's *evidential* and *inferential* practices. The claim is simply that by looking at these practices we will be able to ascertain whether our speaker is using a concept of verification-transcendent truth. With this type of response in mind, Dummett writes:

It thus becomes conceivable that a certain model of meaning is required only in order to validate certain forms of inference, the employment of which is part of our standard practice. That is, that model of meaning would be unnecessary in order to account for the use of that fragment of the language which contained only sentences of a low degree of logical complexity.... And this would mean, therefore, that the meaning which, on such a model, we were taken as assigning to certain sentences, a meaning given in terms of their truth-conditions, was displayed only by our acceptance of certain froms of inference which could not otherwise be validated, rather than by anything involved in the use of those sentences as we learned it when, so to speak, they were on the frontier of the language we were acquiring (the frontier of complexity, that is).

It is just this which an opponent of a realist model of meaning finds incredible: he cannot believe that a grasp of a notion of truth transcending our capacities for its recognition can be acquired, and displayed, only by the acceptance of certain forms of reasoning. He concludes, instead, that these forms of reasoning, though generally accepted, are fallacious.[85]

The realist might respond by claiming that although our classically based inductive and deductive inferential behavior does not itself *explain* how we came by the verification-transcendent conception of truth that governs the inferences we make, it does nonetheless *manifest* such a conception, and since Dummett only requires a manifestation of such knowedge, he should concede that this sort of evidence fulfills his express requirements.

I think there is something right about this response—no "wise monkey" could cook this up. However, it cannot by itself answer Dummett.

What I think is right about the response is this: Suppose we hold, along with many a naturalistic realist, that truth is merely a disquotational property; then if speakers could be coherently attributed a grasp of the classical truth conditions of non-ED statements, we should not expect any philosophically illuminating explanation of what having such a conception consists in, since none is possible. We should rather look to evidence in their behavior that they have a conception of the disquotational features of the truth predicate together with a conception of classical logic. On such a view, it would simply be misguided to seek an explanation in the behavioral evidence of what truth amounted to over and above the cognitive equivalence in a speaker's language of "p" is true with p and their use of the truth predicate to assert or deny unspecified sets of sentences. Truth itself has no interesting nature waiting to be discovered. That it is evidence-transcendent truth rather than some recognition-dependent ersatz is in turn patent in the speaker's use of classical modes of inference.

The reason the response cannot answer Dummett by itself is this: The position is quite consistent with the behavioral evidence being, as always, inconclusive and in need of radical interpretation. Although speakers might all concur in their estimates of the degree to which certain evidence confirmed the (classical) truth of a statement or in their judgments as to which inferences are (classically) valid, this of itself is no guarantee that an explanation of these tendencies of theirs that made the best rational sense of their overall behavior would not construe their grasp of the meanings of non-ED sentences as in reality a grasp of the *assertibility* conditions of those sentences (rather than a grasp of their classical *truth* conditions). As we know, this is precisely the antirealist's claim—the attribution best supported by the behavioral evidence overall, the most parsimonious theoretically and so on, is one that credits speakers with a grasp of verifiable conditions rather than recognition-transcendent ones, for speakers cannot detect that recognition-transcendent conditions hold when they do. Dummett nicely sums up the antirealist response to the suggestion that we view classical inferential practices as by themselves manifesting a grasp of a realist conception of truth:

> It is undoubtedly the case that *if* we have a grasp of some conception of truth ... with respect to which the principle of bivalence holds, then the laws of classical logic are valid; but it is hardly plausible that the mere propensity to reason in accord with those laws should *constitute* a grasp of such a notion of truth. If we consider any other class of statements for which it would be generally agreed that we do not possess a notion of truth subject to the principle of bivalence— for example, counterfactual conditionals—we can readily imagine that we had been induced, by childhood training, to apply the laws of classical logic to them, and we can recognise that, in such circumstances, we might be under a strong compulsion to suppose that we did have a notion of truth for such statements according to which each was determinately either true or false.... Nevertheless, there seems no merit in the suggestion that, merely by undergoing training in applying the laws of classical logic to these statements, we should thereby acquire, what we now lack, a conception of truth for them under which each must be determinately either true or false.[86]

3.4.2 Completing the "Classical Inferential Practices" Response

The problem with this response, in other words, is that it establishes only a *conditional* claim—to wit, *if* we have a grasp of classical truth, then our evidential and deductive practices will adequately attest its existence. Yet what we require is a ground for believing the *unconditional* claim that we *do* have such a grasp, that our inculcated inferential dispositions manifest a *coherent* conception of realist truth rather than a socially transmitted illusion of such. As it stands, this second response resembles an attempt to give a recursive definition of "grasp of realist truth" by supplying only the recursion clauses. We need the base clauses specifying "grasp of realist truth" for the "atomic" cases. These "recursion clauses" specify a grasp of classical inference only after the base clauses state outright what a grasp of realist truth amounts to.

So, we need a reason for thinking that we have a coherent conception of realist truth. I believe that we *do* have a reason for thinking this. To the extent that we grasp the meanings of first-person psychological sentences as these are uttered by others, we have, or so I argued in the previous section, an understanding of the truth conditions of those sentences. Moreover, the notion of truth applicable to those sentences certainly seems to be, as Strawson claimed it was, verification-transcendent. If I am right, the fact that we can understand the utterances of others as these pertain to their conscious experiences serves as a counterexample to Dummett's global antirealism.

3.4.3 Recognitional Capacities

Why does Dummett think that linguistic understanding is manifested primarily by recognitional or, at any rate, nonlinguistic abilities? His reason seems to be this:

> But to suppose that, in general, a knowledge of meaning consisted in verbalisable knowledge would involve an infinite regress: if a grasp of the meaning of an expression consisted, in general, in the ability to *state* its meaning, then it would be impossible for anyone to learn a language who was not already equipped with a fairly extensive language. Hence, that knowledge which, in general, constitutes the understanding of the language of mathematics must be implicit knowledge. Implicit knowledge cannot, however, meaningfully be ascribed to someone unless it is possible to say in what the manifestation of that knowledge consists: there must be an observable difference between the behaviour or capacities of someone who is said to have that knowledge and someone who is said to lack it.[87]

Dummett rehearses this argument in several places, and it is crucial to the success of his attack on realism. But what does it actually establish? Only, I submit, that semantic knowledge is in general implicit and that attributions of implicit knowledge must be constrained by the evidence of a speaker's behavior. But these are theses available to someone who denies on holistic grounds that those who know the meaning of an expression or sentence must evince a certain common pattern of behavior. To have any bite, the argument should at least prove that for each speaker there is some class of expressions whose senses she cannot informatively state for which the model of verbalizable knowledge is inappropriate.

Yet I submit that even this thesis is not warranted by the argument. A speaker might understand a word such as "red" and be unable informatively to state its sense, yet it might be manifest to an interpreter from the speakers's *verbal responses alone* that she understands the term perfectly well insofar as she uses it in precisely the right verbal contexts. Indeed, one crucial ability that Dummett neglects in his many discussions of how to test for semantic understanding is that of a speaker to give appropriate verbal responses to novel or counterfactual circumstances. Can she readily and appropriately project to these?

From the fact that semantic knowledge cannot in general be explicitly formulated, it does not follow that it is not testable by purely verbal means. We test how (or whether) a speaker understands "red" or "square" by observing as best we can the "conceptual role" the word occupies in the intentional organization of the speaker's overall linguistic behavior. Unless she understood "red," certain utterances or responses to questions, particularly those testing for responses within novel and hypothetical contexts, certain discriminatory perceptual evaluations or executions of tasks, all patently presupposing that the agent must understand "red," would appear totally inexplicable. And it might be manifest just from her verbal replies to our questions that she understands the predicate.

Moreover, to reject the sufficiency of verbal responses alone is to take a negative stand on the adequacy of the Turing test as an effective test for intelligence. Although I cannot hope to defend its adequacy here, I would argue that for real-time responsivity, only a genuinely intelligent system can be expected to pass it. Claiming that verbal responses do not provide a sufficient ground on which to base ascriptions of semantic knowledge is equivalent to claiming that the Turing test cannot possibly be an adequate test for intelligence. This strikes me as a very unwelcome consequence of Dummett's view.

3.4.4 *Holism, Meaning, and Use*

If we are not to pair meanings with recognitional capacities in the way demanded by the exhaustive manifestion requirement, in what sort of relation does a theory of meaning stand to the practical linguistic abilities of speakers' on the holistic model that I am recommending? Dummett himself nicely describes this model in *Elements of Intuitionism*, pp. 377–378:

... the platonist is compelled to repudiate the principle that meaning is use.... he may choose to emphasise the *theoretical* character of a theory of meaning. Within such a theory, we explain a speaker's understanding of an expression or sentence by ascribing to him knowledge of some feature of it or by saying that he associates some semantic element or complex with it; but, on the present account, we do not then need to explain what it is for him to have this knowledge or make this association in terms of his linguistic behaviour. In constructing a theory of meaning, we are not, on such a view, attempting to articulate the complex of practical abilities that make up mastery of a language into its constituents, conceived of as isolable, though interconnected, practical abilities; we are merely aiming at what any theory attempts to provide, a picture which, taken as a whole, makes sense of a complex phenomenon, that is, makes it surveyable, even though there is no one–one correspondence between the details of the picture and observable features of the phenomenon. On this view, an acceptance of classical reasoning in mathematics does not *constitute* a grasp of a notion of truth for mathematical statements subject to the principle of bivalence.... rather, it *warrants* the ascription of a grasp of such a notion of truth to the individual concerned. This position does not represent a complete retreat into holism, since it allows the necessity of finding some theory of meaning, some general form of representation of that in which the understanding of a sentence consists, even though a theory of this kind does not need to be justified piece-meal.

Contrary to Dummett's suggestion, however, the realist will not be forced to surrender the thesis that meaning is use, or, at least, that it is determined by use, provided we include under "use" successful scientific practice. What she will deny is that one's grasp of meaning is exhaustively manifest in one's use of language.

3.4.5 *Cognitivism and Meaning*

What drives Dummett's demand for exhaustive manifestation? It is, I believe, a strong antipsychologism inherited from Frege that leads him to insist that the contents of thought must be essentially communicable. Mental *acts* may be private, but when those acts are acts of judging or thinking or believing, their *contents* are in principle communicable and open for all to see. Since a theory of meaning for a given language L is a theory of what every competent speaker knows by virtue of speaking L, knowledge of meaning must also be publicly surveyable. So it must be manifest in the speaker's linguistic behavior. Thus:

(A)   Linguistic understanding is a highly complex practical skill—one that we could not have acquired unless the principles governing its exercise were out in the open for all to see.

It is just this assumption—that language is a *skill* we acquire by being taught the correct use of words—that Chomsky and his followers have effectively undermined, in my view. The theoretical considerations involved seem to me to receive strong support from the empirical evidence. The crucial point, however, is that if the cognitivist's view is so much as *empirically possible*, Dummett's thesis (A) above stands refuted.

So, without expecting to convince the skeptics, let me just set out some of the evidence Steven Pinker adduces for thinking that language development is largely biologically determined. If it is innately determined, the need for exhaustive behavioral manifestation will lapse in the context of language acquisition, at least. A "pidgin" is a makeshift jargon that people from different linguistic backgrounds develop when forced by practical circumstances to communicate but without the time or inclination to learn each other's language. The classic examples come from the Atlantic slave trade and from the South Pacific. "Sometimes a pidgin can become a lingua franca and gradually increase in complexity over decades, as in the 'Pidgin English' of the modern South Pacific," writes Pinker,[88] "But the linguist Derek Bickerton has presented evidence that in many cases a pidgin can be transmuted into a full complex language in one fell swoop: all it takes is for a group of children to be exposed to the pidgin at the age when they acquire their mother tongue." This has actually happened, Bickerton argues, in those cases where children are isolated from their parents and tended collectively by a worker who spoke pidgin to them. Pinker describes the result: "Not content to reproduce the fragmentary word strings, the children injected grammatical complexity where none existed before, resulting in a brand-new, richly expressive language."[89] The new languages are called *creoles*. The difference between a pidgin and a creole is that whereas the former provides its users with "no consistent word order, no prefixes or suffixes, no tense or other temporal and logical markers, no structure more complex than a simple clause, and no consistent way to indicate who did what to whom," some of the words of the host language in the case of creoles "have been converted by the creole speakers into auxiliaries, prepositions, case markers and relative pronouns.... Indeed, creoles are bona fide languages, with standardized word orders and grammatical markers that were lacking in the pidgin of the immigrants and, aside from the sound of words, not taken from the language of the colonizers."

Although claims about historical creolization are difficult to verify, Pinker maintains that Bickerton's basic ideas have been "stunningly corroborated by two recent natural experiments in which creolization by children can be observed in real time." The experiments involved deaf Nicaraguan children. No sign languages existed in Nicaragua at all prior to the Sandinistas since the deaf were isolated from each other. But the Sandinista government created schools for the deaf when they took over in 1979. A pidgin sign language, LSN, was quickly established collectively by the children who pooled the gestures they used at home. LSN is a pidgin, Pinker contends, because there is no consistent grammar and those young deaf adults who learned it from 1979 all use it differently.

But children who joined these schools from around age four are different. They use their sign language in the same way, developing a consistent grammar for the pidgin; the result is the creole ISN. Moreover, similar achievements have been observed at the level of the individual language-user, Pinker relates. Simon, a deaf user of American Sign Language, ASL, was exposed only to his parents' defective grasp of it. Yet "He understood sentences with moved topic phrases without difficulty, and when he had to describe complex videotaped events, he used the ASL verb inflections almost perfectly, even in sentences requiring them in particular orders. Simon must somehow have shut out his parents' ungrammatical 'noise.'"

Is it perhaps just the very intelligent who are capable of such grammatical invention as creolization? No. Linguistic facility, all the evidence suggests, is largely independent of general intelligence. Victims of Broca's aphasia seem to be grammatically debilitated yet not to be cognitively impaired generally. The opposite dissociation—linguistic facility coupled with poor cognition—is evinced by linguistic idiot savants: severely retarded individuals, such as some spina bifida sufferers, make fluent and interesting conversationalists, and other sorts of intellectually impaired individuals can still retain their grammatical abilities: Alzheimer's patients, autistic children, and certain aphasics.

Chomsky's own primary ground for believing grammars to be innate was his famous "poverty of the stimulus" argument. Children are not in any sense taught language; indeed in some societies adults do not deign to talk to prelinguistic children. What children hear is degraded, elliptical, and ungrammatical sentences for the main. Yet they are able to recognize grammatical from ungrammatical sentences in their own language. Thus Chomsky showed that a linear model of question formation was clearly inadequate by showing that children who were confronted with a declarative sentence with two auxiliaries for the first time were still able to convert it into a grammatically correct question:

[a man who is driving a car] is drinking

was not converted to the ungrammatical:

is a man who driving the car is drinking?

but the quite grammatical:

is [a man who is driving a car] drinking?

The skeptical retort "Ah! But this is because the children have grasped the fact that 'a man who is driving a car' is a semantically significant unit that cannot be broken up!" can be answered, it seems, by further empirical research due to Stephen Crain and Mineharu Nakayama. They asked children of three, four, and five years old to pose questions to some dolls. One such question was "Ask Jabba if it is raining in the picture." The significance of this is that the "it" is just a "dummy element" in Pinker's words, there only to satisfy the rules of English syntax. Other questions with dummy elements included "Ask Jabba if there is a snake in this picture."

It might be countered that Pinker's evidence for an innate grammar coded in the brain is not relevant to the question of semantics, which is what Dummett's argument deals with. But I think this is a mistake. We do not first learn sounds and then attach meanings to acoustic units. Rather, we cannot even properly distinguish the sounds without simultaneously marking in some way, however crude, their semantic significance. The fact is that structure is a significant part of meaning: From the very start there is an interanimation between grammar and meaning. Indeed, it may be that logic itself is to be accounted for on structuralist grounds, as has recently been suggested by Arnold Koslow following a tradition that derives from Heinrich Hertz and Gerhard Gentzen and has been championed by Nuel Belnap in more recent times.

Cognitivists can therefore take issue with Dummett's claim that the realist's explanations of the logical constants is vacuous because we cannot possibly pair practical recognitional abilities with the classical truth conditions that fix their meaning. Why should this matter, if we have the requisite realist conception implicitly defined for us by the classical structural laws of logic coded in our brains?

I do not mean to endorse this speculation. The point is simply that Dummett's manifestation constraint looks inescapable only if one assumes that the meanings of our sentences and expressions have to be learned—for then what else could we possibly base our guesses about meaning on other than what was manifest in our language-teachers' behavior? But the Chomskyan claim is that we come to the learning of language with a detailed and complex cognitive structure prewired in a language module in our brains. Even if there is no language of thought and our brains are connectionist machines, the "weightings" of the nodes of the network have already been determined biologically. Dummett's manifestation constraint is an attempt to mandate how a language *must* be learned. It is, arguably, at variance with the empirical facts about how it actually is learned.

4
Intuitionistic Foundations of Antirealism

4.1 Intuitionism

In this section we look at some basic features of intuitionism[1]—the view of mathematics as a science of mental constructs, the attendant emphasis on constructive reasoning and the rejection of nonconstructive modes of inference, a brief outline of various aspects of intuitionistic mathematics, particularly intuitionistic attitudes to the infinite and to set theory, a brief description of intuitionistic conceptions of truth and validity, a formulation of intuitionistic logic, and an introduction to intuitionistic semantics by means of Kripke trees. We begin with a brief history.

4.1.1 History of Intuitionism

Intuitionism was invented by the Dutch mathematician L. E. J. Brouwer (1881–1966). Recalling Kant, Brouwer held that the "basal intuition" on which all of mathematics was founded was the intellectual separation of time into "qualitatively different parts, to be reunited only while remaining separated by time."[2]

Brouwer called this "the intuition of the bare two-ity." Since he thought we are able to repeat this process indefinitely, we arrive at the concept of an infinite progression as a process of constructing one element after another without end. In this way, Brouwer was led to think of the infinite sequence of natural numbers **N** as only potentially infinite—we could always construct another number in the sequence, and since this process was endless, the whole sequence could never be completed. Moreover, this construction occurred in time, each element in the sequence **N** being quite literally a mental construct.

Brouwer thus rejected Cantor's view that the sequence of real numbers, **R**, was a completed whole. Such a totality could not possibly be constructed from intuitions of the intellectual separation of time into discrete moments. Individual real numbers could be so constructed but only by specifying laws for generating their decimal expansions. Unlike the natural numbers, where the successor operation permitted the construction of any item in the sequence from its predecessor, there was no single law for constructing each real number. Hence, although it was meaningful to talk of the whole set of natural numbers **N** if only as a way of adverting to the principle of generation of each number in **N**, the same could not be said for the real numbers. There was thought to be no such thing as the set of all reals, **R**.

What was to be made of Cantor's work, then? Didn't Cantor prove that the set of real numbers **R** was nondenumerable, a larger set than **N**? How could such comparisons even make sense if there was no such thing as **R**? Brouwer's attitude to Cantor's diagonal argument was the same as Poincaré's: Instead of proving the nondenumerability of a determinate set of all reals, what Cantor had actually done was to demonstrate that the reals did not form a determinate totality in the first place. The constructive import of diagonalization was its provision of a recipe for generating for any given list of real numbers a further real number not on the list. *The real numbers were, in this sense, indefinitely extensible.* Given that mathematics was firmly rooted in temporal experience and as a consequence that the objects mathematics dealt with were mental constructs, some forms of mathematical reasoning had to appear dubious. One could not assume that a given mathematical object either did or did not have a certain property if there was no construction that would determine which. The law of the excluded middle could not be blithely assumed to hold.

4.1.2 Constructive Reasoning

Here is a simple illustration of the difference between *constructive* and *nonconstructive* proof. Consider the following question: Are there irrational numbers a and b such that a^b is rational? Classically, we can reason as follows:

Consider $\sqrt{2}^{\sqrt{2}}$. Either $\sqrt{2}^{\sqrt{2}}$ is rational or it is irrational. (A)

Suppose that it is rational. Then we have a solution to the problem by setting $a = \sqrt{2}$ and $b = \sqrt{2}$.

Suppose on the other hand that $\sqrt{2}^{\sqrt{2}}$ is irrational. Then $(\sqrt{2}^{\sqrt{2}})^{\sqrt{2}}$ will be rational. So we have a solution by setting $a = \sqrt{2}^{\sqrt{2}}$ and $b = \sqrt{2}$.

Hence, either $a = \sqrt{2}$ and $b = \sqrt{2}$, or $a = \sqrt{2}^{\sqrt{2}}$ and $b = \sqrt{2}$. (B)

The constructivist rejects this reasoning on the grounds that we have no warrant at (A) for asserting that either $\sqrt{2}^{\sqrt{2}}$ is rational or irrational. There is no construction determining which of the alternatives holds. The grounds for asserting this are precisely those grounds that would determine which of the two alternatives holds at the final step (B). To determine which alternative holds, moreover, we have to engage in some serious number theory rather than content ourselves with the general reasoning above.

4.1.3 Truth and Validity

Classically, truth is not constrained by what we can recognize, whereas intuitionistically, it is: *A statement is intuitionistically true if and only if we have (conclusive) grounds for asserting it.* The intuitionist, then, operates with a notion of truth that differs from the classical notion. Hence, the law of bivalence is not generally valid. It holds for restricted domains but not for all domains, intuitionists maintain.

As a direct result of this alternative notion of truth, many classical inference rules are not validated in intuitionistic logic. The law of the excluded middle (LEM), the proof-theoretic counterpart to the law of bivalence, is perhaps the most notable example. However, double negation elimination (DNE), which licenses the inference of $\emptyset$ from $\neg\neg\emptyset$ in classical logic, does not hold either. We should take care to grasp what the intuitionist is claiming in declaring this inference not generally valid. She is not committed to the strong claim that DNE is *invalid* in the sense that there are cases in which the premise might be true (i.e., assertible) and the conclusion false (i.e., refutable). The claim is, rather, that there are many cases in which we can recognize that there is no prospect of our ever refuting $\emptyset$ (so that the assertion of the double negation of $\emptyset$ is justified) that do not by themselves constitute any ground for asserting $\emptyset$. Hence $\neg\neg\emptyset$ may be assertible in situations that do not warrant the assertion of $\emptyset$. So the intuitionist maintains that LEM and DNE do not generally hold. There are cases where the inference rule holds—when $\emptyset$ is a *decidable* statement, that is, when the truth-value of $\emptyset$ can be decided. But it fails to hold generally because of the way intuitionistic negation is understood.

One might worry that if the notion of truth varies from the classical one, the notion of validity might suffer a similar dramatic reinterpretation. It undoubtedly does undergo some significant reinterpretation as we shall see. But at least the *relation* between truth and validity remains common ground for classical and intuitionistic logic—it is still the case that an argument is valid, intuitionistically, if and only if whenever all its premises are true its conclusion is also true. From the classical point of view, there is an intimate connection between the notions of entailment and consistency such that $\Gamma \vDash \varnothing$ iff $\Gamma \cup \{-\varnothing\}$ is inconsistent. However, this cannot be an acceptable explication of the notion of entailment to an intuitionist, because although $\neg\neg\varnothing$ and $\neg\varnothing$ *are* inconsistent, we cannot infer from this intuitionistically that $\neg\neg\varnothing \vDash \varnothing$. So what *does* the notion of semantic entailment amount to for the intuitionist? *To assert that $\Gamma \vDash \varnothing$ is to assert that we have an effective procedure for transforming any grounds for asserting all the well-formed formulas (wffs) in Γ into grounds for asserting $\varnothing$.*

4.1.4 Intuitionistic Logical Constants

So how does the intuitionist understand her logical constants? In the following way:

$\varnothing$ & Ψ is assertible iff we have grounds for asserting $\varnothing$ and we have grounds for asserting Ψ.

$\varnothing \vee \Psi$ is assertible iff we have grounds for asserting $\varnothing$ or we have grounds for asserting Ψ.

$\varnothing \rightarrow \Psi$ is assertible iff we have a general procedure by which grounds for asserting $\varnothing$ can be transformed into grounds for asserting Ψ.

$(\exists x)\varnothing(x)$ is assertible iff we know of an object k in the domain for which we have grounds for asserting $\varnothing(k)$.

$(\forall x)\varnothing(x)$ is assertible iff we have a general procedure, applicable to each object k by which grounds for asserting that k belongs to the domain can be transformed into grounds for asserting $\varnothing(k)$.

Like its classical counterpart, the intuitionistic biconditional is definable in terms of an (intuitionistic) conjunction of two (intuitionistic) conditionals. In sharp contrast to the classical connectives, for the intuitionistic connectives we can prove that no intuitionistic logical constant, aside from the intuitionistic biconditional, can be defined in terms of any of the others.

What of intuitionistic negation, though? As with classical negation, it is definable by taking "$\neg\varnothing$" to abbreviate "$\varnothing \rightarrow \bot$" where "$\bot$" denotes an atomic statement whose falsity can be directly perceived, for example, "$0 = 1$." Because we can directly recognize the falsity of "$\bot$" we know that there can never be any grounds for asserting "$\bot$," so that to say that we have a procedure for converting any grounds for asserting

∅ into a ground for asserting ⊥ is equivalent to claiming that we have grounds for asserting that there can never be any grounds for asserting ∅—that is, "¬∅," which is often read as "∅ is absurd."

4.1.5 Natural Deduction for Intuitionistic Logic (I)

All the inference rules of classical logic apart from double negation elimination are validated by the (informal) semantics of intuitionistic logic. That is, with the notion of (conclusive) assertibility or proof replacing the classical notion of truth, those classical inference rules hold good under this reinterpretation of the logical constants. Let us call our system of intuitionistic logic **I**. To give an example of how the reinterpretation is supposed to go, take disjunction elimination (∨E):

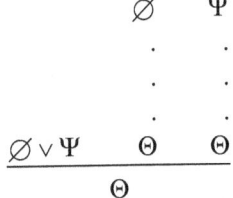

The intuitionist explains the validity of (∨E) as follows:

"Suppose we have a derivation of Θ from ∅ and also from Ψ. Then the assertibility of ∅ yields the assertibility of Θ and the assertibility of Ψ yields the assertibility of Θ. Suppose in addition that ∅ ∨ Ψ is assertible. This means that either ∅ is assertible or that Ψ is assertible. But since the assertibility of Θ is guaranteed in either case, Θ must be assertible." The natural deduction rules for the constants &, ∨, ∃ are complete for these constants in the sense that any intuitionistically valid sequent that contains no constants other than these three may be derived from the rules for these constants alone, and as these rules are common to classical and intuitionistic logic, it follows that *a sequent of this kind is intuitionistically valid if and only if it is classically valid.*

In contrast to the situation with the three constants above, → and ∀ are not complete for the classical understanding of them. To prove some sequents containing just those constants and ∨ (for which the rules (∨I) and (∨E) are complete), LEM is required. This means that there are sequents containing → (and ∀) that are classically valid but *not* intuitionistically valid.

Here are some examples involving →:

(1) ⊢ ∅ ∨ (∅ → Ψ)

(2) $(\varnothing \to \Psi) \to \Psi \vdash \varnothing \vee \Psi$

(3) $(\varnothing \to \Psi) \to \varnothing \vdash \varnothing$

That the rules for $\forall$ are not complete follows from the fact that if they were, then since the rules for $\vee$ are complete, we could prove the classically valid sequent $\forall x(\varnothing(x) \vee \Theta) \vdash \forall x \varnothing(x) \vee \Theta$ from the inference rules for $\forall$ and $\vee$ alone. But we cannot do this without LEM (or some other nonconstructive rule such as nonconstructive dilemma or double negation elimination). It is important to note that the existential and universal quantifiers are not interdefinable with the aid of negation as is the case with their classical counterparts. Although it is the case that $(\forall x)\neg\varnothing(x) \dashv\vdash \neg(\exists x)\varnothing(x)$ and $(\exists x)\neg\varnothing(x) \vdash \neg(\forall x)\varnothing(x)$, it is not the case that:

(4) $\neg(\forall x)\varnothing(x) \vdash (\exists x)\neg\varnothing(x)$

The reason (4) fails to hold is that one may be able to prove that the supposition that every object is $\varnothing$ leads to absurdity without knowing of an object in the domain that is not $\varnothing$. We shall return to the intuitionistic understanding of the quantifiers later in section 4.2.

The most obvious difference between intuitionistic systems and classical systems is in the theorems and sequents involving negation that are derivable in these different systems. We can set this out most clearly by listing some of the sequents and theorems that are derivable in the classical systems and indicating whether they are derivable in **I** or not:

Rejected in **I**	Accepted in **I**
(1*) $\vdash \varnothing \vee \neg\varnothing$	$\vdash \neg\neg(\varnothing \vee \neg\varnothing)$
(2*) $\neg\neg\varnothing \vdash \varnothing$	$\varnothing \vdash \neg\neg\varnothing$
(3*) $\neg\varnothing \to \varnothing \vdash \varnothing$	$\varnothing \to \neg\varnothing \vdash \neg\varnothing$
(4*) $\neg\varnothing \to \neg\Psi \vdash \Psi \to \varnothing$	$\varnothing \to \Psi \vdash \neg\Psi \to \neg\varnothing$
(5*) $\neg\varnothing \to \Psi, \neg\varnothing \to \neg\Psi \vdash \varnothing$	$\varnothing \to \Psi, \varnothing \to \neg\Psi \vdash \neg\varnothing$

Note that if we set $\Psi = \bot$ in the classically but not intuitionistically valid (1) to (3) earlier, we end up with the rejected sequents on the LHS of (1*) to (3*) above. We can formulate an inference rule for $\bot$, namely, *ex falso quodlibet*, which states that from $\bot$ one may derive any wff $\varnothing$ one chooses. This inference rule ($\bot$) is complete in the above sense for *both* the classical and the intuitionistic understandings of $\bot$.

What of the remaining constants? It turns out that ($\to$I) and ($\to$E) are complete for the intuitionistic understanding of $\to$. As for negation, if we do without $\bot$ and instead take negation as primitive, then we can obtain a complete pair of inference rules for intuitionistic negation if we take reductio ad absurdum (RAA) as a (quasi) introduction rule and ex falso quodlibet (EFQ) as our elimination rule. The rules are set out below:

$$(\text{RAA}) \quad \frac{\overset{\varnothing}{\Psi} \quad \overset{\varnothing}{\neg \Psi}}{\neg \varnothing} \qquad (\text{EFQ}) \quad \frac{\varnothing \quad \neg \varnothing}{\Theta}$$

4.1.6 Semantics for Intuitionistic Logic: Many-valued Truth-tables

We have seen from the informal explanation of the meanings of the intuitionistic logical constants that they cannot be given in terms of the simple structures that suffice for the meanings of their classical counterparts, embodied in the truth-tables. This is because the classical truth-tables do not exhaust *all* the logical possibilities as far as the intuitionist is concerned: *A given sentence may be unassertible in a given situation though not refutable (and therefore, not false) in that situation.*

So it is natural to inquire whether a modification of the classical two-valued truth-tables to include a *third* truth value for statements that are neither intuitionistically true nor intuitionistically false may suffice to convey the meanings of the intuitionist's sentential connectives. To achieve greater generality let us allow for the possibility of an arbitrary finite number of intermediate truth values. So for any number $n \geq 2$ we take the set of numbers $\{0, 1, 2, \ldots, n-1\}$ as representing our truth values, with truth and falsity represented by the extreme values 0 and $n-1$ respectively.

However, it turns out that for *every* $n \geq 2$ there are wffs that always take the value 0 on all truth-tables with less than n truth values, but which take a different value on an n-valued truth-table. We might still be hopeful that for every invalid wff there is *some* n-valued truth-table or other that refutes that invalid wff. Yet even this hope cannot be fulfilled. One wff that serves as a counterexample is $(\neg\neg p \to p) \to (p \vee \neg p)$. This wff is verified by every n-valued truth-table and yet it is not intuitionistically logically true. It cannot be proven in our intuitionistic system for ND. What this means is that *even the many-valued truth-tables cannot, as their classical counterparts can, provide a decision procedure for the logical truth of intuitionistic SL wffs.*

4.1.7 Semantics for Intuitionistic Logic: Kripke Trees

The partial success of our many-valued truth-tables prompts us to look for richer structures that are semantically complete—ones that suffice to refute all intuitionistically invalid inferences and validate all intuitionistically valid inferences. So let's take stock of the situation with respect to intuitionistic semantics: Intuitionistic logic does not accept the universal applicability of bivalence, as we have seen. That is, it is not generally true, intuitionistically, that in any situation every statement is either true or false. However, intuitionistic logic does assume that any situation will either provide grounds for asserting a statement or fail to provide grounds for asserting it. Moreover, it is also usually assumed by intuitionistic logicians that we can actually *recognize* whether a situation does or does not provide grounds for asserting the statement. The question of whether a given situation does or does not provide grounds for asserting a given statement is, in other words, assumed to be decidable.

The other assumption crucial to intuitionistic logic is that sentences may change their semantic status in response to the evidence so that a state of information Σ_1 may fail to warrant the assertion of a given sentence $\varnothing$, but its augmentation Σ_2 in response to further evidence may provide the necessary warrant for $\varnothing$ that Σ_1 lacked. Moreover, the grounds for asserting any given sentence are assumed to be conclusive—no further evidence could overturn the grounds for asserting a sentence once it is genuinely assertible.

So what is an *n*-valued truth-table? It is a model of a sequence of evolving *states of information*, each state evolving from its predecessor state. A wff $\varnothing$ is assigned the value 0 in a state of information Σ_k if $\varnothing$ is true in the present state of information Σ_0. Once true, a wff remains true, since we are assuming that the grounds for asserting a given wff are always conclusive. A wff is assigned the maximum value n on the other hand if it fails to be true in all the possible states of information (in which case its negation has value 0 for all possible states—i.e., is true).

```
  .   .   .    . . .   .
  0   1   2          n − 1
```

But what do the intermediate values represent? They are intended to represent the state of information, if any, in which a given wff becomes true. So if $\varnothing$ is assigned the intermediate value k, this indicates that conclusive grounds for the assertion of $\varnothing$ are not available until node k of the linear array of nodes representing states of information.

Perhaps it would be more accurate to conceive of the situation as one in which the notion of truth was replaced by the temporal notion of a sentence's *coming to be true*? Then it would be possible to verify that the original rules for asserting a sentence hold good for this interpretation. That is, a conjunction becomes true as soon as both its conjuncts become true; a disjunction becomes true as soon as one of its disjuncts becomes true. A conditional $\varnothing \to \Psi$ becomes true as soon as it becomes true that if $\varnothing$ ever becomes true (in the present state of information or within some future state) then so does Ψ. For one case, $\varnothing$ becomes true before Ψ does, and then the conditional becomes true when (if at all) Ψ becomes true. For the other case, Ψ is already true when, if ever, $\varnothing$ becomes true, and so the conditional receives the value 0.

So why aren't these many-valued structures complete? The answer is that they assume that the only future situations or states of information that are possible are *linearly ordered* ones: Each state of information, if it has a successor at all, has *just one* successor so that branching is not even considered. Yet on reflection, it should be clear that the intuitionist *ought* to allow for branching states of information in order to explicate her semantics. Suppose *P* fails to be true now in our present state of information Σ_0. What can we say about the structure of Σ_0's *successor* state of information? In the general case, there is not going to be any *unique* successor. It may be that evidence for *P* does become available in our next state of information but equally no such evidence may arise. So we need coordinate possible successor states of information, neither of which temporally precedes the other. Let us denote these coordinate possibilities as Σ_α and Σ_β. Then to represent our epistemic situation with respect to *P* we need to have a branching structure as shown in figure 4.1 in which in our present state of information Σ_0, *P* is not true, and although in Σ_α it does become true, in Σ_β it does not.

The situation shown in figure 4.1 represents *partially ordered* states of information (partially ordered since neither Σ_β nor Σ_α comes before the other in the ordering). Kripke's semantics for intuitionistic logic uses such partially ordered tree structures to explicate the meanings of the intuitionistic logical constants. Think of an idealized human knower who is constantly in the process of extending not only his knowledge but also his universe of objects. At every moment of time *t*, the "creative subject" (as such an idealized mathematician is known) has some stock of sentences Σ_τ that he has established and a domain D_t of objects that he has constructed. Since at *t* our creative subject has various choices for future mathematical activity, the stages of that activity represented by states of information must be thought of as only partially ordered. A *Kripke model*, as such branching tree structures are known, is given by a set of elements K with one element α to serve as the origin of the tree

126   Chapter 4

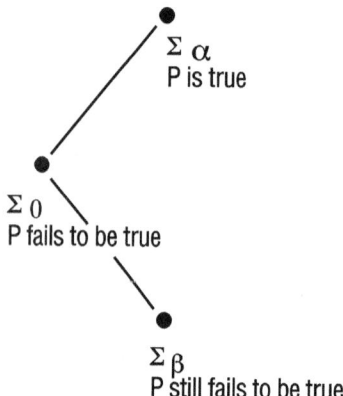

Figure 4.1

and a relation ≤ to generate the structure. The model itself is then just a quintuple, $\langle K, \alpha, \leq, D, \Vdash \rangle$, where:

(i) K is a set and α is an element of K.

(ii) ≤ is a relation which generates on K a tree structure with minimal element α.

(iii) D is a domain function which assigns to each element β of K a non-empty set of individuals D_β subject to the constraint that if $\beta \leq \gamma$ then D_β is a subset of D_γ.

(iv) ⊩ is a relation between elements β of K and closed wffs subject to the following conditions [noting that β, γ range over all elements of K, including α]:

(a) Where $\Psi(x_0, \ldots, x_n)$ is atomic, and $a_0, \ldots, a_{n-1} \in D_\beta$ we have that if $\beta \Vdash \Psi(a_0, \ldots, a_{n-1})$ then $\gamma \Vdash \Psi(a_0, \ldots, a_{n-1})$. Where Ψ is a sentence letter, there is no reference required to elements of the associated domain.

(b) For every β we have that $\neg \beta \Vdash \bot$

(c) $\beta \Vdash (\emptyset \,\&\, \Psi)$ *iff* $\beta \Vdash \emptyset$ and $\beta \Vdash \Psi$

(d) $\beta \Vdash (\emptyset \vee \Psi)$ *iff* $\beta \Vdash \emptyset$ or $\beta \Vdash \Psi$

(e) $\beta \Vdash (\emptyset \rightarrow \Psi)$ *iff* for every $\gamma \geq \beta$, if $\gamma \Vdash \emptyset$ then $\gamma \Vdash \Psi$

We can work out the clause for negation from the clauses (b) and (e):

(f) $\beta \Vdash \neg \emptyset$ iff for every $\gamma \geq \beta$, $\neg(\gamma \Vdash \emptyset)$.

What of the quantifiers?

(g) $\beta \Vdash (\exists x)\varnothing(x)$ *iff* there is some $a \in D_\beta$ such that $\beta \Vdash \varnothing(a)$

(h) $\beta \Vdash (\forall x)\varnothing(x)$ *iff* for every $\gamma \geq \beta$ and every $a \in D_\beta$, $\gamma \Vdash \varnothing(a)$

The relation $\Vdash$ defined above, which clearly means "is true in" goes by the name of the *forcing relation*. Notice that if a wff is true at any node in the tree structure it will be true for all such nodes. Truth is preserved from node to node. All that remains is to say when a wff is true in a Kripke model. This is achieved simply by requiring that *for a wff $\varnothing$ to be true in such a model it must be true at the minimal element α of that model, that is, that $\alpha \Vdash \varnothing$*.

It can be proved that a wff is true in a given Kripke model if and only if it is provable in the ND system I for intuitionisitic logic—that is, that intuitionistic logic is both sound and complete with respect to the Kripke semantics.

4.2 Intuitionism and Antirealism

Dummett advocates intuitionistic logic and mathematics by way of revision of classical inferential and mathematical practice, which he deems unintelligible. In this section and the next I will be concerned to trace his route to intuitionism and his argument for revisionism.

4.2.1 Dummett's Advocacy of Intuitionism

There are several points of contact between Brouwer's intuitionism as outlined in section 4.1 and Dummett's antirealism as set out in chapters 2 and 3. Both reject verification-transcendent truth, both insist on a means of determining the truth value of a statement before licensing its assertion, and both call for a radical revision in some of our inferential practices. There are also some clear disanalogies and a real question as to whether intuitionism can be generalized from the mathematical to empirical domains in the way that a global antirealism, of the sort Dummett envisages, would require.

For a start, Brouwer subscribed to a mentalistic (in fact, a solipsistic) theory of meaning for mathematical statements to which Dummett is so implacably opposed. As we have seen, Dummett is committed to the Wittgensteinian thesis that since thought is essentially communicable, meaning cannot transcend use. Second, there is no obvious empirical analogue to the notion of mathematical proof. Empirical confirmation is probabilistic and thus intrinsically nonmonotonic, whereas mathematical proof is intrinsically monotonic. Third, it is not obvious that the sentences whose truth conditions are in dispute between realists and antirealists are non-ED sentences in general rather than *barely true* non-ED sentences. Yet the crucial notion of a *barely true* sentence does not even apply in the mathematical context, and the notion of "decidability" will almost surely have to be weakened to confirmability for the empirical case. All these problems are going to exercise us in the sections ahead, so I shall not dwell on them now.

Platonism conceives of mathematical objects as mind-independent abstract objects. Mathematical assertions are then held true or false insofar as they correspond or fail to correspond to the determinate, mind-independent reality comprising of such objects. Intuitionism denies this thesis—the meaning of a mathematical statement must be given in terms of those constructions that prove it, rather than by reference to mysterious platonistic states of affairs that happen to correspond to it. So mathematical sentences are to have their meanings explained by citing the *grounds for asserting* them. Adhering as he does to a truthmaker principle, Dummett also contends that such constructions make these statements true.

4.2.2 *Constructions and Constructive Proof*

So what are these "constructions" that the intuitionist charges with the complex semantic role of content-specifier-cum-truth-maker? Intuitionists' own talk of constructions is apt to mislead. As Göran Sundholm has noted, intuitionists often equivocate between constructions-as-processes (constructions$_p$) and constructions-as-objects (constructions$_o$) in their use of the single term "constructions." Henceforth, I will use subscripts to avoid any ambiguity where ambiguity threatens.

Charles McCarty gives a nice informal explanation of "construction":[3] "Generally, constructions are mathematical operations which are completely performable in principle. They are operations which we can, barring limitations of time and memory, carry to completion on any argument from the relevant domain. And once we've finished with the operation, we can recognize that it has been properly carried out." But which constructions are they? Intuitionism parts company with finitism in holding that we can "in principle" determine whether $10^{11^{10}} + 11^{10^{11}}$ is either prime or composite. Similarly, we can in principle "carry to completion" the constructive procedure for determining the greatest common divisor (GCD) of any numbers at all, be they as huge as our addends, $10^{11^{10}}$ and $11^{10^{11}}$. *Euclid's algorithm* tells us that if we wish to discover the GCD of any two numbers m and n, first divide m into n to obtain a remainder r_1. Then iterate the procedure obtaining on the way the sequence of decreasing remainders $r_1, r_2, r_3, \ldots, r_j, \ldots$ until we find some k for which $r_{k+1} = 0$. We then take as our GCD the term r_k in the sequence of remainders.

McCarty remarks that Euclid's algorithm is a bona fide constructive method because it gives us not only a routine for the explicit calculation of the GCD of any m and n, but also a simple computational check that the putative GCD, g say, *really is* the greatest common divisor.[4] Yet given such an apparently liberal conception of what we can in principle construct, what is to stop the classical mathematician from claiming that we can *in principle* construct *any* mathematical function, or, at least, that suitably idealized extensions of ourselves unconstrained by time and memory could do so? Thus, faced with the intuitionist's claim that the characteristic function of the rationals as a total function on the reals is a "nonconstruction,"[5] such a realist might object that under just the same types of idealizations as support the intuitionist's claim that we can establish the GCD of any two m and n at all, irrespective of how huge m and n might be, or whether the effort would require more time than for the heat death of the universe and so on, a superhuman calculator could determine whether Euler's constant given by the formula below is rational or irrational:[6]

$$\gamma = \lim n \to \infty \left[\sum_{(k=1 \text{ to } n)} 1/k - \log n \right]$$

Why should there be any intuitionistic objection under the idealizations permitted so far to a (super)human calculator doubling his speed every two minutes to complete the precise calculation of the limit within finite time? This question is of some concern to an antirealist who looks to intuitionistic semantics for her theory of meaning, for unless some principled basis can be found for distinguishing the *super*human from the idealized human mathematician, the manifestation demand may well judge intuitionistic meaning to be meaning that cannot be made fully manifest in use. Crispin Wright has provided a plausible initial response to this worry: "I propose that we should count any feat as within our compass in principle just in case some *finite* extension of powers we actually have would enable us to accomplish it *in practice*."[7] "Hypertasks" such as the calculation of Euler's constant, γ, then, would seem to fail this criterion.

4.2.3 The Method of Weak Counterexamples

The example of Euler's constant is also useful to introduce the method of "weak counterexamples," which intuitionists use to *reject*[8] certain classical notions and principles. Thus the intuitionist rejects the existence of the characteristic function of the rationals—let's call it F—that assigns 1 to a real if it is rational and 0 otherwise because to construct such a function in order to justify the claim that it exists we'd have to know whether γ is rational or irrational, which we do not know. We have not thereby shown that F does *not* exist, that there is *no* such function; rather, we've merely shown that there is no ground for asserting that F *does* exist since the assumption that we have such a ground entails a claim that is *not intuitionistically true*, namely, that either γ is rational or it is irrational.

The counterexamples used to reject the classical inferential principles are thus *weak* in that they do not show the principles to be false, they merely show them not to be intuitionistically true (demonstrable). Quite generally, the method of weak counterexamples rejects a classical principle by showing that were the principle to hold without exception some currently unsolved problem would become intuitionistically decidable. We shall see how such a weak counterexample can be given to LEM.

Now the claim that it is *not* intuitionistically true that either γ is rational or else irrational is apt to sound incoherent to classical mathematicians. How could one possibly doubt that it is one or the other when it is a perfectly determinate matter whether any given number p is either rational or irrational: it is rational if it can be expressed in the form m/n with $(m, n) = 1$, and irrational if it can't. *So what is the problem?* The problem from the intuitionistic point of view, as we saw in section 4.1, is that we have no construction (or even any effective method, EM, for discovering one) that permits us to decide *which* of the two alternatives holds. A mathematical statement is true, however, only if we have a construction (or at least an EM for finding one) that proves it, and a disjunction of statements is true only if we have an EM at least for determining which of its disjuncts holds. In contrast to our means of determining whether a given number is prime, however, there is no EM for determining whether a given number is rational (in the sense that it can be expressed in the form m/n with $(m, n) = 1$).

I cannot refrain from registering my dissatisfaction with this response. It is just not obvious to me why the unavailability of an EM should matter. Might not some of our artifacts or constructs possess properties that we might not be able to ascertain they had? Couldn't there be a fact of the matter as to whether Sherlock Holmes's attitude to Watson was paternalistic even if neither Conan Doyle himself nor any of his Victorian readers could so much as detect such a property? More pertinently, isn't there a fact of the matter from the intuitionistic point of view as to whether a given sentence Θ is an intuitionistic logical consequence of some set of sentences Γ? Yet since first-order intuitionistic logic is not decidable there may be no EM for detecting that Γ does not entail Θ if it in fact does not. Without a means of determining which of two complementary properties a given construct has we may well choose to refrain from asserting that it must have either one or the other, but that might have more to do with an ethics of assertion keyed to what one can prove than with any underlying antirealism. We might think there is a fact of the matter as to whether the construct has R or not R even if we are not able to determine which it has.

4.2.4 Natural Deduction System for Intuitionistic Logic

Proof-theoretically, intuitionistic logic is just a subsystem of classical logic, since every sequent valid in the former is valid in the latter, but not conversely. The principles of intuitionistic reasoning can be codified in an intuitionistic natural deduction system **I**, which has inference rules as shown in figure 4.2.

4.2.5 Translation between Intuitionistic and Classical Languages

We can define a translation-mapping, $*$, such that:

$$\bot^* = \bot$$
$$\varnothing^* = \neg\neg\varnothing$$
$$(\varnothing \,\&\, \Omega)^* = (\varnothing^* \,\&\, \Omega^*)$$
$$(\varnothing \vee \Omega)^* = \neg\neg(\varnothing^* \vee \Omega^*)$$
$$(\varnothing \to \Omega)^* = (\varnothing^* \to \Omega^*)$$
$$(\forall x.\varnothing)^* = (\forall x.\varnothing^*)$$
$$(\exists x.\varnothing)^* = (\exists x.\varnothing^*)$$

The $*$-mapping replaces well-formed formulas (wffs) with their double negations. It can be proved that:

(1) $\Delta \vdash_{CPL} \varnothing$ iff $\Delta^* \vdash_{IPL} \varnothing^*$

where Δ, Δ^* are sets of wffs and CPL, IPL denote classical and intuitionistic predicate logic, respectively. From the classical semantic

Chapter 4

$$(\&I) \quad \frac{\emptyset \quad \Omega}{(\emptyset \,\&\, \Omega)} \qquad (\&E_l) \quad \frac{(\emptyset \,\&\, \Omega)}{\emptyset} \qquad (\&E_r) \quad \frac{(\emptyset \,\&\, \Omega)}{\Omega}$$

$$(\vee I_l) \quad \frac{\emptyset}{(\emptyset \vee \Omega)} \qquad (\vee I_r) \quad \frac{\Omega}{(\emptyset \vee \Omega)}$$

$$(\vee E) \quad \frac{\emptyset \vee \Omega \quad \overset{[\emptyset]}{\underset{\Theta}{\vdots}} \quad \overset{[\Omega]}{\underset{\Theta}{\vdots}}}{\Theta}$$

$$(\rightarrow I) \quad \frac{\overset{[\emptyset]}{\underset{\Omega}{\vdots}}}{\emptyset \rightarrow \Omega} \qquad (\rightarrow E) \quad \frac{\emptyset \rightarrow \Omega \quad \emptyset}{\Omega}$$

$$(\bot) \quad \frac{\bot}{\emptyset} \qquad (\neg I) \quad \frac{\overset{[\emptyset]}{\underset{\bot}{\vdots}}}{\neg \emptyset}$$

$$(\neg E) \quad \frac{\neg \emptyset \quad \emptyset}{\bot}$$

$$(\forall I) \quad \frac{{}^{*}\emptyset(a/x)}{\forall x.\emptyset} \qquad (\forall E) \quad \frac{\forall x.\emptyset}{\emptyset(t/x)}$$

$$(\exists I) \quad \frac{\emptyset(t/x)}{\exists x.\emptyset} \qquad (\exists E) \quad \frac{{}^{\dagger}\exists x.\emptyset \quad \overset{[\emptyset(a/x)]}{\underset{\theta}{\vdots}}}{\theta}$$

* provided a does not occur in ∅ or in any of the assumptions on which ∅(a/x) depends.
† provided a does not occur in ∅ or in θ or in any of the assumptions used in the derivation of θ from ∅(a/x) — except ∅(a/x) itself.

Figure 4.2

viewpoint the topological structures used to interpret IPL (among which the Beth trees and Kripke trees are special cases) appear as complicated *classical* structures with their own languages that can be interpreted in the ordinary classical model-theoretic way. But from the intuitionist's standpoint, these classical appraisals of intuitionistic logic and semantics are of dubious coherence. A completeness theorem for IPL proved in a classical metatheory will clearly not be faithful to the intended meanings of the intuitionistic logical constants. The intuitionist might even claim that the *-mapping shows CPL to be a *weaker* subsystem of IPL, since a classical proof of a formula such as $\exists x.\varnothing x$ will be mapped onto an intuitionistic proof of $\neg\neg\exists x.\varnothing x$. But neither the classicist nor the intuitionist should accept an identification of classical wffs with their *-translations. The fact is that they each *mean different things* by their logical constants—a classicist who asserts $\exists x.\varnothing x$ is *not* claiming that the supposition that $\exists x.\varnothing x$ cannot be proved leads to absurdity (which is how the intuitionist understands $\neg\neg\exists x.\varnothing x$), but that $\exists x.\varnothing x$ is *true*. The intuitionist for her part rejects such classical interpretations of the constants as incoherent.

As Dummett observes, the intuitionist's attitude to classically valid laws such as LEM and DNE will seem arbitrary until we see that it is based on a complete rejection of bivalence:[9] "$A \vee \neg A$" is assertible only when either A can be proved or $\neg A$ can be proved—that is, only when A is decidable. Precisely what concept of truth (if any) the intuitionist can avail herself of is a difficult question. Dummett searches for an interpretation of "is true" more liberal than "has been proved" (which has the consequence that any sentence not yet decided is neither true nor false), but not so liberal as to entail that there exists something that, were we to become aware of it, we would regard as a proof (a notion Dummett finds unacceptably platonistic).[10]

4.2.6 *Quantification*
The divergence between the intuitionistic and classical understanding of logical constants is most clearly in evidence over the quantifiers. Classically, the only significant difference between domains of quantification lies in their cardinality. This is not the case intuitionistically—the intuitionist requires not just that a domain D of quantification be *nonempty* ($\neg\forall x.\neg x \in D$), but that it be *inhabited* ($\exists x.x \in D$)—that is, that we can produce at least one element that we can assert belongs to D.

In addition, the intuitionist sharply distinguishes *decidable* from *undecidable* domains: A *decidable* domain is one specified by some finite

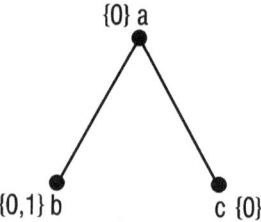

Figure 4.3

description that allows us to recognize of any element whether it belongs to the domain or not. There can be no general requirement that a domain be decidable—a domain can be specified by any meaningful predicate whatsoever.

An example of an *undecidable* domain would be the following:

$D_g = \{x | x = 0 \lor (GC \ \& \ x = 1)\}$, where GC abbreviates Goldbach's conjecture (that every even number greater than two is the sum of two primes). We could represent our possible states of knowledge with respect to D_g by a simple Kripke tree, as shown in figure 4.3. Since GC has not been decided, we're in the state of information represented by node a: we know that $0 \in D_g$, but we do not know whether 1 belongs to D_g or not. Were GC to be proved, we would be in the state represented by b— we'd know that $D_g = \{0, 1\}$. Were GC to be disproved, on the other hand, we would be in the state of information at c—we'd know that $D_g = \{0\}$.

Dummett writes: "the crucial assumption of classical logic is that the interpretation of the quantifiers remains the same, whether their domain be finite or infinite, denumerable or non-denumerable."[11] The intuitionist's complaint with this assumption, he goes on to say, is that it erroneously assimilates infinite structures to finite ones—for, from the intuitionistic viewpoint, the infinite is precisely that which cannot be completed or surveyed in its entirety.

With finite processes, we can distinguish the *outcome* of the process from the *process* itself—distinct finite processes might generate a result that is recognizable *independently of* either process. But if we take an infinite structure such as the totality of natural numbers, **N**, we can grasp that structure *only insofar as* we know its process of generation, a process that has no final result. Infinite structures are therefore of necessity incomplete and always in growth. Every mathematical object is a construction$_o$ and generated by a construction$_p$, but infinitary objects, unlike finite objects, can be understood *only* through the constructions$_p$—the processes—that generate them. Thus, although each real number is extensional, it is incomplete, and can be given to us only through its corresponding generator, which is intensional and complete.[12]

There is some doubt as to whether the notion of an incomplete object is really coherent. In number theory, although we're concerned with an infinite domain, **N**, the elements of the domain are finite objects; in analysis, however, the objects of the infinite domain **R** are themselves infinite—real numbers generated by Dedekind cuts or Cauchy sequences or sequences of nested intervals of rationals. Perhaps it would be better to regard the reals intuitionistically not as objects at all, but as abstractions from uncompleted and uncompletable processes—their generators. On this proposal, the intuitionist would no longer be ontologically committed to infinitary objects: Terms denoting infinite structures could then be assigned a semantic value just as Frege assigned a semantic value for directions, though, just as directions could be reduced to classes of parallel lines, the reals would be eliminable in favor of classes of (in this case) uncompletable processes.

According to Dummett, the Platonist regards the truth value of a quantified sentence as if it were the outcome of a process of running through the values of its instances: on the assumption that the application of a well-defined predicate F to each element of the infinite domain has a determinate truth value, true or false, the classicist concludes that its universal closure has a determinate truth value, arrived at by forming the logical product of the values of its instances, and that its existential closure similarly has a determinate truth value—the logical sum of the values of its instances. The intuitionistic objection to this thesis is that no mathematical or logical entity—truth value or otherwise—can be the result of an infinite process for the simple reason that infinite processes *have no* finished result. Because an infinite domain can be grasped intuitionistically only as a process that generates the totality, when the domain of quantification is infinite, an existentially quantified sentence cannot be thought of as determinately either true or false in advance of our possessing a proof of it;[13] nor can a universally quantified sentence whose domain is infinite such as GC be thought of as being true accidentally, that is, that each of its instances might all be true, but coincidentally, so to speak—each true for a different reason.

I do not believe the classicist really does think of quantification over an infinite domain in the manner Dummett alleges, since he sharply distinguishes the process whereby we come to *know of* the domain from the *domain* itself. In the case of spatial and temporal continua, which the classicist alleges have the cardinality of the classical continuum, there is nothing to be found in human experience—no "smallest perceivable spatial (or temporal) point (or moment)"—with which the points of these continua could be paired. Hence it cannot be right to assimilate the classical conception of such nondenumerable physical domains as one wherein an interminable process of determining the values of the instances of a sentence quantified over that domain somehow, mysteriously, comes to an end. The classical spatiotemporal continua are precisely not "in growth." Rather, they are conceived as literally consisting in a nondenumerable number of unextended spatiotemporal points.

How then *does* the intuitionist understand "$\exists x.Fx$" and "$\forall x.Fx$" where x ranges over an infinite domain? For simplicity's sake, take the domain of quantification to be $\mathbf{N}$ and let F be a decidable predicate. Our domain is generated by the operation of forming the successor of each number starting at 0. Since F is a decidable property of the natural numbers, there exists a second process that generates truth values in the following manner: Fa is true when the object denoted by a that is formed at the corresponding stage in the process that forms the domain has F; Fa is false otherwise. "$\forall x.Fx$" is to be interpreted as asserting that this second process coincides with a third process generating only truths $\langle T, T, T, \ldots \rangle$. For "$\exists x.Fx$," we consider a third process generating only falsehoods $\langle F, F, F, \ldots \rangle$, and "$\exists x.Fx$" asserts that our second process does not coincide with this one. So, "$\forall x.Fx$" means that the rule governing the second process guarantees that it yields the sequence $\langle T, T, T, \ldots \rangle$, and "$\exists x.Fx$" that the rule yields some sequence other than $\langle F, F, F, \ldots \rangle$.

4.2.7 Classical Constructive Operators

Let us see how the differing interpretations of the constants manifest themselves in the mathematical practice of the classicist and of the intuitionist. It might be thought that the intuitionistic constants could be embedded in a classical fragment. Thus we could classically define a constructive operator, "∪," such that "A ∪ B" meant:

(i) We have a constructive proof of A ∨ B.

Similarly, we could define a classical constructive operator "3," such that "$3x.Ax$" meant:

(ii) We have a constructive proof of $\exists x.Ax$.

Although the intuitionist will reject (i) and (ii) as unintelligible, this complaint would have no force antirealistically if the observable practice of the classical mathematician interested in constructive proof differed not at all from his intuitionistic counterpart.

But that there are differences in inferential practice can be seen from the intuitionistic invalidity of (the classically sound) *Markov's principle*, Dummett claims:[14]

(MP) $[\forall x(Fx \vee \neg Fx) \,\&\, \neg\forall x\neg Fx] \rightarrow \exists x.Fx$

(MP) is still assertible classically even when we replace '∃' by '∃' to obtain:

(MP*) $[\forall x(Fx \vee \neg Fx) \,\&\, \neg\forall x\neg Fx] \rightarrow \exists x.Fx$

Classically, "$[\forall x(Fx \vee \neg Fx) \,\&\, \neg\forall x\neg Fx] \rightarrow \exists x.Fx$" expresses the classical truth that if we have an EM for deciding of every n whether Fn or $\neg Fn$ and we know that not every number falsifies Fx, then we can find a number satisfying Fx, since if $\neg\forall x\neg Fx$ holds, the process of running through each number in the domain $0, 1, 2, \ldots$ and testing whether it satisfies Fx, breaking off as soon as we find one that does, must terminate. But the corresponding *intuitionistic* interpretation of (MP) generates an intuitionistic *falsehood*: "$\neg\forall x\neg Fx$" does not mean, intuitionistically, "Fx will not as a matter of fact be found to fail for every natural number," as it does classically, but rather "the supposition that Fx fails for every natural number leads to absurdity," which does *not* guarantee that by testing each natural number in turn we shall eventually chance on one satisfying Fx.[15] So, rather than there being a special constructive reading of "∃" and "∨" alongside a more general nonconstructive reading that the intuitionistic reading of these constants captures, Dummett takes his example to show that *both* constructive and nonconstructive *classical* readings are senseless: "$\exists x.Fx$" *can mean only that* we have a proof (or can provide an EM for proving) of a specific element of the domain that it satisfies Fx. Dummett goes on to argue that as a consequence the truth-tables do not render the classical meanings of the constants intelligible, and the crucial assumption required to effect this—that every statement is determinately either true or false—must be rejected.

I think this argument is completely spurious. How could the failure of certain classical translations to render classically intelligible the meanings of the intuitionistic constants *possibly* show that the *classical* readings of the constants are senseless? At best this could secure incommensurability for the *intuitionistic* readings, at worst unintelligibility for *those* readings, not for the classical ones. It is clear what has gone wrong in the argument: Dummett has not provided constructive classical readings for *all* the constants in (MP*), the putatively constructive classical reading of (MP). In particular, the *conditional* has not been fully "constructivized." Negation is definable both classically and intuitionistically in terms of $\bot$ and $\to$. Yet the reading Dummett provides for "$\neg \forall x \neg Fx$" is *Fx will not as a matter of fact be found to fail for every number n* rather than the correct constructive classical one that *we can refute the claim that we have an EM for showing of any object that it fails to satisfy Fx*.[16] We shall return to this argument after reviewing the Heyting explanations of the meanings of the constants, which we first encountered in section 4.1.

4.2.8 Heyting's Recursive Definition of Assertibility

How, then, are the intuitionistic constants to be understood? Assuming that we understand what it is for a construction$_0$ C to be a proof of a mathematical wff $\emptyset$,[17] we can give a recursive definition of the proof conditions of a complex wff in terms of those of its parts following Heyting's informal exposition.

For simplicity's sake, we assume that the variables of our language range over the natural numbers:

(i) Construction C is a proof of $(\emptyset \,\&\, \Omega)$ iff C is a pair (C_1, C_2) such that: C_1 is a proof of $\emptyset$ and C_2 is a proof of Ω.

(ii) Construction C is a proof of $(\emptyset \vee \Omega)$ iff C is a pair (C_1, C_2) such that: $C_1 = 0$ and C_2 is a proof of $\emptyset$ or $C_1 = 1$ and C_2 is a proof of Ω.

(iii) Construction C is a proof of $(\emptyset \to \Omega)$ iff C is a construction that converts each proof p of $\emptyset$ into a proof $C(p)$ of Ω.

(iv) No construction is a proof of $\bot$.

(v) Construction C is a proof of $\exists x.\emptyset x$ iff C is a pair (c_1, c_2) such that: c_1 is a proof of $\emptyset c_2$.

(vi) Construction C is a proof of $\forall x.\emptyset x$ iff C is a construction such that: for each natural number n, Cn is a proof of $\emptyset n$.

Kreisel and Goodman have incorporated these intuitive explanations of the constants into a mathematical theory of constructions. Dummett believes that although their theory is as yet still in an imperfect state of development ... there is no doubt that these standard intuitive explanations of the logical constants determine the intended intuitionistic meanings, so that anything which can be accepted as the correct semantics for intuitionistic logic must be shown either to incorporate them, or, at least to yield them under suitable supplementary assumptions.[18]

4.2.9 Evaluation of the Heyting Definition

There is a prima facie ground for doubting the adequacy of these intuitive explanations that Dummett acknowledges: They are highly *impredicative* inasmuch as they require us to ascertain what effect a construction$_0$ will have when applied to an arbitrary proof of a conditional or to an arbitrary proof of a negated sentence before we can determine whether the construction genuinely is a proof of the relevant conditional or negated sentence. As this seems to require that we must in *some* sense be able to grasp a totality of constructions for a given conditional or negated sentence that includes all possible proofs of such sentences, these explanations might appear to be viciously circular.[19]

Another feature of the Heyting explanations that is more easily resolved is their apparent lack of fit with the actual practice of intuitionists. Disjunctive statements are often asserted in their writings without a proof of one or the other disjunct—it is common practice for a constructivist to assert $A \vee B$ when she merely has an EM for obtaining a proof of either A or of B (e.g., when A is a decidable statement and $B = \neg A$). An informal proof of $A \vee B$ (or of $\exists x.Fx$) that merely cites an EM for finding a proof of either disjunct (or for finding an object k such that Fk) should not in the strict sense be regarded as a proof, but only as an EM for finding one, Dummett contends. Hence, we should acknowledge a distinction between strict or *canonical proofs* and *informal demonstrations* that supply EMs for constructing canonical proofs. The first step in making Heyting's informal semantics a rigorous explication of the meanings of the intuitionistic logical connectives will then be to replace each occurrence of "proof" throughout with "canonical proof."[20]

4.2.10 Classical Expressibility of the Intuitionistic Constants

In actual fact, contrary to Dummett's claims about the impossibility of expressing the intuitionistic readings as special sorts of constructive classical ones, it would appear that there are a number of ways of doing just that. Here is one of the more familiar ways via the modal logic S4:

$\nabla(\varnothing \mathbin{\&} \Omega)$ asserts that $\nabla\varnothing \mathbin{\&} \nabla\Omega$
$\nabla(\varnothing \vee \Omega)$ asserts that $\nabla\varnothing \vee \nabla\Omega$
$\nabla(\varnothing \rightarrow \Omega)$ asserts that $\nabla(\nabla\varnothing \rightarrow \nabla\Omega)$
$\nabla(\neg\varnothing)$ asserts that $\nabla(\neg\nabla\varnothing)$

The connectives to the left of "asserts that" are the intuitionistic ones; the connectives to the right, their classical counterparts. "∇" means "we have a proof that...." We can now provide a translation of any ISL wff into a wff of S4 by working from the outside inward and eliminating every intuitionistic constant in favor of its classical counterpart. Call $\varnothing^*$ the *modal translation* of an ISL wff $\varnothing$. Then:

$P^* = \nabla P$ (P atomic)
$(\varnothing \mathbin{\&} \Omega)^* = \varnothing^* \mathbin{\&} \Omega^*$
$(\varnothing \vee \Omega)^* = \varnothing^* \vee \Omega^*$
$(\varnothing \rightarrow \Omega)^* = \nabla(\varnothing^* \rightarrow \Omega^*)$
$(\neg\varnothing)^* = \nabla(\neg\varnothing^*)$

It can be proved that: *A formula of ISL is intuitionistically valid iff its modal translation is S4-valid.*

Moreover, we can give an argument for the failure of LEM similar to the one a supporter of S4 might give to reject the definitive S5 axiom: $\nabla A \vee \nabla\neg\nabla A$, for the modal translation of $A \vee \neg A$ is just that axiom. Reading "∇A" as "we have a proof of A," the S5 axiom states that "it is either the case that we have a proof of A or that we can prove that no proof of A will ever be forthcoming," which is clearly false for currently unsolved mathematical problems such as Goldbach's conjecture.

4.2.11 *Denying the Doctrine or Changing the Subject?*

We can no longer afford to ignore the problem that has been simmering under the surface throughout our discussion: *in what sense does the intuitionist reject classical principles like that of the excluded middle or Markov's principle?* The putative rejection takes the form of reinterpreting the constants that figure in these principles *intuitionistically* and showing that *thus construed* they express principles that are not intuitionistically true. But that *by itself* can constitute no grounds for rejection of the classical readings of those constants, as we saw above with the partially constructive classical reading of Markov's principle (MP*). Moreover, *thus construed*, not only are the principles not true intuitionistically, they are not true classically either. It would seem, then, that in the very act of denying the doctrines Dummett really does just change the subject.

In a powerful article criticizing the intuitionist's program in logic and mathematics, Geoffrey Hellman writes:

> It is highly misleading to speak of "the law of the excluded middle": we have not one, but two "laws," depending on which connectives are employed. And the fact that the component sentences generally have distinct meanings for the intuitionist and the classicist—and the fact that the above explanations of the connectives are intimately bound up (perhaps inseparably so) with the distinctive intuitionistic assertibility content of any mathematical statement—these facts only enhance the necessity of distinguishing formally analogous "laws." ... *everyone* can see that the intuitionistic "law of the excluded middle" (LEM_i) is not generally correct for arbitrary propositions p. If p is a problematic statement (say, the Goldbach conjecture) for which we possess neither a constructive proof nor a constructive refutation (nor any method of finding either), then *no one* would want to assert *this* instance of (LEM_i). And, of course, this is entirely irrelevant to the corresponding instance of (LEM_c), which makes no claim whatsoever about anyone having constructive proofs.[21]

Hellman argues that the intuitionistic constants are indeed intelligible when interpreted in a classical metalanguage and that there are strong grounds for suspecting that they may *only* be so intelligible—for the explanations that the intuitionists themselves give seem to make use of the officially discredited classical interpretation of the quantifiers. We shall examine Hellman's claims further in section 4.5 when the issue of the meanings of the constants is looked at in more detail. Despite Dummett's claims, then, we have found no reason so far to suspect any genuine conflict between classical and intuitionistic systems. Moreover, the only reason for revising classical inferential practice that Dummett gives has to do with the way we actually acquire and manifest an understanding of the meanings of the constants in the course of acquiring a grasp of a natural language.

This reason Dummett gives had better be a very good reason, for there are powerful empirical arguments in support of classical as opposed to constructivistic logic and mathematics for the purposes of overall scientific practice. Hermann Weyl, one of intuitionism's supporters, put the point well when he said: "It is the function of mathematics to be at the service of the natural sciences."[22]

4.2.12 Intuitionism and Quantum Theory

What might these empirical considerations be? Geoffrey Hellman has argued that constructivistic logic and mathematics is theoretically stunted in the arena of quantum mechanics (QM). In the first place, he has provided evidence for thinking that Gleason's theorem is not constructively provable. In QM, the lattice of subspaces L(H) of a Hilbert space, H, constitutes the domain over which probability measures are defined. Gleason's theorem proves that, provided only H has dimensionality ≥ 3, any possible probability measure on L(H) is generated from some pure or mixed quantum state. The reason this result is significant philosophically is that it has as a corollary that there can be no dispersion-free ($\{0, 1\}$-valued) measures on L(H), which is to say that there can be no definite value assignments to the quantum magnitudes since all quantum states do exhibit dispersion for some magnitudes. "Thus," Hellman observes, "a major type of hidden-variables theory for quantum mechanics was ruled out."[23]

There are, to be sure, other ways of proving there are no hidden-variables theorems, including constructivistically acceptable ways, Hellman notes, but the Weyl point remains: One wants one's mathematics and logic to be the servant, not the master, of overall science.

Second, Hellman shows that QM cannot be constructivistically presented in the standard way via unbounded operators since constructive unbounded operators do not exist. He regards this as a limitative result about constructivism provable in a classical metatheory.

On behalf of the constructivist, Keith Hossack replies that there are "constructive results that cannot be proved classically, so constructivists can symmetrically claim to know what classicists cannot."[24] This is not really to the point, however, since the issue is the adequacy of constructivism within the domain of QM. Moreover, whether this *tu quoque* is successful at all will depend largely on whether the various classical translations of constructive mathematics and logic—such as those deploying the various modal and epistemic translations of the connectives studied by Stewart Shapiro and others—are unable to reproduce the constructivistically valid but classically "invalid" results. To recall our previous discussion, we have yet to be convinced that classical and constructive readings of the connectives really do conflict.

More significant is Hossack's response on behalf of the constructivist to Hellman's Weylian point. As Hossack interprets Hellman: "The objection to constructivism is that it bars us from theoretical insight and gives a less elegant overall theory." His constructivist reply is that such an argument, though possibly effective against the nominalist, who wishes selectively to place credence in the concrete rather than the abstract objects to which she is theoretically committed, "is powerless against constructivists." The reason is that "it requires prior agreement on what our best theory is," something that is, he thinks, genuinely controversial for the constructivist. As he puts it: "Constructivists will not accept that a classical theory is a best theory. They will say that the feeling of insight from a classical presentation is mere illusion, for the classical theory with its meaningless logical constants is radically unintelligible."[25] Philosophers are, of course, masters at feigning incomprehension. They are also seldom short of a response. However, this imaginary constructivist reply will simply not do. For a start, it begs the question against a holist who sees the issue of the meanings of the logical constants as itself a highly theoretical one to be assessed in the light of our best overall semantic, logical, and empirical theories and not one to be decided on purely encapsulated a priori meaning-theoretic grounds. Such a holist has a reply to the only serious argument we have so far for the unintelligibility of the classical constants—to wit, the manifestation argument, or so I argued in section 3.4.

Second, and more important, what is at issue is QM. So to the extent that QM as standardly presented can be formulated only in a classical framework, the constructivist must be holding *this* theory to be "radically unintelligible." Then what alternative constructivist theory is on offer? Until the constructivist can frame an alternative to classical QM, say, QM*, a Hossackian-styled response is just bluster for the simple reason that QM is a terminus for current scientific explanation. I can find no better illustration of this feature of QM than that provided by Steven Weinberg in his lucid *Dreams of a Final Theory* when he poses the simple question "Why is chalk white?" and answers:

Chalk is white because the molecules of which it is composed do not happen to have any state that is particularly easy to jump to by absorbing photons of any color of visible light. *Why?* Why do atoms and molecules come in discrete states, each with a definite energy? Why are these energy values what they are? Why does light come in individual particles, each with an energy inversely proportional to the wavelength of the light? And why are some states of atoms or molecules particularly easy to jump to by absorption of photons?... It turns out that light, like atoms, can exist only in certain quantum states of definite energy.... *Why?* Why are the quantum-mechanical equations that govern the particles in atoms what they are? Why does matter consist of these particles, the electrons and the atomic nuclei? For that matter, why is there such a thing as light? Most of these things ... have only become reasonably well understood in the last fifteen years or so, with the success of what is called the *standard model* of elementary particles and forces ... all these particles are ... quanta of various sorts of fields.... The reason that ordinary matter is composed of electrons, protons, and neutrons is simply that all the other massive particles are violently unstable.... the structure of the standard model is largely fixed once one specifies the menu of fields that it should contain and the general principles (like the principles of relativity and quantum mechanics) that govern their interactions.[26]

Weinberg goes on to show how the explanation of chemical properties again traces a path through the tree of explanations that ends in QM and the standard model and remarks, that modulo the part played by historical happenstance,

> ... no one doubts that with a large enough computer we could in principle explain all the properties of DNA by solving the equations of quantum mechanics for electrons and the nuclei of a few common elements, whose properties are explained in turn by the standard model. So again we find ourselves at the same point of convergence of our arrows of explanation.[27]

The indispensability of QM in fact bites the constructivist far harder than the nominalist, for the nominalist does not complain of the *unintelligibility* of the classical theory. She understands it well enough, she claims—indeed, her understanding is more sophisticated, she thinks, than the realist's. But the constructivist contends that the theory is radically unintelligible. As feigning aphasia is cheap, we're consequently owed an explanation as to how a radically unintelligible theory could possibly have the explanatory and predictive power QM has—how, for instance, whole new technologies such as those involving lasers could be dreamed up as empirical consequences of an incoherent or meaningless theory. We've become inured enough to the claim that false theories can have such consequences to not be too nonplussed by it. But *incomprehensible* ones?

Pace Hossack, then, this style of indispensability argument is not at all "powerless against constructivists." Indeed, unless they can come up with a constructivistically sanitized QM* and a demonstration that QM* preserves the theoretical and empirical power of QM, as well as an explanation of how we were duped into believing we understood QM in the first place, they are in danger of being completely overwhelmed by it—that, at least, is what any naturalistic realist will say.

4.3 *Antirealism and Proof Theory*

Dummett's main argument for revising our classical inferential practices depends crucially on certain proof-theoretic ideas and results that Prawitz and Dummett have developed between them. In this section, I will be chiefly concerned to bring out those of Prawitz's results that bear on this argument; in the following section we will look at Dummett's more recent ideas.

4.3.1 Quine's Web and Dummett's Model of Understanding

Dummett endorses Quine's image of a web of interconnected sentences as a theoretical model for our understanding of language (see the discussion of holism in sec. 3.2). This model is essential for Dummett's own account of verification.[28] For Dummett, the understanding of a single sentence in general presupposes an understanding of a fragment of the language, which may be quite extensive. Unlike Quine's holistic model, however, no sentence features in that fragment that does not contain components of the given sentence. Dummett therefore denies the essential doctrine of semantic holism—that any given sentence has inferential relations with every other sentence in the web; on the contrary, we can impose a definite structure on the web that will approximate at least a quasi-ordering. From this perspective, holistic theories of meaning are indeed structureless.

4.3.2 The Language Acquisition Argument

With Dummett's model of semantic competence in hand, we can now offer a rough outline of Dummett's language acquisition argument (LAA) against classical reasoning:

(1) Our understanding of our language may be represented as (at least) a quasi-ordered structure, the order being determined by our progressive acquisition of the sentences of the language.

(2) What we acquire in acquiring our language is a knowledge of the assertibility conditions for its sentences. Insofar as we have a concept of truth for these sentences, it is constrained by what we recognize in practice as establishing truth.

(3) Thus, the concept of truth applicable to the atomic fragment of the ordered structure will be a recognizable one—something like intuitionistic truth.

(4) Hence, the concept in terms of which the deducibility relation between sentences is to be characterized will be (something like) intuitionistic truth.

(5) But, relative to such a concept, the use of classical modes of reasoning in relation to the atomic fragment induces a nonconservative extension of that fragment.

(6) On that basis, we can criticize those classical practices and seek to revise them—for the conditions for asserting a sentence can no longer be expected to be in harmony with the consequences that can be drawn from its assertion once we are able to infer sentences by those classical rules that we were previously unable to infer prior to their introduction.

Clearly, (2), (3), and (4) constitute the crucial premises of the argument. So how does Dummett hope to establish that the concept of truth speakers acquire through their training in the use of the sentences of a natural language is a *nonclassical* one? This looks like an empirical claim; so to establish it Dummett needs some empirical evidence. As far as I am aware he provides none. In actual fact, I doubt that Dummett really sees the issue as an empirical one. He takes himself to have already established, via his manifestation argument, that no speaker *could* acquire a knowledge of classical truth—by default, then, the only conception of truth available must be a nonclassical one. I provided reasons in sections 3.3 and 3.4 for doubting this claim, including evidence that we *do* have a grasp of the classical truth conditions of an important class of sentences.

Even if he himself feels no need to provide empirical evidence for his premises, however, the fact is that Dummett's argument is hostage to empirical fortune. He claims that our understanding of the sentences of our language approximates a quasi-ordering, the structure imposed being induced by the conceptual complexity of the sentences we actually acquire at any given stage in our learning of language. This is presumably *not* intended as a psychological hypothesis about the temporal order of acquisition but rather as an attempt to chart the growth of a certain sort of idealized cognitive structure. That there be some such structure to our semantic competence is crucial to his argument against holism, as we have already seen. It is worth pointing out, then, how difficult it is simultaneously to satisfy Dummett's demands *if* competence is taken to consist in a grasp of *assertibility* conditions. Dummett envisages our understanding of a sentence S as consisting in a grasp of some direct way of verifying S that maps the internal structure of the sentence, crucially: *No sentence of logical complexity greater than S will feature in a direct verification of S, and thus no one who understands S will need to grasp the meanings of any sentences more complex than S.*

Thus is a structure induced on our semantic competence and holism defeated.

4.3.3 *Fermat's Last Theorem and Dummett's Model of Semantic Competence*

I now want to show why the above requirements look almost impossible to satisfy in the very domain they were originally designed for—mathematics. I take it to be incontestable that every numerate adult can understand what Fermat's last theorem (FLT) asserts. I take it to be equally incontestable that few have any hope at all of grasping the proof of that theorem due to Andrew Wiles and his coworkers. So in what sense do I (and the millions of numerate, not to mention mathematically literate, adults like me) "understand" FLT at all, according to Dummett, *unable as I presently am to recognize the proof when presented with it*?

To get a fix on *how* implausible it is to credit numerate adults who have no apparent difficulty in comprehending FLT when it is put to them with a grasp of the proof of that theorem, even granted the most exotic sense of "grasp," just consider how Wiles actually proved FLT. In 1986, Kenneth Ribet noticed that FLT is true provided that the Taniyama–Shimura–Weil conjecture held for a certain class of elliptical curves. In June 1993, Wiles established this conjecture for a large class of such curves. What remained uncertain until 1995 was whether the class of curves for which Wiles's argument held included those necessary to deduce FLT as a corollary. It does not matter whether we regard Wiles's proof of FLT as a "direct" or "indirect" verification of it; trouble attends either alternative for Dummett. If it is *direct* then those numerate adults who do not grasp the proof simply do not understand FLT, which is intolerable since it numbers them with the innumerate who *cannot* understand FLT. If it is *indirect*, as it presumably must be, then the mathematical world awaits the discovery of some EP for transforming it into a direct proof that is restricted to using sentences no more complex than FLT itself. Even if this just means "limit the number of quantifiers in every sentence featuring in the Wiles proof to four" we'd have no guarantee at all that this could be done. Moreover, what possible philosophical interest would it have if it *could* be done?

It is no reply to point out that for the antirealist generally and the intuitionist in particular, semantic competence is compositional. Of course it is and so it should be. But the problems occur as soon as one tries to tie one's compositional understanding of FLT to its *actual* Wilesian proof conditions. Our compositional understanding, according to the antirealist, is somehow supposed to confer on us the ability to recognize a proof of FLT when presented with one. I submit that for the vast majority of perfectly numerate, even semi-(mathematically) literate adults who grasp the meaning of FLT as well as Wiles or even Fermat himself but who haven't a prayer when it comes to understanding the proof, this demand is quite exorbitant. This demonstrates yet again, I believe, that there is no simple argument from theses about meaning to theses about semantic competence. It is one thing to require that meaning be determined by use, a thesis entirely congenial to the holist, and quite another to require that our *grasp* of meaning be *exhaustively manifest* in use.

If the viability of intuitionism as a theory of meaning for mathematical statements is to depend on whether numerate adults can recognize Wiles's proof as a proof of FLT when presented with it then we have to conclude that, conceived thus, intuitionistic semantics is quite indefensible. *But what else can it possibly mean to claim that individuals who grasp mathematical statements do so by virtue of grasping their proof conditions than that the ungodly multitude who do understand FLT are to be numbered among the chosen few who grasp Wiles's proof?*

One basic problem with Dummett's claims about language acquisition is that they may well be confuted or at least disconfirmed by the empirical facts (as we already observed in sec. 3.4)—intended as they are to be claims about how our competence *must be* structured, they are vulnerable not just to a considerable body of disconfirming evidence about how it *actually* is so structured but, more crucially, to any ground for thinking that the competing theory that disconfirming evidence does support is at least empirically possible.

4.3.4 The Language Acquisition Argument and Circularity

To return to his actual language acquisition argument, LAA, as presented above: Dummett tells us that disputes about the general validity of logical laws are to be settled either by seeing which laws are justified by the meaning theory or by determining which of two rival theories of meaning is correct. Clearly, only the second of these two methods is applicable here.[29] So, premises (2), (3), and (4) of the LAA, which assert that the concept of truth we actually acquire is a recognizable one in terms of which the deducibility relation must be explained, will depend on the success of Dummett's meaning-theoretic argument against realism.

Yet, if this is Dummett's strategy for establishing (1), there is an obvious flaw in it: One natural realist reply to Dummett's demand for a practical manifestation of a speaker's knowledge of the truth conditions of non-ED sentences was to cite our classical deductive practices involving those sentences as evidence that we'd grasped a classical concep-

Intuitionistic Foundations of Antirealism   149

tion of truth for them. I agreed that our practices do not *constitute* a grasp of classical truth but insisted that they might yet *manifest* such a grasp. Moreover, even though this reply needed augmenting by a demonstration that some set of non-ED sentences patently has evidence-transcendent truth conditions that competent speakers could all grasp, it is an important part of the considered response to Dummett of section 3.4. *It would therefore be question-begging on Dummett's part to presume the success of his manifestation challenge in order to mount an argument for the revision of a practice that the realist contends meets that challenge.*

Dummett must therefore avoid the threat of vicious circularity in his strategic argument for the revision of classical modes of reasoning. I will later suggest one way in which this circularity can be avoided.

4.3.5 Do the Introduction and Elimination Rules for the Logical Constants Fix Their Meanings?

As I noted in the previous section, the introduction and elimination rules in a natural deduction system **I** run parallel with Heyting's explanations of the meanings of the logical constants. Gerhard Gentzen hinted at an idea Prawitz and Dummett have sought to make precise when he wrote:

> an introduction rule gives, as it were, a definition of the constant in question.... an elimination rule is only a consequence of the corresponding introduction rule, which may be expressed somewhat as follows: when making an inference by an elimination rule, we are allowed to "use" only what the principal operator of the major premiss "means" acording to the introduction rule for this sign.[30]

Can the introduction rules in a ND system really be thought of as defining the meanings of their associated constants? One logician unconvinced that they could was Arthur Prior.[31] Prior invented a propositional connective "TONK" with the following introduction and elimination rules:

	A	B
TONK I	A TONK B	A TONK B
TONK E	A TONK B	A TONK B
	A	B

Prior showed that it was possible, using TONK I then TONK E, to prove false conclusions from true premises—for example, we could prove the absurd thesis that any two arbitrary propositions A and B are identical:

	A (1)	B (2)	
(TONK I)	A TONK B	A TONK B	(TONK I)
(TONK E)	B	A	(TONK E)
	A ↔ B	1, 2 (↔I)	

There must therefore be *some* constraints placed on an introduction rule before it can serve as definiens for some logical constant.

In response to Prior's TONK, Nuel Belnap urged that there was a purely proof-theoretic way of ruling out such operators as illicit. There must, in a sense yet to be made precise, be a certain type of *harmony* between the introduction and elimination rules.[32]

Suppose, with Gentzen, that we regard the introduction rules for a constant as synthetic, supplying the canonical condition for asserting a sentence with the constant as main operator, and the elimination rule for that constant as a analytic, specifying the consequences that can be drawn from an assertion of a sentence with that constant. Then, the intuitive requirement of *harmony* is that one not be able to deduce any sentence previously not deducible from a fragment of a language when the sentence containing that constant is added to that fragment. Clearly, in this intuitive sense, there is no harmony between the introduction and elimination rules for TONK, since an application of (TONK I) to an arbitrary sentence A followed by an application of (TONK E) allows us to deduce a sentence previously not deducible—namely, A ↔ B. Belnap said that these rules *nonconservatively extended* the fragment. The notion of a *conservative extension* can be defined as follows:

A set of sentences Δ^* is a *conservative extension* of a set of sentences Δ iff for every wff $\emptyset$ of Δ, if $\Delta^* \vdash \emptyset$ then $\Delta \vdash \emptyset$.

As we shall see, we can make this constraint precise for first-order logic, but Dummett maintains that *some* version of this constraint holds not just for first-order theories but for all sentences of a natural language. An elimination rule can be seen as the *inverse* of the corresponding introduction rule in the sense that a proof of the conclusion of an elimination is already available if the major premise of the elimination is inferred by the corresponding introduction rule.[33]

This principle, due to Prawitz, is known as the *inversion principle* and can be formulated more precisely in the following way:

Let * be a logical constant and (*I) and (*E), respectively be the introduction and elimination rules for *. Then if C is a consequence of applying the elimination rule (*E), then a deduction of the major premise of (*E) whose last step consists of an application of (*I), already contains a deduction of C.³⁴

As an illustration, consider modus ponens (→E). The introduction rule for "→" stipulates the condition for inferring B → C: B → C can be inferred whenever we have a proof of C available from the hypothesis of B.

B
.
.
.
$\dfrac{C \quad (\to I)}{B \to C}$

Modus ponens, the elimination rule (→E):

$\dfrac{B \quad B \to C}{C}$

is the *inverse* of (→I) in the sense that if the condition for inferring B → C as stated by (→I) is satisfied (i.e., there is a proof of C from the hypothesis of B), then a proof of C is already available by replacing every hypothesis B by the given proof of B. The deduction of the major premise B thus already contains a deduction of C, the consequence of the elimination inference.

The inversion principle gives rise to certain reductions that apply whenever a sentence obtained as the conclusion of an introduction rule is then used as the premise of an elimination rule. The reduction removes this "loop" in the proof. In our example:

B
.
.
.
$\dfrac{C \quad (\to I)}{B \quad B \to C \ (\to E)}$ *reduces to*   B
                                                               .
                                                               .
                                                               .
C   C

That is, we can deduce C without the detour of first introducing B → C and then applying (→E). When all such reductions have been carried out, the proof is said to be in *normal form*—a normal derivation proceeds directly from certain hypotheses to its conclusion without introducing any sentences in the proof that are not deployed to build up the conclusion of the proof.[35]

A *normal form theorem* states that if $\Delta \vdash \varnothing$, then there exists a normal derivation of $\varnothing$ from Δ. A *normalization theorem* states that any derivation reduces to a normal derivation where the relevant notion of reduction is as above. A *strong normalization theorem* states that every sequence of reduction steps terminates in one in normal form.

Dummett requires that for all sentences of a natural language there be a *harmony* between two identifiable aspects of their use:

(1) the conditions under which their assertion is warranted; and

(2) the consequences that flow from their assertion.

This broader requirement generalizes the proof-theoretic constraint that holds between the introduction and elimination rules for first-order logic. There is good reason to believe that the constraint can be imposed on constructive mathematical sentences: Martin-Löf has analyzed intuitionistic mathematical proofs with inductive and iterated inductive definitions into introduction and elimination inferences and proved a corresponding normalization theorem.[36] He has also formalized a considerable fragment of constructive mathematics by means of an intuitionistic theory of types that he developed for the task. In his system, the notion of introductions and eliminations applies not just to logical constants but to atomic predicates as well.

4.3.6 Harmony between Conditions for Assertion and Consequences of Assertion

Outside of a mathematical or logical context wherein the notion of proof can be clearly defined, can we legitimately demand that any proof-theoretic constraint be met? Does the constraint even make sense in the wider context? Although sensitive to the perils of generalizing to the natural language case, Dummett is convinced that we can impose *some* version of the constraint. So, let us assume for now that some such requirement can be justified. Dummett insists that there be a harmony between *(1) the conditions* and *(2) the consequences of an assertion*.

Suppose that by "conditions for assertion" for p, we understand the verification or falsification conditions of p. Does Dummett mean by "consequences" simply the *logical* consequences a hearer is entitled to draw from a sentence asserted in his presence? Apparently not, for he considers the possibility of taking the meaning of a sentence as being given not by (1), its assertibility conditions, but by (2), its "consequences," in the following passage:

> Would it not be equally feasible to adopt the reverse procedure, and take the meaning of a sentence as given in terms of the consequences of uttering (asserting) it, that is, roughly, what accepting it would lead you to do that you would not otherwise have done? In the general case, this seems highly problematic, because of the often remarked fact that what difference a belief makes to your behaviour depends upon your wants.[37]

So, by "consequences," Dummett apparently means behavioral differences pursuant on accepting the sentence as true. Then the general requirement of harmony between (1) and (2) would be:

(A) *There must be harmony between the conditions that suffice to justify the assertion of a sentence p and any behavioural differences the assertion of p would produce in the speaker or hearer.*

Take a simple example: Jones utters "I'm in pain," acting all the while as if he's on top of the world. Because there is no harmony between his assertion and his actions, we have good reason to suspect that he *might* misunderstand the meaning of "pain,"[38] a suspicion, let us suppose, borne out by further behavioral evidence. On those grounds, we can criticize his use of "pain."

As for Jones's pain-behavior, so for his logical behavior: We find that his use of "or" and "not" is in disharmony with his understanding of the atomic fragment of his language—he asserts "$p \vee \neg p$" even where p is non-ED, or he assents to $\neg \neg p \rightarrow p$. We thus have precisely the same grounds for criticizing his use of "or" and "not" as we had for criticizing his use of "pain." The obvious objection to this is that it is simply more grist for the holist's mill: Any evidence supporting the thesis that Jones meant "happy" by "pain" is equally evidence that he wished to demonstrate that he rejoiced in his temporary affliction, or that he believes that pain subsides if one acts as if one is untroubled by it, and so on, and so the revisionist's project is doomed unless she can show that the classical meanings an interpreter might read into Jones's words are straightforwardly incoherent. The problem is that although Dummett does indeed have a powerful argument purporting to establish precisely this conclusion, it is unavailable to him to use against the holist who cites Jones's use of classical modes of reasoning as evidence that Jones does in fact possess the very conception Dummett declares to be incoherent. To use this argument would be question-begging on Dummett's part. So, is there any way around the question-begging strategy suggested at the beginning of this section by the argument (1) through (6)?

4.3.7 Tennant's Argument for Revisionism

Neil Tennant has suggested an argument for revisionism that does not appear to involve any *petitio* against the realist:[39]

(1*) Valid arguments must preserve some desirable semantic property. The classicist claims that this is classical truth; the intuitionist claims that it is intuitionistic truth or provability.

(2*) Whatever the property, it must be such that it yields a warrant for asserting Ω whenever there are warrants for asserting each of $\varnothing_1, \varnothing_2, \ldots \varnothing_n$ in the derivation $\varnothing_1, \varnothing_2, \ldots \varnothing_n \vdash \Omega$. (AC)

(3*) So, let us compare the classical and intuitionistic ND systems **C** and **I** and ask for each system whether it satisfies our adequacy constraint (AC). The answer is that although **I** satisfies (AC), **C** fails to satisfy it.

There is no known *classical* method, M_c, for transforming warrants for asserting $\varnothing_1, \varnothing_2, \ldots \varnothing_n$ into warrants for asserting Ω in the derivation $\varnothing_1, \varnothing_2, \ldots \varnothing_n \vdash \Omega$. Letting "$\nabla$" denote "we have a warrant for asserting ...," we can represent this diagramatically as:

$\nabla \quad \nabla \quad \ldots \nabla \quad M_c? \quad \nabla$
$\varnothing_1, \varnothing_2, \ldots \varnothing_n \rightarrow \quad \Omega$

Take a simple example to illustrate this—the derivation of q from p in classical logic by the use of nonconstructive Dilemma (NCD). Suppose then that we have established $p \vdash_c q$ by (NCD) and that we have a warrant for asserting p:

$$\nabla \qquad\qquad\qquad \nabla$$
$$p \qquad r\ (1) \quad p \qquad \neg r\ (1)$$
$$\text{Sub-proof (a)} \quad \text{Sub-proof (b)}$$
$$\underline{\qquad q \qquad\qquad\qquad q \qquad}$$
$$q \quad (1)$$

Subproof (a) has r as an undischarged assumption; subproof (b) has $\neg r$ as an undischarged assumption. Yet, the classicist claims that one is still justified in asserting q on the basis of a rule he takes to be sound, namely, (NCD).

(4*) The intuitionist's criticism of the classicist's claim is this: just because there is no demonstration that (NCD) does in fact preserve warranted assertibility, we have no demonstration that the rule really is sound.

Note that the intuitionist is *not* making the stronger claim that (NCD) does *not* preserve assertibility; he claims only that it has not been established that it *does*.

The classicist might be tempted to respond that the subproofs do preserve that semantic property which the proof theory establishes, namely, classical truth. But this would be to beg the question against the intuitionist—since to establish that the semantic property in terms of which the deducibility relation between wffs ($\vdash_C$) in C is to be made out is classical truth, (NCD) (or else (LEM) or (DNE) from which (NCD) can be derived) would have to be used in the metalogic.[40]

The argument in (1*) through (4*) is markedly superior to the original argument in (1) through (6), for it does *not* presuppose, as the original argument did, that speakers have a grasp of intuitionistic truth. Instead, it challenges the classicist to show why, even if speakers were attributed a notion of classical truth on the strength of their deductive practices, we should imagine that that notion is sound.

4.3.8 The Meanings of the Logical Constants—A Structuralist Alternative

We will see in the ensuing sections that the intuitionist in particular and the antirealist generally have great difficulties in explicating the semantics of their logical operators. A sticking point is truth, which, predictably, the antirealist finds difficult to explicate. It would be better for her to be rid of it, if she could, replacing it with warranted assertibility or somesuch.

Dummett's antirealist cannot replace truth in this way: Her whole case is fashioned around a contrast between incoherent realist meaning and its coherent antirealist counterpart. The problem is that truth is needed to explicate antirealist meaning—or so I argue in section 4.5. Would an antirealist achieve anything by adopting a minimalist attitude to truth? In many ways this seems the more natural reading of her objection to realism: It is truth that is incoherent—warranted assertibility or idealized rational acceptability are not truth's pure core, occluded by the realist's metaphysical distortions; they are, instead, replacements for a wholly bogus notion.

In fact, I do not think that it makes much difference how one describes the antirealist's project—whether debunking truth entirely or revealing its true nature, the antirealist professes to find realist semantics and realist epistemology incomprehensible. What *is* comprehensible is what we have grounds for asserting. It is this connection between assertibility and comprehensibility that my arguments in the following sections put pressure on—truth gets into the picture only because it seems to be needed to explicate antirealist content. In the following sections one recurring theme concerns the meanings of the logical constants. The choices seem limited to a *proof-theoretic* or *model-theoretic* explication of those meanings. These need not be conceived of as mutually exclusive or even as in competition at all—indeed, Dummett does not so regard them. But we might wonder whether there are alternatives.

The answer to that query may well be "Yes." Arnold Koslow, building on work of Nuel Belnap, Gerhard Gentzen, and Heinrich Hertz, has developed a "structuralist" approach to the logical constants that, in his own words: "does not presuppose that the elements upon which the operators act are distinguished by any special syntactic or semantic features."[41] The key theoretical notion is that of an *implication structure* where this is conceived of as any nonempty set with a finitary implication relation defined on it. *Implication relations*, in Koslow's sense, can hold between wholes and parts just as readily as between sentences. As regards the latter though, Koslow shows how to define the logical constants in terms of such structures.

What is a Koslowian implication relation? It is simply a binary relation, $\Rightarrow$, on a nonempty set S that holds between nonempty finite subsets of S and elements of S subject to the following conditions:

(i) For any finite subset of S, A we have that $A \Rightarrow a_i$ for all $a_i \in A$.
(ii) If $\Gamma \Rightarrow a_i$ for all $a_i \in \Sigma$ and $\Sigma \Rightarrow \Theta$ then $\Gamma \Rightarrow \Theta$.

Koslow explains the difference between his structuralist approach to the meanings of the connectives and traditional (proof-theoretic, model-theoretic) approaches thus:

We shall not be concerned directly with questions about those conditions under which hypotheticals, conjunctions, negations, and the other logical operators are true, or assertible, or those under which they are false or refutable. Instead, we shall focus on a question that appears to be much simpler: What are the conditions under which a certain item is to count as a hypothetical, a conjunction, a negation, or a disjunction, or as existentially or universally quantified? Our question concerns what it is like to be a hypothetical or a conjunction, for example, not what it is for a hypothetical, conjunction or other logical type of item to be true, false, assertible, or refutable.[42]

What is interesting about Koslow's approach for the intuitionist is this: *The valid inferences on Koslow's account are precisely those that are intuitionistically valid.* Vann McGee remarks: "This is quite a dramatic result. Intuitionistic logic emerges, naturally and almost inevitably, from considerations that have nothing to do with the usual motives for intuitionism."[43]

4.4 Model Theory, Proof Theory, and the Meanings of the Logical Constants

Dummett rejects "modest" theories of meaning that fail to explicate the logic of the object language. How then will his preferred "full-blooded" theory of meaning fulfill this task? There are two ways in which this responsibility might be discharged: proof-theoretically or model-theoretically. These differing methods correspond to two different ways in which the relation of logical consequence can be characterized, namely, syntactically or semantically.

4.4.1 Derivability and Logical Consequence

On a Tarskian semantic approach, one analyzes what it is for an arbitrary sentence to be "true-in-a-model." A sentence θ is then said to be a *logical consequence* or a *semantic consequence* of a set of sentences Δ if θ is true in every model in which all members of Δ are true.

Although Dag Prawitz[44] and more recently John Etchemendy[45] have expressed some skepticism on this point, most logicians would agree that Tarski's method does explicate what it is for the truth of all members of Δ to necessitate the truth of θ—that is, for θ to be a logical consequence of Δ.

We shall review Prawitz's criticisms of Tarski later but first we need to try to clarify the relation between the syntactic notion of derivability in a formal system and the semantic notion of logical consequence. On a *proof-theoretic* approach, one syntactically specifies effective rules for forming and transforming wffs of a formal language L, and a sentence θ is then said to be a syntactic consequence of Δ if one can move from Δ to θ using only the specified rules. The syntactic rules are, naturally, selected with an eye to preserving the semantic consequence relation, and, if these rules can be proved to be sound with respect to a given semantics, it will appear plausible that we have succeeded in characterizing proof-theoretically that same relation of logical consequence which we could have characterized semantically within the given model theory.

I am taking it that there is one relation of logical consequence that we can characterize either proof-theoretically or model-theoretically, even if for the logician's purposes it may be necessary to bifurcate this relation into separate relations of "syntactic consequence" and "semantic consequence." We should therefore distinguish the relation of *logical consequence*, properly so called (symbolized by "⊨"), from the relation of *formal derivability* (symbolized by "⊢"), which holds between uninterpreted wffs of a formal language. Because the wffs are uninterpreted, the notion of one wff following of necessity from another has no application there.[46]

To characterize the deducibility relation proof-theoretically, one must be able to determine whether a given string of symbols is a formal derivation *without* adverting to its interpretation. Even so, the deducibility relation between sentences, although syntactically specified, must still be conceived as holding between meaningful statements. This point will be important in what follows.

4.4.2 The Belnap–Prior Debate on the Meanings of the Constants

Nuel Belnap thinks it sheer mystification to attribute any meaning to the constants outside of their inferential roles. Prior's TONK is to be ruled out on purely *structural* grounds.[47] Given that we've made certain assumptions about the deducibility relation sufficient to characterize it completely in proof-theoretic terms, TONK can be shown to be inconsistent with those assumptions: a nonconservative extension of the language ensues upon addition of TONK to the original fragment.

It is crucial to the success of Belnap's response to Prior that the characterization of deducibility be *complete*—that is, that we have a characterization that can itself be treated as a formal system that is taken to express *all and only the universally valid statements and rules expressible in the given formalism*. Only then can the context of deducibility be fully determined.[48]

Belnap chose Gentzen's structural rules to determine deducibility:

Axiom $A \vdash A$

Rules

(i) Weakening: From $A_1, A_2, \ldots, A_n \vdash C$ infer $A_1, A_2, \ldots, A_n, B \vdash C$

(ii) Permutation: From $A_1, A_2, \ldots, A_i, A_{i+1}, \ldots, A_n \vdash C$ infer $A_1, A_2, \ldots, A_{i+1}, A_i, \ldots, A_n \vdash C$

(iii) Contraction: From $A_1, A_2, \ldots, A_n, A_n \vdash C$ infer $A_1, A_2, \ldots, A_n \vdash C$

(iv) Transitivity: From $A_1, A_2, \ldots, A_n \vdash C$ and $B_1, B_2, \ldots, B_m, C \vdash D$, infer $A_1, A_2, \ldots, A_n, B_1, B_2, \ldots, B_m \vdash D$

Relative to the notion of deducibility *thus characterized*, TONK constitutes a nonconservative extension.[49] Had we included $A \vdash B$ as an axiom or omitted transitivity, TONK would have conservatively extended the original formalism.

4.4.3 Dummett, Canonical Proof, and the Heyting Clauses

It is clear from Dummett's writings (especially in his *Logical Basis of Metaphysics*) that he would wish to endorse Prior's rejection of the *conventionalism* he (mistakenly in my view) attributes to Belnap without surrendering the thesis that a restricted class of inferential rules can be used to give the meanings of the logical constants. Prior thought that Belnap's structural characterization of the constants could apply at best only for symbolic games devoid of semantic significance.[50] Both Dummett and Prawitz think that the notion of a *conservative extension* can be freed from its moorings to the structuralist view of the meanings of logical constants and pressed into service for the intuitionist. If inferential rules are to be of any use in fixing the meanings of the constants, then we must choose a *restricted* class of rules and accord them some privileged status, unless we are to side with the conventionalist. As noted previously, intuitionists have generally agreed with Gentzen in regarding the introduction rules in a ND system as conferring meanings on the constants, since the introductions of the constants run parallel to Heyting's informal semantics for intuitionistic logic.[51]

I also noted that to explicate the meanings of the connectives in the Heyting explanations, we need to replace the informal notion of proof with a restricted type of proof. The reason given was that we could better account for the actual practice of intuitionists by doing so. But Dummett gives a more compelling reason for choosing to restrict the notion of "proof" in the Heyting clauses to a special type of proof, "canonical proof," rather than expand it to include EMs for finding canonical proofs, in *Elements of Intuitionism*, pp. 392–393. It is this: *Unless we restrict the notion of "proof" in these explanations, the explanations of the meanings of "$\to$" and "$\forall$" will be circular.*

Without certain restrictions, we might use the constant in question as a major premise in an application of the elimination rule for that constant in the constructions alleged to prove a statement with the constant as main operator (its introduction).

Thus, in explaining the meaning of "→" we cannot allow unrestricted use of modus ponens, the elimination rule for "→," since the explanation of the meaning of the constant would be vacuous if we did. That explanation held that we have a proof of A → B iff we have an EM for transforming any proof of A into a proof of B. Were we to allow unrestricted use of modus ponens in the context of that explanation, we could admit *any* construction we liked as a proof of A → B and it would still be true that we had an EM for transforming any proof of A into a proof of B—namely, add the proof of A → B to the proof of A and infer B by modus ponens. So we cannot admit modus ponens as a major premise in the EM for transforming proofs of A into proofs of B.[52] To explain the meanings of "→" and "∀" in the Heyting clauses for the connectives, we must therefore replace each occurrence of "*proof*" with "*canonical proof*." A recursive specification of the concept of canonical proof can then be obtained by including a clause for the atomic case.

Dag Prawitz has shown how this can be done for wffs of first-order logic.[53] Call a system of first-order logic S an *atomic* system if it consists in:

(1) A set of individual, operational, and predicate constants.

(2) A set of inference rules that have atomic wffs as premises and conclusions.

Then, we can provide a precise characterization of canonical proof for wffs of S by adding to the modified Heyting recursion clauses the clause: *A construction C is a canonical proof of an atomic wff A iff it is a proof of A in an atomic system S.*

4.4.4 Canonical Proof and the Introduction Rules

Now suppose that we wished to encapsulate this notion of canonical proof in the intuitionistic ND system **I**. The idea would be to depict canonical proof as comprising applications of introduction rules alone, since the consequences of an application of an introduction rule for a constant fulfill the conditions stated on the left-hand side of the appropriate Heyting biconditional just when its premises meet the conditions stated on the right-hand side.

Consider (&I) by way of illustration. A canonical proof of (A & B) will have the form:

$$\frac{\begin{array}{cc} D_1 & D_2 \\ A & B \end{array}}{(A \,\&\, B)}$$

with D_1 and D_2 canonical proofs of A and B, respectively. So the form of the canonical proof (CP) of (A & B) is:

$$\frac{\begin{array}{c} D_1 \\ D_2 \end{array}}{(A \,\&\, B)}$$

Label this proof D_3. Then it is clear that D_3 will be a CP of (A & B) iff it is a CP of A and a CP of B. The Heyting clause for "&" is thus satisfied by (&I) in the manner indicated above.

But whereas CPs of (A & B), (A ∨ B), and ∃x.Fx can all plausibly be thought of as comprising applications of (&I), (∨I), and (∃I) alone, this is not the case for the CPs of either (A → B) or ∀x.Fx. Even though (→I) and (∀I) satisfy the Heyting clauses for "→" and "∀" respectively, *there are no constraints in* **I** *on the conditions that suffice to infer either (A → B) or ∀x.Fx comparable to those on CPs of those wffs in the Heyting interpretation.*

All that we need to be able to infer (A → B) in **I** is a proof of B from A as hypothesis—*no* restrictions are placed on the *type* of proof involved. So, it is an open possibility that a proof of B from A will consist in applications of (→E) as well as (→I). This is a barrier to our project of encapsulating the requisite notion of canonical proof in **I**, for whereas (→I) assuredly does satisfy the *informal* Heyting recursion clause for "→," it does not, initially, satisfy the given Heyting clause *after* it has been suitably modified in terms of canonical proof.[54]

Yet only the "canonical" clauses can be held to explicate the meanings of their associated constants. The meanings of "→" and of "∀" as represented by (→I) and (∀I) in **I** are therefore *weaker* and more *general* than those meanings conveyed by their canonical Heyting clauses. Moreover, (→I) and (→E) remain in harmony even when the premise of (→I) is permitted to be any deduction whatsoever of the consequent from the antecedent.[55]

Prawitz has suggested a way around this problem:[56] A *closed derivation* D in a system S of a wff ∅ is one that has no open assumptions and no parameters that are not proper. We then stipulate that:

A canonical proof, CP, is to be a construction whose initial premises are atomic sentences, whose final conclusion is a sentence and for which every compound sentence in a closed derivation is deduced from its immediate premises by an introduction rule.

Using this approach, we can encapsulate the notion of canonical proof for first-order logic within an intuitionistic ND system. Yet, as Dummett stresses in *Elements of Intuitionism*, it is important to allow A → B in the general case to be assertible just when we have any deduction whatever of the consequent from the antecedent if we're to remain faithful to our intuitive understanding of "if" in ordinary discourse. So, there remains a doubt as to the applicability of Prawitz's strategy outside the contexts of constructive mathematics and logic.

4.4.5 Can Introduction and Elimination Rules Fix the Meanings of the Constants?

The difficulties caused by conditional and universally quantified statements for the thesis that the meaning of a mathematical statement is given by its canonical proof (or that the meanings of statements in general are given by their direct verifications) ought not to take us by surprise. Just because they cannot be conclusively verified, it cannot be correct to take the meaning of universal or negative existential empirical statements such as "nothing travels faster than the speed of light" as given by their conclusive verification conditions. It is far more plausible to regard the meanings of such statements as fixed not by the *grounds* on which we assert them but by the *consequences* that flow from an assertion of them. In the ND case, this would be to take the elimination rules (→E) and (∀E) as fixing the general meaning that "→" and "∀" carry in all contexts.

On this approach, H knows what S is saying in asserting a conditional or a universally quantified statement just in case he knows what he, H, is entitled to infer from S's utterance of statements of this form. He does not have to know the type of evidence S had in his possession that caused him to issue such an assertion—indeed, in an actual case this might be undiscoverable—but he must understand that modus ponens entitles him to conclude that S *commits himself* to q insofar as he *commits himself* to p and $p → q$, that universal elimination entitles him to impute the belief that Fa to S who asserts "∀x.Fx," and so on. Dummett is opposed to such "mixed theories" and thinks we must choose *between* an assertibility-conditional theory of meaning and a consequentialist theory such as the above: We cannot have both.

4.4.6 Prawitz on Tarski

Tarski analyzed logical consequence along the following lines:

Let $A(c_1, c_2, \ldots, c_n)$ and $B(c_1, c_2, \ldots, c_n)$ be sentences with $c_1, c_2, \ldots, c_n$ standing for the nonlogical constants in A and B; and let $A(v_1, v_2, \ldots, v_n)$ and $B(v_1, v_2, \ldots, v_n)$ be open wffs corresponding to $A(c_1, c_2, \ldots, c_n)$ and $B(c_1, c_2, \ldots, c_n)$, respectively, which are obtained by replacing the constants c_i by variables v_i. Then $B(c_1, c_2, \ldots, c_n)$ is said to be a *logical consequence* of $A(c_1, c_2, \ldots, c_n)$ iff *every model satisfying* $A(v_1, v_2, \ldots, v_n)$ *also satisfies* $B(v_1, v_2, \ldots, v_n) \ldots (V)$.

Although Prawitz acknowledges the correctness of Tarski's criticisms of the view that logical consequence and derivability in a formal system are one and the same, and maintains that "almost regardless of foundational viewpoint, the Tarskian ... account must be accepted as far as it goes," his complaint is that "it does not go very far."[57]

The reason he gives is that once we make the domains of the quantifiers explicit, rewriting (V) as:

(V*) $(\forall v_1 \in D_1) \ldots (\forall v_2 \in D_n)((A(v_1 \ldots v_n) \rightarrow B(v_1 \ldots v_n))$ is true,

we see that Tarski's explication simply amounts to the claim that:

A sentence S is *logically true* if the logical sentence obtained by taking the universal closure of the wffs arising from S by replacing nonlogical constants by variables is true irrespective of the choice of independent domains.

But this just shifts the original question, Prawitz contends, to the question of what it means to call a logical sentence true—that is, to the meaning of (V*), and, although Tarski has an analysis of truth, this analysis does not distinguish logical truth from factual truth. Prawitz concludes in "Approaches to Logical Consequence," p. 154: "Tarski gives no analysis of the necessity of logical truth nor to answering the question of the ground for a universal truth like (V*) or how we can come to know even with certainty that a logical sentence is true in all domains."

Prawitz's criticisms of Tarski do not seem wholly justified to me. It is true that Tarski does not answer the question of how we can come to know that a given sentence is logically true or is a consequence of another sentence, nor does he set out to. Antirealistically, this might appear as a serious failing, but from the classical standpoint it is not.

The more serious accusation concerns the necessity of logical truth and of logical consequence, and here, it seems to me, Prawitz's criticisms are unfounded. Logical truths are precisely truths that hold good in all structures, according to Tarski. Quantification over all structures is supposed to capture the relevant notion of logical necessity in exactly the same way as quantification over all possible worlds is supposed to capture the more general notion of necessity. Moreover, just because logical truths are true in *all* models and empirical truths true only in *some*, we do have, on a Tarskian account, a means of distinguishing logical truths from empirical truths.

4.4.7 Canonical Arguments and Prawitz's Proof-theoretic Characterization of Logical Consequence

As a result of his dissatisfaction with Tarskian characterizations of logical consequence, Prawitz has recently developed a more general proof-theoretic approach to this notion and to the meanings of the connectives[58] in which the fundamental explanatory role is played not by the notion of canonical proof that Dummett, following Heyting, has sought to develop, but by the more general notion of a *canonical argument*. An *argument* here is simply an arbitrary collection of linked inferences, preferably arranged in tree form to make the links explicit.[59] As before, the approach is based on an assertibility-conditional theory of meaning. But Prawitz's innovation is that the condition for asserting a sentence is now not to know a proof of it, but rather to know a closed valid argument for it.[60] To know that B can be correctly inferred from the assumption of A is to know that we can correctly assert B in just those situations in which we can correctly assert A. So, if we have an account of the conditions under which A is assertible, we will eo ipso know when an inference involving A is valid on such a theory of meaning.

Prawitz wants to make precise Gentzen's idea that the introduction rules are *self-justifying*: They are self-justifying in the sense that by stipulating what is to count as a proof of a certain conclusion, the introduction rules thereby determine the meaning of that conclusion. The elimination rules are then justified in light of those meanings. A *closed argument*, Prawitz stipulates, is one for which all its assumptions and parameters are bound by some inference; otherwise it is said to be *open*. Open arguments are schemas for obtaining closed arguments in this sense: One can obtain from them a closed argument by replacing free occurrences of parameters by terms and free assumptions by closed arguments. To know a closed argument for a sentence *p* is not to have a proof of it—to have *that*, the closed argument must be a valid one. But how do we decide when a closed argument is valid? Prawitz makes two assumptions to answer this question:

(1) For each form of sentence occurring in the argument, there exists an introduction rule for that sentence.

(2) For each inference in the argument that is not an application of an introduction rule, there is associated with it a *justifying operation* that transforms certain arguments to another argument for the same wff depending on not more assumptions than the transformed one.

The idea is that by stating the introduction rules, one thereby determines the canonical forms of arguments for the sentences in question, and in so doing the meanings of those sentences are determined by those of their constituents. So, an argument that has a certain compound sentence as its conclusion should have the relevant introduction rule as its last inference if it is to be in canonical form. Canonical arguments, like canonical proofs, are correct forms of argument (proof) for the sentence in question, which are such that *any correct closed argument (proof) for the sentence in question could always be given in these forms.*[61]

Thus, if we ask why (&I) is a correct form of argument, the only possible answer is that it is part of the meaning of "and" that a conjunction is proved by proving both its conjuncts (i.e., the introduction rules are self-justifying). But what of closed arguments involving elimination inferences—when are they valid? Prawitz thinks that certain *justifying procedures* can be assigned to these inferences that transform a given closed argument containing them into a *valid* canonical argument. A canonical argument is *valid* iff its immediate subarguments are valid.[62]

An argument A is valid just when it is valid with respect to some justifying procedure $\emptyset$. An inference rule is judged valid just when each application of it preserves the validity of arguments. Introduction rules are then (trivially) valid because, being in canonical form, they consist in valid immediate subarguments. Elimination rules are valid iff one has a justifying procedure $\emptyset$ such that if A is an argument whose last inference is R and whose immediate subarguments are valid with respect to justifying procedures β, then A is also valid with respect to $\beta \cup \{\emptyset\}$. Let us take a simple example to illustrate Prawitz's idea: Consider modus ponens once more. Let A be an argument whose last inference is ($\rightarrow$E). A will be of the form

$$\frac{\emptyset \to \Omega \quad \emptyset}{\Omega} \quad (\to E)$$

Suppose that A consists of subarguments A_1 and A_2 for $\emptyset \to \Omega$ and $\emptyset$, respectively, which are valid with respect to justifying procedures μ_1 and μ_2. Then we can use μ_1 and μ_2 to transform A_1, A_2 into arguments in canonical form A_{1c}, A_{2c}, respectively. Then we can use A_{1c} to find an argument A_3 in canonical form establishing Ω from $\emptyset$ as hypothesis. But then we have a justifying procedure π for transforming our original argument for Ω, A, into one in canonical form: Use A_{2c} to provide a canonical argument for $\emptyset$, and then use A_3 to argue canonically for Ω from $\emptyset$ as hypothesis. The resultant argument:

A_{2c}
$\emptyset$
A_3
Ω

is valid with respect to the justifying procedure $\pi \cup \{\mu_1, \mu_2\}$.

Hence, in accord with the definition above, the elimination rule ($\to E$) is valid (since it preserves the validity of certain canonical arguments assumed already to be valid). So, modus ponens is a *sound* rule of inference. The soundness of the other elimination rules can be demonstrated in an equally straightforward way. Prawitz goes on to give a definition of logical consequence based on this approach:

A sentence p is said to be a *logical consequence* of a finite set of sentences Δ when there is a logically valid argument for p from Δ (i.e., all its free assumptions belong to Δ).[63]

In fact, Prawitz's general assumption—that if a complex sentence can be asserted at all, it must be derivable from atomic sentences via some valid argument—seems questionable (unless we permit, as Prawitz clearly does not, classically valid arguments). Thus I might select one ball bearing from a box of one hundred, christen it "Alphonse," return it to the box without looking or noting its position in any way, and, though quite unable to distinguish Alphonse from the rest, still be entitled to assert "one of these ball bearings is called 'Alphonse.'" Or, to use one of Dummett's favored examples, I might observe that I have crossed every Königsberg bridge without observing that I, as I must, have crossed some bridge twice—that I crossed all the bridges is the content of my observation; I have not reached it (and now cannot do so) as a conclusion from discrete observations of my crossing each individual bridge (and one of these twice).[64] Prior claimed that it is one thing to define "conjunction-forming sign" and quite another to define "and."[65] A definition of the former could be achieved either by stipulating that its introduction and elimination rules (&I) and (&E) were to hold, or by providing a truth-table for "&."[66]

Someone who already understood the meaning of "and" would, Prior thought, in all probability realize that it was *that* meaning that the inferential or truth-tabular definition sought to capture. Now Prawitz, following Gentzen, takes the introduction rules to be self-justifying, and he claims it as a chief virtue of a Gentzen-styled approach that it shows how the meanings of complex sentences depend on the meanings of their parts.[67] Belnap might also have declared his inferential definitions "self-justifying" in the sense that if we simply know how a sign such as "&" is to be *used*, we do not need to *appeal to* any independent extrasystemic *semantic* concepts to justify its use—rather, provided we use "&" consistently, its use is already justified *within the context of the whole system*. He need not be committed to claiming, à la Prawitz, that Tarskian model-theoretic accounts of logical consequence are all but useless.[68]

4.4.8 Dummett on the Relation between Proof-theoretic and Semantic Approaches to Logical Consequence

In contrast to Prawitz, Dummett does not see a proof-theoretic account of the meanings of the connectives as a genuine *competitor* to a model-theoretic account. On the contrary, even when we choose a suitably restricted class of inference rules to perspicuously represent the meanings of the logical constants, these rules can succeed in doing so only if we already have an implicit grasp of how the semantic value of a sentence depends on the semantic values of its parts. Proof-theoretic characterizations of the meanings of the constants are for Dummett *supervenient on* that provided by a semantic theory.[69] To grasp the meaning of a connective such as "or" simply *is* to have a tacit understanding of how the semantic value of complex sentences involving it are determined by the semantic values of their parts.

Dummett lays down some conditions that a set of inference rules must satisfy if it is to provide a perspicuous representation of the meanings of the connectives. But, even if we take the meanings of the constants to be determined by the stipulation that these inference rules are to hold, Dummett contends, we still do not have a genuine *alternative to* the above semantic conception of their meaning. Each inference rule in the set has to be understood as contributing to the determination of the meaning of the constant by displaying either a necessary condition for the truth of a complex sentence involving it (in the case of an elimination rule), or a sufficient condition for the truth of such a sentence (in the case of an introduction rule). A complete set of (suitably constrained) introduction rules, by displaying all possible sufficient conditions for the truth of the comlex sentence, or a complete set of (suitably constrained) elimination rules by displaying all possible necessary conditions for the truth of that sentence, gives a necessary and a sufficient condition for the truth of the sentence.[70] But just because the proof-theoretic characterization yields a truth condition for the relevant compound sentence, *the precise meaning that the inference rules confer on the constants will depend on the concept of truth we're appealing to.*

On Dummett's view, however, the concept of truth will be determined by the theory of meaning—which, to recall, is a three-tiered structure consisting in a semantic theory as base, a theory of sense correlating speakers' grasp of truth conditions with practical abilities, and a theory of force connecting the sense of each sentence with its actual use in discourse. Hence, since the theory of meaning is founded on a semantic theory, proof-theoretic characterizations of the meanings of the connectives (and thus of validity) must *supervene on* a semantic characterization. In his *Logical Basis of Metaphysics*, largely building on Prawitz's work and, in particular, on the latter's notion of a *canonical argument*, Dummett discusses certain constraints that might be imposed on any putative meaning-revealing set of inference rules. His first question is what formal properties an introduction rule should have in order to be self-justifying.[71] We *could* require each rule to be: (1) single-ended; (2) pure; (3) simple; (4) sheer; (5) direct. We *ought* to require them collectively to be: (6) in harmony; (7) stable.

(1) A *single-ended* inference rule is one that is unambiguously either an introduction rule or an elimination rule. Here, an introduction rule for some logical constant c is one whose conclusion has c as its principal operator; an elimination rule for c on the other hand has c as the principal operator of one of its premises. Thus, according to this way of reckoning things, transitivity is not single-ended, since it is simultaneously an introduction and elimination rule:

$$\frac{\Phi \to \Psi \quad \Psi \to \Theta}{\Phi \to \Theta}$$

(2) A *pure* inference rule is one for which no more than one logical constant appears in the formulation of the rule. Modus tollens is an impure rule.

(3) A *simple* inference rule has any constant c appearing in it as its principal operator.

(4) A rule is *sheer* if it is either (a) an introduction rule for a constant c that does not figure in any premise or discharged hypothesis or (b) an elimination rule for a constant c that does not figure in the conclusion or in any discharged hypothesis.

(5) A rule is *direct* if no constant c figures in any hypothesis discharged by it.

Relative to this classification, Gentzen's inference rules (save those for negation) were *pure, simple,* and *single-ended.* Should we then follow Gentzen's lead, Dummett wonders? His answer is that although in practice we can require our rules to be single-ended, both purity and simplicity cannot be justified theoretically. Although an impure introduction rule involving constants other than some designated c will make a grasp of c depend on a prior grasp of those other constants, provided the relation of dependence is not cyclical, we may yet be able to order these constants so that an understanding of each depended only on the understanding of those preceding it in the ordering. Likewise, the demand for simple rules is excessive, Dummett argues. One might have different rules governing negation introduction depending on what the principal operator of the negated sentence is. Thus, if it is "∨," we might specify that from ¬Θ together with ¬Φ one can derive ¬(Θ ∨ Φ); but if it is "&" these conditions would be excessive, as one can derive ¬(Θ & Φ) from ¬Θ alone or from ¬Φ alone. Dummett terms it the fundamental assumption underlying putative attempts to demonstrate the self-justifying character of the introduction rules that "Wherever we are entitled to assert a complex statement we could have arrived at it by means of an argument terminating with at least one of the introduction rules governing its principal operator."[72] The *minimal* demand that the fundamental assumption dictates, Dummett thinks, is that if an introduction rule is intended to be self-justifying, its structure must guarantee that "the conclusion is of higher logical complexity than any of its premises and discharged hypotheses." He calls this the complexity condition (CC).[73]

The fundamental assumption cannot be reasonably imposed on open sentences, Dummett notes. To see why, consider the derivation of

$\forall x(Ax \vee Bx)$ from the open sentence $Ay \vee By$. Applying fundamental assumption to $Ay \vee By$ would entail that that open sentence could have been derived from Ay or from By, whence we could derive $\forall x.Ax$ or $\forall x.Bx$. Dummett follows Prawitz in appealing to the notion of a *canonical argument* to justify the inference rules. However, his project, unlike Prawitz's, is not simply to justify the *elimination* rules; it is to justify *arbitrary* inference rules. To that end, he assumes we are given certain "boundary rules" for deriving atomic sentences from other atomic sentences that we recognize as valid. He then initially defines a *canonical argument* as (I) "one in which no initial premise is a complex sentence (no complex sentence stands at a topmost node) and in which all the transitions are in accordance either with one of the boundary rules or with one of the given set of introduction rules."[74] He then defines a *supplementation* of an arbitrary argument to be the result of replacing any complex initial premise by a canonical (sub)argument having that premise as its final conclusion.

Then, an arbitrary argument A is deemed *valid* if:

(II) We have an EM of transforming any supplementation of A into a canonical argument with the same final conclusion and no new initial premises.

The notion of a canonical argument has to be broadened, however, to deal with lines that contain open sentences. So to account for these, we define an *instance* of an argument A to be an argument obtained by replacing each free variable in its final conclusion or in any of its initial premises by one and the same constant term. Claim (II) is modified accordingly to read:

(II′) An arbitrary argument is valid if we possess an EM for transforming any supplementation of an instance of it into a valid canonical argument.

Further problems arise, however. Subordinate deductions and lines involving open sentences cannot reasonably be required to involve introduction rules alone. This leads to a more complicated definition where the notion of a valid *canonical* argument is simultaneously defined with that of a valid *arbitrary* argument. We say that a sentence belongs to the *main stem* of an argument A if it and every other sentence between it and the main conclusion depend only on some (all) of the initial premises of A. Then A is deemed to be a canonical argument if:

(i) The final conclusion is a closed sentence.

(ii) All its initial premises are closed atomic sentences.

(iii) Every atomic sentence in the main stem is either an initial premise or derived by a boundary rule.

(iv) Every closed complex sentence in the main stem is derived by means of one of the given set of introduction rules.

A subargument,[75] α, of an argument A is *critical* if its conclusion stands in α immediately above a closed sentence not in the main stem but is itself either an open or a closed sentence not in the main stem.

We then have that an arbitrary argument is valid if:

(II″) we can effectively transform any supplementation of an instance of it into a valid canonical argument with the same final conclusion and initial premises

and

(I″) A canonical argument A^* is valid just when every one of its critical subarguments is valid.

Dummett illustrates how these definitions vindicate the validity of simple inferences. Thus, if we wish to show that the inference of $\forall x(Bx \vee Ax)$ from $\forall x(Ax \vee Bx)$ to be valid we first observe that it will typically assume the following form:

$\forall x(Ax \vee Bx)$
$\overline{Ay \vee By}$
$\overline{By \vee Ay}$
$\forall x(Bx \vee Ax)$

But to justify the initial premise, it is necessary that there exist some supplementation of the argument of the form:

$\nabla \alpha$
$\overline{Az \vee Bz}$
$\overline{\forall x(Ax \vee Bx)}$
$\overline{Ay \vee By}$
$\overline{By \vee Ay}$
$\forall x(Bx \vee Ax)$

The initial premises of the valid canonical argument will contain no occurrences of the free variable z, moreover, since they will perforce be closed. Only the last two lines of the supplemented argument stand in need of justification. All save those two together constitute a critical subargument, and so, by definition (I″), a valid canonical argument. Do the last two lines preserve this property? Yes, provided that any instance of this critical sub-argument is valid. So we take as a typical instance, κ:

$$\frac{\frac{\nabla\alpha}{Az \vee Bz}}{\frac{\forall\xi(A\xi \vee B\xi)}{\frac{At \vee Bt}{Bt \vee At}}}$$

But since $\nabla\alpha$ is a critical subargument proceeding from closed atomic premises for the conclusion $\forall x(Ax \vee Bx)$, a valid canonical argument for the instance of it resulting from the substitution of t for the free variable z, $\nabla\beta$, proceeding from just the same premises as $\nabla\alpha$, must exist. That is, $\nabla\beta$ will be either of the form:

$$\frac{\nabla\beta}{\frac{At}{At \vee Bt}} \quad or \quad \frac{\nabla\beta}{\frac{Bt}{At \vee Bt}}$$

Finally, to transform this into a canonical argument with the same initial premises and final conclusion as the typical instance κ, all that we need do is replace the conclusion $At \vee Bt$ of $\nabla\beta$ with $Bt \vee At$. Thus we have shown that the inference of $\forall x(Bx \vee Ax)$ from $\forall x(Ax \vee Bx)$ is valid. Dummett calls such vindications of validity *proof-theoretic justifications of the third grade*.[76]

4.4.9 Philosophical Significance of Proof-theoretic Approaches for Natural Language

What are the chances of generalizing Dummett's or Prawitz's proof-theoretic approaches to a natural rather than a formal language? To be sure, the notion of a canonical argument for a sentence seems to hold out more promise of application to empirical statements than does the notion of canonical proof, which seems more or less restricted to mathematical and logical discourse. Moreover, the notion of a canonical argument is not restricted to first-order theories. The antirealist claim presumably would not be that speakers could actually *produce* such an argument for the statement (even under epistemically ideal circumstances), but rather that speakers are disposed on reflection to *acknowledge* such an argument as correct when it is presented to them.[77]

But, even so, is it really plausible to credit speakers who grasp the meaning of a statement with implicit knowledge of a closed valid argument for it? The answer is surely "No," for the reasons given in section 4.3—closed valid arguments for mathematical statements are simply mathematical proofs. But whereas children of 12 can understand Fermat's last theorem, they certainly cannot acknowledge Wiles's proof when it is presented to them.

4.4.10 Harmony, Stability, and Other Virtues

As to the constraints regulating sets of meaning-explicating inferences, we have already discussed the need for *harmony* between introduction and elimination rules. The requirement of *stability* arises as follows. Suppose that two alternative proof-theoretic procedures for justifying forms of argument are proposed:

(a) An "upward" justification procedure that appeals to introduction rules as giving the meanings of the connectives, and

(b) a "downward" procedure that appeals to elimination rules as effecting this task.

Suppose we start with some set of elimination rules. Then the set of introduction rules that can be justified with respect to them by a downward procedure is well defined. Now consider this set of introduction rules—the set of elimination rules that can be justified with respect to them is similarly well defined (by an upward procedure). The question of stability has to do with whether we will arrive back at the set of elimination rules with which we started. If so, we call that set of elimination rules *stable*.[78] Stability is not the same property as harmony because the latter is automatically guaranteed by either type of justification procedure. "But, to verify that stability obtains, we have to appeal to both justification procedures," Dummett informs us in *Logical Basis of Metaphysics*, page 287. Dummett believes that no intelligible meanings can be conferred on a set of logical constants by the stipulation of an unstable set of introduction and elimination rules. No assertibility-conditional theory of meaning can be provided for a language with an unstable set of introduction rules governing its logical constants; no theory of meaning based on the consequences of an assertion can be provided for a language with an unstable set of elimination rules.[79]

I do not wish to investigate the plausibility of Dummett's requirements here. Suffice it to say that the need for some such constraints on allegedly meaning-canonical inference rules seems genuine wherever we are dealing with a constructivist semantics that is *itself* based on the central concepts of inference and proof. Here, the threat of impredicativity is ever-present. Whether these constraints can reasonably be imposed on proof-theoretic approaches to the meanings of the classical connectives seems far less certain. At any rate, Dummett seems to me to be entirely correct in his perception of the *relation* between proof-theoretic and model-theoretic characterizations of the meanings of the constants.

Dummett regards a set of pure and simple inference rules as displaying the general form of the meanings that the operators carry in all contexts. Further, specific introduction rules pertain to specific contexts—for example, whereas an intuitionistic understanding of canonical proofs (hence meaning) of "$\forall x.Fx$" is governed by the demand that ($\forall$E) be valid, the means of establishing a universal statement may vary from domain to domain. In the particular domain of natural numbers, for example, a recognition of induction as a (in fact the only) method of proving "$\forall x.Fx$" depends on an understanding of the construction of that domain. This is symptomatic of the general point that inference rules fix the meanings of the constants only against an extensive background of semantic principles governing the language. The inference rules governing "or" (e.g., ($\vee$I) and ($\vee$E)) neither require us to assume nor forbid us from assuming that LEM holds in the object language. But whereas both intuitionist and classicist agree that the truth of A and the truth of B exhaust the possible sufficient conditions for the truth of "A or B," the realist understands truth as something that attaches to the sentence independently of our capacity to establish it, and the intuitionist identifies truth with our capacity to establish it. Dummett remarks at pages 299–300 of *Logical Basis of Metaphysics*:

Logic as a whole can only be thought wholly to rest on stipulated, self-justifying laws if a satisfactory proof-theoretic justification procedure can be based on them which will validate all the logical laws we firmly regard as valid; and this in turn depends on the soundness of some version of the relevant fundamental assumption.

For all that, the laws of intuitionistic logic appear capable of being justified proof-theoretically by any of the procedures we have discussed; and this means that the meanings of the intuitionistic logical constants can be explained in a very direct way, without any apparatus of semantic theory, in terms of the use made of them in practice. Many—possibly most—people who have thought about the matter believe that meanings should be given to the logical constants which cannot be explained in this way, but can only be explained on the basis of some semantic theory at a certain remove from practice (if they can be explained at all).

We shall see in section 4.5 just how difficult it is for the intuitionist to explain the meanings of her constants in semantic terms. A structural or proof-theoretic characterization might then be the only way possible for her to communicate those meanings. Dummett might, in other words, be making a virtue out of necessity.

4.5 Intuitionism and Alethic Eliminativism

4.5.1 Fitch's Argument

Frederick Fitch famously purported to show that the antirealist's thesis that all truths are knowable entailed the absurd conclusion that *all truths are already known*. Strong verificationism is the thesis that all truths are already known. Weak verificationism is the more moderate thesis that all truths are knowable. Fitch purported to show that weak verificationism collapsed into strong verificationism. Alternatively, the recognition that we are not omniscient can be shown by Fitch's argument to lead to paradox. This is often referred to as the *paradox of knowability*. We can derive the absurd conclusion from the distinctive antirealist axiom that it is possible to know any truth together with the two highly plausible axioms that any proposition that is known is true and that for any known conjunction of propositions, each of its conjuncts is also known. In symbols, the three axioms assert:

(KT) $p \rightarrow \Diamond Kp$

(FK) $Kp \rightarrow p$

(K&) $K(p \,\&\, q) \rightarrow Kp \,\&\, Kq$

It is easy to show by classical propositional logic that these three axioms jointly lead to a modal collapse:

1. $p \,\&\, \neg Kp$ Hyp.
2. $\Diamond K(p \,\&\, \neg Kp)$ KT
3. $\Diamond (Kp \,\&\, K\neg Kp)$ K&
4. $\Diamond (Kp \,\&\, \neg Kp)$ FK
5. $\bot$ 4
6. $\neg(p \,\&\, \neg Kp)$ 1, 5 RAA
7. $p \rightarrow Kp$ CPL

The K operator needs an intuitionistically acceptable interpretation. It is plausible to understand it intuitionistically as covertly quantifying over states of information so that Kp means $\exists\sigma K\sigma p$. With this interpretation of "K" secured, the argument can proceed up to line 6 as before but not to the desired conclusion $p \to Kp$ (viz., $p \to \exists\sigma K\sigma p$) needed to secure a 'modal collapse' of weak verificationism's $p \to \Diamond Kp$ to strong verificationism's $p \to Kp$. Even though the step from line 6 to the conclusion at line 7 is classically valid, it is intuitionistically invalid, requiring double negation elimination to justify it.[80] Our real interest lies in the refutation of the principle of limited knowledge ($p \ \& \ \neg Kp$) expressed by line (1) of the derivation above, but it is worth pointing out that although the modal collapse of weak into strong verificationism can be resisted intuitionistically, a difficulty still remains: Even though the formula at line 6 of the derivation, $\neg(p \ \& \ \neg Kp)$, does not intuitionistically entail the formula at line 7, $p \to Kp$, it *does* entail $\neg\neg(p \to Kp)$, which is worrying enough for antirealists as it apparently means that *we can refute the claim that not every truth will eventually be known.*

How could we even contest, let alone *refute*, a truth so patent as that not every truth will eventually be known? The formula to be refuted, $\neg(p \to Kp)$, is one that intuitionists must surely *accept* on pain of not being able to distinguish the provable from the already proven.

Michael Dummett has proposed a solution to Fitch's paradox of knowability.[81] He thinks that the paradox stems from a naive approach to the principle that all truths are knowable. This principle, reflected in (KT) above, should be restricted to "*basic*" statements, Dummett avers, with truth recursively projected from these. Then, however "basic" is to be precisely characterized, "$p \ \& \ \neg Kp$" will not count as a basic statement. The paradox cannot then arise. Berit Brogard and Joe Salerno have recently responded that Dummett's solution fails to rule out other variants of Fitch's paradox. Brogard and Salerno first argue that antirealists such as Dummett ought to accept the (KK) principle ($\Box(K(B) \to KK(B))$):[82] "After all, if '$K(B)$' is constructively true (that is, there is a finite and surveyable discourse that verifies 'it is known that B'), it is arguable that this can be turned into a constructive verification of '$KK(B)$' (that is, there is a finite and surveyable discourse that verifies 'it is known that it is known that B')." They also think it is plausible for antirealists to accept the closure principle (CP): $\Box(p \to q) \to (\Diamond p \to \Diamond q)$. Given (KK) and (CP) together with the factive nature of $\Diamond Kp$: (F) $\Diamond Kp \to p$:

1. $p \,\&\, \neg Kp$ Hyp.
2. $\Box(K(p) \to KK(p))$ (KK)
3. $p \to \Diamond Kp$ (KT)
4. p 1 & E
6. $\Diamond Kp$ 3, 5 → E
7. $\Diamond KKp$ 2, 6 by (CP)
8. Kp 7 by (F)
9. $\neg Kp$ 1 & E
10. $\bot$ 8, 9 & I

Here p is assumed to be a basic statement but Kp is not.

Naturally, Dummett could contest either of the principles (KK) or (CP). Moreover, it has to be acknowledged that the closure principle (CP) does not look at all compelling if "$\Diamond$" is interpreted in terms of *epistemic* possibility, $\Diamond_E$, such that "$\Diamond_E p$" is true if *p is consistent with what we know*. This is a natural interpretation of "$\Diamond$" for an antirealist to adopt, since it seems to be the notion of possibility in play in the Kripke trees.

Antirealists might find Neil Tennant's suggested solution to Fitch's paradox more congenial than Dummett's appeal to "basic" statements.[83] His idea is that *every truth p is knowable provided that "Kp" is not self-contradictory*. Now the Brogard-Salerno derivation above does not fall foul of Tennant's strictures, so his solution is still susceptible to it; but suppose we do interpret "$\Diamond$" on Tennant's behalf as epistemically possible and deny the closure principle (CP). What then?

Brogard and Salerno adduce an argument that purports to show that "epistemic possibility . . . renders anti-realism inconsistent with the claim that there are undecid*ed* statements. Worse, it entails that there are no undecided statements, *necessarily*."[84] This is a pretty astonishing claim on the face of it. How is it to be supported? Brogard and Salerno make use of a further intuitive principle in their demonstration of the above conclusion:

(*)   If $K\neg A$ then $\neg \Diamond_E A$

Brogard's and Salerno's detailed argument then proceeds, in their words:

Let us suppose . . . that there is an undecided statement:

(1) $\exists A(\neg KA \,\&\, \neg K\neg A)$

If (1) is true, then some instance of it is true:

(2) $\neg KA \ \& \ \neg K\neg A$

Since line (2) does not violate Tennant's restriction (that is, $K(\neg KA \ \& \ \neg K\neg A)$ is not self-contradictory), we may apply anti-realism to it. It follows from anti-realism that it is possible to know (2):

(3) $\Diamond K(\neg KA \ \& \ \neg K\neg A)$

Now let the anti-realist suppose for reductio that it is known that A is undecided:

(4) $K(\neg KA \ \& \ \neg K\neg A)$

Knowing a conjunction entails knowing each of the conjuncts. Therefore,

(5) $K\neg KA \ \& \ K\neg K\neg A$

Applying principle (*) to each of the conjuncts gives us

(6) $\neg\Diamond_E KA \ \& \ \neg\Diamond_E \neg KA$

Given the assumption of anti-realism, we derive the contradiction $\neg A \ \& \ \neg\neg A$. So the anti-realist must reject our assumption at line (4):

(7) $\neg K(\neg KA \ \& \ \neg K\neg A)$

Resting only on the assumption of anti-realism, which the anti-realist takes to be known, line (7) is now known:

(8) $K\neg K(\neg KA \ \& \ \neg K\neg A)$

But then, by (*), it is epistemically impossible to know that A is undecided:

(9) $\neg\Diamond_E K(\neg KA \ \& \ \neg K\neg A)$

But this line contradicts line (3), which rests merely upon anti-realism and line (2). Line (2) is the instance of the undecidedness claim at line (1). A contradiction then rests on anti-realism conjoined with undecidedness. The anti-realist must reject the claim of undecidedness:

(10) $\neg\exists A(\neg KA \ \& \ \neg K\neg A)$

Since anti-realism is taken to be a necessary thesis, it must be admitted by the anti-realist that, necessarily, there are no undecided statements:

(11) $\Box(\neg\exists A(\neg KA \ \& \ \neg K\neg A))$

Line (11) says, necessarily, no statement is such that it and its negation are not known. Denying in this way that there is an undecided statement boasts of a kind of epistemic completeness that we are in no position to endorse a priori. After all, it is more likely that we will leave some stones unturned. Denying undecidedness in favour of epistemic completeness is bad enough, but things are worse. We see that anti-realism (a necessary thesis) entails the necessity of that completeness. But whether a statement is known is often a contingent matter. And so, whether such statements are undecided is a contingent matter as well.[85]

Ingenious as it no doubt is, this argument is fundamentally flawed. *It can appear convincing only if we overlook the implicitly indexical nature of all antirealist assessments of undecidability.* Statements are decidable or not *relative to* the information contained in a given TSI. For definiteness, let us choose as our sample undecided statement Goldbach's conjecture *g* that every even number greater than 2 is the sum of two primes. We have that *g* is undecided relative to the information contained in our present TSI, σ_a. That is:

(2*) $\neg K\sigma_a g \ \& \ \neg K\sigma_a \neg g$

It is certainly possible for us to know in σ_a that *g* is undecided:

(3*) $\Diamond_E K\sigma_a(\neg K\sigma_a g \ \& \ \neg K\sigma_a \neg g)$

since we actually *do* know this in our present TSI σ_a:

(4*) $K\sigma_a(\neg K\sigma_a g \ \& \ \neg K\sigma_a \neg g)$

Then of course we must know in σ_a each of the conjuncts:

(5*) $K\sigma_a \neg K\sigma_a g \ \& \ K\sigma_a \neg K\sigma_a \neg g$

Now Brogard's and Salerno's principle (*) states "If $K \neg A$ then $\neg \Diamond_E A$." What (*) really means is:

(**) $\exists \sigma K\sigma \neg A \rightarrow \neg \Diamond_E A$

Our present TSI, σ_a, surely is such a σ. Hence from (5*), by (**):

(6*) $\neg \Diamond_E K\sigma_a g \ \& \ \neg \Diamond_E K\sigma_a \neg g$

But at this point any prospect of a reductio has truly vanished, for (6*) is just a puffed-up way of telling us what we knew from the outset: given our present state of mathematical knowledge as specified in σ_a, it is epistemically impossible to know in σ_a that every even number greater than 2 is the sum of two primes and it is epistemically impossible to know in σ_a that it is not the case that every even number is the sum of two primes—which is just a convoluted way of saying that g is undecidable relative to the available information.

What then of the antirealist principle (AR) $p \leftrightarrow \Diamond_E Kp$? Can this principle be brought to bear somehow on (6*)? Plainly, what (AR) means is:

(AR*) $p \leftrightarrow \Diamond_E \exists \sigma K \sigma p$

Thus the fact that $\neg \Diamond_E K \sigma_a g$ tells us nothing at all as to whether some future TSI σ_K may not emerge wherein $K \sigma_K g$. So we can state succinctly the fallacy in the Brogard–Salerno "proof" above: To derive $\neg g$ from (6*) using (AR), what we'd need is $\neg \Diamond_E \exists \sigma K \sigma g$, whereas what we have from (6*) is merely that $\exists \sigma \neg \Diamond_E K \sigma g$. Failure to respect the indexical nature of the antirealist's epistemic evaluations can thus lead to some pretty egregious errors in interpreting their position.

4.5.2 Whence the Paradox of Knowability?

The puzzle with Fitch's argument for the antirealist is this: Not only "$\neg \neg (p \to Kp)$" but the stronger "$(p \to Kp)$" and indeed "$\neg (p \,\&\, \neg Kp)$" are all perfectly acceptable *if interpreted in the intended intuitionistic way*. Intuitionistically, "$(p \to Kp)$" simply says that any ground for asserting p can be transformed into a ground for asserting that p is known, while "$\neg (p \,\&\, \neg Kp)$" says that we can refute the claim that we can produce a warrant for asserting p and simultaneously refute the claim that a TSI exists that warrants the claim that we know that p, which is surely true since a warrant for the second conjunct would automatically undermine any warrant for the first.

How then can Fitch's argument be thought to "refute" these principles? Provided the warrants for assertion are understood to be, as intended, *conclusive*, the cited claims are almost truistic intuitionistically—for if anything can provide knowledge that p a proof of it can. Moreover, not only are these propositions true intuitionistically, they are true classically as well. Thus the only "paradox" here is why antirealists have thought the "paradox of knowability" was a paradox for them at all.

What of the "modal collapse" of weak verificationism's $p \to \Diamond Kp$ into strong verificationism's $p \to Kp$ (or, at least $\neg\neg (p \to Kp)$)? This is a simple reflection of the fact that the intuitionistic conditional already has modal force (perhaps a case of modal absorption rather than collapse). The recursive clause for "$\to$" in the informal Heyting semantics not only makes reference to (suitably idealized) human epistemic *capacities*, but, more significantly, quantifies over future TSIs that are the antirealist surrogate for possible worlds.[86] Intuitionists can thus legitimately avoid the unwelcome interpretation of "$\neg\neg (p \to \exists \sigma K \sigma p)$" as "we can refute the claim that not all truths will be known" or of "$(p \to \exists \sigma K \sigma p)$" as all truths are already known. *These propositions are strictly unintelligible to them since they are intuitionistically inexpressible.*

This reply comes at a price, however. That price is *truth-conditional semantics*. As soon as "($p \to \exists \sigma K \sigma p$)" is interpreted in terms of *truth conditions*, even if epistemically constrained truth conditions, the "unintelligible" reading can be recovered. There are numbers (infinitely many) whose primality will not at any stage of inquiry be decided even though we could "in principle" decide of any given one of these whether it is prime or not, according to intuitionists. Knowing this, we have conclusive grounds to refute the claim that $p \to \exists \sigma K \sigma p$, *if we construe* $p \to \exists \sigma K \sigma p$ *as* "if p is true, it will eventually be known."

If this assessment is correct, then the moral of the paradox of knowability looks very different from the antirealist perspective. It is that antirealist intuitionistic semantics must be conceived of as *eliminativist* rather than *reductionist* about truth. Of course antirealists can still have a truth predicate—an eliminable disquotational one—but their logical constants cannot be explicated in terms of this or any other notion of truth. Truth is not to be thought of as a construct out of assertibility. "Epistemic" or "antirealist" truth is a chimera. Truth is disquotational (or otherwise minimal) for the antirealist and there's an end to it. Instead, it is meaning that is epistemically constrained for anti-realists.

4.5.3 Truth-conditional Semantics and the Meanings of the Intuitionistic Constants

I have argued that Fitch's argument acts as a limitative result on intuitionistic logic, forcing antirealists to reject truth-conditional semantics, TCS. This by itself is no problem for antirealists who take themselves to be doing this, anyway. I now want to argue that there is a problem nonetheless and it won't go away: Intuitionistic languages are expressively inadequate when interpreted in terms of canonical assertibility conditions—*they systematically misrepresent possibilities that are quite intelligible from their own standpoint.*

Let us first ask in what sense the intuitionist rejects classical principles like that of the excluded middle or Markov's principle.[87] If one looks at the putative grounds for rejection, one finds that these take the form of reinterpreting the constants that figure in these principles *intuitionistically*, showing that *thus construed* they express principles that are not intuitionistically true. But that *by itself* can constitute no grounds for rejection of the classical readings of those constants since, as we saw in section 4.2.11, *thus construed*, not only are the principles not true intuitionistically, they are not true classically either. It would seem that in the very act of denying the doctrines the intuitionist does just change the subject.[88] Since the bearing confirming or infirming evidence has on an empirical statement's truth is not always determinable, it is an intelligible intuitionistic possibility that the warranting relation W that holds between states of information and statements is not a decidable one. How is the intuitionist to *express* this possibility in intuitionistic terms?

We want to formalize intuitionistically the thought that the relation W holding between states of information s and sentences p is or may not be decidable. We already know that we cannot prove intuitionistically that the statement "$W(\sigma, p)$ is undecidable," for then we would be able to transform that proof into a refutation of that very statement (since a proof of unprovability of p just is a refutation of p). But once we recognize this, the intuitionistic reading in terms of assertibility conditions becomes unsustainable. If we attempt to formalize this thought as:

(A) $\quad \Diamond \forall \sigma^* \forall \sigma [\neg(\nabla(\sigma^*, W(\sigma, p))) \,\&\, \neg(\nabla(\sigma^*, \neg(W(\sigma, p)))]$

with "$\nabla(\sigma^*, W(\sigma, p))$" to be read as "There is a warrant in σ^* for the claim that p is warranted in state of information σ," this leads to intuitionistic nonsense. (A) expresses the thought that it is possible that we have an effective method for transforming any ground for asserting $W(\sigma, p)$ supplied by σ^* into a proof of $\bot$ and also of transforming any refutation of $W(\sigma, p)$ supplied by σ^* into a proof of $\bot$. However, this possibility is incoherent: The first part contradicts the second. In similar fashion, in discussing the motivation for the intuitionist's refusal to assert LEM, Geoffrey Hellman notes that "what gives real force to intuitionism's stance"—that it is possible that at any stage of mathematical inquiry, exceptions to LEM can be found—cannot apparently be expressed either since this would be represented as:

$\Diamond \forall s \exists p (\neg \vdash_s (p \vee \neg p))$,

where "$\vdash_s$" means "is assertible at stage s."

However, this claim is to be interpreted intuitionistically as claiming that for all we know, we might actually have an EM for producing an inexhaustible supply of unsolved problems—hardly what we intended when we merely entertained the *possibility* of an inexhaustible supply of unsolved problems. The situation is even more serious for the intuitionist in that the very method used to "reject" classical principles—the method of "weak counterexamples"—again seems expressible only through nonconstructive universal quantification over a potentially infinite, noncanonically generable totality. Dummett explains that the method gains its force from the fact that we have a uniform way of constructing similar "counterexamples" for each unsolved problem of the same form. Since we can be virtually certain that the supply of unsolved problems will *never* dry up, we can conclude with equal certainty that the general statement will *never* be intuitionistically provable. Such a recognition that a universally quantified statement is unprovable does not amount to a proof of its negation....[89]

Hellman comments: "Indeed it does not! But were we to fomalize the 'never' intuitionistically, that is precisely what it would mean. And the very same problem—irrelevant commitment to a method of generating unsolved problems—just encountered in connection with (LEM) plagues us here." And he concludes his searching analysis:

These points confront intuitionism with a dilemma: either it is genuinely incapable of expanding its own framework to express the sorts of possibilities in question, in which case ... it cannot really motivate its own internal logic in a convincing way, it must even renounce some of its quasi-formal methods, and it cannot do justice to mathematics in a great many real scientific contexts; or it is capable of such an expansion, in which case we are led to suspect that it must acknowledge itself as part of a broader, essentially classical framework.[90]

Plainly, many of the expressive inadequacies of intuitionistic languages stem from the intuitionistic account of *quantification*. Indeed, since negation is definable in terms of "$\rightarrow$" and "$\perp$" and the intuitionistic conditional tacitly quantifies over states of information, it is plausible to believe that the problems might all be attributable to deficiencies in the clauses for the quantifiers. Dummett tells us that to understand the intuitionist's "$\forall$," we must realize that

it would be incorrect to characterize a proof of $\forall x A x$ merely as "a construction which, when applied to any number n, yields a proof of An"... since we should then have no right to suppose that we could effectively recognize a proof of $\forall x A x$ whenever we were presented with one. We therefore have to require explicitly that a construction is to count as a proof of $\forall x A x$ only if we can recognize it as yielding *for each* n a proof of An.[91]

So we understand $\forall x A x$ in the intended intuitionistic way when we interpret it as a statement about human recognitional capacities: that we are entitled to assert $\forall x A x$, in the case of number-theoretic statements, when we have the ability to recognize of a construction C that for each n it proves An. There is a doubt that can be motivated from the intuitionist's own standpoint as to whether this definition will do, however. An interesting example of Michael Hand's brings this out. For any two galaxies one cares to nominate, g_k and g_m, there is a fact of the matter intuitionistically as to whether the first is further from Earth than the second—the predicate $d(g_k, E) > d(g_m, E)$ can be assumed to be effectively decidable. So we have a "construction" C that proves either $d(g_k, E) > d(g_m, E)$ or $d(g_k, E) \leq d(g_m, E)$, and, given any such pair g_k and g_m we can recognize of that pair that C does prove this. Yet as Hand says:

> Despite [the predicate $d(g_k, E) > d(g_m, E)$'s] decidability, the claim that for each galaxy there is a further one from Earth may itself turn out not to be decidable.... For any two galaxies there is a fact to the matter as to whether the first is further from Earth than the second, yet there is no fact to the matter as to whether for every galaxy there is a further one.[92]

The universally quantified claim $\forall g_i \forall g_j (d(g_j, E) > d(g_i, E) \vee d(g_j, E) \leq d(g_i, E))$ would in those circumstances not be assertible despite the fact that we have a construction (we recognize as) proving for each pair g_k and g_m either $d(g_k, E) > d(g_m, E)$ or $d(g_k, E) \leq d(g_m, E)$. *Pace* Dummett, the problem with the intuitionistic account of the quantifiers just is that it transforms all quantified claims into statements about human epistemic capacities even when we wish to give expression to general claims about the possible limits of those very capacities. That we may remain in perpetual ignorance as to whether a given claim is or is not assertible, that we may not be able to determine in general whether our evidence warrants a given claim or not, that no state of information will ever warrant a given claim—these are all intelligible epistemic possibilities. Indeed, that we are not omniscient we take to be fact. *Yet these claims all seem to be inexpressible using the semantic framework of any assertibilist semantics. To give expression to such claims, a truth-conditional semantics seems to be required.*

These considerations collectively suggest that intuitionistic languages require a classical metalanguage in order to sustain the intended interpretation of their logical constants. The meanings of these constants must be given by their truth conditions, not their assertibility conditions. Any assertibility-conditional theory of meaning will face the same problem, irrespective of whether it uses intuitionistic or classical logic in its semantic theory. Yet the moral of Fitch's argument was that the antirealist thesis that all truths are knowable is incompatible with TCS. We thus have an argument against antirealism together with its eliminativist notion of truth that can be transformed into one in favor of truth-conditional semantics and a rich notion of truth.

III
Putnam's Internalism

5
The Internalist Critique of Realism

5.1 Hilary Putnam's Antiexternalist Arguments

Whereas the bearing of Michael Dummett's arguments on naturalistic realism is initially hard to discern, there is no comparable problem with Hilary Putnam's writings on the topic. Putnam attacks a doctrine he calls "metaphysical externalism" (ME) with an aim to overthrowing *naturalistic* versions of metaphysical realism, the only version of ME he thinks can be taken seriously. Alternatively, he refers to the view he wishes to attack as metaphysical realism.

If we are to have any hope of understanding Putnam's complex and changing conception of metaphysical realism, it is crucial to realize that he has never disputed the metaphysical determinacy of states of affairs for which we lack any evidence, states of affairs such as our earlier example, σ_s, of Socrates' sneezing in his sleep the night before he took the hemlock. True, he has flirted with the idea that truth is simply an idealization of rational acceptability. But for Putnam the determinacy of the past is just a fixed point of commonsense, one that any plausible metaphysics has to respect.

This respect of Putnam for metaphysical determinacy is why it is completely misleading to think of Putnam as an antirealist in Dummett's sense. Our conception of the past for Putnam is of a domain of facts that either hold or fail to hold irrespective of the ability of any particular person or generation to establish which they do. From Dummett's perspective, this makes Putnam a metaphysical realist about the past, although Putnam would not like the label "metaphysical" to be attached to his views here.

So what *does* Putnam object to in metaphysical realism then? The answer, I submit, is that it is the conjunction of metaphysical realism and naturalistic epistemology and semantics that he means to reject. When

Putnam eschews the title "metaphysical realist," he means to indicate that he is not a naturalistic metaphysical realist—that is, one who believes that all entities, properties, and relations can either be reduced to (or are supervenient on) items in the natural world or else must be eliminated from our total theory of the world. In particular, he means to target physicalism, the doctrine that all existents, properties and relations, are physical.

If this is correct, it ought to be possible to read his arguments either as refutations of naturalism or as refutations of metaphysical realism. In fact, I think that they are more plausible when read as the former, but it is clear that in Putnam's view, these doctrines of naturalism and realism are inextricably linked.

One way of putting Putnam's position, as I understand it, is this: There are certain properties, such as semantic, ethical, aesthetic ones for which not only do we not presently have any plausible account of how they could be derived from physical or biological ones, there almost certainly will never be such an account. Yet these properties are fundamental to our self-conception as thinking, rational beings who construct accurate representations of our world. We cannot conceivably "eliminate" them since they discharge an ineliminable normative role in our thinking about the world and our place in it. However, if naturalistic realism is true, these properties are as they are independently of our perceptions or conceptions of them—that is, of any representation we might have of them. They are wholly external to us. Hence, we do not even know that our representations of them are so much as reliable if this metaphysical externalist view is correct. How then can the naturalist realist explain how these properties discharge the normative role they manifestly do discharge in our theory constructions and evaluations? In a word, if naturalistic realism is true, the representation problem is insoluble.

Read in this light, Putnam's arguments appear formidable, and it is, just as in Dummett's case, a travesty that their full force has not been appreciated by naturalistic realists. There are, I think, three main arguments:

(1) The brains in a vat argument (BIVA)
(2) The argument from equivalent descriptions (EDA)
(3) The model-theoretic argument(s) (MTA)

There are many naturalistic realists who believe the MTA to be either question-begging or to lead to dialectical intractability caused by the clash of incommensurable intuitions. Others believe BIVA to be the most serious on the grounds that it is constitutive of realism that it takes seriously the possibility of global skepticism. I believe that the MTA is the most powerful argument against naturalistic realism of *any* so far produced. Unfortunately, owing largely to its complexity, it is also the most widely misunderstood. It is, on my interpretation, the purest attempt to show that naturalistic realism ought to be rejected on the grounds that such a metaphysical view makes it impossible to see how we could form the beliefs about the world that the naturalistic realist wants to endorse in the first place. It is true that some of these arguments can be "dismissed" by naturalistic realists, and if one thinks there is any value in a theoretical standpoint that refuses to examine in its own foundational assumptions, one might be quite impressed with some of these dismissals. So in this vein, BIVA can, without compromising realist principles in the slightest, be plausibly dismissed by the naturalistic realist. The EDA also can be given the same treatment. Moreover, the MTA itself can and has been rebutted in just this way. We will in the pages ahead catalog some of these realist rebuttals.

For my part, I cannot see the point of these "rebuttals" unless they are tempered by a genuine attempt to see what drives the arguments in question. Philosophy is the attempt to understand the world and our place in it. Of course anyone can dismiss an attack on their view by laying claim to assumptions they cannot in the end justify. But that is the way of ideological intransigence, the very antithesis of the desire to understand that should mark out the philosopher.

The task now is to outline briefly Putnam's alternative to naturalistic realism, or, as he prefers to call it, metaphysical externalism, before turning to his arguments against this view.

5.2 *Internalism and the God's-eye View*

I have argued that metaphysical realism is indeed a metaphysical thesis about the nature of the world and what it contains—that the world is as it is independently of how we conceive or perceive it to be. We saw how in Dummett's hands this thesis was transformed into a thesis in the theory of meaning and we saw that there was also a simple explanation for this transformation—Dummett believes quite generally that metaphysical claims are reducible to meaning-theoretic claims.

For Putnam as well, metaphysical realism is a complex doctrine embodying specific epistemological and semantic commitments. In rejecting this doctrine, Putnam originally opposed it to his alternative view, which he called "Internal Realism," a label he now regards as unfortunate. This in itself is interesting, I think, since many vigorously contested Putnam's justification for thinking of his view as a type of *realism* at all. Michael Devitt, for instance, claimed: "In a vivid and comprehensive way, Putnam has captured most of the intuitions that motivate antirealism."[1] What was it that Putnam meant to reject, though? Did he mean to reject the existence of the world as anything other than a mental construct in the fashion of idealists of yore? Surely not, even though Devitt for one interpreted him thus in alleging that internal realism was nothing other than a version of radical idealism.[2]

It is not my intention to delve into the exegetical niceties here, but one telling point against any such interpretation is that, even though he now confesses to having subscribed to a "residue of idealism" in his *Reason, Truth, and History*, in his hope that truth could be reduced to idealized rational acceptability,[3] Putnam's commitment to the fundamental soundness of basic common-sense intuitions about the world has never wavered, as his written "Responses" to Gary Ebbs and David Anderson demonstrate.[4] Nowhere is this clearer than in his well-known example of Lizzie Borden:

We certainly regard the statement that Lizzie Borden murdered her parents with an axe as one that has a determinate truth-value (either she did or she didn't administer the famous "forty whacks"). But the reason isn't that we could believe that if we carried out certain investigations, we could warrantedly assert now that she did or she didn't, nor is it that we believe that in some ideal state of scientific inquiry in the future it will be possible to warrant one claim or the other. (Lizzie Borden may well be forgotten and all records obliterated in the remote future.) I have repeatedly argued that any theory of truth that makes the truth or falsity of a historical claim depend on whether that claim can be decided in the future is radically misguided.[5]

In Dummett's view, this makes Putnam a *metaphysical realist* about the past: Putnam believes that there is a fact of the matter as to whether Lizzie Borden administered the famous forty whacks or not. One or the other of these events is contained in the world's past even though we may never be able to determine which. This seems to commit Putnam to a verification-transcendent notion of truth. How then could he have ever thought, if this is, as he claims, what he has always thought, that truth could be identified with some construct out of rational acceptability? Putnam's response is interesting:

On the other hand, the fact that the corresponding present tense claim, the claim that Lizzie Borden is now murdering her parents with an axe, if it had been made by someone in that house at that time, is one that would have been either established or ruled out by the perceived facts has everything to do with the possession of a truth-value by the past-tense (and also by the future tense) version of the same statement. For one of the norms underlying our rational inquiries, to use Ebbs' language, is that if a claim has a truth-value when made in the present tense, then the corresponding past tense and future tense versions also have a truth-value. To give up that norm would be to regard past generations as little more than constructions out of present and future evidence. (In effect, it would be to adopt a species of solipsism with respect to past human beings.)[6]

The view endorsed in his internal realist phase must then have been that truth is circumscribed by what human beings across time would recognize as true under sufficiently good epistemic conditions. This indeed is precisely how Crispin Wright interprets even Putnam's most recent views. However, I shall argue in section 7.2 that Wright's exegesis of those recent views is not correct and that the view he formulates, which I call new internalism, is unstable. I think it is correct, though, that this represents what Putnam was at least aspiring to in his "internal realist" period.

What can we say about the conjunction of the two theses below?

(I) The world determinately either contains e or does not contain e irrespective of whether we could ever have any means of deciding which it does.

(II) The world's containing e or not containing e is something that some human beings at some time could have decided.

I think we can say this: (I) and (II) are manifestly compatible with metaphysical realism. These theses in no way distinguish a (nondisquotational) notion of truth as epistemically constrained (Putnam's "residue of idealism") for the simple reason that they distinguish no (nondisquotational) notion of truth at all. In fact, I do not believe that Putnam ever had a settled conception of *how* truth was to be defined in terms of rational acceptability. Rather, I think he believed such a view to be the only live option once one rejected the idea of truth as correspondence with an external reality rationally impervious to human conceptions of it and rejected also the notion of truth as merely disquotational or otherwise minimal.

To be sure, he did, in *Reason, Truth, and History* adhere to the view that "truth is an idealization of rational acceptability. We speak as if there were such things as epistemically ideal conditions, and we call a statement 'true' if it would be justified under such conditions."[7] However, Putnam soon came to disavow the gloss he had put on "epistemically ideal conditions" in that book:

> "Epistemically ideal conditions," of course, are like "frictionless planes": we cannot really attain epistemically ideal conditions, or even be absolutely certain that we have come sufficiently close to them. But frictionless planes cannot really be attained either, and yet talk of frictionless planes has "cash value" because we can approximate them to a very high degree of approximation.[8]

So what exactly did Putnam think was wrong with truth as correspondence to reality? What was wrong with "metaphysical externalism"? It was the burden of Putnam's internal realism that metaphysical realism was incoherent. But what he meant by "incoherent," he tells us in retrospect, is that the metaphysical realist's distinctive claims could not be made out. Every attempt to say what the metaphysical realist wanted to say ended in failure: All the metaphysical realist's substantive claims could be endorsed by an internal realist.

One natural response for a metaphysical realist to make to this criticism is that since any such equivalence is symmetric, the reason for it may rather be that internal realism just is a version of metaphysical realism, one that is a little optimistic epistemologically. Putnam's reply is this:

> The main point was that metaphysical realism cannot even be intelligibly stated. I expressed this by saying that metaphysical realism is "incoherent." I did not mean by that that it is inconsistent in a deductive logical sense, but rather that when we try to make the very vague claims of the metaphysical realist precise, we find that they become compatible with strong forms of "antirealism." Thus the attempts at clear formulation never succeed in capturing the content of "metaphysical realism" because there is no real content there to be captured.[9]

I am puzzled by these comments. To be sure, metaphysical realism is a vague thesis—ineradicably so, in my view. That is because of the generality of its content. Yet the thesis of metaphysical realism can be intelligibly stated. I have done so many times throughout the book, a particular instance of it occurring at (I) above. Thesis (I) is precisely what the Dummettian global antirealist denies when he denies that the world determinately either contains the event of Lizzie Borden murdering her parents with an axe or determinately does not contain that event. The conclusion seems inescapable: *Putnam cannot mean by "metaphysical realism" what we have been meaning.*

So what does he mean? Putnam tells us this:

> In "Realism and Reason," I argue that certain realistic theses, first formulated by Richard Boyd and defended by me in *Meaning and the Moral Sciences*, could, in principle, be accepted by an antirealist as well, and hence cannot, as they stand, express what the metaphysical realist is trying to say. Those theses, taken without commitment to either the particular metaphysical realist way of understanding them or the antirealist way of understanding them, I referred to as "internal realism." To be sure, I did accept "internal realism," so understood; but "internal realism" was not a term for my new position; it was rather a term for a kind of scientific realism I had already accepted for some years, for a position (I now argued) both realists and antirealists could accept. (I agree with Ebbs that the connotations of the word "internal" have proved to be unfortunate; which is why in later writings, I have tended to speak of "pragmatic realism," or simply "realism with a small 'r'." The reason I used the term "internal," by the way, is that I saw this sort of realism as *science's* explanation of the success of science, rather than as a metaphysical explanation of the success of science.)[10]

This then was the core of *internal realism* for Putnam: *the theses common to realism and antirealism.* What was the "metaphysical realism" he meant to reject, then? He goes on to explain this in the passage quoted immediately above:

> According to Boyd (and myself in the Locke Lectures), metaphysical realism can be formulated as an overarching empirical theory about the success of science, namely the (meta-)theory that the success of the mature physical sciences is explained by the fact that the terms used in those sciences typically refer, and that the statements that constitute the basic assumptions of those theories are typically approximately true.[11]

The problem with this formulation, in my view, is simple—it is not metaphysical realism that Putnam is discussing here but *scientific* realism. It is easy to conflate the two when the version of metaphysical realism one is interested in investigating is a naturalistic one, since naturalistic metaphysical realists tend to be scientific realists. However, one can be a metaphysical realist without being a scientific realist and still consistently with accept a broadly naturalistic epistemology—witness Bas van Fraassen who is agnostic over the question of whether theoretical (i.e., non-observational) terms refer and, though this is controversial, Quine who is uniformly instrumentalist in his attitude to the theoretical posits of science. Van Fraassen and Quine do accept, on my understanding of their views, that there is a world out there whose nature is independent of human conceptions and perceptions of it. But they are not scientific realists—van Fraassen, at least, manifestly is not.

Putnam's novelty, in his internal realist period, then, according to this interpretation, was the discovery that an influential argument for scientific realism, which he had himself accepted and helped refine and promulgate, was in fact compatible with metaphysical antirealism. By way of contrast, it was already well attested that scientific antirealisms (such as constructive empiricism and instrumentalism) are clearly compatible with metaphysical realism. If this is correct, though, as an interpretation of what was driving internal realism, and we have Putnam's own testimony to back it up, the most that we should conclude is not that metaphysical realism is incoherent or that its distinctive claims cannot even be formulated, but rather that a highly influential argument for *scientific* realism wasn't cogent. Internal realism was not a distinctive metaphysical view at all—it had nothing to say about metaphysics in its opposition to the standard scientific realist argument that defined it. A "residue of idealism" only managed to creep in through the back door, so to speak, in the view (or, more accurately, the hope) that truth was to be reduced somehow to idealized rational acceptability. Can this be *all* there was to "internal realism"?

Surely not. In fact, I think there is a deeper reason why during his "internal realist" phase Putnam believed (and still believes in his newer "common-sense realist" incarnation) that metaphysical realism is *incoherent*. This has to do with *the nature of our conceptual involvement with the world*. The metaphysical realist, according to Putnam, assumes that the conceptual schemes we deploy to make sense of the world are somehow dictated to us by that very world. There is such a thing as the God's-eye point of view, as Bernard Williams calls it, or the view from nowhere, as Thomas Nagel describes it, which we cognitively appropriate in our most successful and presumptively true theories about the world. It is the burden of his equivalent descriptions argument (see sec. 5.4) to demonstrate the incoherence of this idea.

Hence, metaphysical realism for Putnam is not simply the thesis of metaphysical determinacy that we have been taking it to be, following Dummett. It is a much richer and more contentious doctrine. Putnam tells us in chapter 3 of *Reason, Truth, and History* that it consists of three claims:

1. The world consists of some fixed totality of mind-independent objects.

2. There is exactly one true and complete description of "the way the world is."

3. Truth involves some sort of correspondence relation between words or thought-signs and external things and sets of things.

The conjunction of these theses is intelligible only if one assumes a God's-eye point of view, Putnam contends. Internal realism connoted the denial of all three claims above:

1*. There is no fixed totality of mind-independent objects.

2*. There are a number of true descriptions of "the way the world is."

3*. Truth is an idealization of warranted assertibility or rational acceptability rather than some sort of correspondence relation between our words or thought-signs and external (sets of) things.

What should we make of Putnam's richer requirements for full metaphysical realism? We have already seen that metaphysical realists need not be saddled with a correspondence theory of truth. So (3) is not obligatory for the realist. Claim (1), on the other hand, surely is a thesis no metaphysical realist can gainsay. That leaves (2). Is a metaphysical realist committed to the claim that there is exactly one true and complete description of "the way the world is"?

I don't see why. Why couldn't a metaphysical realist allow the possibility that the world is simply too rich in structure and complexity for any one language or theory to countenance? Perhaps the world is infinitely complex, even at the microphysical level? If so, it may just be our lot to aspire in our theories to a number of true partial descriptions of "the way the world is" with no genuine prospect of ever integrating these into a single "final theory." So my assessment is that Putnam is requiring more of the metaphysical realist than is reasonable.

On the other hand, Putnam was clearly responding to the epistemological and semantic worries that attend acceptance of metaphysical realism. Indeed, that it was precisely the representation problem that was bothering him is manifest from early on. Witness his words in his introduction to his collection *Realism and Reason: Philosophical Papers*, volume 3:

The issue that first made me uncomfortable with my hard-line "realist" position was one with which every philosopher is familiar: the notion that our words "correspond" to determinate objects (where the notion of an "object" is thought to have a determinate reference which is independent of conceptual scheme) had long seemed problematical, although I did not see any alternative to accepting it.... What are those problems?

As far back as Berkeley and Kant it had been pointed out that the notion of a "correspondence" is difficult once one becomes even a little bit psychologically sophisticated. If one is not psychologically sophisticated, then it appears easy to say how we "put our words in correspondence with objects." We teach a child a word, say "table," by showing him the object and by using the word in various ways in the presence of that object (or, rather, kind of object) until the child comes to "associate" the word with the object. In some sense, this is undeniably true. (As an ordinary language remark about, say, pedagogy, it is unproblematical; for, in such a context, the notions of "object" and of "showing someone an object" and of "associating a sound with a kind of object" are all taken for granted, as part of the linguistic background we assume.)

However, psychology is something that came on the scene at the same time as modern philosophy. Early philosophical psychologists—for example, Hume—pointed out that we do not literally have the object in our minds. The mind never compares an image or word with an object, but only with other images, words, beliefs, judgments etc. The idea of a comparison of words or mental representations with objects is a senseless one. So how can a determinate correspondence between words or mental representations and external objects ever be singled out? How is the correspondence supposed to be fixed?[12]

It is this last question, I maintain, that constitutes Putnam's problem with metaphysical realism—all of his arguments against metaphysical realism can be read in one way or another as attempts to show that *if metaphysical realism is correct, the representation problem is simply insoluble.* It is to the first of those arguments that we now turn.

5.3 Brains in a Vat?

Much has been written about Putnams's brains in a vat argument (BIVA)—too much to possibly review. I do not intend to try. I simply wish to show that even on the assumption that the argument is sound a naturalistic realist has some plausible initial responses to it. I will then investigate whether the argument really is sound.

BIVA attacks an externalist theory of reference and truth on which the contents of our thoughts are determined in part by the relations they bear to a mind-independent world. It is, note, not externalism per se that is under attack—to the contrary, this doctrine, for Putnam, when properly understood (i.e., freed from its entanglement with MR) is both true and important; it is its admixture with the incoherent notion of a mind-independent world graciously and miraculously supplying for us exactly the right referents for our words (or mental representations) that the argument seeks to undermine.

What BIVA aims to show is that, *given externalism,* MR, committed as it is to the real possibility of our being brains in a vat, entails that we could not have the thought that we are brains in a vat. Therefore, MR is incoherent. Accordingly, there are two obvious responses to such an attempted reductio of MR that can be made from the outset without examining its detail:

1. Give up externalism; or
2. deny that MR is committed to the genuine possibility of our being brains in a vat.

The reason that naturalistic realism is better placed than more "metaphysical" versions of MR should be clear: Both (1) and (2) can be motivated from the naturalistic perspective.

Before seeing how (1) and (2) can be motivated by naturalism, let me briefly rehearse the BIVA: Externalism holds that the referents of our words (or mental representations generally) is determined partially by contingent relations we have to the world. Consequently, were we to be envatted brains we could not possibly mean by the word "brain" or "vat" what unenvatted folk mean, and the thought we pondered in posing the question "Am I a brain in a vat?" could not possibly be the thought the unenvatted think when they pose the homophonic query in English. Yet MR entails that we could indeed be brains in a vat. As we have just shown that were we to be so we could not even entertain this as a possibility, MR is incoherent.

No doubt this rendition of the argument lacks subtlety. The point, though, is that irrespective of how the finer details go, both (1) and (2) above represent responses that can be motivated from the naturalistic viewpoint. Consider (1). Can a naturalistic realist really give up externalism without reinvoking mysterious Fregean senses or other undesirable intensional entities mediating between us and a mind-independent external world?

Of course. We already know how. Such a realist might be a semantic minimalist. Truth and reference might be mere disquotational devices—in saying things like "'cat' refers to cats," we're simply registering our dispositions to call everything we consider sufficiently cat-like "cat." The relation between words and their referents and sentences and states of affairs will then be a "logical" or at least an "immanent" one—one that is, in Michael Resnick's words, "a consequence of the syntax for the object language, the listlike definitions of name and predicate reference and the logic (set theory) of the metalanguage."[13]

Surrendering externalism in this way clearly undercuts the BIVA, for even if we were brains in a vat, if minimalism is right, "'vat' refers to vats" would still register our disposition to call everything we consider sufficiently vatlike "vat." It is just that this disposition will have a very different ground from the one it has in our real, unenvatted circumstances. So "'vat' refers to vats" comes out true in the counterfactual envatted case just as in the actual unenvatted case. Moreover, "we might be brains in a vat" will still express the genuine possibility that we might be brains in a vat. At least, it needs an argument other than the one Putnam gives to show that it doesn't. Hence the BIVA fails.

Consider (2): This is the option of denying, on naturalistic grounds, that it is a genuine possibility that we might be brains in a vat. This has to be done without compromising realism. Can it be done? I think it can. Daniel Dennett has indicated how. He imagines that the brain in the vat is being given impulses leading it to think it is housed in a body that is relaxing on its back on the beach. The "brain-nappers" who, predictably, are evil scientists, then have to try to convince you, whose brain they've napped, that "you are not a mere beach potato, but an agent capable of engaging in some form of activity in the world."[14]

How could they convince you of this? They seek to do this by removing the "paralysis" of your phantom finger to let you have a sensation as of wiggling your finger in the sand:

> Suddenly, they are faced with a problem that will quickly get out of hand, for just how the sand will feel depends on just how you decide to move your finger. The problem of calculating the proper feedback, generating or composing it, and then presenting it to you in real time is going to be computatationally intractable on even the fastest computer, and if the evil scientists decide to solve the real-time problem by pre-calculating and "canning" all the possible responses for playback, they will just trade one insoluble problem for another: there are too many possibilities to store. In short, our evil scientists will be swamped by a *combinatorial explosion* as soon as they give you any genuine exploratory powers in this imaginary world.[15]

Possibilities that require combinatorial explosions, that would consume exponential computational time if actually implemented, are a fortiori not *real* possibilities for the naturalist.

The antirealist might respond that Dennett's reply begs the question against the skeptic by presuming that our theory is correct in its prediction of combinatorial explosion. But this is a bad reply. Mathematical considerations alone force the conclusion that there will be such an explosion, given the tree of possible choices. If the BIVA supporter wants to claim that those mad scientists (or an all-powerful evil genie) might have fooled us about the mathematical facts, good luck to him. In doing so he abnegates any claim to being taken seriously: If we do not assume fundamental mathematics and logic the very hypothesis that the skeptic wants to pose becomes inexpressible. We really *would* then lack any reason to think that any intelligible hypothesis at all either has been or could be expressed by the sequence of words: "We might be brains in a vat."

I cannot imagine that Putnam himself would endorse the idea that we might be wrong about the logico-mathematical facts.[16] I think his own response to Dennett would be more subtle. He would want to deny, I think, that *Dennett's* reply really is available to a *metaphysical* realist. On his view MR and naturalism are incompatible. Indeed, that is the real burden of his model-theoretic argument (MTA). It is a moot question at this stage whether MR and naturalism are incompatible. I think we have seen enough, though, to be confident that the BIVA does not pose the threat to *naturalistic* realism that it poses to the more "transcendental" versions of realism.

Is Putnam's BIVA sound? The task now is to evaluate Putnam's "internal realist" response to the skeptic, according to which we can know that we are not brains in a vat since if we were we could not have the thought that we were. To do this, we will need a more precise formulation of the argument. Anthony Brueckner has provided one:[17]

	(1) Either I'm a BIV or I'm not a BIV.	LEM
2	(2) I'm not a BIV.	A
2 Ext	(3) I speak English and not Vattish.	2
2, Ext	(4) My utterances of "I'm a BIV" are not true.	3, Ext
5	(5) I'm a BIV.	A
5, Ext	(6) I speak Vattish and not English.	5, Ext
5, Ext	(7) My "BIV" tokens refer to BIV-images.	6, Ext
5, Ext	(8) My "BIV" tokens do not refer to BIVs.	7, Ext
Ext	(9) My utterances of "I'm a BIV" are true only if my "BIV" tokens refer to BIVs.	Ext
5, Ext	(10) My utterances of "I'm a BIV" are not true.	8, 9 Modus Tollens
Ext	(11) My utterances of "I'm a BIV" are not true.	1,2,4,5,10 ∨ E
T_D, Ext	(12) It is not the case that I am a BIV.	11 T_D

In this formulation of Brueckner's reconstruction of the BIVA, "Ext" refers to externalism, the thesis that the referents of our words are determined by contingent facts outside our heads, facts about the world and about how we are situated within it, about the contexts in which we utter our words and the linguistic community to which we belong, and so on. A background assumption is that "I" refers to a putative English-speaker who will be speaking English if and only if he is not speaking Vattish, and which language he is speaking will, as prescribed by externalism, depend on whether he is a brain in a vat or not—if he is a BIV, he will be speaking Vattish, if not, English. Finally, "T_D" refers to a disquotational principle that Brueckner argues for:

(T_D) My utterances of "I am a BIV" are true if I am a BIV.

Brueckner sees Putnam arguing to his conclusion that he knows he is not a brain in a vat by arguing that he knows that both (T_D) and externalism are true and that the conclusion at (10) above, that he is not a brain in a vat, follows from these theses. If we are unpersuaded by this argument, which of the principles (T_D) or Ext should we take issue with? The argument appears unquestionably valid with the conclusion that I am not a brain in a vat resting solely on (T_D) and Ext as hypotheses.

However, "appears" is the operative word. It is not at all obvious that some of the alleged consequences of externalism are genuine consequences of it. In particular, lines (7) and (9) look to be problematic. Why should the fact that, *were* I to be a brain in a vat, and my tokens of "brain in a vat" would fail to refer to brains in vats for want of the appropriate causal and contextual links to such entities, bring it about that these tokens *do* refer to "BIVs-in-the-image"? Why should we believe that a solipsistic symbol-manipulator has contentful thoughts in the first place? Absent a genuine external linguistic community with a genuine external history of use for the symbols the BIV finds itself crunching and genuine extracerebral causal connections to at least some genuine extracerebral entities, any claims about semantic content can only look brittle from the externalist point of view. Worries about the contents of a brain in a vat's words or mental symbols ought be put to one side, though, since they undermine the whole point of Putnam's argument, which is to respond to the skeptic who claims that we have no way of telling whether we are, as we think we are, flesh and blood humans thinking thoughts that are largely true or massively deluded brains in vats, thinking the same thoughts or else thoughts that we cannot distinguish from the thoughts we take ourselves to be entertaining. Henceforth we shall simply assume that there is something it is like to be a brain in a vat and that such creatures do have the power to represent their world in thought and language.

But the world they would represent would be their world. So why, if I were to suffer the misery of being a brain in a vat speaking Vat-English, should my utterances of "I am a brain in a vat" not come out as true expressions of the thought that I am a BIV-in-the-image? If, as a brain in a vat, I thought in a language of thought—and what *other than the manipulation of neural symbols* could thought possibly consist in for a brain in a vat?—and my LOT was Vattish then, if the correct semantics for Vattish were to assign BIVs-in-the-image as the referent for my expression "brain in a vat," how *could* my utterance "I am a brain in a vat" express any thought other than the true thought that *I am a BIV-in-the-image*?

In short, (9) seems to require us to supply an *English* semantics for *Vat-English* expressions. Yet externalism itself suggests this demand is incoherent. We must therefore take care to specify which language we have in mind when we evaluate the truth value of my utterances in each of the possible scenarios—BIV and non-BIV.

So let's recast the argument with these points in mind:

	(1) Either I'm a BIV or I'm not a BIV.	LEM
2	(2) I'm not a BIV.	A
2 Ext	(3) I speak English and not Vattish.	2, Ext
2 Ext	(4) My "I" tokens refer to me, my "BIV" tokens refer to brains in vats.	3 Ext
2, Ext	(5) My utterances of the English sentence "I'm a BIV" are true iff I am a BIV.	3, Ext
2, Ext	(6) My utterances of the English sentence "I'm a BIV" are not true.	4, 5 ↔ E
7	(7) I'm a BIV.	A
7, Ext	(8) I speak Vattish and not English.	7, Ext
8, Ext	(9) My "I" tokens refer to me-in-the-image, my "BIV" tokens refer to brains-in-vats-in-the-image.	8, Ext
8, Ext	(10) My utterances of the Vattish sentence "I'm a BIV" are true iff I-in-the-image am a BIV-image.	9, Ext

Here things grind to a stop. To derive the desired subconclusion that my utterances of "I am a BIV" are not true from the left-hand disjunct above, we need it to be the case that I-in-the-image am *not* a BIV-image. Yet "I-in-the-image" is merely one of the poor envatted Brain's *representations*—that is, it *is* a brain-in-the-vat-image! So although I cannot express the true thought that I am a brain in a vat, in my envatted predicament, I can and do express a *different* true thought every time I utter the words or think the symbols "I am a brain in a vat"—the thought that the representation I refer to by "I" is but one of those representations generated by the brain that, epistemically inaccessible though this be to me, I in reality am. Brueckner's reconstruction of Putnam's argument therefore collapses. It cannot possibly support the conclusion that my utterances of "I am a brain in a vat" are not true irrespective of whether I am a BIV or a non-BIV, since precisely the opposite conclusion can legitimately be drawn from the assumption that I am a BIV. Of course, the fact that this particular reconstruction fails does not show that there might not be a sound argument from externalist premises to the conclusion that I am not a brain in a vat. So we need to examine the underlying hypotheses that are thought to sustain this conclusion. There are two of these: (1) externalism, and the (2) disquotation principle:

(T_D) My utterances of "I am a BIV" are true if I am a BIV.

It is tempting to think that externalism and disquotation might pull in opposite directions. Externalism prescribes that there are substantive causal and contextual constraints on reference and truth that disquotationalists precisely deny: For them, all that it takes for the sentence "I am a brain in a vat" to be true is for me to be a brain in a vat; causal/contextual constraints on this sentence are simply irrelevant since the connection between my being a brain in a vat and the sentence "I am a brain in a vat" being true is *logical*, not causal or contextual. At least one writer, Stephen Leeds, has been persuaded by some such line of reasoning to seek out some moral about the nature of truth in the failure of the Brueckner argument.[18]

Briefly, Leeds's view is that where an externalist theory of truth will make it plausible that my utterances of "I am a brain in a vat" are not true and make it dubious that my utterances of "I am a brain in a vat" are true if I am a brain in a vat, a disquotationalist theory of truth will do precisely the opposite. Leeds sees Putnam and others responding to this by attempting to develop a conception of truth distinct from both the causal/contextualist one and the disquotationalist alternative. Such a conception would have to be a substantive one. But, according to Leeds, any such notion is just a chimera from the naturalistic point of view: Either truth is as the externalist says it is, truth$_C$, or truth is as the disquotationalist says it is, truth$_D$. *Tertium non Datur.*

We can agree with part of this view. We have already seen at (10) above that my utterances of the Vattish sentence "I'm a BIV" are true iff I-in-the-image am a BIV-image. This certainly looks to be incompatible with disquotationalist principles, for a disquotationalist condition governing reference would be:

(R$_D$) In my utterances of "I am a brain in a vat," "I" refers to me, "brain" refers to brains, "in" refers to the inclusion relation, "vat" refers to vats.

This looks flatly inconsistent with (9) above, according to which my "I" tokens refer to me-in-the-image, and my "BIV" tokens refer to brains-in-vats-in-the-image. If we call this latter referential assignment (R$_C$), then (R$_C$) and (R$_D$) are, apparently, inconsistent with one another. Moreover, were we to replace (R$_C$) with (R$_D$) at line (10) of the above proof, perhaps we could accomplish what eluded us before—a derivation of the desired conclusion that my utterances of "I am a brain in a vat" are not true? Let's see:

	(1) Either I'm a BIV or I'm not a BIV.	LEM
2	(2) I'm not a BIV.	A
2 Ext	(3) I speak English and not Vat-English.	2, Ext
2 Ext	(4) My "I" tokens refer to me, my "BIV" tokens refer to brains in vats.	3 Ext
2, Ext	(5) My utterances of the English sentence "I'm a BIV" are true iff I am a BIV.	3, Ext
2, Ext	(6) My utterances of the English sentence "I'm a BIV" are not true.	2, 5 ↔ E
7	(7) I'm a BIV.	A
7, Ext	(8) I speak Vattish and not English.	7, Ext
7, Ext	(9) My "I" tokens refer to me-in-the-image, my "BIV" tokens refer to brains-in-vats-in-the-image.	8, Ext

7, R_D	(10) My utterances of the Vattish sentence "I'm a BIV" are true only if my "I" tokens refer to me and my "BIV" tokens refer to BIVs.	7, R_D
7, R_D, Ext	(11) My utterances of the Vattish sentence "I am a BIV" are not true.	9, 10 MT

It might be thought that we could drop the restriction to the language I am actually speaking, since if I'm a BIV I cannot speak English, and if I am not a BIV, I cannot speak Vattish. So why not simply say that in both cases my utterances of "I am a BIV" are not true simpliciter if the qualification "in English," "in Vattish" drops out as redundant? This would then permit us to derive the same conclusion in each of the subderivations and allow us to reach the desired end in the following way:

	(1) Either I'm a BIV or I'm not a BIV.	LEM
2	(2) I'm not a BIV.	A
2 Ext	(3) I speak English and not Vat-English.	2, Ext
2 Ext	(4) My "I" tokens refer to me, my "BIV" tokens refer to brains in vats.	3 Ext
2, Ext	(5) My utterances of "I'm a BIV" are true iff I am a BIV.	3, Ext
2, Ext	(6) My utterances of "I'm a BIV" are not true.	2, 5 ↔ E
7	(7) I'm a BIV.	A
7, Ext	(8) I speak Vattish and not English.	7, Ext
7, Ext	(9) My "I" tokens refer to me-in-the-image, my "BIV" tokens refer to brains-in-vats-in-the-image.	8, Ext
7, R_D	(10) My utterances of "I'm a BIV" are true only if my "I" tokens refer to me and my "BIV" tokens refer to BIVs.	7, R_D
7, R_D Ext	(11) My utterances of "I am a BIV" are not true.	9, 10 MT
Ext, R_D	(12) My utterances of "I am a BIV" are not true.	1, 2, 6, 7, 11 ∨ E
T_D Ext, R_D	(13) I am not a BIV.	12, T_D

However, if that is the intended argument, it is just as flawed as the original. There are now two different and apparently incompatible notions of reference and truth in play, not one—disquotational truth and reference and externalist truth and reference—and for the argument to succeed *both* are required since the crucial modus tollens transition from (9) and (10) to (11) cannot be effected otherwise:

(9) My "I" tokens refer$_C$ to me-in-the-image, my "BIV" tokens refer$_C$ to brains-in-vats-in-the-image.

(10) My utterances of "I'm a BIV" are true$_D$ only if my "I" tokens refer$_D$ to me and my "BIV" tokens refer$_D$ to BIVs.

But then what notion of truth is in use in the conclusion?

(11) My utterances of "I am a BIV" are not true.

Leeds's analysis would thus appear to be vindicated.

In fact, I think this analysis is flawed and appears plausible only because we have studiously avoided discussing a crucial issue: *In what language is the argument itself supposed to be cast?* We have used the terms "true" and "refers" with gay abandon without ever specifying the metalanguage in which they are formulated. The answer to our question, we suppose, is (isn't it?): *English*.

If the argument is formulated in English, then we have no straightforward way of applying disquotational principles governing truth and reference to Vattish. For disquotational truth is defined only for languages one understands. So we need a translation manual between English and Vattish that will involve systematically matching English expressions with Vattish expressions. Thus where Vattish talks of "brains in vats," our translation manual will replace each occurrence of this Vattish expression with the English "brains-in-vats-in-the-image," and it will replace each occurrence of the Vattish "I" with the English "I-in-the-image," and so on.

The upshot is that our two disquotational principles governing reference and truth are erroneous when applied to Vattish since, as stated, they apply only to reference-in-English and truth-in-English and have no application to Vattish in the absence of any translation manual:

(ER$_D$) In my English utterances of "I am a brain in a vat," "I" refers$_D$ to me, "brain" refers$_D$ to brains, "in" refers$_D$ to the inclusion relation, "vat" refers$_D$ to vats.

(ET$_D$) My English utterances of "I am a BIV" are true$_D$ iff I am a BIV.

Extending these disquotational principles to Vattish results in extended disquotational principles governing reference-in-Vattish and truth-in-Vattish:

(VR$_{ED}$) In my Vattish utterances of "I am a brain in a vat," "I" refers$_{ED}$ to me-in-the-image, "brain" refers$_{ED}$ to brains-in-the-image, "in" refers$_{ED}$ to the inclusion image relation, "vat" refers$_{ED}$ to vats-in-the-image.

(VT$_{ED}$) My English utterances of "I am a brain-in-a-vat" are true$_{ED}$ iff I-in-the-image am a brain-in-the-vat-in-the-image.

But then (10) in the argument above is revealed as flawed:

(10) My utterances of "I'm a BIV" are true only if my "I" tokens refer to me and my "BIV" tokens refer to brains in vats.

So BIVA, on this way of formulating it, is quite unsalvageable. Some analogue of (10) is surely required to prove the crucial lemma that if I am a brain in a vat, my utterances of "I am a brain in a vat" are uniformly false. Nothing interesting about the nature of truth follows from these investigations other than that it cannot be purely disquotational, that is, undefined for any language that I do not understand, if the background metalanguage in which the argument is cast is English. Neither could it be purely disquotational if the background metalanguage were to be Vattish.

Can we tell which language the argument is formulated in? No. If we could, we would know whether we are brains in a vat or not. But parallel considerations governing the assumption that the metalanguage is English will suffice to show that if the metalanguage is, in fact, Vattish, the subderivation of the conclusion that my utterances of "I am a brain in a vat" are not true will not go through if I am not a brain in a vat.

5.4 Equivalent Descriptions

We now turn to the equivalent descriptions argument (EDA). In Putnam's view, metaphysical realism (MR) entails that there is exactly one true theory of the world. MR is therefore incompatible with the existence of equivalent true descriptions of the world that are inconsistent, inconsistent from the metaphysical realist's point of view, that is. As against MR's "totalizing" tendency to produce the *one true description of the world*, we should therefore admit a *plurality* of possible descriptions of the world.

Putnam is aware that the realist will try to dismiss any inconsistency between theories that are in some sense equivalent as merely apparent, holding that when genuinely equivalent theories T and T^* *appear* to conflict, this conflict can always be resolved by demonstrating either that they are merely different versions of the same theory or that within some more comprehensive theory the appearance of incompatibility can be satisfactorily accounted for.

What sense of "equivalence" is in play then? Putnam tells us that he has in mind *cognitive* equivalence—it is the notion of cognitively equivalent theories that are nonetheless incompatible that raises problems for the MR thesis of *the one true theory of the world*. This would be fine, except that Putnam tells us that he is particularly interested in "theoretical systems which are, taken literally, incompatible." To the realist who tries to demonstrate that prima facie incompatible T and T^* are simply different formulations of the same theory, he replies: "the realist who does gloss his belief in one true theory in such a way is admitting that theories which are different at the level of "surface grammar," and even at the level of mathematical and logical equivalence—i.e., which are different and even incompatible, in literal meaning—may simultaneously be true."[19]

The notion of literal meaning is then being called on to bear some theoretical weight in Putnam's EDA. The realist will claim, from the outset, that it is simply impossible that logically incompatible theories could both be true. Putnam thinks that he can confute him by producing genuinely equivalent theories that are from the realist's perspective recognizably logically incompatible. After surveying and rejecting on Quinean grounds Reichenbach's attempt to provide a probabilistic criterion of cognitive equivalence, Putnam apparently concludes that the whole notion of cognitive equivalence cannot be informatively characterized. So he proposes an alternative: Two theories T and T^* are equivalent, Putnam suggests, if we can interpret each theory in the other and they each explain the same phenomena. Putnam's explication of equivalence combines a *formal* requirement—that T and T^* be mutually *relatively interpretable*, with the *informal* requirement that precisely the same phenomena are *explained* by both.[20] Putnam turns to relativity theory to provide his examples of logically incompatible but nonetheless equivalent (in the newly defined sense) theories: Suppose we have two descriptions A and B of two events, X and Y, framed relative to two different inertial systems S_A and S_B. X might be an explosion on the moon, and Y might be an explosion on Mars, for example. Suppose that description A says that X and Y were simultaneous and description B denies just this, claiming that X preceded Y.

What are we to make of this description? Just what Reichenbach and most other philosophers of science made of it, one would have thought: that "the incompatibility between the sentences 'X and Y happened simultaneously' and 'X and Y did not happen simultaneously' is only a *real* incompatibility when these sentences are uttered by an observer in the same frame...."[21]

However, this is not *all* Putnam makes of it. He goes on to gloss Reichenbach's view as: "Description A and Description B are equivalent, then, in the sense of being *notational variants* of each other." He then proceeds to argue against Reichenbach's use of the idea of notational variance and the assumption of a neutral observation language to which Reichenbach appealed in formulating his idea of coordinating definitions.

When folk situated in S_A say that their clocks are synchronized and those situated in S_B say that *theirs* are, neither is making empirical claims, according to Reichenbach—they are instead *defining* temporal duration within their respective inertial frames. But, once more on Quinean grounds, "*There is no such thing as analyticity in scientific theory,*" Putnam tells us. That is why we need a different explication of cognitive equivalence—to wit, the one above. It then transpires that relative to this new sense of equivalence, description A and description B are, indeed, equivalent.

Are they or are they not incompatible, genuinely incompatible, though? Putnam goes only as far as saying that they are *apparently* incompatible and then shows how a realist can completely sidestep any worries she might have had with these apparently incompatible frame-bound descriptions by describing the situation using the invariant notions of space-time distance for the frame-relative concepts of "temporal separation" and "spatial distance." It is, consequently, difficult to see what purpose the original example serves if the incompatibility is *merely* apparent and the appearance of incompatibility can be effectively explained away. Description A and description B are equivalent in Putnam's sense of that phrase but they are not genuinely incompatible. What then does the example illustrate?

I think that the notion of literal meaning must have some part to play here in Putnam's thinking. "X is simultaneous with Y" literally means the same uttered in inertial frame S_A as it does when uttered in S_B. If theories T and $T*$ thus assign different truth values to this statement, then they must be logically incompatible. So to the extent that description A and description B are two such theories, they are logically incompatible, equivalent theories from the realist's point of view. That there exists a more comprehensive theory in which this apparent incompatibility can be explained away is to the point only if we can always back up to such a theory when faced with any apparent incompatibility between equivalent theories. But there is no good reason to believe that we can, and, indeed, there are grounds for thinking that we cannot. That, at any rate, is a first attempt at reconstructing Putnam's reasoning. Before we look at the examples that Putnam thinks really do clinch his case, let me just present a naive response to the relativity example that Putnam's argument obfuscates. The reason the apparent incompatibility between theories formulated in one inertial frame and theories formulated in another is *merely* apparent is simply that expressions such as "simultaneous" are token-reflexive.[22]

To be sure, it was Einstein's great discovery that a term unanimously believed to be absolute was token-reflexive. But what the relativity example really shows is that terms like "simultaneous" contain a further hidden parameter. So in the light of the special theory of relativity (STR), there is not even a prima facie case for believing in genuine incompatibility—or, if there is, it is precisely the same case that exists for believing "I am Australian" as uttered by me and "I am not Australian" as uttered by Hilary Putnam are genuinely incompatible. Nothing *should* be made of simple token-reflexivity.

I think this response is too naive. It is not at all obvious that the STR case is *just* a matter of token-reflexivity. I shall return to discuss it later. The example that Putnam thinks really does show that there can be genuinely incompatible equivalent descriptions concerns the alleged theory-dependence of the notion of an object. To illustrate this, Putnam gives us two "stories" about space-time:

Story 1 Space-time consists of objects called points (point-events). These have no extension, and extended space-time is built up out of them just as, in classical Euclidean geometry, the extended line, plane, and solid bodies are built up out of unextended spatial points.

Story 2 Space-time consists of extended space-time neighborhoods. All parts of space-time have extension. This corresponds to the theory (advanced by Whitehead) that classical Euclidean space consists of extended spatial neighborhoods. On Whitehead's view, "points" are mere logical constructions, not real spatial objects: A point is (identified with) a convergent set of solid spheres (i.e., spheres together with their interiors).

By Putnam's criteria, these two "stories" count as equivalent descriptions since theories incorporating them will certainly be mutually relatively interpretable and will, one can presume, explain just the same phenomena. The crucial question is, again, whether they are *genuinely incompatible* descriptions.

I claim that they are not genuinely incompatible: Putnam says that if, following story 2, you start with regions, points will then just be sets of concentric spheres. But there will just be too many such sets to identify with the points, for "'Points' can be sets of spheres whose radii are negative powers of 2, for example, or sets of spheres whose radii are negative powers of 3," and then we will be forced either into skepticism where we say: "we can't know whether the 'correct' translation of story 1 into story 2 is the one that identifies points with sets of spheres which converge and whose radii are powers of 2 or some other translation"; or else an indefensible dogmatism: "transcendental metaphysics (if we claim *a priori* knowledge of which is *the* correct translation)."[23] When the choice is either skepticism or dogmatism, the realist can be forgiven for looking elsewhere. Why do we need to *identify* the points with *any* of these regions in the first place? The realist need not claim that points just *are* sets of convergent spheres with radii of negative powers of 2 rather than sets of spheres with radii of negative powers of 3. That such a claim is unmotivated is evident from the very procedure of interpreting story 1 in a theory that incorporates story 2. All that such relative interpretations achieve is the setting up of a bijection between the regions of story 2 and the points of story 1.

Rather than attempt to push beyond the technical facts to the outer reaches of transcendental metaphysics, the realist should simply acknowledge the facts for what they are: we can use regions to identify points and we can use points to define regions. That is all that the constructions *do* show mathematically; that is all they should therefore be taken to show "metaphysically." *They simply attest the existence of a one–one correlation between regions and points, and there's an end to it.* Putnam may have been assuming that a theory of space-time formulated in terms of spatiotemporal regions is committed to holding that points do not exist. But that assumption is not warranted, as one can hold that points exist but are not mereological parts of space-time.

There is indeed a more substantive topological issue lurking in the background of Putnam's discussion of theories of the continuum and of space-time. It is this: In many accounts of either pure or physical geometry, points are taken to be parts of the space. Yet one can develop topological accounts of continua in which points are not parts of the space but are, instead, locations within the space. One who holds to such a theory will not want to deny that points exist. For these locations in the space most certainly exist. Moreover, it does not follow from the denial that points are parts of space that one can do geometry without taking points as primitives in one's geometrical theory. But even if it could be shown that the relevant geometrical axioms have to quantify over points, this still would not settle the issue of whether they are genuine parts of space. It turns out that it *is* possible to formulate topology in terms of regions or three-dimensional volumes, formulating as one's axioms those that use as their only entities three-dimensional volumes and their relations. So geometrical description is indeed possible without quantifying over points.

At this stage we are a long way off making sense of Putnam's claim that there can be, from the realist's point of view, logically incompatible yet descriptively equivalent theories of the same phenomena that are nonetheless both true. Our difficulty might stem from the fact that the allegedly incompatible theories have not been formulated with anything like the precision necessary to test Putnam's claim. Lacking any precise specification, when we restrict ourselves to the topology of space-time, the punctate and the region theory appear to be descriptively equivalent in the sense that each can be translated into the other: points as convergent sets of regions, regions as sets of points. So it is hard to see how the two theories could be incompatible *topologically*.

Differences between the theories do emerge over the *contents* of space-time, though—the properties, relations, and functions definable on space or time. Punctate theories may contain details that are not duplicated in the region theories: Thus, at the stroke of midnight, Cinderella's carriage changes into a pumpkin. It is a carriage up to midnight, a pumpkin thereafter. According to the region-based theory, which takes temporal intervals as primitives, that's all there is to it. But if there are temporal points or instants, there is a further fact left undecided by the story so far—namely, at the moment of midnight, is the carriage still a carriage or is it a pumpkin?

So does the region-based theory fail to recognize certain facts or are these putative facts merely artifacts of the punctate's theory descriptive resources, reflecting nothing in reality? We cannot declare the two theories descriptively equivalent until we at least resolve this question and we cannot do that without a precise formulation of the theories.

The original demonstration that such theories can indeed be constructed occurs in Carnap's *Logical Construction of the World*. Following Carnap's lead, Thomas Mormann has constructed a simple example that does seem to vindicate Putnam's claims:[24] The empirical domain for the two competing theories, T_1 and T_2, is a "similarity structure" (S, δ). The task is to explain the similarity by "discovering" or, at any rate, postulating certain properties responsible for the empirical similarity. Two objects x and y are deemed to be similar if and only if they share at least one common property. Each theory must then set up a correlation between objects and their properties that obeys this basic law. Then an empirically adequate theory will be a distribution of properties obeying the basic law. Mormann then shows quite generally that for a given (S, δ), the "empirical domain" of the theories, there are indeed logically incompatible property distributions, that is, theories.

I am uncertain as to the wider implications of this work, however. It may yet be that for actual theories of space-time or of the early stages of the universe, say, cases of apparent logical incompatibility between two presumptively true empirically equivalent theories can always be dismissed as merely apparent, or else that the descriptive equivalence of the two theories can be questioned by showing that one theory but not the other can account for some phenomenon. This is what the realist needs to prove Putnam wrong. It is uncertain whether one or the other of these two routes will always be available.

Are there some more general philosophical considerations that can be brought to bear on the issue of whether there can be genuinely incompatible theories that are nonetheless true from the metaphysical realist's point of view? Two recent explications of Putnam's argument may be of assistance here. The first is due to Ernest Sosa. Sosa argues that EDA with its recommendation of conceptual relativity can be understood as a response to a problem he sees with our ordinary ways of identifying objects:

I am supposing a snowball to be constituted by a certain piece of snow as constituent matter and the shape of (approximate) roundness as constituent form.

That particular snowball exists at that time because of the roundness of that piece of snow. More, if at that time that piece of snow were to lose its roundness, then at that time that snowball would go out of existence. Compare now with our ordinary concept of a snowball, the concept of a snowdiscall, defined as an entity constituted by a piece of snow as matter and as form any shape between being round and being discshaped. At any given time, therefore, any piece of snow that constitutes a snowball constitutes a snowdiscall, but a piece of snow might at a time constitute a snowdiscall without then constituting a snowball. For every round piece of snow is also in shape between discshaped and round (inclusive), but a discshaped piece of snow is not round.

Any snowball SB must hence be constituted by a piece of snow PS which also then constitutes a snowdiscall SD. Now, SB is distinct (a different entity) from PS, since PS would survive squashing and SB would not. By similar reasoning, SD also is distinct from PS. And again, by similar reasoning, SB must also be distinct from SD, since enough partial flattening of PS will destroy SB but not SD. Now there are infinitely many shapes S1, S2,... between roundness and flatness of a piece of snow, and, for each i, having a shape between flatness and Si would give the form of a distinctive kind of entity to be compared with snowballs and snowdiscalls. Whenever a piece of snow constitutes a snowball, therefore, it constitutes infinitely many entities all sharing its place with it.

Under a broadly Aristotelian conception, therefore, the barest flutter of the smallest leaf hence creates and destroys infinitely many things, and ordinary reality suffers a sort of "explosion."[25]

Sosa then responds to this problem in the following way:

If I am right, we have three choices:

Eliminativism: a disappearance view for which our ordinary talk is so much convenient abbreviation. Problem: we still need to hear: "abbreviation" of what, and "convenient" for what ends and whose ends? Most puzzling of all is how we are to take this "abbreviation"—not literally, surely.

Absolutism: snowballs, hills, trees, planets etc. are all constituted by the in-itself satisfaction of certain conditions by certain chunks of matter, and the like, and all this goes on independently of any thought or conceptualization on the part of anyone. Problem: this leads to the "explosion of reality."

Conceptual relativism: we recognize potential constituted objects only relative to our implicit conceptual scheme with its criteria of existence and of perdurance. Problem: is there not much that is very small, or far away, or long ago, or yet to come, which surpasses our present acuity and acumen? How can we allow the existence of such sorts at present unrecognized by our conceptual scheme?

Right now, I cannot decide which of these is least disastrous. But is there any other option?[26]

I confess to being more than a little bemused by the original problem Sosa identifies. To be sure there are great problems in identifying any thing at or across time. I don't see Sosa's "explosion of reality" as among them, though. I cannot see his problem as anything other than a pseudo-problem. The only "explosion" I can detect in Sosa's description of the problem occurs precisely *there*—at the linguistic or representational level, not at the level of the things themselves. Thinking of new ways of classifying things cannot itself multiply entities beyond necessity in the way that Sosa worries about. There is, after all, only one piece of cold wet matter in Sosa's original snowball example, variously describable at any given time t as a collection of molecules, a piece of snow, a snowball, a snowdiscall. Flattening it, drying it, and so on at $t + \delta$ will lead to some of these predicates no longer being applicable. But it will not itself spirit into existence any new matter. Where is the explosion of reality Sosa worries about, then? I think that Sosa has confused our various actual and possible representations of reality with reality itself.

Furthermore, even if there is a genuine problem here, it doesn't seem to be the problem for which Putnam proposes conceptual relativity and metaphysical pluralism as the solution. Putnam's EDA and the pluralism he puts forward as a response to it are supposed to show that the metaphysical realist is mistaken in thinking that there is such a thing as the *one true description* of the world, whereas in Sosa's "explosion of reality" problem the notion of a *privileged* description does not even feature.

In his *Truth in Context*, Michael Lynch presents a particularly clear discussion of an example Putnam uses to support his EDA:[27]

Suppose ... Smith and Johnson ... are asked to look in a bag containing some marbles and count how many objects there are in the bag. Johnson looks inside and announces, "There are exactly three objects in the bag: x, y and z." Suppose that Smith is a "mereologist," that is, a logician who believes that every part of an object is an object and that the sum of any two objects is an object. When Smith looks in the bag, she says, "There are *really* exactly seven objects in the bag: x, y, z, x $\oplus$ y, x $\oplus$ z, y $\oplus$ z, x $\oplus$ y $\oplus$ z."

Qua metaphysical pluralist, Lynch claims that the following four propositions are all true:

(1) Smith and Johnson are expressing distinct propositions.

(2) Smith and Johnson are expressing incompatible propositions.

(3) Smith and Johnson are expressing true propositions.

(4) Smith and Johnson are not employing completely different concepts of "object" or "exist" or "number"; they are not talking past one another.

I think the metaphysical realist who believes in the *one true privileged description* of the world should not quibble with (1). And, if Smith does indeed insist that she has the correct number of objects and Johnson for his part does the same, then the realist should also assent to (2): "There are exactly three objects in the bag" and "There are exactly seven objects in the bag" are flatly inconsistent, provided of course both Smith and Johnson mean the same by "object."

But there's the rub. By "object" Johnson means what folk ordinarily mean by "object," object in the quotidian sense of "object," whereas Smith patently does not. Smith means "*mereological* object." These two senses of "object" are related (the mereological objects include the ordinary ones), so in one sense (4) is true: Smith and Johnson are not completely talking past each other. However, if they are rational at all, Smith and Johnson could both be brought to assent to the following proposition: *If by "object" it is meant ordinary material object, then there are, indeed, three objects in the bag, but if by "object" it is meant mereological object there are, instead, seven objects in the bag.*

Given this conditional, though, the apparent incompatibility simply evaporates: Smith and Johnson do indeed mean different things by "object." So (4), in the sense relevant to pluralism, is false. Lynch defends the claim that Smith and Johnson are expressing incompatible propositions by appealing to a counterfactual sense of "incompatible":[28]

According to the pluralist, [Smith and Johnson] are (or could be) extending their shared minimal concept of an object differently. Thus the propositions they are expressing are relative to different conceptual schemes and are therefore logically consistent. At the same time, there is a clear and important sense in which the pair of propositions are incompatible: *if these propositions were relative to the same scheme, they would be inconsistent.*

The italicized point is no doubt right but I'm unsure how it is supposed to help the pluralist, or, indeed, precisely how Lynch means to interpret it. Suppose someone asks me how many children I have and I reply "I have exactly four of them" and then follows up with the question "And how many boys?" to which I reply "I have exactly three of them." Relative to a scheme wherein "child" means "male child" I would be contradicting myself if I maintained both that I had four children and that I had three boys. But no one who deployed such a scheme would be tempted to maintain both these propositions. So it is unclear to me how there could be a possible world wherein Smith and Johnson could rationally disagree in the way Lynch's view seems to require. In spite of this exegetical uncertainty, I think that Lynch is on to something important in this notion of counterfactual incompatibility as we'll see below. In fact, I think we can edge a little closer to what Putnam has in mind through this example. Suppose Smith says:

Look, the commonsense conceptual scheme with which you are working Johnson is all very well old chap but it is simply not up to the task of limning the ultimate structure of reality. For that you need mereology. So when I say that there are *really* exactly seven objects I am using "object" in the precise sense demanded by ultimate theory. To say that there are only three objects is therefore not strictly true.

Johnson might respond to this in a number of ways. He might concede the point if his metaphysical views happen to coincide with Smith's. He might disagree if they do not, insisting that ultimate theory has no need to recognize mereological objects, replying *tu quoque* to Smith, that strictly speaking *her* claim is not true. He might, alternatively, declare all such metaphysical wrangles completely irrelevant to the ordinary request to count the number of marbles in a bag.

There is no better formulation of the sort of view Putnam means to attack in his EDA than Frank Jackson's version of physicalism. According to this view, everything that exists supervenes on the microphysical. The main task for "serious metaphysics," according to Jackson, is thus to find microphysical truthmakers for claims about supervenient aspects of reality that are conceived of as *a priori deducible from the microphysical facts.* Even the putatively necessary a posteriori bridge laws that link the manifest way things are to the fundamental way they are follow a priori from contingent a posteriori premises made true by the microphysical facts. Jackson's view, enthusiastically endorsed by David Lewis, is precisely a version of metaphysical realism that holds to the idea of the one true theory of the world—the microphysical description of how things are is *privileged.* That Putnam regards any such reductionist program as seriously flawed is clearly brought out in his response to one of its sympathizers, Simon Blackburn:[29]

Philosophers have long disagreed, and disagree today, over the relation of commonsense objects—tables and chairs—to their matter. Quine believes that a table is identical with its matter, that its matter is the electromagnetic, gravitational, etc., fields that occupy the volume in question, that fields are simply collections of space-time points with certain properties, and that, in consequence, tables and other physical objects are, in the last analysis, identical with space-time regions. David Lewis believes that they are identical with mereological sums of time-slices of molecules. Saul Kripke believes that they are distinct from their matter, on the grounds that they have different modal properties from their matter (the table could have consisted of different molecules; it could have occupied a different place).

Putnam's response to these competing views is pure Carnap:[30]

> Our ordinary language can be rationally reconstructed (i.e. formalized) in accordance with any of these doctrines, and our description of such states of affairs as there being three glasses on the table will not be affected. Indeed—and this is what Blackburn objects to—I would say that these different formalizations just provide us with different ways of describing what is, by commonsense standards, the same state of affairs.

I confess to finding extremely attractive this Carnapian response of Putnam's to the question of how the manifest way things are relates to the microphysical way they are, but a vindication of this claim must await the final chapter where I provide independent reasons for doubting the Lewis–Jackson "analytic functionalist" view and for accepting the Carnap–Putnam "nonfactualist" alternative. It is worth recording Putnam's final remarks on this matter so that we grasp exactly what his pluralism amounts to:[31]

> Blackburn complains that "we are not given ... any help [by Putnam] in understanding how much of the commonsense standard we are being asked to abandon, or why we should do so," but of course I am not asking us to abandon any part of the commonsense standard, of the commonsense practice (for such I take it to be) of regarding it as no real question at all whether a table is "identical with the region it occupies in space-time or with the mereological sum of time-slices of molecules that it contains." *What I am asking us to "abandon" is the idea that such a question must have a non-conventional answer.*

Once more, echoing Carnap, Putnam judges (at least some of) these ontological questions to be just "pseudo-questions." It is Putnam's Carnapian conventionalism about "ultimate theory" that lies at the heart of his EDA, as I understand it.

Let us return to the relativity theory case in a final effort to expound the basis for the EDA. Consider 2 different inertial frames of reference, IF_1 and IF_2, such that event A precedes event B relative to IF_1 and B precedes A relative to IF_2. I said before that I thought it naive to assimilate the relativity case to simple indexicality. The reason is that such an evaluation ignores the *conventional* nature of relativizing to an inertial frame.

Suppose now that Lynch's Smith and Johnson switch the topic of debate to temporal precedence and that Smith declares that A preceded

B, while Johnson declares B preceded A. Do they disagree? Not necessarily. If they are both absolutists about temporal precedence, then although both certainly disagree about the absolute temporal order of events, both are wrong since there is no *absolute*, that is inertial frame-independent, fact as to which of A or B preceded the other. If they both accept this latter fact and mean to be talking only relative to some inertial frame, then whether they disagree or not will depend on whether they have adopted the same frame. So we can say with Lynch that *were* Smith and Johnson to have adopted the same inertial frame, Smith's claim "$A < B$" and Johnson's counter "$B < A$" *would* indeed conflict. Putnam's Carnapianism can now be expressed in the following way: Just as all talk of absolute temporal precedence is nonfactual, so all talk of the objects the world contains *absolutely*, "from the God's-eye point of view," is likewise nonfactual, and just as attributions of temporal precedence contain a hidden parameter, so too do attributions of existence, identity, and number. For the relativistic case, the parameter ranges over inertial frames, for the object identity case, over conceptual schemes.

Isn't this Carnapianism just straightforward conceptual relativism of the sort Putnam is at pains to avoid? No, for two reasons. First, we can say "absolutely" exactly what objects, properties, and so on exist relative to a given scheme of classification in just the same way as we can say "absolutely" whether A preceded, coincided with, or succeeded B relative to a given inertial frame. Every conceptual scheme is conceptually accessible to and from every other conceptual scheme, and there are scheme-independent facts of the matter about what exists relative to each scheme. The point is that the metaphysical realist who believes in the one true theory of the world is, from Putnam's perspective, in exactly the same position as the Newtonian or absolutist about simultaneity—pretending that God or nature fixes the facts about temporal priority independently of any decision on our part as to inertial frame. This, I think, is part of what Putnam means when he declares metaphysical realism "incoherent."

Second, and more important, schemes of classification for Putnam are *conceptual norms* in the sense that they tell us what we *ought* to regard as the same object—relative to the commonsense or quotidian scheme of classification there were three objects in the bag containing three marbles; relative to the mereological scheme there were seven. Any other answers are *incorrect* relative to each scheme.

We cannot cognitively engage with the world at all without such schemes. But the schemes themselves are not dictated to us either by

God or by nature—*pace* Jackson and Lewis, they are not necessitated by the microphysical or any other facts. Hence selection of a classification scheme is every bit as conventional as selection of a frame of reference in the temporal order case. Putnam, on this reading, is a *nonfactualist* about norms in the sense that our adherence to a norm cannot be explained in purely cognitive terms.

I know of no better discussion of the status of norms and noncognitivist attitudes toward them than can be found in Hartry Field's lucid essay "Disquotational Truth and Factually Defective Discourse."[32] Putnam would certainly not wish to endorse Field's view that evaluative discourse is somehow "second-grade" or, as Field himself puts it, "not fully factual." Indeed, he has argued forcefully against noncognitivism in ethics. However, a generalization of Field's view is available to Putnam that helps make sense of many of the otherwise puzzling features of Putnam's own position with which we've so far struggled.

Field takes his lead from Alan Gibbard's theory of evaluative statements. According to Gibbard, an evaluative assertion such as (σ) "Spearing someone in the leg for killing a dog is wrong" is not straightforwardly true. Rather, (σ) is true or false only relative to certain norms. The debate between factualists and nonfactualists in ethics is thus concerned with whether evaluative assertions such as (σ) are straightforwardly true or not.

Putnam regards evaluative claims such as (σ) as every bit as factual as scientific claims since he rejects the fact–value dichotomy. That's fine, since it is precisely scientific and other straighforwardly factual assertions to which we are going to apply the Field–Gibbard "nonfactualist" approach on Putnam's behalf. So, we shall continue to take (σ) as our paradigm nonfactual assertion to explicate the Field–Gibbard approach. Field's proposal is this:

(NF) An evaluative utterance such as (σ) is true for me iff it is true relative to those norms I regard as appropriate to associate with its evaluative terms.

Field operates with an individualistic notion of truth (truth for me) but this is not obligatory. We might instead follow Bernard Williams in developing a notion of ethical truth that holds for various communities or cultures at various times. Thus, in sharp contrast to contemporary Western cultures, within a warrior culture that esteemed dogs, (σ) would not be true as, indeed, in some contemporary Aboriginal or Koori communities in Australia (σ) is definitely false. It is the contrast between claims such as (σ) that are, according to the nonfactualist, not fully factual and other favored claims that is of interest to us, for:

(FF) A fully factual utterance is true irrespective of the norms one associates with it.

One cannot simply identify the fully factual assertions as those that do not contain evaluative terms since the following claim is fully factual even though it contains evaluative terms: "Spearing someone in the leg for killing a dog is wrong *relative to* present Western norms of right and wrong."

Thus in general when the relativization to norms is made explicit, Field notes, the result is a fully factual assertion. It may help to convey the character of the Field–Gibbard view if we develop things a little further with (σ). So consider three people, Namatjari, Ernie, and Charlie, with respectively decreasing involvement with traditional Koori communities—Namatjari an elder of one such community, Ernie an erstwhile member now local councillor in an outback town, Charlie a successful Koori lawyer and wealthy resident of Sydney whose connections with traditional Koori communities have only ever been indirect. Whereas Namatjari's norms license, under certain strict conditions, the spearing of someone who kills a dog—if that dog is thought to harbor the spirit of an ancestor, for instance—Charlie's do not. Indeed, Charlie's norms, exclusively Western as they are, expressly prohibit such actions. The most interesting case is Ernie's. Ernie has competing norms. On the one hand, he does not *literally* believe that a dog can house the spirit of an ancestor, for he construes all such talk in mythopoeic terms—which leads him to regard the practice of spearing those who kill dogs as morally dubious. On the other hand, recognition of who he is and the culture to which he belongs impels him to allow that there is at least a prima facie case for taking such drastic action against a Koori person who does share traditional Koori beliefs and kills a dog despite believing it may house the spirit of an ancestor.

Relative to the norms that Namatjari accepts, (σ) is false; relative to those norms Charlie acknowledges, (σ) is true. As for Ernie, though, (σ) is indeterminate in truth value as it is true relative to some norms he accepts and false relative to others. Nonetheless, there is a clear sense in which Namatjari, Charlie, and Ernie *disagree* with one another, as their beliefs about the morality of spearing the killer of a dog are incompatible. If the nonfactualist explanation of this type of disagreement is correct, this cannot be a *pure* conflict in belief about the facts; it must involve in addition a conflict about which norm to respect, as Field notes. This is a conflict in *attitude,* not *belief,* according to the nonfactualist.

My suggestion now is to transpose this nonfactualist framework for dealing with evaluative statements to conceptual schemes. Smith's assertion "There are exactly seven objects in the bag" is not fully factual to the extent that it includes a normative conceptual component that is not reducible to any purely physical or otherwise nonnormative elements. On the other hand, the assertion "there are exactly seven objects in the bag relative to the mereological conception of an object" is, indeed, fully factual and thus straightforwardly true. Smith's unrelativized assertion that there are exactly seven objects in the bag is no more straightforwardly true than is her unrelativized claim that event A temporally preceded event B.

We can also see why the question "what objects does the world contain?" strikes Putnam, as it did his teacher Carnap, as a pseudo-question: *If no scheme of conceptual classification has yet been imposed,* the question is as empty as the parallel one about absolute temporal precedence. There is simply no fact of the matter as to what the world contains absolutely. More precisely, though, "There are exactly three objects in the bag" will come out true in the quotidian classificatory scheme Q, and it will come out false in the mereological scheme M. Hence, *if Q and M both provide acceptable classificatory norms for me,* "There are exactly three objects in the bag" comes out neither true nor false relative to the norms I accept.

This conclusion looks alarming. But the appearance here is deceptive since the italicized antecedent above is not fulfilled. It is implicit in our ordinary practice that the classificatory scheme we use is Q, not M. Consequently, the sentence "There are exactly three objects in the bag" should be understood as implicitly indexed to Q, and once thus indexed, from the nonfactualist perspective it is straightforwardly true.

Still, there is no denying that if the nonfactualist appraisal of conceptual schemes is correct, a consequence of so explicating Putnam's ideas on conceptual relativity is that Johnson's quotidian claim that there are three objects (i.e., three marbles) in the bag turns out not to be straightforwardly true either. This is a wholly unacceptable consequence for Putnam who thinks with Wittgenstein that our ordinary prephilosophical ways of speaking about ordinary objects are not susceptible to philosophical disconfirmation of this type.

But the moral of this for Putnam might simply be that the invidious contrast between straightforward and nonstraightforward truth that

Field and Gibbard seek to draw cannot be sustained, since *all* truths turn out to be not fully factual in *their* sense. *Putnam would then have "deconstructed" the factual–nonfactual distinction from within.* What survives, or could survive, from the above "nonfactualist" articulation of Putnam's views on conceptual schemes are two things:

(I) The idea that truths are always relative to norms of classification and always contain a conventional element with which they are inextricably intertwined.

(II) The idea that acceptance of a norm is at least partially a conventional rather than a physically determined matter.

Would recognition of the inextricability of conventional classificatory norms and objective fact compromise metaphysical realism *qua* the thesis of the metaphysical determinacy of evidence-transcendent states of affairs? I think the answer to this is a clear "No" for reasons that Michael Dummett has eloquently enunciated:

> Unquestionably there have been philosophers whose views have embodied both externalist and internalist doctrines, held in apparent harmony. Frege is a clear example. His celebrated principle that a term has meaning only in the context of a sentence is a strongly internalist one. It involves a rejection of the conception whereby to treat a term as referring to some particular object is to make a mental association between the term and the object, considered as directly apprehended by the mind from a standpoint outside our language and thought....
>
> Equally internalist is the corollary derived by Frege from the context principle, that with any term there must be associated a criterion of identity. This says, essentially, that *the world does not come to us already dissected into discrete objects; rather, it is we who, by adopting particular criteria for what is to count as being presented with the same object as before, slice it up into objects in one manner rather than another.*
>
> Despite his propounding these internalist theses, Frege was, notoriously, a staunch realist. The mathematician's task is to discover what is there; truth is to be utterly distinguished from what is taken to be true; the sun is what it is, regardless of what we think it to be. We express our thoughts in language, but, in grasping those thoughts, recognize them as being determined as true or false in virtue of how things are and independently of whether we do or can judge of their truth or falsity. The conception that reconciles the internalist and externalist components of Frege's philosophy is expressed in the *Tractatus* in the metaphor of the grid. *To describe the world at all, we need a grid, and might use one or another; but, given the grid, what constitutes a correct description is wholly independent of us.*[33]

I think the Frege–Wittgenstein position is essentially right and that it compromises naturalistic realism not one whit to acknowledge this. We owe to Frege the recognition that the question "How many objects are there in this room?" is ill formed until we specify some sortal relative to which we can count and identify things. The alleged conflict between the mereologist's inventory of objects and the quotidian middle-sized dry good inventory is then easily resolved by distinguishing identity claims from methods of identifying objects.

However, in contrast to Putnam, I hold that there *is* indeed a privileged conceptual framework—the framework of the sciences—and that in a clear sense physics is the foundational theory within that framework. The reason is partially the one alluded to in Quine's remark that "Nothing happens without a redistribution of particles," but it has been clearly articulated once again by Field:

> The methodological role of the doctrine of physicalism is double-edged. On the positive side, the doctrine tells us that when we have a putative body of facts and causal explanations that we are quite convinced are basically correct, we need to find a physical foundation for them. (If the facts and explanations are sufficiently "high-level," we will not look directly for a physical foundation: we will simply look for a foundation in terms of "lower-level" facts and explanations that we think are clearly unproblematic in that their having a physical foundation is relatively uncontroversial.) For instance, the implicit acceptance of the doctrine of physicalism on the part of most scientists has led to the successful search for the molecular foundations of genetics and the quantum-mechanical foundations of chemical bonding. The other, negative, aspect of the doctrine of physicalism is that when faced with a body of doctrine (or a body of purported causal explanations) that we are convinced can have no physical foundation, we tend to reject that body of doctrine (or of purported causal explanations).[34]

I am unsure whether Putnam means to reject physicalism in even this rather weak sense—the supervenience of all facts on the physical facts, which we shall call the physical supervenience thesis. In commenting on Bernard Williams's thesis that it is implicit in the very idea of scientific knowledge that science should converge on the one true theory ("But one is hard put to know why one should believe this," says Putnam), he writes in his "Objectivity and the Science/Ethics Distinction," pp. 170–171:

> At the level of space-time geometry, there is the well-known fact that we can take points to be individuals *or* we can take them to be mere limits. States of a system can be taken to be quantum mechanical superpositions of particle interactions (a la Feynman) or quantum mechanical superpositions of field states. (This is the contemporary form of the wave-particle duality.) Not only do single theories have a bewildering variety of alternative rational reconstructions (with quite different ontologies), but there is no evidence at all for the claim (which is essential

to William's belief in an "absolute conception of the world") that science converges to a single theory.... It could be, for example, that although we will discover more and more approximately correct and increasingly accurate equations, the *theoretical picture* which we use to explain those equations will continue to be upset by scientific revolutions. As long as our ability to predict, and to mathematicize our predictions in attractive ways, continues to advance, science will "progress" quite satisfactorily; to say, as Williams sometimes does, that convergence to one big picture is required by the very concept of knowledge is sheer dogmatism.

The dream of the one true theory may be no more than a dream, for all proponents of the physical supervenience thesis care. It may, in point of fact, be wholly unlikely that we shall ever formulate a "final theory." This needn't dull in any way our conviction that if we were only clever enough, or better informed, apprised of crucial pieces of information we are unable for some reason to get, and so on, we would be able to find a physical basis for all that we take to be factual in this world. That various rational reconstructions of physical theory appear equally acceptable, that physical theories permit of alternative axiomatizations, that the foundations of physics itself are constantly in flux does not in any way show that the physical supervenience thesis is unlikely, much less that it is false. The physical supervenience thesis is grounded in the knowledge that everything that exists is made of physical stuff of some sort or other. What remains unclear to me is whether Putnam genuinely doubts *this*.

In the end, I don't believe Putnam has any decisive argument against metaphysical realism in his equivalent descriptions argument. The virtue of exploring the argument, though, does not depend on its ultimate effectiveness in discharging that role, in my view; it is in the many issues it raises in regards to conceptual schemes, reduction, uniqueness of physical theory, and so on that its real value lies. Moreover, naturalistic realists have a lot to learn in this connection. Putnam's conceptual pluralism is in no way irrelevant to a plausible version of naturalistic realism. Indeed, as we shall see in the final chapter, it gives, arguably, exactly the *right* general account of the relation between the manifest and scientific understandings of the world.

6
Models, Representation, and Reality

6.1 The Model-theoretic Argument

Hilary Putnam's model-theoretic argument (MTA) continues to fascinate and frustrate readers. What precisely is the problem supposed to be? Putnam seems to impute to realists theses they explicitly disavow and to stress over and over claims they have never disputed. As Steven Wagner puts it:

> ... Putnam continues to uphold the MTA while his opponents still advance an objection that appeared immediately. Each side accuses the other of question-begging. One suspects a failure to communicate. I believe neither side has understood the argument. Resolving the impasse depends on giving the MTA the right target: not realism, as Putnam thinks, but a complex view within which realism standardly appears.[1]

I think Wagner is right in this assessment, although I demur from his idea of the target Putnam is stalking. My ultimate purpose is to defend naturalistic realism against the MTA. I believe that the MTA in its various forms highlights some sort of problem for realism. But what?

My claim is that the various MTAs constitute attempts to show that *metaphysical realism is inconsistent with a representationalist theory of mind (RTM)*.[2] Since Putnam has not explained clearly what the problem is, realists have not observed the epistemic strictures imposed by RTM. Consequently their replies seem question-begging to him. To rebut Putnam's MTAs one therefore needs to show not that they do not refute realism but rather that RTM and realism are compatible. Plainly, the MTAs refute realism if and only if RTM is a consequence of it.

But how *could* RTM *qua* bold conjecture about the mind possibly follow from naturalistic realism *qua* thesis about the existence of a mind-independent world? The relation between the two surely is much looser, so without even surveying the arguments, talk of refutation appears overblown.

Even so, perhaps the best naturalistic theory of mind is RTM and the best naturalistic theory of the world realist. If so, then to the realist, a successful MTA should at the least reveal an unexpected anomaly, one comparable to our accepting both relativity theory and quantum theory though no one knows how to make the two theories consistent, but, equally, no one can conceive of how either theory could be false. In fact, by now the connection ought not to be surprising. RTM affords a naturalistic explanation of how mental representation is possible. So then the MTA should be conceived as an attempt to show that if metaphysical realism is true, the best naturalistic explanation of mental representation is thereby undercut.

6.2 Skolem's Paradox

Putnam tells us that the inspiration for his MTA came from the Löwenheim–Skolem theorem and Skolem's paradox. The MTA is supposed to somehow generalize Skolemite worries about the referent of "set"[3] to (in the first instance) the referents of the theoretical terms of our best theories. The simplest description of Skolem's paradox is perhaps this:

In axiomatic set theory one can prove that there are sets with a nondenumerable number of elements, such as the set of real numbers. The Löwenheim–Skolem Theorem (LST) asserts, on the other hand, that any consistent, countable set of first order formulae has a denumerable model—indeed, a model in the set of integers, **I**. The axioms of ZF, for example, comprise just such a consistent, countable set of formulae. Hence, by LST there exists a model in **I** for this set. Yet one can prove theorems within ZF asserting that there exist sets with uncountably many elements. How can this be if there are only denumerably many elements in the domain as is the case for **I**?[4]

It is not my purpose to examine this "paradox" here. The interest lies in its connection with the MTA. Putnam thinks Skolem's paradox constitutes a real worry for a mathematical realist who refuses to ascribe to us unmediated insights into the Platonic universe of abstract mathematical objects. Such a realist will hold that the only means we have for establishing epistemic contact with sets, numbers, and so on is through our understanding of set theory, number theory, and so on. Our knowledge of abstract objects for this moderate realist is theory-mediated.

The standard way of resolving Skolem's paradox has it that the reason we can prove the existence of nondenumerable sets in the countable models of ZF is that the domains of those models do not contain the functions that would serve to enumerate the sets that these models judge "nondenumerable." An appeal is therefore made to what can be verified inside and what can be verified outside such models. The standard resolution presupposes the standard interpretation of terms like "uncountable," "set," "enumeration," and the like. How do we come by the *standard interpretation* of these terms? As far as the moderate realist is concerned—by understanding the relevant mathematical theories. It is just *that* which Putnam wants to know more about.

Suppose we take in the contributions of overall theory to our understanding of the notion of set. Will this fix the referent of "set"? It is the burden of "Models and Reality"[5] to argue that it will not, even for an ideal theory that passes every conceivable operational and theoretical constraint. A natural response is that the inscrutability of the reference of "set" at least will not ramify through the rest of the theory—we can be more confident that "electron" refers to electrons than that "uncountable set" refers to uncountable sets since we have causal contact with the former though not the latter. At any rate, we can be sure that "cat" refers to cats.

Holism and representationalism conspire to defeat this hope, holism by tying the fate of the reference of theoretical terms to that of all other terms of one's total theory, representationalism by interposing mental representations between objects in the world and our cognition of them. Given the naturalistic realist's epistemic commitments, it is as if all objects were abstract objects and our cognitive contact consisted in "grasping" truths about them. Thus is Skolem's paradox writ large.

6.3 The Model-theoretic Arguments

So far we have what appears to be a standard Quinean argument for referential inscrutabililty. How can this make trouble for realism? We can surely do science without worrying about whether our theoretical terms uniquely designate the objects our theories are ontologically committed to. Indeed, the upshot of the MTA might simply be that reference and truth are not language–world relations at all but are to be conceived of disquotationally.

My aim in this section will be to outline the MTAs and to develop in some detail the one that does apparently threaten realism directly. I will argue that it fails as a refutation of realism but highlights a worrying tension in the realist's overall theory of nature. If I am right, it is this tension that the MTAs argue to be a genuine incompatibility. It is no simple matter to work out how the MTAs are supposed to go. I discern three interrelated arguments:

(1) The argument based on Löwenheim–Skolem theorems. Henceforth, LSA.

(2) The argument based on the Gödel completeness theorem for first-order logic. Henceforth, GCA.

(3) The argument based on permutations of a universe of a model. Henceforth, PA.

LSA contends that the truth values of all the sentences of a language can be held constant as the language is given a vast number of distinct, even nonisomorphic, interpretations. GCA contends that realism is either incoherent or false since it implies the absurdity that even an ideal theory could be false. PA establishes a more elegant and general version of the result that LSA aims for.

An immediate limitation of both LSA and PA is that they assume that realism is committed to a nonminimalist[6] theory of truth and reference. GCA, on the other hand, carries no such presumption and challenges realists who are semantic minimalists.

It would be useful to set out Putnam's assumptions before we develop the GCA. The three philosophical theses distinctive of metaphysical realism according to Putnam are:

(1) The world is a totality of mind-independent objects.

(2) Truth is radically nonepistemic—even an ideal theory could be false.

(3) At least for an ideal language, one and only one reference relation R connecting our words with that totality is singled out by our very understanding of the language.

That (1) and (2) are distinctive realist theses is, I take it, uncontroversial. Claim (3), however, is not, as we have noted.

Putnam now invites the realist to suppose the following:

(4) There exists a theory containing all and only those sentences that we would accept in the ideal limit of rational enquiry. Call it T_I.

(5) We have succeeded in formalizing the language of this theory, L_I, say, up to some (perhaps transfinite) level of the Tarskian hierarchy of metalanguages.

A reference relation R for L_I will assign appropriate extensions to each predicate and function symbol of L_I and to each individual constant of that language. We can then define the set of true sentences of L_I à la Tarski:

(T_R) s is true, under R, iff the predicate "$x = x$ & s" refers to at least one object.

Putnam makes the following assumptions about the ideal theory, T_I:

(i) T_I is first order.

(ii) T_I is syntactically consistent.

(iii) T_I implies all and only true observation sentences.

(iv) T_I passes all conceivable theoretical constraints such as simplicity, mathematical elegance, inductive plausibility, fecundity, and so on.

(v) It is a true thesis of T_I that the world is infinite.

I shall now set out the GCA. Henceforth I shall sometimes refer to the proponent of any MTA as "The Skolemite":

From assumptions (i) and (ii) above, by Gödel's completeness theorem, T_I has a model, M_0, say. The Skolemite then claims that since this model either already constitutes an intended model or can be extended to one that does, the theory T_I has to be true since truth is truth in the intended model. Thus the realist's thesis that T_I might nonetheless be false becomes incoherent.

Of course, M_0 may itself consist in merely syntactic expressions or integers, thereby excluding the concrete denizens of the world.[7] Furthermore, there may not be enough objects if the domain is denumerable.

So the Skolemite has to ensure that M_0 cannot be faulted with respect to either the cardinality of its domain or the objects contained therein. We need some solid reasons for believing that the domain of M_0 will contain the right sorts of entities to appear in the extensions of the theoretical predicates—electrons, or at the very least, entities of that ilk to appear in the extension of "electron" rather than syntactic expressions pathologically satisfying the theses of T_I that, intuitively, talk about electrons. Otherwise we will have no reason at all to believe that the constraints T_I allegedly satisfies have not been pathologically reinterpreted in the model M_0.[8]

But the Skolemite can, apparently, provide us with some reasons, as Michael Resnick[9] makes clear. To obtain a model whose domain consists in just the objects in the world, the Skolemite applies the hidden inflation theorem of model theory to increase the size of the model M_0 served up to us by the Gödel completeness theorem (if that be necessary) so that the cardinality of the newly inflated model M_0+ is now the same as that of the world. Then another theorem of model theory—the same size theorem—is used to project M_0+ onto the world to obtain as a new model our M^*, whose domain is now the set of objects in the world and which assigns subsets of that set to the predicates of T_I as their extensions.

So now we can be sure, the Skolemite claims, that M^* is an intended model since it interprets the theses of T_I as truths about the world (rather than about numbers or linguistic expressions) and it satisfies all operational and theoretical constraints. Thus we've ensured that T_I is true since it is true in M^* and M^* is an intended model. So T_I is true and realism is wrong, right? Wrong! The conclusion depends on a crucial lemma that the model satisfies all operational and theoretical constraints, and Putnam's justification of this lemma is opaque.[10]

Before we examine this lemma, we should take note of a natural objection to Putnam's initial assumptions: *If the MTAs are reductios of anything, they are reductios not of realism but of the assumption that first-order resources suffice to frame an ideal theory, one that passes all conceivable operational and theoretical constraints.* Putnam takes himself to have adequately answered this objection, I think, since his PA applies to intensional and higher-order logics. However, he does not distinguish the different forms of MTA. They are all in his mind reductios of realism in one way or another. This is not so, as the realist who is a minimalist about semantics will take the LSA and PA as reductios of the assumption that truth and reference are language–world relations. The adequacy of first-order logic is still a real issue, then.[11] Within the context of GCA, at least, lack of categoricity of the first-order theory T_I plays a crucial role (as it does for LSA as well). Putnam's quick response to the proponent of second-order logic is that such logics have nonstandard Henkin models wherein the quantified variables of the theory are not taken to range over the full power-set.

Without going into details at this stage, we can note that this reply is by no means decisive. There are "schematic" second-order logics that are quasi-categorical and that do not assume we have a grasp of all subsets of the domain of individuals. It is a real possibility, as far as I can see, that T_I formulated within a schematic second-order logic might justifiably evade Putnam's "Skolemite" interpretative maneuvers.

There is a general point here. Putnam's MTAs apparently ask us to take sides on some highly controversial issues in the philosophy of logic, and no argument that does that can hope to refute a given thesis, much less show it to be "incoherent." So, *do* we have to take sides? In fact, the issue of the adequacy of first-order languages is subsidiary to some more general and urgent questions concerning formal languages:

(1) Why should we have to formalize T_I in the first place?

(2) Why should the realist be wedded to model-theoretic semantics as a theory of meaning for L_I?

As regards (2), model theory is simply applied set theory and, it could be argued, we already know that in the light of LST and the various independence results, the notion of a set is itself too *indeterminate* to ground determinate reference. Therefore:

(3) What is wrong with using one's home language to specify the reference of "set" and "boson," no less than "cat," directly in homophonic clauses of the form "'set' refers to sets," "'boson' refers to bosons," "'cat' refers to cats"?

From a certain perspective, the MTAs can seem all but worthless. Putnam gives the realist so little to determine reference (or the "intended" model) that the exercise looks futile. All that she is allowed to assume, it appears, is determinacy for the logical constants and perhaps for observational terms. Yet we manifestly do understand our *own* language. The MTAs may well reveal certain limitations in the powers of first-order (or higher-order) formalisms to categorically specify a given domain and undoubtedly constitute interesting generalizations of extant limitative results.[12] But the expressive weakness of certain languages reveals nothing about the domains those languages essay to describe.

This assessment is understandable, and Putnam has not clearly explained why questions such as (1), (2), and (3) above are misconceived, if he thinks they are. I believe that he does have a way of justifying his assumptions about T_I and about its language L_I. The justification, we shall see, comes from assuming RTM.

I now want to turn to the central lemma of the GCA and to the debate surrounding Putnam's notorious "Just more theory" response to realists.

6.4 Just More Theory?

6.4.1 The Central Lemma of GCA

M^* is the intended model, Putnam argues, because it satisfies every conceivable operational and theoretical constraint. This is the central lemma of the GCA. How does Putnam try to justify it?

M^* is conceived to be one of a (still vast) number of models of T_I in which all observation sentences come out true. Putnam then claims that M^* satisfies all the theoretical constraints we may reasonably impose since it makes T_I true.

Realists such as Michael Devitt and David Lewis have replied that there is at least one theoretical constraint that T_I does not satisfy—to wit, a right reference constraint (RRC). The RRC is that the terms of the language L_I of T_I stand in the right referential relation, R, say, to their referents. That is:

(RRC) Term τ refers to object x iff $R\tau x$.

Putnam's original respose to the RRC suggestion in "Models and Reality" was that adding RRC *as a body of theory* to L_I was just adding more theory. To this point, Putnam's critics have replied, in strident unison, that this represents a misunderstanding of the way in which the RRC is supposed to work. RRC, they claim, is supposed to be a *condition that is to be satisfied by an intended model*; it is not just *another sentence to somehow be made true by the model*. In David Lewis's words: "The constraint is not that an intended interpretation make our account of RRC true. The constraint is that an intended interpretation conform to RRC itself."[13] It beggars belief that Putnam has simply *missed* this distinction, which I will henceforth call "Lewis's distinction." So why *does* he talk of "just more theory" (JMT)? Barry Taylor has provided a lucid reconstruction of the JMT gambit, based on David Lewis's exegesis of Putnam. Informally, the idea is this: We consider a metalanguage for L_I that is adequate for the formulation of a truth-theory for that language. Call that language L_I+. To ensure that this new language L_I+ contains the expressive power of L_I, the language of our ideal theory, we assume that it contains L_I as a proper part. Thus translation into the metalanguage will be homophonic. The truth theory for L_I will contain as axioms sentences such as the following:

"Hilary Putnam" refers-in-L_I to Hilary Putnam.

y satisfies-in-L_I "x is a cat" iff y is a cat.

But the conjunction of all such assignments of extensions in L_I to individual and predicate constants expresses the requirements of any acceptable (RRC). What (RRC) demands is precisely that the terms of L_I be connected to their correct referents, so that conjoining these disquotational reference assignments will amount to an explicit formulation of that requirement.

Call this conjunction (RRC+) to indicate that this represents the translation into L_I+ of (RRC). Then Taylor has (Lewis's) Putnam arguing as follows:

(i) Form in L_I+ a new theory T_I+ by adding (RRC+) as a new axiom to T_I along with the recursive clauses necessary to formulate a complete truth-theory for L_I.

(ii) Unless (RRC) ought not to be complied with in the first place, we can safely assume that adding its truth-theoretic analogue (RRC+) along with the other recursive clauses as axioms to T_I will induce no inconsistency.

∴ (iii) T_I+ is consistent.

∴ (iv) By GCT, T_I+ has a model M^*+.

(v) Cut down M^*+ into a model M^* of L_I by deleting assignments of referents to all semantic predicates (such as "refers-in-L_I to," "is satisfied-in-L_I by ...," "is true-in-L_I")

(vi) Since M^*+ semantically explicates M^* by dint of T_I+'s containing a truth-theory for L_I, no semantic mismatch between the extensions M^*+ assigns to semantic predicates and the extensions it assigns to nonsemantic predicates can have been generated.

∴ (vii) paring down M^*+ in this way, we will ensure that M^* is a model of L_I that satisfies (RRC).

Now Lewis maintains "... The constraint is not that an intended interpretation make our account of RRC true. The constraint is that an intended interpretation conform to RRC itself."[14] If this is to constitute an effective rejoinder to JMT as it is represented above, the final inference from (v) and (vi) to (vii) is not warranted. Lewis's claim just *is* that there is no legitimate way of bridging the gap between the model M^*+ making (RRC+) true and (RRC)'s holding for a model M when $M = M^*+$.

Is this inference warranted, then? Taylor provides plausible reasons for believing it is: The fact that M^*+ semantically explicates its embedded

M^* means that the assignments M^*+ makes to semantic predicates such as "is true-in-L_I" will match the assignments it makes to nonsemantic predicates. The consequence of this is that as the expanded model M^*+ interprets it, "refers-in-L_I" means precisely the same as "refers to, relative to M^*." Hence, if M^* *is* the intended model, the sorts of clauses that (RRC) is invoked to regulate will come out aright:

"Hilary Putnam" refers-in-L_I to Hilary Putnam.

y satisfies-in-L_I "x is a cat" iff y is a cat.

This is because the semantic explicability of M^* by the expanded model M^*+ ensures that we can move from:

(I) "'Hilary Putnam' refers-in-L_I to Hilary Putnam" is true relative to M^*+

to

(II) "Hilary Putnam" refers relative to M^* to (Hilary Putnam)$_{M^*}$.

In (II), "(Hilary Putnam)$_{M^*}$" simply indicates that the name "Hilary Putnam" is being used as M^* interprets it. Thus, *if M^* is* the intended model, we will have as desired:

(III) "Hilary Putnam" refers relative to M^* to Hilary Putnam.

As a verification that the conjunction of all such clauses as (III) simply *is* what the satisfaction of (RRC) by M^* demands, we would then have shown *contra* Lewis that we can indeed move from:

(1) M^*+ makes (RRC*) true.

to

(2) (RRC) holds when the model of T_I is M^*.

All of this raises anew the very question that a right reference constraint was invoked to answer: *is M^* an intended model or not?*

Taylor concludes his excellent discussion of the JMT ploy and the satisfaction of (RRC): "In short, no noncircular argument can be mounted against the Putnamian from Right Reference Constraints, because *the unavailability of an independent and stable metalanguage* means that in this case such conditions yield no independent criterion for judging the hypothesis [that M^* is an intended model] under dispute."[15] Now the realist will scarcely agree that there is no independent and stable metalanguage. Yet, Putnam's Skolemite is no semantic skeptic. Putnam's point is, rather, that realism *engenders* such intolerable skepticism. To claim that there is no stable metalanguage, though, is to deny that clauses like "'cat' refers to cats" are meaningful or, at least, have the meaning we think they have. Taylor's discussion consequently raises, without resolving, all the worries about formalization and model-theoretic interpretation aired at (1) to (3) above.

So, recalling question (3) above, why isn't *English* augmented by such informal and formal mathematical, logical, and theoretical notions as are deemed necessary, a suitably "independent and stable meta-language" for determining whether M^* does or does not satisfy (RRC)? The answer, I think, lies in the epistemic constraints imposed by RTM and the other naturalistic assumptions that Putnam's moderate realist makes. *If mental states are computational states and thought consists in processing syntactic formulae, we are owed an account of how determinate relations between words and things can be established in the first place.*

Viewed from this perspective, a formal language is precisely the *right* sort of language in which the realist should frame an ideal theory since such is the language of thought. Hence Putnam's realist cannot lay claim to an interpreted informal metalanguage without begging an important question. Our epistemic access to reality consists in testing a theory holistically against experience, on the view Putnam ascribes to the moderate realist. Reality has an impact on us cognitively by causing in us the tokening of "mental representations"—syntactic formulae of some sort. That's why the cognitive content of any such constraint as (RRC) for the realist must be "just more theory." To read more content than that into it is to suppose that the world itself somehow interprets our words for us, that "noetic rays stretch from the outside into our heads," as Putnam puts it in his *Dewey Lectures*, page 461.

But how do these considerations show that M^* actually passes (RRC)? Putnam's reply as developed by Taylor is, in effect, that:

(A) If M^* is the intended model then M^* will satisfy the RRC by being the restriction of a model of an extension of the theory obtained by adding RRC+ (the translation of RRC into the metalanguage for L_I, L_I+) to the theory T_I.

Now (A) seems trivial since it represents part of what makes M^* the intended model in the first place. But this, I take it, is precisely Taylor's point. The realist thinks RRC can be used as a substantive theoretical constraint to distinguish the intended model from the pretenders, but it cannot, since it is simply part of what is *meant* by calling a model M "intended" or "standard."

Despite its popularity, then, I do not think that an RRC is able to do the job realists ask of it. The fact of the matter is that Putnam has a very different understanding of *what it is* for an RRC to hold—it is just for our best possible theory to *warrant the assertion that it does*. Moreover, he thinks that this not only is how his antirealist understands Lewis's distinction, but also that it is how the realist, given commitment to naturalistic principles and RTM, really understands it. Anything over and above this presupposes some Archimedean vantage point outside total theory from which we compare our beliefs with reality.[16]

To convince the Skolemite that Lewis's distinction *needs* to be read, or, indeed, *can* be read, in Lewis's way, the realist needs some hard evidence that it needs to be—evidence that cannot be dismissed.[17] So can we find such evidence? I believe we can. There are two sorts of considerations. The first, due to Michael Resnick, urges that there are many mathematical and logical results that bear out Lewis's distinction. The second urges that on pain of paradox some such distinction must hold with respect to the metatheoretical properties of the ideal theory T_I itself.

Recall that Putnam argued for the central lemma of GCA by contending that M^* satisfied every conceivable theoretical constraint since it made T_I true. Michael Resnick contends that this inference is a non sequitur unless some reflection principle of the following general form holds:[18]

To any condition χ that a model of a theory satisfies, there corresponds a condition ζ expressible in the theory that that theory satisfies.

What might the justification for this reflection principle be? Unfortunately, there can be none, for the principle is false. The simplest counterexample to it, Resnick points out, is Tarskian truth. A condition that a model of a theory T might be required to satisfy is that it make all of T's theses come out true. But unless T is either inconsistent or too weak to permit the derivation of basic arithmetic, no truth predicate will be definable in T. So there will be no condition ζ expressible in T corresponding to the condition χ on models of T that they render T's theses true. As Resnick says: "... there is a difference between imposing some constraint C on models of T and requiring that T assert that C is satisfied.... Any true interpretation of T whatsoever—even one which does not satisfy C—will make true every thesis of T, including T's assertion that C is satisfied. Which suffices by itself to block the 'just more theory' gambit...."[19] Resnick is right about this. Putnam's "just more theory" gambit depends on a false assumption to the extent that it accepts the reflection principle above in its unrestricted generality.[20]

But need Putnam accept the reflection principle Resnick imputes to him? Perhaps not. Putnam could say that it is only in the case of an *ideal* theory, an idealized *global* theory of nature, that such a reflection principle would apply. This is because our imagined ideal theory will make explicit every implicit methodological desideratum as part of total theory. That is why the constraints on *models* appear as axioms or theorems within the *theory* T_I.

However, he might claim global theory to be *unique* in this respect. There is no general result connecting conditions on models with conditions expressible in theories, as Resnick rightly points out. Nor can there be. But the cases that Resnick discusses—Tarskian truth, nonnormal models, Skolem's paradox, inner models of ZF—are all cases of theories contained *within* global theory; they are local theories for which a gap can indeed open up between the conditions that models of the given theory satisfy and conditions expressible within the given theory that that theory satisfies.

To take the example that Resnick thinks Putnam's argument appears most plausible for, that of inner models of ZF, the Skolemite can explain why it is that *truth-in-an-inner-model* is no failsafe guide to *truth simpliciter*: "It is indeed the case," she might say, "that if the ideal theory T_I contains ZF one can express the fact that T_I has inner models satisfying all the theoretical constraints, including nondenumerability of the domain of T_I's intended models, standard identity predicate, and a standard truth predicate within the theory T_I itself. So one might be tempted to believe that such inner models constitute intended models of T_I."[21] But as Resnick points out, we can show that *truth-in-an-inner-model* need not coincide with *truth simpliciter* because we can specify in ZF an inner model wherein ZF + AC (axiom of choice) holds yet still prove within ZF itself that AC is independent of the other axioms of ZF. But ZF is simply a local theory within global theory, and the proof that there is such a mismatch between its inner models and its intended models is, again, a proof that is constructed from *within* global theory. Assuming, that is, that we know which models of ZF are intended ones, we can dismiss from within global theory, the identification of ZF's inner models with its standard models.[22] This is possible for local theories where their interpretation is assumed already known and known from within the standpoint of total theory. But none of this will aid us in the slightest when the question at issue is "*What might the correct interpretation of global theory be?*"

The Skolemite contends that Resnick's argument fails because it does not make any allowance for the crucial difference between the models of local theories and models of global theory.[23] In fact, the attempt to privilege the ideal theory T_I in this way ultimately backfires as soon as we inquire about *its* metatheoretical properties.

(I) How do we know that T_I is *consistent*, for example? On Putnam's view this can only be because some theory which we have good grounds for believing asserts that T_I is consistent. If this theory were T_I itself we would ex hypothesi have the best possible grounds for believing its assertion of consistency for T_I. But *can* that theory be T_I? Not without falling foul of Gödel's second theorem. So the consistency of T_I must depend on some other theory, T' say, verifying it as one of its theorems. But this gives rise to a dilemma that Steven Wagner[24] has drawn attention to. Either T' is *independent* of T_I or it is *stronger* than it. If T' is *stronger* than T_I then its assertion of the consistency of T_I is circular since it presupposes the consistency of T_I. On the other hand, if T' is *independent* of T_I then we face an infinite regress in which T''s assertion of the consistency of will only have value if there exists some T'' asserting the consistency of T', which of course only has value if there exists some T''', and so on.

Putnam clearly cannot allow it to be an unknowable fact that T_I is consistent since this would be to adopt an Archimedean vantage point. Yet all need not be lost. Putnam might argue, building on work by Solomon Feferman, that there are perfectly acceptable senses of "consistency" in which the consistency of a system can indeed be proven within the system.

(II) More generally, what is it for the ideal theory T_I to satisfy any desirable constraint according to Putnam? Can it simply be for T_I itself to contain theorems asserting it does? This can't be right. We wouldn't believe the theorems were true unless we already believed the theory itself and the reason we have for believing the theory just is, inter alia, that it satisfies every conceivable operational and theoretical constraint. So once more it must be by virtue of some independent or stronger theory T', and we face a similar problem to that afflicting the consistency of T_I. Only here our reasons for believing the metatheorems of some independent T' concerning T_I will be that some independent ideal theory T_I^* warrants the assertion of T' and our grounds for holding T_I^* to be ideal will likewise be the existence of some independent T'', for which we require an independent ideal T_I^{**}, and so on.

I take it that the considerations at (I) and (II) show that the ideal theory T_I's position is no different from "local" theories' with respect to its metatheoretical properties. So to the extent that Putnam is relying on the reflection principle Resnick imputes to him, his argument breaks down.[25]

I can conceive of only one other way in which the central lemma of the GCA could be salvaged. Putnam might argue that we can be certain, given the vast number of models available for T_I, that there will be at least one in which the constraints we impose on a model to ensure that it is intended are genuinely satisfied.[26] So if we let the sentence s be "M^* is simple," we require proof that M^*+, the model that semantically explicates M^*, preserves our favored interpretation of simplicity. However, it would suffice for Putnam's purposes if there simply *were* such a model M^*+. Of the many interpretations that extend M^*, there is surely at least one that interprets "M^* is simple" as M^* is simple. So we just select that one.

However, there is an unjustified assumption here: there do exist interpretations that interpret the sentence "M^* is simple." But how can we be sure that any of those interpretations constitutes a *model* of T_I? In fact, we *can* be certain of this if the LSA goes through. So let us turn to that argument now.

6.4.2 The Löwenheim–Skolem Argument
The crux of the LSA is a demonstration that for certain languages the truth values of all their sentences can be held constant as they are given a vast number of distinct, even nonisomorphic, interpretations. The upshot of the argument is, then, that reference thereby becomes massively indeterminate, a problem for realism only to the extent that it incorporates an assumption of referential determinacy. For realists disposed to accept determinate word–world relations, a natural response is "So much the worse for the assumption that the total distribution of truth values of sentences suffices to fix reference! This is precisely why we introduced a right reference constraint in the first place."[27] Once more Putnam *appears* to be attacking a position his opponents explicitly disavow. In fact, however, given RTM and accompanying naturalistic assumptions, it is arguable that all that is *available* to fix reference is the

truth values of the sentences we accept, so the problem cannot be dismissed so simply.

Michael Hallett has presented both LSA and PA in an elegant form.[28] It is a direct consequence of the Löwenheim–Skolem theorem that for any distinguished set of objects in the infinite domain $D(M)$ of a model M of a countable, consistent set of first-order sentences, Γ, given any infinite cardinality χ_1 different from that of $D(M)$, some structure W of just that cardinality χ_1 can be found that differs *only* in its cardinality from $D(M)$. In particular, the distinguished objects of $D(W)$ will be the same as for $D(M)$, and the properties and relations of those objects will be preserved also.

To the realist who insists that terms be referentially related to just the right objects, the LSA Skolemite replies that they *can* be so related across these nonisomorphic models. Thus "cats" may well refer to all and only cats, "electrons" to all and only electrons, "Socrates" to Socrates, and so on. The only difference between the domain of the intended model M_I of ideal theory T_I and the domains of its nonisomorphic brethren might just be that the latter are generated from $D(M_I)$ by adding inaccessible parts to it. Thus the (RRC) can be satisfied by nonisomorphic models of T_I.

That the contents of our ideally rational beliefs could be so indeterminate as to be satisfiable in nonisomorphic models is a striking and deeply disquieting result.[29] Does Putnam's LSA really establish *that*? Fortunately, there is reason to doubt that it does. The LST theorems are restricted in range of application and do not apply to second-order languages *as standardly interpreted*. Of itself this is just grist for the Skolemite mill. However, as mentioned before, schematic second-order logic does not require a conception of all subsets of a domain, and since there is at least a strong prima facie argument for a richer logic than first-order even for the purposes of present-day physical theory, the realist can mount a plausible defense for the irrelevance of the LSA, even given commitment to RTM.[30] For this reason, it is the permutation argument, PA, which applies to higher-order and intensional logics, that is the more serious one for the realist to rebut.

6.4.3 *Permutation and Identity*

In the *Meaning and the Moral Sciences* (MMS) theorem on which the permutation argument is based, two interpretations I and J constitute *different* interpretations, according to Putnam, when they assign different *intensions* to each predicate of the language L that has a nontrivial extension. So models or interpretations are identified by their assignments of intensions to each predicate of L.

Putnam claims in "Model Theory and the Factuality of Semantics"[31] (MTFS) that there can be two entirely different reference relations assigning the *same* intension to the sentences of L, where an intension for a sentence s of L is just a function mapping s onto a truth value in every possible world.

The first thing to note about Putnam's theorem is that it does not apply directly to L_I, the language of the ideal theory T_I—at least not as that language is described in MTFS. There, Putnam allows L_I to contain individual constants, and the language L described in his MMS theorem contains *no* individual constants. So can the MMS result be extended to handle individual constants? That will depend on whether those constants are conceived of as *rigid* or *nonrigid* designators. If they are nonrigid, then they can be assimilated to predicates and the MMS result will obviously apply. However, if some or all of these constants are conceived of as *rigid* designators, the MMS result will no longer apply. Sentences of the form Fτ with τ rigid will *not* maintain their truth values across possible worlds, as can be seen from the construction shown in figure 6.1.

We set I as the identity permutation. Vertically arrayed individuals are then deemed identical under I: the individual 1 in world w_1 is identical to the individual directly above it in world w_2, which is identical to the individual directly above *it* in world w_3. For J, the individual 1 in world w_1 is not identical to the individual 1 in world w_2 but rather to the individual 3, the individual 2 in w_1 is identical to the individual 2 in w_2 but

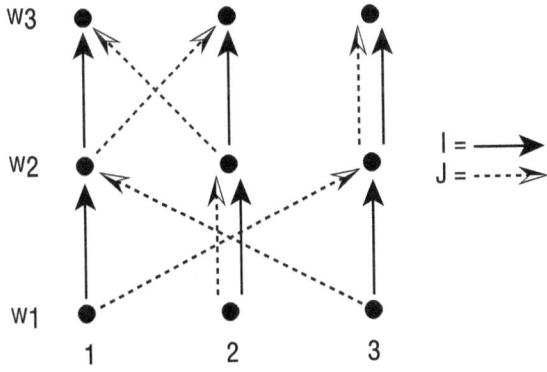

Figure 6.1

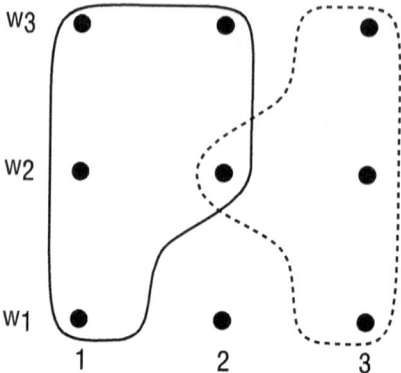

Figure 6.2

not to individual 2 in w_3 but rather to individual 1, and so on, according to the lines.

Now suppose we add some rigid designators to the language L to which the MMS theorem applies such that in our diagram the individual constant k_1 picks out the individual 1 in each world. Suppose also that we represent the individuals in the extension of the predicate F under I and J as indicated in figure 6.2. Then, from the construction, we see that whereas at w_2 Fk_1 is *false* under J, at that same world w_2 it is *true* under I. Hence, the addition of rigid designators to the language L will not preserve the crucial thesis that the intension of a designated *sentence* remains constant from possible world to possible world, since Fk_1 is just such a sentence. Moreover, the construction itself is surely a permissible one since the permutation imposed on one possible world's domain is independent of the permutation imposed on the domain of any other world.

The absence of rigid designators from L_I might not worry a Quinean. Such devices may be entirely unnecessary for serious science, which is presumed to have reached its apotheosis in our hypothesized ideal theory T_I. However, it *does* create problems for Putnam. Whatever else rigid designators are useful for, they are primarily a means of recording the identity of individuals across possible worlds. To debar such devices from L is then to relinquish our certainty that we can track Socrates from possible world to possible world. But if this is so, *Putnam's claim that the interpretations I and J really constitute different interpretations begins to look shaky.*

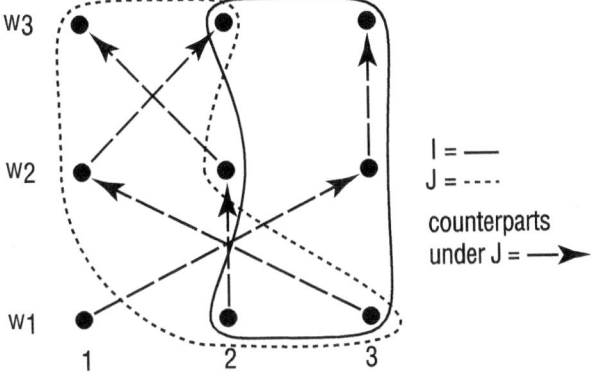

Figure 6.3

Hence, the crucial claim that different *intensions* are assigned to the predicates of L under I and J respectively also becomes dubious. Putnams's justification for that claim is that by permuting domains the extension of a predicate differs under I from its extension under J. The extension of the predicate F in the diagram in figure 6.2, for example, allegedly differs at all the worlds w_1, w_2, and w_3 under I and J respectively. However, we have just seen that rigid designators cannot be incorporated into L. So there is no *absolute* account of identity across possible worlds. So the only sense that we can make of the claim that, say, individual 1 in world w_1 is identical to individual 3 in world w_2 under J is in terms of Lewis-styled counterparts. The identity of individuals across possible worlds is then to be constituted (or approximated) by sufficient similarity of their counterparts. If we do construe identity in terms of counterpart similarity, however, the claim that the extension of F genuinely differs across possible worlds becomes highly dubious as the construction in figure 6.3 shows.

As before we set I as the identity permutation so that vertically arrayed individuals are the most similar counterparts from world to world. With respect to J, however, the arrows indicate the counterparts of individuals 1, 2, and 3 in worlds w_2 and w_3.

It is a simple matter to verify that if the counterparts of individuals 1, 2, and 3 are as indicated by the arrows under J, the extension of F does not vary from world to world. Under both I and J we have that:

(i) $|F|_{w_1}$ = {Individual 2, Individual 3}

(ii) $|F|_{w_2} = \{\text{Individual 3}\}$

(iii) $|F|_{w_3} = \{\text{Individual 2, Individual 3}\}$

It is immaterial which of these worlds we take as the actual world for the structure. So the assumption of an identity permutation is not necessary for the actual world. Indeed, an assumption of an identity permutation for *any world* is not necessary and is made only to simplify the example. My argument is that in the absence of rigid designators from the language, individuals have no identity across possible worlds other than that conferred on them by the satisfaction of predicates. The allegedly different permutation P, then, becomes empty, because it leaves the relations between extensions intact.

So Putnam's permutation argument does not work against the realist. We have been given no convincing reason to believe, even for the simple language L that Putnam considers, that the permutations really *do* produce different models. In fact, we have seen that there are grounds for doubting that this is so. Moreover, if L_1 does contain rigid designators, the permutations cannot possibly go through; and there are some weighty reasons, some of which Putnam has himself adduced, for believing that our language at least *does* contain such devices. If, on the other hand, concurring with Quine, we agree to "Pegasize" our individual constants away, Putnam's MMS theorem still should not disturb us. The crucial claim that the permuted interpretation, J, constitutes a *different* interpretation from the intended one, I, does not survive close scrutiny.

6.5 *Representationalism Skolemized?*

I have argued that none of the MTAs construed as arguments against realism goes through. I have also claimed that, in spite of what Putnam says, this is not the right way to construe them in the first instance. Instead, they are attempts to show that realism and RTM are incompatible. Do they succeed in that endeavor?

I find this a difficult question to answer. Perhaps there is some right reference relation, R, hooking "cat" to cats, but how could we ever get to know about it if RTM is right? Realists who believe in language–world relations of truth and reference should worry about the MTAs for exactly the same reason that theists who believe in miracles should worry about Hume's arguments—they may not establish that miracles do not occur, but they do establish, according to naturalists at least, that we could never have any reason to believe they do.

Is belief in R likewise a matter of faith rather than reason? We need a plausible realist semantics and epistemology to show that it is not. Matters are not helped by declaring that we do not need a reduction of semantic notions to vindicate them. What *do* we need, then? The available reductionist fare—teleosemantics, causal covariationism—is too stunted, semantically and epistemically, to be taken seriously in my view. Austere externalism *appears* to be in trouble from a Humean construal of the MTAs. But perhaps this is to miss the externalist's point that the *world* sets up reliable causal relations that ultimately make for meaning and knowledge. Then we need to know more.

What of realists who are semantic minimalists? No one knows at this stage—at least not until we're given some account of how thought is possible for the minimalist. And what are the prospects for that? Verificationist semantics? Conceptual-role semantics? No semantics? All of these are, in my estimation, nonstarters. The fact of the matter is that realists are committed to verification-transcendent states of affairs, and even if they do not believe such states of affairs make particular beliefs true, epistemic contact between the wffs in our heads and those states of affairs must have something to do with what those beliefs are intuitively "about." Otherwise, how do we become apprised of them in the first place? Starving intentional notions or spiriting them away just exacerbates the epistemic and semantic (if not, then *cognitive*) problems.

So perhaps we should just give up on RTM. That's what Putnam himself has done in his *Dewey Lectures* and subsequently. We shall investigate Putnam's own solution to the representation problem—common sense realism—in section 7.1. Pending that, what are the alternatives? All the things that make realist metaphysics attractive seem to conspire to make realist epistemology and semantics intractable. Should realists then just give up and admit Quine is right? I think this would be an unduly pessimistic response to these difficulties. If holism is right our scientific and linguistic practices implicitly subtend truth conditions for our sentences and referents for our words. Whether there is indeterminacy in these truth conditions and extensions is a matter to be decided by our best logical, grammatical, and semantic theories in concert with other relevant theories—in particular, theories of cognition.

We do not have any direct access to reality either perceptually or cognitively; this is simply not the way nature has designed us. So our cognitive interaction is propositional—theory-mediated, in other words. If the MTA does not succeed in proving that realism is false, as I have argued it does not, this prospect is still open to the naturalist unless it is assumed that only a recognitional grasp of truth conditions can confer meaning on our sentences.

Somehow, in ways we are only beginning to discover, nature has coded in enough cognitive complexity and subtlety to permit us to theorize. Moreover, it is surely no illusion that our theories are approximately true. We may not understand how this is possible. The evidence, though, suggests that it is.

7
Internalism, Pluralism, and Antirepresentationalism

7.1 Common Sense Realism and Antirepresentationalism

I wish now to look at Putnam's more recent position, which he calls "common sense realism" or "natural realism." His intention is to develop a version of realism that does not involve adopting a "God's-eye view" toward our linguistic practices. To that end, along with Wittgenstein, Putnam now believes that it is not possible to circumscribe our linguistic practices in any way other than demonstratively—that is, by pointing to "the way paradigmatic expressions are used in a paradigmatic language by paradigmatic speakers," as Barry Taylor expresses it.[1]

As Taylor points out, Putnam is committed to two basic theses about content that together define his common sense realism (CSR). They are:

(1) Content is internal.
(2) Content is world-embedded.

The internality of content is just the claim above, that it is only by demonstratively circumscribing the use of expressions in a language that we can understand the meanings or contents of those expressions. The world-embeddedness of content, on the other hand, is what Putnam's antirepresentationalism consists in.

Thesis (1), that content is internal, may be inescapable for anyone committed to the view that content is determined purely by use. As Wittgenstein emphasized over and over again,[2] formulations of the assertibility conditions of even the simplest expressions are apt to be misinterpreted—nothing can forestall misunderstandings of how an expression is intended to be used. There does seem to be a need for something like *Verstehen* in the context of linguistic practice if one is to catch on to how speakers intend to use at least certain of their expressions.

The more important reason for demonstrative elucidations of content within the context of "use" theories of meaning is this: Kripke has argued, persuasively in my view, that once one rejects the idea that truth conditions can be assigned to meaning-theoretic clauses specifying the meanings of sentences, one incurs the burden of explaining how it is that there is any fact as to what we mean by them. Internalist views of content such as Putnam's and McDowell's concede at least this to Kripke by way of response—there is no fact *sub specie aeternitatas* as to what one's words mean; there is only a fact within the context of one's linguistic community that by "cat" one means cat, say. This internal meaning fact is then held to be visible only within the framework of those practices that implicitly imbue our words with meaning.

The disquotational clause "'Cat' refers to cats" can thus sweep wildly divergent understandings of "cat" under one label: It simply signals the speaker's intention to call anything he considers sufficiently catlike "cat." But what does he consider sufficiently catlike? Only by attending closely to the circumstances in which he uses "cat," it might seem, can we figure out the pattern of his use. We shall examine the wider impact of Kripke's views for internalism in section 8.3. Having said this, I remain unpersuaded by thesis (1). My basic worry is that the semantic content of words and other linguistic symbols appears to derive from those of mental states. But it is not at all obvious what the analogue of thesis (1) is for mental states. Is it that the mental content of my thought symbol "cat" can be understood only by attending to the functional role that that symbol occupies in my mental economy whereas the mental content of your "cat" symbol can be understood only by delineating the functional role "cat" occupies in your mental economy?

If this is the analogue, and it is hard to see what else it might be, then there seems to be no reason in principle why this should preclude the formation of a hypothesis by an interpreter about what those mental contents are: *that by "cat" I mean cats whereas by "cat" you mean cats-or-mongooses*. The reason we need *Verstehen* in the social setting, if indeed we do, is not replicated in the individualistic context. We need *Verstehen*, the thought goes, because any attempt by a theorist to formulate semantically how participants in a common linguistic practice use their words in the form of a theory of meaning for their language, say, is open to misinterpretation in the sense that someone could accept the formulation as truly describing the way they use their words yet use them in ways quite different from the way other participants in the common practice use them. Such a speaker would be using the words incorrectly by the lights of the other speakers of that language.

In the individual setting, though, where we are discussing the contents of the mental symbols of an individual agent, even though there is indeed an important normative dimension constraining the use the agent himself puts those symbols to in thought and decision making, this normative dimension is not the social dimension of learning to so use your words that others do not misunderstand what you mean or what you want, learning to "go on in the same way," as Wittgenstein puts it. That is a coordination problem that has no analogue in the case of the individual thinker. Relative to the problem of solving this coordination problem, then, it is at least arguable that something like *Verstehen* is required on the part of the would-be participant in the linguistic practice in question.

As Davidson has reminded us, though, interpreting the words of an agent is part of a larger project of interpreting his actions. This involves ascribing propositional attitudes to the agent in such a way that the agent appears rational on the whole. How then is thesis (1) to help us in this part of the interpretative task? Thesis (1) is a corrective against the facile assumption that the interpreter's use of "cat" coincides with the interpretee's use of "chat," to take a simple example. It is also a corrective against a more subtle error—that the interpreter's "cat" coincides with the interpretee's "cat." But it gives the interpreter no purchase at all on how to ascribe contents to the interpretee's propositional attitudes, a sine qua non for the putative pattern recognition involved in discerning the interpretee's use of linguistic expressions to begin. Linguistic use has to be an intentional activity. Davidson nowhere suggests that *Verstehen* and semantic pattern recognition are not necessary in the context of radical interpretation. He would, I think, resist the suggestion, I think quite rightly, that such pattern recognition is sufficient.

So we can agree that some content is internal without agreeing that all is. In particular, the mental content of some typical mental states is not. More than that, unless, as Saul Kripke's skeptic avers, there is no fact of the matter as to what our words mean, we must be able to formulate meaning-theoretic clauses of the form "*'cat' refers to cats*" where the notion of reference is nondisquotational. Unless there were determinate conditions under which at least some predicates are satisfied, names refer, and sentences are true, the strategic problems of communication would appear impossible to solve. This claim is consistent with the thesis that the only humanly feasible entrée into what such conditions are is in general by means of the pattern recognition alluded to in thesis (1). But this falls short of establishing the *internality* of semantic content in the desired sense of that phrase, since other creatures might have other ways of discerning these truth and satisfaction conditions—such as by constructing a recursive truth theory for the languages concerned, in the context of radical interpretation of the speakers' words and actions.

Let us turn now to thesis (2) since this is the more radical of the two theses that define CSR. What does it mean to think of content as world-embedded? In his *Dewey Lectures*, Putnam argues that the representational theory of mind, RTM, which he also calls the Cartesian conception of mind, CCM, is seriously flawed. Putnam does not mean to restrict his attack to a language of thought version of RTM. Rather, any view of the mind will be a RTM or CCM if it entails that the mind is an entity whose contentful states are fixed by connections with the world that are purely causal. The RTM or CCM is then the thesis that the world acts on the agent by producing ideas in his or her mind and the mind in turns acts on the world through behavior that is caused by these ideas. Since all that is available to fix content on this conception are the causal input and output relations the mind bears to various parts of the world, Putnam concludes that since these massively underdetermine content, the CCM has to be rejected.

If the CCM is to be rejected, what does Putnam propose to put in its place? Putnam follows John McDowell in holding content to be world-embedded. What does this mean? Schematically, this is easy to describe. The mind is to be conceived of as connected to the world through the peripheral states that are its perceptions of that world in such a way that the contents of those peripheral states simply are bits of the world. There are no causal or rational intermediaries such as sensory impressions or sensory information interposing between our minds and the states of the world that perception reveals to us in perceptual transactions with that world. As McDowell puts it: "In experience, one takes in, for instance sees, that things are thus and so. That is the sort of thing one can also, for instance, judge."[3] Or again, this time talking of linguistic meaning: "There is no ontological gap between what one can mean and what can be the case."[4] Barry Taylor nicely sums up the Putnam–McDowell picture of the mind when he says: "The mind acquires representational content through the way it is embedded in the world—its peripheral states (perceptions) assume a content identical with bits of the world, whilst interior states assume content through connections with each other and ultimately with the periphery."[5] Taylor goes on to emphasize the crucial point of this picture: As a result of the mind's peripheral states having contents identical with bits of the world, on this model mental contents are *supercausally* related to the world.

This is an ingenious and intriguing view. However, I have several worries. The first concerns *perceptual misrepresentation*. How is this so much as possible if the content of perceptual judgment is a worldly fact or state of affairs? McDowell says: "When we are not misled by experience, we are directly confronted by a worldly state of affairs itself, not waited on by an intermediary that happens to tell the truth."[6] Maybe so. Once one identifies contents of (perceptual) judgments with facts, though, this leaves unexplained what type of contents, if any, perceptual misrepresentations might have.

Second, and more generally, how is it that unmediated cognitive connections between states of the world and veridical perceptual judgments are set up? McDowell seems to think that this is achieved by a type of passive receptivity toward the world. Yet this cannot be the whole story, since we are equally passive on his view to receiving impressions of inner sense—the contents of our thoughts and sensory states. McDowell's way of distinguishing outer from inner seems to go by way of the active faculty of understanding, à la Kant. As Michael Friedman characterizes it:

passively received impressions become experiences of an objective world (and thus impressions of outer sense) only by being taken as such by the active faculty of understanding: by being subject, that is, to the perpetually revisable procedure through which the understanding integrates such impressions into an evolving world-conception.[7]

However, if this is also to be Putnam's answer, it faces a nontrivial task, which Friedman notes, of distinguishing itself from idealism in the form of coherentism:

Relation to an independent objective world is thus not secured by the idea of receptivity, but rather by the spontaneous conceptual activities of the understanding as it rationally evolves an integrated picture of the world. Hence, given McDowell's own conception of what impressions of outer sense amount to, I do not see, in the end, how he has fully rebutted the charge of idealism. I do not see why his conception itself is not finally a version of Coherentism.[8]

Friedman goes on to explain that the problem for McDowell at any rate is not the veridicality of perception but rather the source of the idea of the world. Given that the deliverances of perception (outer sense) are themselves in the end products of spontaneity (the understanding), what we have is that "(perceptual impressions) become expressions of constraint by an independent world precisely through the integrative activities of the understanding. In this way, the crucial notion of independence is, in the end, given a purely coherence-theoretic reading."[9]

My third worry is that I suspect the highly schematic picture of the mind's connections with the world against which both Putnam and McDowell seem to be objecting—the Cartesian conception of mind—is a little too simplistic since it masks the fact that highly complex natural mechanisms whose operation is causal through and through can and have evolved to represent the world reliably in perception. The theory-sketch of CCM makes it appear to the unwary as if these "links" are both simple and direct. Of course, nothing could be further from the truth. As Jerry Fodor notes, in commening on McDowell:

You might have thought that seeing a tree goes something like this: Light bounces off the tree and affects your eyes in ways that determine the sensory content of your experience. Your mind reacts by inferring from the sensory content of your experience something about what in the world might have caused it. The upshot, if all goes well, is that you see the world as locally entreed.

So, then, perception is a hybrid of what the senses are given and what the mind infers. The process is causal through and through: It's part of psychophysics that encounters with trees bring about the kinds of visual sensations that they do. And it's part of cognitive psychology that the visual sensations that encounters with trees provoke occasion the perceptual inferences that they do in the minds with the right kind of history and structure.... So what, exactly, is supposed to be wrong?[10]

McDowell's answer is that this whole psychological account relies on an indefensible myth of the given, which in the end "offers at best exculpations where we wanted justifications.... the best it can yield is that we cannot be blamed for believing whatever our experiences lead us to believe, not that we are justified in believing it."[11] But as Fodor observes, it may be the demand for justification that is at fault here, not the account of perception just given:

Granting something unconceptualized that is simply Given to the mind in experience has generally been supposed to be the epistemological price one has to pay for an ontology that takes the world to be not itself mind-dependent.... Maybe sometimes exculpation is justification and is all the justification that there is to be had?

Why not, after all? If the situation is that I can't but believe that I'm looking at a tree, and if, in that situation, it's the case that I am looking at a tree, and if there is a workable account of why in such situations, I reliably come to believe that there's a tree I'm looking at (viz., because they are situations where trees cause the kinds of sensations that cause minds like mine to think that they are seeing trees) why isn't that good enough for my judgment that I'm seeing a tree to make it into the Realm of Reason? Why, in short, mightn't fleshing out the standard psychological account of perception itself count as learning what perceptual justification amounts to?[12]

Fodor concludes with an observation close to Friedman's: "What McDowell has to pay for demanding that his account of perception conforms to the apriori constraints that his normative epistemology imposes is that he leaves us with no idea at all how perceiving could be a process in the world."[13] The upshot of this brief sketch of Putnam's common sense realism appears to be this: *The representation problem is no easier to solve for proponents of this direct realist view than for metaphysical realists. Hence naturalistic realists gain nothing in their attempts to fend off the antirealist challenge to their views by accepting it.*

7.2 Wright's New Internalism

7.2.1 Some Varieties of Internalism

Crispin Wright has recently argued for a more moderate version of internalism wherein truth, though not definable in epistemic terms, is subject to significant epistemic constraint. As Wright expresses it: "Every kind of state of affairs of which we are capable of conceiving must be one of which we can attain a concrete conception of what kind of powers and situation would place us, or relevantly similar beings, into a position from which it would be assured that our, or their, opinion that it did or did not obtain would be correct."[14]

Internalists propose to constrain truth epistemically by making truth contingent on what would be believed under sufficiently favorable epistemic conditions. But this formulation is both ambiguous and elliptical. It is ambiguous in that it may mean either that a truthbearer p is true if and only if it would be believed under sufficiently favorable epistemic circumstances or, alternatively, that were circumstances sufficiently favorable epistemically, p would be true if and only if it we would come to believe it. The formulation is elliptical in that it does not specify *whose* beliefs are supposed to carry such epistemic authority. We can clarify the alternative readings if, following Wright, we distinguish some actual instances of the first version from the second. Thus Charles Peirce and Hilary Putnam can both be construed as having supported the first version:

(1) Peircean convergentism: p is true ↔ were p to be appraised under conditions holding at the ideal limit of enquiry, p would be believed.

(2) Putnam's internal realism: p is true ↔ were p to be appraised under conditions sufficiently good for the appraisal of p, p would be believed.

Wright argues that both (1) and (2) suffer from insuperable problems. However, he believes that there is a version of internalism, motivated by the second reading of the formulation above, that is *not* vulnerable to these problems. Wright's analysis of the difficulties faced by (1) and (2) leads him to the conclusion that they commit a conditional fallacy in their identification of truth with what would be believed under sufficiently favorable epistemic circumstances. Instead of identifying truth with what would be believed under the right circumstances, we should rather see truth as significantly constrained by the beliefs that we would form given the right epistemic circumstances.

As Wright formulates it:

(3) Wright's moderate internalism: Were p to be appraised under sufficiently good epistemic conditions, p would be true ↔ p would be believed.

Note the right-side of the biconditional, "p would be believed." Believed *by whom?* For Peirce, by *all* enquirers investigating p at the limit of inquiry. For Putnam and Wright, nothing so ambitious is required—instead, any creature with the right cognitive capacities, with access to just the information made available in just those circumstances that are sufficiently favorable for the appraisal of p will come to form the belief that p; no mythical limit of enquiry is needed.

Wright's thesis is that the realism of moderate internalism is just the realism of common sense oblivious to the affront to it caused by metaphysical realism. He defends this by first ascribing to the metaphysical realist a conception of how states of affairs such as the ones involving Socrates' sneezing and BP fluctuations, σ_s and σ_β, may elude our recognitional capacities. This conception he regards as untenable. This is the error-theoretic approach to metaphysical realism that I alluded to above. According to it, we can have no direct access to states of affairs as they are in themselves, owing to the fact that we are subject to, as Wright puts it, *necessary limitations*, which "interpose an irremovable veil or interface between how things are and how we believe them to be such that large sweeps of fact are essentially inaccessible not just to us ... but to any sentient, intelligent creature no matter where and when situated."[15] Is this really metaphysical realism, though? It sounds more like transcendental idealism with its talk of noumenal states of affairs that, of necessity, we can know about only indirectly. Metaphysical realists are perfectly entitled to hold that how things are in themselves is everywhere rationally discoverable. Whence the irremovable interface? Significantly, Wright cites the writings of no contemporary metaphysical realists in support of his claim that "The essence of metaphysical realism ... is thus interface realism" where the "interface" derives from the "necessary limitations" that, according to his understanding, metaphysical realism supposes all rational creatures to be subject to. I see no reason why the metaphysical realist has to be committed to any source of undecidability or evidence-transcendence other than the sort Wright terms "contingencies of epistemic opportunity":

... in all cases where we have a conception of this kind of how the truth value of a particular statement could be unverifiable, a developed account of that conception will consist in detailing limitations of opportunity, or spatiotemporal situation, or perceptual or intellectual capacity, which stop us getting at the relevant facts but to which we, or others, might easily not have been subject—or at least, to which we can readily conceive that an intelligible form of investigating intelligence need not be subject.[16]

A contrast with radical internalism as Dummett conceived it is apposite. Dummett contends, recall, that what distinguishes the metaphysical realist from his antirealist (radical internalist) is the thesis that states of affairs that we currently have no evidence for either hold or fail to hold independently of our ability to find out which. We saw earlier that the resultant notion of undecidability or evidence-transcendence was implicitly indexed to the speakers of a linguistic community in a particular epoch with the specific conceptual resources, means of detection, and total evidence available then and there to them. For Dummett's metaphysical realist, then, it is indeed true that:

In all these cases we have a conception of how the truth-value of a particular sentence could be unverifiable and this conception is backed up by a specific account of our limitations in the relevant case which details:

(1) limitations of opportunity, or (2) limitations of spatio-temporal situation, or (3) limitations of perceptual/intellectual capacity

which limitations prevent us from getting at the relevant facts but which are such that we or others or at least an intelligible form of investigating intelligence need not be subject.[17]

This is precisely the issue between Dummett's realist and his antirealist: that *the facts are there to be got at*, if not by us, then by some hypothetical investigator with suitably enhanced powers. As he put it in his classic paper "Truth" when discussing the sense in which claims such as (S) or (B) are incapable of being known: "The fundamental difference between the anti-realist and the realist lies in this: the anti-realist interprets 'capable of being known' to mean 'capable of being known by us' whereas the realist interprets it to mean 'capable of being known by some hypothetical being whose intellectual capacities and powers of observation may exceed our own.'"[18] If nothing stronger than the notion of undecidability due to contingencies of epistemic opportunity is needed to distinguish Dummett's realist from his antirealist, why is it needed to distinguish Wright's realist from his moderate internalist?

Pace Wright, it seems clear that it is *sufficient* for metaphysical realism that there be states of affairs that obtain independently of our best efforts to find out they do. As our discussion of determinacy showed, it is no step in the direction of internalism to add that the obtaining of such states of affairs is a result of mere contingencies of epistemic opportunity in Wright's sense. Why then does Wright insist that the essence of metaphysical realism is interface realism? Why does he believe the metaphysical realist is committed to an impenetrable veil of representation?

7.2.2 Moderate Internalism and New Actualism

The answer might lie in a striking similarity between moderate internalism and a recent version of actualism in modal metaphysics. Actualists hold that the only things that exist are actual—possibilia do not exist. Though natural, this view is hard pressed to account for the compelling intuition that there really are other ways the world might have been, some of which we may be unable to conceive. If, as Lewis has so persuasively argued, the best explication of the latter intuition involves ontological commitment to possible worlds, actualism is no longer defensible. Enter the new actualist who argues along the following lines:

> The modal realist is quite right to hold that the truth-condition for "Socrates might have been a fisherman" is that there be a possible world containing Socrates in which he is a fisherman. However, pace modal realism, this carries no commitment to possibilia. Rather, this only commits us ontically to the existence of an actual nonconcrete object which might have been a fisherman.

As Christopher Menzel explains:

> ... unlike mathematical objects, which are nonconcrete at *every* possible world, the actual objects required by the truth of modal claims are only *contingently* nonconcrete—they are nonconcrete at our world but concrete at other possible worlds. Similarly, ordinary concrete objects (like the rocks, tables, planets, etc. of our world) are assumed to be contingently concrete—they are concrete at some worlds (including ours) and not at other worlds.[19]

Wright's moderate internalist argues, in precisely analogous fashion, that the truth condition for "Socrates sneezed in his sleep the night before he took the hemlock" is indeed the evidence-transcendent state of affairs σ_S. But although evidence-transcendent, and so epistemically inaccessible, for twenty-first-century human investigators, σ_S is not *necessarily* evidence-transcendent. It is only contingently so. Classical (radical) internalism and metaphysical realism can then be seen to arise as opposite reactions to a shared false presupposition: that states of affairs that are evidence-transcendent are necessarily so. Where the metaphysical realist insists that *in spite of their epistemic inaccessibility*, such states of affairs determinately either hold or fail to hold, the classical internalist concludes that *because of their epistemic inaccessibility*, such states of affairs could not possibly hold or fail to hold.

Following the new actualist's lead, the new internalist contends that common sense is not committed to the existence of "pure possibilia" in the form of epistemically inaccessible states of affairs when it correctly assigns σ_S as the truth condition for (S). For us twenty-first-century humans, σ_S is indeed epistemically inaccessible, but it could have been accessible. It is thus an abstract state of affairs whose epistemic inaccessibility is merely contingent.

Realism about possibilia begins with the correct intuition that there are other ways the world might have been; it then wrongly infers, according to the new actualist, that these possibilia are necessarily nonconcrete. Metaphysical realism starts with the correct observation that some states of affairs are undetectable, mistakenly inferring, the new internalist contends, that these states of affairs are *necessarily* undetectable. New actualists view modal realism as involving an unwanted and unnecessary commitment to possibilia whose inclusion in our ontology comes at an impossibly high epistemic cost. These entities are supposed to be both knowable, yet wholly independent of our minds. They are deemed to exist in a certain state—that of necessary nonconcreteness—that eludes any ordinary means of detection.

Metaphysical realism, according to our new internalists, gives rise to a comparable commitment to mind-independent possibilia in the form of necessarily undetectable states of affairs (or other objects) like our past states of affairs σ_S or σ_B involving Socrates' sneezing or blood pressure fluctuations. An impossible epistemic cost is incurred when we *erroneously* take these states of affairs to ground the commonsense conviction of metaphysical determinacy. Yet there is nothing we twenty-first-century humans can ever do to access either σ_s or σ_B. Hence, the commonsense conviction that Socrates either did or did not sneeze or suffer BP fluctuations that night must have a very different origin if it is to be well founded. What could this source *be* other than the structure of our own cognitive capacities? The means of detecting σ_S that Xanthippe might plausibly have actually exercised that night in 399 B.C. differ not at all from our means of detecting when someone sneezes in their sleep today. This fact justifies the claim that states of affairs such as σ_s and σ_B can be thought of as *contingently nonconcrete* only in the sense that it is a contingent matter that they fail to activate the recognitional capacities of twenty-first-century humans—for us they are abstract entities that could indeed have been concrete.

So we have a tight analogy between new actualism and new internalism. Internalism stands to externalism as actualism stands to possibilism. The classical internalism of Dummett's antirealist refused to endorse the existence of states of affairs that are not actually detectable by our twenty-first-century human recognitional capacities. Thus was the classical internalist distinguished from the externalist, that is, the metaphysical realist, who did endorse the existence of these mere possibilia. Now, just as the new actualist charges his classical forebear with drawing a crucial distinction in the wrong place, so does Wright's new internalist charge his classical forebear. The distinction for the new internalist is *not* between those states of affairs that are actually detectable and those that are not actually detectable. Rather, since the only states of affairs that exist are actually detectable states of affairs, the real distinction is between those detectable states of affairs that are *contingently detectable* ("contingently concrete") and those that are *contingently nondetectable* ("contingently nonconcrete"). Internalists reject merely possible objects of cognition, on this interpretation, just as surely as actualists reject merely possible objects. The diagram in figure 7.1 illustrates this.

What are we to make of new internalism? One welcome feature is that it imputes to the metaphysical realist no irremovable interface between objects and our knowledge of them. We saw earlier that this attribution

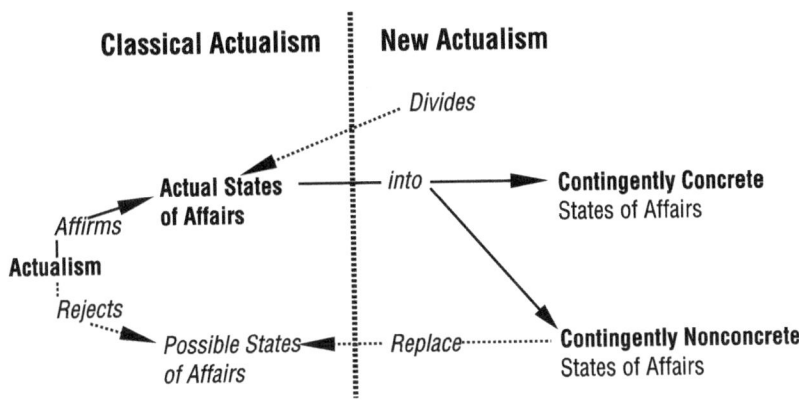

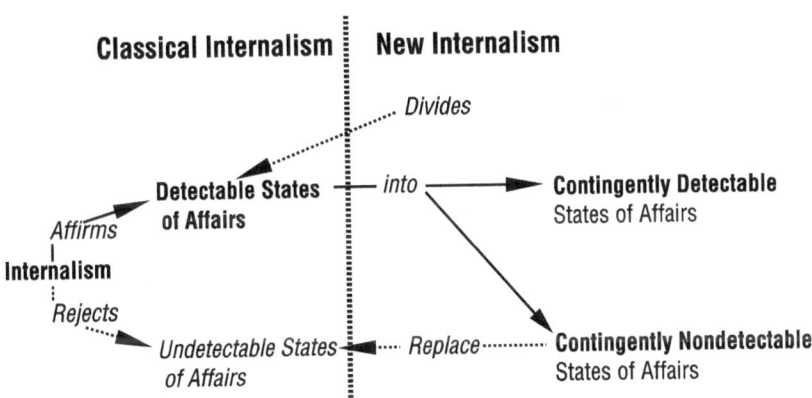

Figure 7.1

is highly problematic, painting metaphysical realists as transcendental idealists. For the new internalist, not only is there no *need* to level such an accusation against metaphysical realism, there is no justification for doing so. The problem with metaphysical realism, according to the new internalist, is not that it interposes a veil of representations between objects in the world and our knowledge of them. The problem is much more fundamental: There are no representations to be had in the first place if metaphysical realism is true.

Why? Because if undetectable states of affairs (or objects of any sort) are *necessarily* undetectable, there is no possible world in which they are detected—no possible world w in which states of affairs such as our σ_s

and σ_B lie at the source of a causal chain that activates the detectional mechanisms of any investigator in that world w. The epistemological problem with metaphysical realism, on this interpretation, is thus not representationalism but rather Platonism. Scientific realists standardly seek to quash instrumentalist qualms about theoretical entities by pointing to cases where previously unobservable theoretical entities have become observable. Such realists take this as strong confirmation that their theoretical entities do indeed lie at the origin of causal chains. Unlike his scientific realist counterpart, the metaphysical realist, on this interpretation, is consigned to admitting his theoretical posits lie at the origin of *no* causal chains. *That* is the problem with metaphysical realism, according to the new internalist.

Stated thus, however, new internalism's objection to metaphysical realism is just a nonstarter for reasons that are by now familiar. The metaphysical realist is *not* committed to the extravagant claim that epistemically inaccessible states of affairs are *necessarily* inaccessible. To the contrary, there are indeed possible worlds accessible from ours wherein states of affairs like σ_S and σ_B can be and *are* reliably detected. How can it be incompatible with metaphysical realism to believe otherwise?

As far as presenting a cogent objection to metaphysical realism, then, new internalism fares no better than moderate internalism. This should be no surprise if, as we've argued, new internalism *just is* moderate internalism. True enough, the new internalist does not attribute any gratuitous beliefs to the metaphysical realist (such as the representational interface). On that score he appears to do better than Wright's moderate internalist. However, by refusing to allow metaphysical realists the right to believe in states of affairs that are only *contingently* undetectable, he does much the same thing.

There is a way of fixing this latter defect open to the new internalist. But it comes at considerable cost to the integrity of his own position. It begins by noting that the epistemological problems with metaphysical realism are not at all trivial and do indeed derive from a genuine problem with mental representation. *Pace* Wright, McDowell, and the recent Putnam, though, that problem has nothing to do with the metaphysical realist's interposition of a veil of representations between real objects and the inquiring mind. It has to do with how mental representation could be so much as possible if the world is as it is independently of how we perceive or conceive it to be.

Given this statement of the representation problem, the particular difficulty twenty-first-century humans have with mentally representing states of affairs such as σ_B at least can indeed be cast in terms of necessary epistemic inaccessibility—there is no world (metaphysically) accessible from our world in which creatures with *just our* conceptual resources Ψ, means of detection Δ, and total information Σ are able to acertain whether (B) holds or not. In every such $\Psi\Delta\Sigma$ world the status of σ_B thus remains indeterminate. How then can any reliable means of mentally representing just that state of affairs be established in the first place? In reinstating cognitive parochialism, a genuine problem for metaphysical realism reemerges, but at considerable cost to the new internalist. The cost is incurred because the new internalist has simply recast classical (or radical) internalism's original objection to metaphysical realism in slightly different terminology. In so doing, the new internalist effectively undermines any basis for preferring his version of internalism to classical internalism and, as a direct and disastrous consequence, thereby undermines his own ground for believing in metaphysical determinacy.

Consider the new internalist's claim that classical internalism draws the distinction between detectable and undetectable states of affairs in the wrong place. The classical internalist took the epistemically relevant distinction to be between states of affairs we twenty-first-century humans can detect and those states of affairs we cannot detect. As metaphysical determinacy had thereby been assimilated to detectability by twenty-first-century humans, the detectability–undetectabililty distinction for the classical internalist simply marked the divide between determinate and indeterminate states of affairs. The new internalist's innovation was to separate issues of metaphysical determinacy from issues of detectability on the grounds that some perfectly determinate states of affairs, such as our σ_S and σ_B, are only *contingently* undetectable. But if "contingently undetectable" is to mean, as it apparently must for the argument against metaphysical realism to get off the ground, *contingently undetectable by us twenty-first-century humans with our quirky psychology Ψ, means of detection Δ, and information Σ*, the classical internalist's original distinction between states of affairs detectable by us and states of affairs not detectable by us has simply been recast—as between those states of affairs *contingently* detectable by us twenty-first-century humans and those *contingently* undetectable by us.

The result is that the new internalist is left squaring off against the classical internalist over the issue of metaphysical determinacy of states of affairs such as σ_S and σ_B. The difference now is that having ceded his basic conceptual resources (contingent versus noncontingent detectability) to the classical internalist in order to issue a genuine challenge to metaphysical realism, he no longer has any *theoretical* basis for defending his belief in metaphysical determinacy. Alternatively, if the new internalist insists on metaphysical determinacy and on the theoretical integrity of his basic division between contingently detectable and contingently undetectable states of affairs, he thereby rejects the classical internalist's cognitive parochialism. But then his challenge to metaphysical realism lapses. Worse, his own position tacitly presupposes metaphysical realism: to secure the metaphysical determinacy of some given state of affairs σ_p, the circumstances suitable for detection and the powers suitable for detecting must be specified in advance. But this cannot be done without parametric dependence on σ_p. It is noteworthy that just this type of objection, which we might call the *terminological transcript* objection, has been leveled at new actualism in modal metaphysics. Christopher Menzel puts the objection thus:

> ... one might argue that it is no surprise that new actualism retains the theoretical power of possibilism, because new actualism is nothing more than thinly veiled possibilism: the new actualist's "actuality" is just the possibilist's being, and contingent nonconcreteness is nothing but the possibilist's mere possibility; nothing but the terminology distinguishes a mere *possibile* from a possibly (but not actually) concrete individual.... the new actualist does indeed maintain a single sense of being; but in place of the possibilist's division of being into two modes—actuality and contingent nonactuality—the new actualist substitutes a division of actuality into two modes: concreteness and contingent nonconcreteness. It is difficult not to see this as a mere relabeling of the possibilist's distinction. Most classical actualists will, therefore, regard new actualism as having the form of actualism without having the content necessary to serve as a genuine solution to the possibilist challenge.[20]

By substituting "internalism" for "actualism," "externalism" (or "metaphysical realism") for "possibilism," and "detectability" for "concreteness," a forceful objection to new internalism can be formulated. In summary, then, Wright's moderate internalism, explicated in most plausible form as new internalism, either presents no alternative to classical, that is, radical, internalism or else presents no credible challenge to metaphysical realism. To achieve the latter, it must reclothe the classical or radical internalist's original objection in its own vocabulary, but then it becomes a mere terminological transcript of radical internalism. Alternatively, by insisting on the distinctness and integrity of its own conceptual framework, moderate internalism faces a far more worrying terminological transcript objection—and to the extent it does so insist, moderate internalism loses its capacity to distinguish itself from the metaphysical realism it purports to oppose: The new internalist's crucial distinctions aimed at securing metaphysical determinacy already tacitly presuppose it. It then becomes a terminological transcript of metaphysical realism. Moderate internalism is the realism of common sense, then, only when it is metaphysical realism in thin disguise. In itself, it is essentially unstable.

7.3 Superassertibility and Alethic Pluralism

7.3.1 Alethic Pluralism

An unattractive sort of alethic pluralism holds that the truth predicate varies in meaning from domain to domain—the sense in which ethical claims are true is not the sense in which scientific claims are true. Such a view is best countered in the way Quine countered a similar thesis about existence: although there may be great variety among existing things, there is no variety in their existence; *pari passu* for truths and truth. Crispin Wright holds a saner version of alethic pluralism: "The contention ... is not that 'true' is ambiguous, that it means different things as applied within different regions of discourse. On the contrary, the concept admits of a uniform characterisation wherever it is applied— the characterisation given by the minimal platitudes, which determine everything that is *essential* to truth." Whence the pluralism then?

> The form of pluralism ... is one of, roughly, *variable realisation*. What constitutes the existence of a number may be very different to what constitutes the existence of a material object. The identity of persons is generally held to call for a special account, contrasting with that appropriate to the identity of material continuants generally. And what constitutes truth in ethics may be quite different to what constitutes truth in theoretical physics.... Evidently, there is space for a corresponding contention about truth. *There need be no single, discourse-invariant thing in which truth consists.*[21]

Does Wright's view entail, as Wright himself requires, that there is a robust property of truth "variably realized" by discourse-relative constituent properties? It does not, for it does not even entail that there is a *property* of truth to begin with. The view is consistent, in other words, with an eliminativist thesis about truth—there is no property of truth per se, but only a disjunction of properties like robust assertibility,[22] ideal coherence, and so on such that the possession of any one of these by a suitable truth-bearer suffices for the predicate "is true" to apply to that truth-bearer. However, disjunctions of properties are not further properties, according to this eliminativist view, which goes back to F. P.

Ramsey. Hence, Wright cannot simply assume the existence of a robust property of truth, given his conviction that "there need be no single, discourse-invariant thing in which truth consists." Whether such a property exists at all will depend on the correct metaphysics of properties.

Further, even if there is a unitary property of truth, it appears to follow from Wright's claims that

For each discourse D and true sentence s of D for which s's truth is realized or constituted by some property that minimally satisfies the alethic platitudes there will necessarily be a determinate set, finite or infinite, of properties $P_1, P_2, P_3, \ldots, P_k, \ldots$ (properties such as superassertibility, convergence of best opinion, optimality of belief, correspondence with a state of affairs ...) each of which realizes or constitutes the property of truth for s in the sense that s is P_1 and s is true or s is P_2 and s is true or ... or s is P_k and s is true or ... and the disjunctive property $P_1 \vee P_2 \vee \ldots P_k \vee \ldots$, is necessarily coextensive with the property of truth.

The reduction or elimination of truth to the disjunctive property $P_1 \vee P_2 \vee \ldots P_k \vee \ldots$ is explicitly modeled on Jaegwon Kim's reduction of mental kinds to disjunctions of physical kinds. Whether one takes the reductionist or eliminativist option depends on whether one thinks disjunctive properties exist to begin with or, supposing they do, whether such properties explain anything over and above whatever their disjunct properties explain. To the extent one thinks either that the complex property does not exist or else that it has no additional explanatory power, one is a serious pluralist about truth.

The platitudes concerning the predicate "true" will have done their work when they point us in the direction of the relevant substantial alethic properties, such as coherence or superassertibility, which ground the applications of the truth predicate within a given discourse. "True" might then discharge an important *expressive* role in a discourse but by itself could discharge no genuine explanatory role distinct from the discourse-relative roles of coherence, superassertibility, convergence, and so on.

7.3.2 Problems for Pluralists

Naive alethic pluralism holds that the predicate "true" is ambiguous, its interpretation discourse-relative. One problem for this view is posed by the *open question argument* against ethical naturalism: Consider any true ethical judgment such as (t), "Torturing innocent children is wrong."

I. Ethical naturalism entails that if (t) is true at all, then it is deducible from true natural (nonevaluative) statements.²³

II. But (t) cannot be deducible from any true natural statements, since for any putative natural reduct (t_n) of (t) formed by replacing the ethical term "wrong" with a term denoting some natural property F, such as "... inflicts pain on them," it is coherent to ask whether torturing innocent children is really wrong simply in virtue of F.

III. Hence, ethical naturalism is false.

If true ethical judgments differ from true natural (nonevaluative) judgments in that a different notion of truth applies to them, this argument fails because of an equivocation in its premises (I) and (II). There is no univocal "true"; there is instead only true$_E$ and true$_N$. But now not only is the open question argument exposed as fallacious, the proponent of (this version of) ethical naturalism cannot so much as coherently *state* the reductionist ambitions of that theory. Yet irrespective of whether they agree or disagree with it, *everyone* appreciates the force of the open question argument, just as readily as they appreciate the force of the ethical naturalism it seeks to undermine. Any theory that disputes this simply beggars belief.

Wright can avoid this unpalatable consequence since on his version of alethic pluralism, "true" is univocal. But the victory is short-lived. Suppose that the truth of (t), a sentence in which evaluative terms appear, reduces to its superassertibility—that is, to the existence of a robust warrant for asserting (t). We suppose also that truth for (t_n), a sentence referring only to natural (nonevaluative) properties, is a mind-independent correspondence between (t_n) and some specific mind-independent fact (f_n). Then we have that for the open question argument to go through it must be the case that:

(1*) If ethical naturalism is true, the property that grounds the truth of (t) is reducible to the property that grounds the truth of (t_n).

(1*) is completely unobjectionable for alethic monists. The property that grounds the truth of (t_n) is, let's say, the propensity for torture to induce pain. Then this same property is what grounds the truth of the claim (t) that torture is wrong. But for Wright's pluralist, things are far more complicated. Given alethic pluralism, (1*) commits the ethical naturalist to defending the claim that the property that constitutes the *superassertibility* of (t), that is, some robust warrant W for (t), can be reduced to some *mind-independent correlation* between (t)'s natural reduct (t_n) and some mind-independent fact, (f_n).

Assuredly, ethical naturalism can now be expressed but in grossly distorted form since what it expresses is patently false. This is because the whole point of introducing the notion of superassertibility is to *displace* correspondence truth. As Wright himself puts it, superassertibility "is a language-game internal notion, as it were"; it is

> a projection of whatever internal discipline informs a discourse.... To think of a discourse as dealing with truth-apt contents, accordingly, need involve, when truth is conceived as superassertibility, no work for a type of idea which is absolutely central to traditional realist thinking: the idea of correspondence, of representation of real, external states of affairs.[24]

Ethical naturalism thus is not committed to (1*) above in any case where the property grounding truth for the evaluative language *L* diverges from the property grounding truth for the nonevaluative language *L** within which the natural reducts of evaluative sentences of *L* are formulated. So the problem remains even for Wright's more sophisticated form of alethic pluralism: Given that different properties may constitute truth from domain to domain, ethical naturalism and reductionist views generally cannot so much as be coherently stated—a problem indeed for a theory whose primary motivation is to *oppose* reductionism.

7.3.3 Superassertibility and Truth

In addition to developing a version of alethic pluralism, Wright has also championed the cause of epistemic theories of truth. His notion of superassertibility, which he intends as a deliberate generalization of intuitionistic provability, is supposed to apply to empirical as well as mathematical statements. He defines it thus: "A statement is superassertible ... if and only if it is, or can be, warranted, and some warrant for it would survive arbitrarily close scrutiny of its pedigree and arbitrarily extensive increment to or other forms of improvement of, our information."[25] If we let "S" be the superassertibility predicate and "W" stand for "is warranted," then, quantifying over states of information, σ, we can express Wright's notion thus:[26]

$$S\Theta \leftrightarrow (\exists \sigma)(W\Theta \text{ in } \sigma \,\&\, (\forall \sigma^*)(\sigma^* \geq \sigma \rightarrow W\Theta \text{ in } \sigma*))$$

In this formula "$\sigma^* \geq \sigma$" is to be read: "σ^* is an extension of σ." Superassertibility is just stable assertibility, in other words.

One difficulty with Wright's proposal concerns the nature of his warrants. These are meant to be defeasible. Yet intuitionistic warrants are standardly *in*defeasible. Are we supposed to obtain an indefeasible warrant for Θ by simply stringing together indefinitely many states of information in which Θ is not as a matter of fact defeated? Wright seems to think that it is just persistent nondefeat that matters.[27] But if that is correct there should be nothing surprising about the possibility of Θ's being superassertible while false, or true while not superassertible. Yet, as we shall see, Wright demurs. These questions are pertinent to the project of formalizing superassertibilist semantics, for in Kripke models states of information *are* identified by the wffs assertible therein, and the "stability" clause of the definition of superassertibility, $(\forall\sigma^*)(\sigma^* \geq \sigma \to W\Theta\sigma^*)$, drops out as redundant since the monotonicity of $\Vdash$ automatically ensures this condition is satisfied.

In fact, there is a serious doubt as to whether superassertibility *is* a generalization of intuitionistic warranted assertibility. The reason is that the forcing relation $\Vdash$ of the Kripke semantics does not satisfy the definition of superassertibility when "$\Vdash$" is substituted for "W" in the definiens:

$$S\Theta \leftrightarrow (\exists\sigma)(W\Theta\sigma \,\&\, (\forall\sigma^*)(\sigma^* \geq \sigma \to W\Theta\sigma^*))$$

Substituting "$\Vdash$" in this definition for "W" gives us:

(S) $S\Theta \leftrightarrow (\exists\sigma)(\sigma \Vdash \Theta \,\&\, (\forall\sigma^*)(\sigma^* \geq \sigma \to \sigma^* \Vdash \Theta))$

However, as the following simple Kripke tree illustrates, intuitionistic assertibility and superassertibility *can* come apart:

$\sigma_\alpha \quad\quad \sigma_\beta$
$\quad\quad\quad\;\; p$

p is superassertible at σ_α, hence superassertible simpliciter, *according to the definition of this notion at (S) above* since it is assertible at σ_β and at all extensions thereof. However, in the Kripke semantics, only $\neg\neg p$ is assertible at σ_α. Since p is not intuitionistically assertible at σ_α, neither is Sp given, as required, that $Sp \to p$ (where the meaning of "$\to$" is given by its assertibility conditions). So we have that in the structure above, whereas p is superassertible according to the definition at (S), only $\neg\neg p$ is intuitionistically assertible. Intuitionistic logic is both sound and complete relative to the Kripke semantics, and the addition of double negation elimination to intuitionistic logic transforms it into classical. This suggests that the logic necessary to systematize reasoning with a superassertibility predicate might be classical rather than intuitionistic.

At the very least, the meaning of existential quantification needs to be made clear in a way that is acceptable to antirealists (since Wright's project is to develop a notion of truth on which both realists and antirealists can agree). As it is, it can be superassertible in σ_α (as in the Kripke tree above) that a state of information σ_i warranting Θ *exists* even though we may not be able to recognize *in σ_α* that it does. There is no requirement that we be able to produce *in σ_α* any witness for this claim.

By way of contrast, in the Kripke Semantics $\exists x \Theta x$ is assertible in β only if we can supply *in β* such a witness:

$\beta \Vdash \exists x \Theta x$ iff there is some $a \in D_\beta$ $\beta \Vdash \Theta(a)$

In an effort to explicate a notion of truth acceptable to both realists and antirealists, Wright aspires to de facto absoluteness and timelessness for his superassertibility predicate.[28] Even more ambitiously, he attempts to establish that superassertibility is a bona fide notion of truth.[29] This is because he advocates a certain minimalism about truth according to which any predicate that satisfies certain minimal conditions is a truth predicate. These conditions are:

(I) The predicate satisfies the disquotational schema, (DS) $T(p) \leftrightarrow p$

and

(II) The predicate commutes with the logical operators.[30]

We can agree that these are at least necessary conditions for a predicate to be a truth predicate even if we are not persuaded that they are sufficient. At first glance it looks unlikely that superassertibility will commute with negation. It seems rash to infer from the fact that p is not superassertible that its negation is. Yet Wright does argue for this very entailment, which he must if "S" is to be a truth predicate. He assumes the following two principles, which he labels (K) and (L): (K) $\Diamond K\Theta \to S\Theta$ and (L) $\Theta \leftrightarrow \Diamond K\Theta$.

His proof of $\neg S\Theta \to S\neg\Theta$ then proceeds straightforwardly:

(1) $\neg Sp$ H
(2) $\neg \Diamond Kp$ (K)
(3) $\neg p$ (L)

(4) ◇K¬p   (K)
(5) S¬p   (K)

Wright also argues for the converse entailment, from S¬Θ to ¬SΘ, as is required if "S" is to be a truth predicate. There is, however, a strong reason for doubting the equivalence between ¬SΘ and S¬Θ. This stems from what might be termed *states of perpetual ignorance*. Wright is well aware of the need to acknowledge such states when he writes: "if the theorist is unwilling to accept that both 'Not P' and 'Not Not P' are assertible in a neutral state of information, that seems dangerously close to an arbitrary insistence that the metalanguage should have no means for expressing such neutrality; which seems quite unsatisfactory."[31] Neutral states of information are one thing, states of perpetual ignorance quite another. The problem for Wright is that although neutral states of information can be expressed easily enough as ones in which S(¬W¬p & ¬W¬¬p),[32] the attempt to represent states of *perpetual* ignorance using a superassertibility predicate results in gibberish. The natural formulation of the relevant possibility is just: S(¬S¬p & ¬S¬¬p). However, given Wright's equivalence, ¬SΘ ⇔ S¬Θ, this amounts to S(S¬¬p & ¬S¬¬p). States of perpetual ignorance apparently license the claim that a contradiction is superassertible—a rather swift (but completely unpalatable) route to dialethism.

It is no use looking for any intensionality in the "S" predicate. It is supposed to be a truth predicate according to Wright and thus subject to the disquotational schema. Therefore:

(1) S(¬S¬p & ¬S¬¬p)   Df
(2) ¬S¬p & ¬S¬¬p   Tr. E
(3) S¬¬p & ¬S¬¬p   Equivalence
(4) S(S¬¬p & ¬S¬¬p)   Tr. I

Wright might wish to contest the representation of states of perpetual ignorance as S(¬S¬p & ¬S¬¬p), perhaps along the following lines: "When we consider the possibility that a given state of information may not warrant a given statement *p*, we are envisaging a neutral state of information. But a state of perpetual ignorance would require us to survey all possible states of information, and given that the totality of such states is indefinitely extensible this is incoherent. In that case even if we can assert of any such σ that it is neutral with regard to *p*, and even if we believe that such neutrality is more than likely to persist through any foreseeable extension of σ, we would never be in a position to assert ¬S¬p or ¬S¬¬p."

That is, according to this argument, it might be superassertible that: $(\exists \sigma)(\neg W \neg p \sigma \,\&\, \neg W \neg \neg p \sigma)$ for any σ and p. It may also be superassertible that: $(\exists \sigma)((\neg W \neg p \sigma \,\&\, \neg W \neg \neg p \sigma) \,\&\, (\forall \sigma^*)(\sigma^* \geq \sigma \rightarrow \neg W \neg p \sigma^* \,\&\, \neg W \neg \neg p \sigma^*))$. Let us call these latter states of information *states of persistent ignorance*. Of special concern to us is the case where it is the present state of information σ_α and all foreseeable extensions thereof that sustain persistent ignorance with respect to p:

$$(\neg W \neg p \sigma_\alpha \,\&\, \neg W \neg \neg p \sigma_\alpha) \,\&\, (\forall \sigma^*)(\sigma^* \geq \sigma_\alpha \rightarrow \neg W \neg p \sigma^* \,\&\, \neg W \neg \neg p \sigma^*)$$

Wright's response might then be to deny the intelligibility of states of perpetual ignorance in favor of states of persistent ignorance.

As against this, I contend that there are empirical cases, such as the one to be developed below, that are cases of *perpetual* rather than just *persistent* Ignorance. Even if it has no problems with neutral states of information (ones that neither warrant p nor warrant ¬p), intuitionism in fact has its own problems with states of perpetual ignorance—or, at least, it *would* have if such states could arise.

Intuitionistically if "∇" means "we have a warrant for," from $\nabla(\neg \nabla \neg p \,\&\, \neg \nabla \neg \neg p)$ we can also prove that we have a warrant for a contradiction:[33]

(1) $\nabla(\neg \nabla \neg p \,\&\, \neg \nabla \neg \neg p)$
(2) $\nabla \neg \nabla \neg p \,\&\, \nabla \neg \nabla \neg \neg p$
(3) $\nabla \neg \neg p \,\&\, \nabla \neg p$
(4) $\nabla(\neg \neg p \,\&\, \neg p)$

However, it is plausible to believe that at least in intuitionistic logic and mathematics states of perpetual ignorance *cannot* arise. For them to do so, it would need to be the case that we could obtain conclusive evidence that for some currently undecided mathematical statement p, we could never prove p and never prove its negation. But it is hard to see how we could be in such a position since this seems tantamount to allowing the possibility of absolutely unprovable intuitionistic mathematical statements. There are no bounds on what we might discover mathematically that could resolve the status of any currently undecidable mathematical statement p; it would seem that from the intuitionistic point of view we could never refute the claim that p was superassertible nor refute the claim that its negation was either. This is a good reason, I believe, why intuitionism ought *not* to be generalized to the empirical case since for empirical statements there are indeed bounds on what we can discover. So there is something deeply mistaken about an account of negation such as the superassertibilist's that licenses the denial of an empirical statement on the grounds that we can be stably certain that no stable warrant for its truth will ever be forthcoming.

Consider the statement, j: "Julius Caesar's systolic blood pressure rose by 30 mmHg just before he crossed the Rubicon." Since there is a fact of the matter about *any* person's systolic BP at *any* time, j is either true or false, realism be hanged.[34] Since people cannot detect when their systolic blood pressure is raised and since no one in Caesar's day possessed the relevant concept nor the techniques for measuring systolic blood pressure, we can be stably certain that no stable warrant for j's truth or falsity *could* ever be forthcoming. Yet intuitionistically this fact licenses us to assert $\neg j$. Worse, it also licenses us to assert $\neg\neg j$, hence $\neg j$ & $\neg\neg j$.[35] As regards superassertibilism, this example also provides excellent grounds for believing that our state of information with respect to j is one of *perpetual* rather than just persistent ignorance—that is, we are justified in believing not only that:

$$(\neg W\neg j\sigma_a \ \& \ \neg W\neg\neg j\sigma_a) \ \& \ (\forall \sigma^*)(\sigma^* \geq \sigma_a \rightarrow \neg W\neg j\sigma^* \ \& \ \neg W\neg\neg j\sigma^*)$$

but also that:

$$\neg(\exists\sigma)(W\neg j\sigma \ \& \ (\forall\sigma^*)(\sigma^* \geq \sigma \rightarrow W\neg j\sigma^*))$$

and:

$$\neg(\exists\sigma)(W\neg\neg j\sigma \ \& \ (\forall\sigma^*)(\sigma^* \geq \sigma \rightarrow W\neg\neg j\sigma^*))$$

That is, this is a case in which we really do have $S(\neg S\neg j \ \& \ \neg S\neg\neg j)$: a situation of *perpetual* rather than *persistent* ignorance.

Furthermore, the objection that this requires us to survey all possible states of information is lame. All we need intuitionistically to demonstrate $\neg S\neg j$ $(/\neg S\neg\neg j)$ is a refutation of the claim that any state stably warranting $\neg j$ $(/\neg\neg j)$ can arise. But we clearly have such a refutation: We can be certain no warrant for $\neg j$ $(/\neg\neg j)$ will ever be forthcoming since no record attesting to $\neg j$ $(/\neg\neg j)$ could possibly have existed and no traces could possibly have survived. The upshot is that superassertibilism does not have an acceptable account of negation. Moreover, and relatedly, if part of what it is to be a truth predicate is to satisfy the recursion clause for negation, the predicate corresponding to superassertibility is not a truth predicate since it does not commute with negation.

Truth and Superassertibility in Mathematics In fact, given his official alethic pluralism, it is unclear that Wright really *would* wish to defend superassertibility as the "realizer" of the truth role in the empirical domain. No matter. There is, in fact, a far more worrying and surprising result with which the friend of superassertibility will have to contend since it apparently shows that *superassertibility cannot serve as a model of either truth or meaning in the one domain for which it is tailor made: mathematics*. I take my lead from George Boolos's delightful article "Gödel's Second Incompleteness Theorem Explained in Words of One Syllable":

Now: two plus two is not five. And it can be proved that two plus two is not five. And it can be proved that it can be proved that two plus two is not five, and so on.

Thus: it can be proved that two plus two is not five. Can it be proved as well that two plus two is five? It would be a real blow to math, to say the least, if it could. If it could be proved that two plus two is five, then it could be proved that five is not five, and then there would be no claim that could *not* be proved, and math would be a lot of bunk.

So, we now want to ask, can it be *proved* that it can't be proved that two plus two is five? Here's the shock: no, it can't. Or to hedge a bit: *if* it can be proved that it can't be proved that two plus two is five, *then* it can be proved as well that two plus two is five, and math is a lot of bunk.[36]

Gödel's second incompleteness theorem applies to formal systems adequate for arithmetic. So let f represent the falsehood $2 + 2 = 5$ and let "$\wp\Theta$" represent the claim that Θ can be proved in a specified formal system Σ—that is, that there exists a proof in Σ of Θ. Boolos imagines a formal system Σ rich enough to represent all of mathematics and his claim is then that we cannot prove in Σ that we cannot prove f in Σ. If by "mathematics" one means intuitionistic mathematics, what are the prospects of finding a system rich enough to represent all of intuitionistic mathematical reasoning?

Surprisingly good, as it turns out. Intuitionistic ZF set theory, IZF, is plausibly just such a system. IZF is the result of interpreting the axioms of classical ZF set theory intuitionistically. With the sole exception of the axiom of regularity, which is replaced by the principle to which it is classically though not intuitionistically equivalent, that of transfinite induction on '$\in$', the ZF axioms are acceptable to constructivists. Neil

Tennant reports that all of Bishop's constructive mathematics can be formalized in IZF.[37]

Boolos's first claim is that $\neg f$ can be proved in any formal system adequate for arithmetic:

(I) $\wp \neg f$

In addition, Boolos observes that from (I) we can derive the sequence:

(II) $\wp\wp\neg f, \wp\wp\wp\neg f, \ldots$

However, by Gödel's second incompleteness theorem (GSIT), it is impossible to disprove the claim that we can also prove f:

(III) $\neg\wp\neg\wp f$

Recall now Wright's Equivalence:

(WE) $\neg S\Theta \Leftrightarrow S\neg\Theta$

Since a mathematical sentence Θ is superassertible if and only if there is a canonical proof for it, then on the assumption that IZF is both rich enough to represent all of intuitionistic mathematics and sound, we also have:

(SP) $S\Theta \leftrightarrow \wp\Theta$

with "$\wp\Theta$" representing the claim that there is a proof in IZF of Θ. Subject to the assumptions about IZF above, (SP) and (WE) then give us:

(WE*) $\neg\wp\Theta \leftrightarrow \wp\neg\Theta$

So we obtain from (III) using (WE*):

(IV) $\wp\neg\wp\neg f$

Using truth elimination on the putative truth predicate $\wp$ in (IV):

(V) $\neg\wp\neg f$

But now we have derived from Gödel's second incompleteness theorem at (III), the coextensiveness of "S" and "$\wp$," and Wright's equivalence (WE) a patent mathematical falsehood in (V) itself. Alternatively, a more careful statement of GSIT, as Boolos notes, yields not (V) but:

(VI) $\wp\neg\wp f \to \wp f$

which by (WE*) yields:

(VII) $\wp\wp\neg f \to \wp f$

which, using the fact at (II) that $\wp\wp\neg f$ gives:

(VIII) $\wp f$

thus, in Boolos's charming monosyllabic language, "math is a lot of bunk."

That $\neg S\Theta \leftrightarrow S\neg\Theta$ is inconsistent with Gödel's proof of the unprovability of consistency *on condition that there exists a sound formal system rich enough to represent all of intuitionistic reasoning and hence to warrant the assertion of* (SP) $S\Theta \leftrightarrow \wp\Theta$ is a surprising and disturbing result for constructivists, if indeed the informal reasoning that led to it is constructivistically valid. So *is* it valid? The only inference rule used in the derivation of (VIII) from GSIT at (III) is modus ponens, together with the principle of substitution of logical equivalents. Nothing constructivistically awry about either of those two principles. Is there some problem with GSIT itself, then, according to the constructivist? This there cannot be since Boolos's derivation of GSIT can be formalized in Heyting Arithmetic (Peano Arithmetic subject to intuitionistic logic), let alone IZF.

A different sort of doubt might be raised at this point. Perhaps $\neg\wp\Theta \leftrightarrow \wp\neg\Theta$ holds only when Θ is either atomic or at least free of any occurrences of $\wp$. This suggestion is, however, not a viable one for antirealists, at least. The reason is simple: the semantic version $\neg V\Theta \leftrightarrow V\neg\Theta$ (Wright's $\neg S\Theta \leftrightarrow S\neg\Theta$) of the equivalence $\neg\wp\Theta \leftrightarrow \wp\neg\Theta$ is a direct logical consequence of a principle no antirealist can afford to gainsay: (AR) $V\Theta \leftrightarrow \Theta$.

This latter principle has to be endorsed by anyone who subscribes to the general thesis that *the meaning of a statement is given by a canonical warrant for its assertion*, which is, of course, the antirealist's distinctive credo. Let's be clear on what (AR) says, though, since if construed in terms of classical truth conditions it appears patently false. Its intended reading is that *we are entitled to assert Θ if and only if we have a canonical warrant for it (in the form of a proof when Θ is a mathematical statement)*.[38] On pain of our not being able to understand them at all, sentences asserting that a canonical warrant holds for some sentence must also be subject to the fundamental meaning-theoretic principle (AR) and thus, given that IZF adequately formalizes intuitionistic reasoning and is sound, also to the principle (AR*) $\Theta \leftrightarrow \wp\Theta$, if the antirealist's understanding of them is to be defensible.

So let us just intuitionistically derive the conclusions in the manner indicated informally above:

(A) (1) $\wp\neg f$
 AR* (2) $\neg\wp f$ (AR*) on (1)
 AR* (3) $\wp\neg\wp f$ (AR*) on (2)
     (4) $\neg\wp\neg\wp f$ GSIT
 AR* (5) $\bot$ 3, 4 & I

The first line of the proof rests on no assumptions since it is derivable within IZF. (A) furnishes us with nothing less than a constructive refutation of the reduction principle (AR*), $\wp\Theta \leftrightarrow \Theta$, using an argument that can be fully formalized in IZF. The consequences of this are dire indeed for antirealists—absent (AR) and if truth is not robust assertibility, neither can the meaning of mathematical statements be given in terms of canonical proof conditions. So to the extent that (AR), the semantic principle that (AR*) encapsulates, is founded on the distinctive antirealist principle that *all truths are knowable*, this principle in turn has been decisively refuted. We shall shortly produce this refutation. The conclusion we have reached about superassertibility, though, is therefore this: Superassertibility is not truth, nor can it be used to explicate meaning.

7.3.4 Not All Truths Are Knowable

Let me now present a refutation of the key principle of antirealist epistemology, the principle that all truths are knowable, Wright's principle (L), which I shall label (KT). The refutation is based on the derivation (A) above. Assume once more that there is some system such as IZF adequate for the representation of intuitionistic mathematical reasoning. Within IZF, all theorems of intuitionistic mathematics can be derived, we will suppose.

Here are three principles to which an antirealist appears to be committed:

(KT) All truths are knowable.

(MK) It is possible to know some mathematical statement is true if and only if we have a proof for it.

(FK) Whatever is knowable is true.

Our three principles are:

(KT) $\Theta \Rightarrow \Diamond K\Theta$; (MK) $\Diamond K\Theta \Leftrightarrow \wp\Theta$; (FK) $\Diamond K\Theta \Rightarrow \Theta$

Note that (MK) and (FK) express principles that realists accept also.

Now consider the formulae of IZF, our formal system encoding intuitionistic mathematics. We shall write "$\Box\Theta$" as an abbreviation for "$\exists x.$ Proof (x, Θ)," where "Θ" is the numeral for the Gödel number of Θ in IZF. Let "f" abbreviate $2 + 2 = 5$. We now proceed to derive a contradiction from our three principles above within IZF:

	(1)	$\Box\neg f$	
MK	(2)	$\Diamond K\neg f$	(1) by (MK)
MK, FK	(3)	$\neg f$	(2) by (FK)
4	(4)	$\Box f$	Hyp
4, MK	(5)	$\Diamond K f$	(4) by (MK)
4, MK, FK	(6)	f	(5) by (FK)
4, MK, FK	(7)	$\bot$	3, 6 & I
MK, FK	(8)	$\neg\Box f$	4, 7 $\neg$ I
MK, FK, KT	(9)	$\Diamond K\neg\Box f$	(8) by (KT)
MK, FK, KT	(10)	$\Box\neg\Box f$	(9) by (MK)
	(11)	$\Box\neg\Box f \to \Box f$	GSIT
MK, FK, KT	(12)	$\Box f$	10, 11 $\to$ E
MK, FK, KT	(13)	$\bot$	8, 12 & I

At line (1), the formula "$\Box\neg f$" can be easily proved in IZF. At line (11) "GSIT" refers to Gödel's second incompleteness theorem, which is (with considerable difficulty this time) also provable in IZF.

Given that IZF is indeed able to codify all of intuitionistic mathematics, then (MK) is difficult for a constructivist to deny *provided that the formal system IZF proves only truths*. It is possible to know Θ according to constructivists only if there is a canonical proof for Θ, and on our assumption that such canonical proofs can be formalized in IZF, we have that $\Diamond K\Theta$ only if $\Box\Theta$. Conversely, if $\Box\Theta$ then it is possible to know Θ *provided the system in which proofs are being carried out is consistent*. Hence, (MK) is antirealistically secure if IZF is consistent. (FK), the thesis that knowability is factive, is, if not analytically true, then surely a priori. Yet (KT), the thesis that all truths are knowable, is a principle no antirealist can afford to gainsay since it is definitive of antirealism. Since (MK) and (FK) are both acceptable to realists, they will have no qualms in identifying (KT) as the principle that has been refuted.

Antirealists might balk at the background assumption that intuitionistic mathematics can be fully represented in any formal system such as our hypothetical exemplar IZF. Correspondingly they will wish to challenge the earlier demonstration involving the principles (AR). Thus Dummett:

> The intuitive conception of a valid mathematical proof, even for statements within some circumscribed theory, cannot in general be identified with the concept of proof in some one formal system; for it may be the case that no formal system can ever succeed in embodying all the principles of proof that we should intuitively accept; and that is precisely what is shown to be the case by Gödel's Theorem.[39]

Irrespective of whether Dummett is correct in holding that no formalization can exhaust the notion of contentful proof, what stymies any identification of the latter notion with formal derivability within IZF or any other formal system is that the conjecture that the system proves only intuitionistically sanctioned truths cannot be *known* to hold precisely because of Gödel's second incompleteness theorem. That is, if $\vdash_{IZF} \Theta$ then we can be sure there will be a canonical proof of Θ in intuitionistic mathematics, assuming the latter is indeed consistent, *only if IZF is consistent*, which cannot be proved within IZF itself unless IZF is inconsistent. We no more *know* that IZF is consistent than we know that intuitionistic mathematics itself is. On the *assumption* that it is indeed consistent, then (MK) seems justified.

My conclusion is that the antirealist cannot plausibly maintain they know a priori that the notion of mathematical proof as it features in (MK) must elude capture within a fully formalized system of intuitionistic mathematics such as IZF. Hence, it is not a serious option for antirealists to take our derivation as a reductio of (MK). Neither can it be a serious option for them to dispute the factive nature of knowledge in (FK). Since both of these principles are acceptable to realists who deny the only remaining principle used in the reductio, we thus have, by default, a refutation of the antirealist's distinctive credo that all truths are knowable.

IV
Prospects for Naturalistic Realism

8
Realism, Facts, and Truth

8.1 Does the Representation Problem Rest on a Mistake?

I have claimed that there are no really credible theories of how our minds are able to forge links with mind-independent states of affairs—that is, of how mental symbols get to have such states of affairs as their truth conditions. It would be nice if we did not have to solve this problem in the first place, however. We have already assessed Hilary Putnam's antirepresentationalism in section 7.1 and found it problematic in many ways. But there are other determined critics of representationalism, none more so than Richard Rorty.

8.1.1 Rorty on Representationalism
Richard Rorty has consistently argued that representationalism lies at the heart of many of our epistemic and metaphysical woes and that it should be rejected. With the rejection of representationalism, the realist–antirealist dispute simply dissipates, according to Rorty, since both sides erroneously assume that there is something that *makes* our statements and beliefs true. We have already seen that Rorty's reading of the realist–antirealist dispute is inaccurate. The dispute is not about the nature of truthmakers. Indeed, there is no reason at all why either side should acknowledge truthmakers in the first place—antirealists, just as much as realists, can be deflationists about truth. However, that is not really germane to the discussion at this point. We wish to see instead whether Rorty is right in his critique of representationalism. If representationalism is false, there is no representation problem. One preliminary puzzle concerns what Rorty has to say about truth. He denies that our beliefs are responsible to any external cognitive authority that could determine whether they are true or false. In particular, no appeal to the nature of the world can do this. So far this is just standard pragmatist fare.

We shall see in the next section, though, that this line of argument just won't wash. There is indeed a difference between what is instrumentally or pragmatically best for us to believe and what is true. What is more than a little puzzling, however, is what Rorty wishes to put in the place of the world, namely, human consensus. Not that human consensus is for him an external cognitive authority. To the contrary. We no more need external authorities for our cognitive practices than we need divine external authorities for our moral practices.

Rorty believes representationalism is false. Suppose, however, that Rorty runs out of luck, and realism wins the day philosophically such that everyone (save Rorty himself) who thinks about these issues comes to believe both that realism is true and that for it to be true our mental representations must be linked to the right mind-independent objects. Would this bring in its train a belated conversion in Rorty's thinking? If not, what type of cognitive authority over him, internal or external, does or could consensus enjoy? Apart from the social pressure of having one's ideas in such a circumstance laughed at or howled down or declined publication, the fact that everyone happened to disagree with him, need not, I submit, move Rorty to so much as reexamine his position, let alone commit what would, by his present thinking, amount to apostasy—confess faith in representationalism. Furthermore not only need such disagreement not move him, I conjecture that it would not, and with good reason. Rorty thinks that representationalism is false yet seductive in its appeal. It is but a further manifestation of humanity's need to prostrate itself before some nonhuman authority, according to him—it was the great legacy of the Enlightenment to dethrone God from this position with respect to our moral judgments; it is the great task of philosophy and other cultural criticism to do this for the world with respect to our judgments about how things are.

This means that Rorty has an error theory about truth as correspondence to reality. Yet some illusions are hard to overturn and can become entrenched over time precisely because they are so useful—they earn their keep by satisfying human needs. This observation plays an essential part in any believable error theory. Attempts to expose these illusions and root them out can actually lead to their entrenchment. Hence Rorty should be the last person to be surprised if the unlikely situation mooted above ever became a reality—it is precisely what his error theory deems likely. Rorty believes representationalism is false. What is it that he believes when he believes that it is false? He does not believe that our world is a world in which humans mistakenly take themselves to form beliefs about the world that are true or false according to how the world is, whereas in reality these beliefs are only ever acceptable or not to their fellow human beings. He does not believe this because this would be to make the world an external arbiter of our beliefs, something it cannot be. Neither does he believe that the intuitive explanation just given of the falsehood of representationalism in terms of its failure to correspond to reality is just a misleading metaphor, a convoluted way of saying that he, Rorty, is inclined to deny representationalism for reasons that he thinks he could defend before his fellows. If he believed truth-as-correspondence to be a mere metaphor, there would be no need for an error theory to explain away the allure of representationalism.

No, Rorty thinks there is a real issue here. The world is not an arbiter of our judgments about it any more than God is an arbiter of our moral judgments. Anyone who thinks it is, and that could in principle include everyone apart from Rorty himself, has simply got it wrong. If there is a difference between this claim and the one we're supposed to reject, I confess I cannot see what it might be. To the extent that he thinks he has exposed a pervasive and seductive error in our thinking, Rorty patently does believe that there is a gross mismatch between how we intuitively take things to be and how they really are. Moreover, this mismatch cannot possibly be explicated in terms of actual rational consensus if the consensual facts break the wrong way for Rorty, as they do in the imagined circumstance. Could the mismatch not be explained in terms of an idealized rational consensus departing from the projected actual one? Not for Rorty, at least, for this would simply be to imagine being in conversation with others who agreed with him on this matter. That, at any rate, is the only sense Rorty can give to "the otherwise thin and useless notion of 'rationality.'"[1]

8.1.2 Alston on the Representation Problem

Rorty is not the only philosopher who thinks the representation problem is a pseudo-problem. William Alston has expressed similar views, though for very different reasons. According to him:

> Putnam's idea that the metaphysical realist is, by virtue of his position, faced with an extra step of hooking up each term of the theory with things and sets of things in the world rests on a radical misunderstanding of the situation. Not only is there nothing in the realist position that engenders any such requirement; the most basic facts of language, and our use thereof, make the requirement thoroughly gratuitous. The acquisition, use and understanding of language just doesn't work that way. People do not learn general terms by having the

extension of each laid out for them. If that were necessary, a first (or any subsequent) language would never be acquired. It is not within human powers to teach someone the meaning (use) of "cat" by enumerating or pointing out all cats—past, present and future, throughout the whole universe. Hence, our mastery of the term, our ability to make use of what we learned when we learned the term, does not involve the employment of any such "interpretation." Suppositions to the contrary come from hypnotic fascination with the procedure of formal logic in describing ... the procedure of setting up formal, artificial "languages" by such an extensional "interpretation." If one allows this model to blind one to the most obvious facts of the human use of actual languages, one may be led to suppose that something like this is what a realist would have to do to attach a definite meaning to a language. But once we get the actual facts of real language use before us, this supposition vanishes like the morning mist with the noonday sun.[2]

Alston takes Putnam to be saddling the realist with a type of hyper-extensionalism ("teaching someone the meaning of 'cat' by enumerating all cats"). This is not correct. Putnam is challenging the realist to explain how "cat" picks out all and only cats, given that cats are mind-independent objects. Appealing to how realists actually learn to use the term "cat" is no answer to this question, for the facts of language acquisition and use may actually militate against realism in just the way Dummett and Putnam believe they do.

Nonetheless, Alston's insistence that the representation problem is a pseudo-problem for realism is widespread among realists, and his rejection of it does merit consideration:

There is something else behind Putnam's supposition that the Model-Theoretic Argument tells against metaphysical realism. The whole discussion hinges on an unwarranted picture of the metaphysical realist vainly struggling to connect his terms with items in a wholly transcendent realm. If we think of the metaphysical realist as committed to a domain of "transcendent" entities, out of any contact with our thought, experience, and discourse, then it can look as if he is faced with an extra, and insuperable, task of relating the terms of our thought and discourse to that transcendent reality.[3]

This is a fair statement of the representation problem for realism. Why is it a pseudo-problem? Alston explains:

But this is, at best, constructing an artificial position in order to have a target for refutation. No living, breathing realist, to my knowledge, takes any such stand. I certainly do not. I don't think of realism as implying that one must, by some supreme metaphysical effort, "reach outside" our experience, thought, and discourse, to make contact with a transcendent realm. On the contrary, the real, independently existing world, the nature of which makes our statements true or false, is one with which we are in contact already through our experience, thought, and discourse. The constituents of that world—people, trees, animals, buildings, oceans, galaxies, God—are things we perceive or otherwise experience, think about, and talk about. They are not wholly external to us and our cognitive and linguistic doings, though they don't depend (for the most part) on those doings for what they are. No sensible realism supposes or implies that the realist is faced with the task Putnam takes the position to require.[4]

As far as I can tell from this passage, Alston's sole reason for dismissing the representation problem is that realists assume that they already *are* in perceptual and cognitive contact with items in a mind-independent world, which of course they do. That, after all, is what makes them realists. But how does that show that the representation problem is based on confusion or error? Precisely the same reasoning could be used to defend color realism against antirealist attacks—no sensible color realist doubts that we are already in contact with the real colors of things through color experience, so there cannot be a serious question as to how we are able to enjoy mental states directed onto mind-independent colors, how the link between mind and those particular mind-independent properties is forged in this instance. Anyone who believes there is a genuine problem here has simply imbibed too much formal semantics, assuming erroneously that the problem of how my term "red" refers to real redness is a matter of vainly trying to get my mental symbol "red" to lasso the set of red things, something a model-theoretic semantics solves by fiat. In fact, color experience itself puts us in contact with real redness and all that remains then is to learn to use the word "red" to refer to that property rather than some other.

If there is a deficiency with this piece of reasoning, and I think it is patent that there is, there is likewise a problem with the general pattern of which it is an instance. Just as no color antirealist is going to agree that color experience puts us in contact with mind-independent color properties, no global antirealist is going to agree that perceptual or cognitive experience generally puts us in contact with mind-independent objects and their properties. Moreover, and crucially, the main reason for dissent in the global antirealist's case just *is* that the facts of how we come to learn to use "red," "blue," and so on are simply inconsistent with our targeting mind-independent properties of redness, blueness, and so on. Far from revealing the representation problem to be a pseudoproblem, then, Alston's counterargument actually underscores its centrality—glib appeals to common sense and experience, error-theoretic attempts to explain away its hold on the philosophers who press it as a problem for realism, simply backfire, raising anew the very question that was supposed to have been spirited away. The representation problem is a genuine problem.

8.1.3 Lewis on Realism and the Representation Problem

The representation problem is a real problem. But is it a problem for realism? David Lewis thinks not. It is worth looking at Lewis's reasons for thinking that this problem is simply irrelevant to realism. Lewis is discussing the model-theoretic argument, the argument that most forcefully trades on the difficulties for realism posed by the representation problem:

> ... even if the model-theoretic argument worked, it would not blow away the realist's picture of the world and its relation to theory. Something vital would be destroyed, but a lot would be left standing. There would still be a world, and it would not be a figment of our imagination. It would still have many parts, and these parts would fall into classes and relations—too many for comfort, perhaps, but too many is scarcely the same as none.
>
> There would still be interpretations, assignments of reference, intended and otherwise. Truth of a theory on a given interpretation would still make sense, and in a non-epistemic way. Truth on all intended interpretations would still make sense. Despite Putnam's talk of the "collapse" of an "incoherent picture," he has given us no reason to reject any of the parts of the picture. The only trouble he offers is that there are too many intended interpretations, so that truth on the intended interpretation is too easily achieved. That is trouble, sure enough. But is it *anti-realist* trouble, except by tendentious definition? It seems to me exactly opposite to traditional anti-realism.
>
> The traditional anti-realist doubts or denies that there is any world save a figment of our imagination. Or he doubts or denies that the world divides into parts except insofar as we divide it, or that those parts fall into any classes or relations except such as are somehow of our own making. Or he doubts or denies that we can achieve reference to parts of the world, he questions that there can be even one intended referential interpretation. Or he doubts or denies that we can ever achieve truth on the intended interpretations, or that we can ever have reason to believe that we have done so.
>
> Putnam ... gives us no argument that discredits the realist's conception of truth of a theory on an interpretation which assigns referents in the world.... It is an exaggeration to say that the realist's picture "collapses" ("Realism and Reason," pp. 126 and 130). That suggests destruction more total than has actually been accomplished. And it is quite uncalled for to say, however metaphorically, that "the mind and the world jointly make up the mind and the world" (*Reason, Truth and History*, p. xi). No; we make theories, not worlds. The metaphysics of realism survives unscathed. What does suffer, if Putnam has his way, is realist semantics and epistemology.[5]

Lewis is right in thinking that it is realist semantics and epistemology that are directly called into question by the model-theoretic argument.

He is wrong in thinking that "the metaphysics of realism survives unscathed." The MTA aimed to show that no mental representation of a mind-independent world was possible on pain of perfectly determinate reference to ordinary recurrent objects and features of our experience such as cats and rain turning out massively indeterminate. To maintain that these are but problems with our representation of such objects and features, not with their mind-independent existence, is to side with the credulist who responds to Hume's attack on the credibility of miracles by claiming that the *metaphysics* of miracles still survives unscathed. Of course one can still believe in a mind-independent world in the teeth of the MTA just as one can still believe in miracles in the teeth of Hume's argument—any such belief, however, will be rationally indefensible if Putnam (or Hume) is right.

8.2 Refutation of a Pragmatist Theory of Truth

It is a consistent theme of pragmatism that our beliefs and statements do not stand in need of any justification beyond those practices in which they are formed. In this vein, William James famously claimed that truth is what is best, all things considered, to believe and it is a non negotiable tenet of pragmatism that there are no differences in what's true without differences in practice. In recent times, James's claim has been endorsed and developed by Rorty and Brandom, among others. Rorty gives expression to the pragmatist view:

> The pragmatist tells us that it is useless to hope that objects will constrain us to believe the truth about them, if only they are approached with an unclouded mental eye, or a rigorous method, or a perspicuous language. He wants us to give up the notion that God, or evolution, or some other underwriter of our present world-picture, has programmed us as machines for accurate verbal picturing, and that philosophy brings self-knowledge by letting us read our own programs.[6]

Again, commenting on William James's idea that "The 'true' is that which is best, all things considered, to believe," Rorty writes:

> James's point was that there is nothing deeper to be said: truth is not the sort of thing which *has* an essence. More specifically, his point was that it is no use being told that truth is "correspondence to reality." ... Given a language and a view of what the world is like, one can, to be sure, pair off bits of the language with bits of what one takes the world to be in such a way that the sentences one believes true have internal structures isomorphic to relations between things in the world.... undeliberated reports like "This is water," "That's red," "That's ugly,"

"That's immoral" ... can easily be thought of as pictures.... Such reports do indeed pair little bits of language with little bits of the world....

James's point was that carrying out this exercise will not enlighten us about why truths are good to believe, or offer any clues as to why or whether our present view of the world is, roughly, the one we should hold. Yet nobody would have asked for a "theory" of truth if they had not wanted answers to these latter questions.[7]

Pragmatists claim that we do not need facts or other truthmakers to epistemically secure our beliefs. Hilary Putnam, himself sympathetic to pragmatist ideas, agrees when he writes:

The idea of a statement's corresponding to the way things are, the idea of a term's having a correspondence to a language-independent class of things, and the idea of a predicate's having a correspondence to a language-independent attribute are ideas which have no metaphysical force at all unless the correspondence in question is thought of as a genuine relation between items independent of us and items in language, a correspondence which is imposed by the world as it were, and not just a tautological feature of the way we talk about talk. What I have in mind by this remark, which may sound puzzling, is this: if you think it is just a *tautology* that *snow* corresponds to snow, or that "Snow is white" is true if and only if snow is white, then you regard the "correspondence" between the word *snow* and snow as a correspondence *within* language. Within our language we can talk about snow and we can talk about the word *snow* and we can *say* they correspond. To this even a philosopher who rejects the very idea of a substantive notion of reference can agree. But if, as Williams believes, the fact that we are "fated" to accept the sentence "Snow is white" is *explained* by something "out there" and by the fact that the sentence corresponds to that something "out there," then the correspondence too must be "out there." A verbal correspondence cannot play this kind of explanatory role. Williams's picture is that there is a *fixed* set of objects "out there," the "mind-independent objects," and a fixed relation—a relation between words and sentences in any language in which "absolute" truths can be expressed and those mind-independent Reals—and that this relation *explains* the (alleged) fact that science converges. If this picture is unintelligible, then the notion of an "absolute conception of the world" must also be rejected as unintelligible.

Now, I have argued for a number of years that this picture *is* unintelligible.[8]

I want to make a start on this question of perceived irrelevance by examining what I think is the most serious threat to the correspondence theory of truth—the pragmatist's claim that our beliefs and statements do not need facts or any other sorts of truthmakers in order for them to be true since our practices already provide all the security, and indeed the only possible security, our beliefs need.

What I have to say applies, I think, to both reductionist and eliminativist pragmatist approaches to truth. Whether we construe the pragmatist as claiming that we should dispense with the notion of Truth (or truth) altogether since it is irredeemably tainted by its association with the metaphor of true beliefs as a mirror of Nature, or whether we construe the pragmatist as maintaining, rather, that the concept of Truth can and should be salvaged from the misleading philosophical illusions that overlay it, the result is the same: Whether the concept of Truth is reduced to or eliminated in favor of "that which is best all things considered to believe," the pragmatist's claim is false.

Truth *is not* that which is best all things considered to believe, neither can it be *eliminated in favor of* that which is best all things considered to believe. Sometimes illusion and ignorance are far better, and we should choose those if we have our wits about us and we wish to flourish. The justification for these claims comes from an intriguing phenomenon that arises in certain interactive situations where agents have an opportunity to inquire or to refrain from inquiring about the situation in which they find themselves acting.[9] But before developing the description of these situations, it may be wise to say something first about why we need to look at situations that are quite so complex as the "games" we shall shortly consider and what, exactly, pragmatists mean by claiming that truth is (or should be replaced by) that which is best all things considered to believe.

First, it is not at all surprising that for a single agent what it is best to believe and what is true can come apart. Jon Elster's *Ulysses and the Sirens* provides many illustrations of this phenomenon, some of them quite unexpected. More humdrum cases include the spouse who cannot maintain the relationship she desires and needs to maintain unless she believes in the teeth of the evidence to the contrary that her unfaithful partner is not unfaithful. James was not talking about such relatively trivial cases. Like the other pragmatists, he was considering the context of inquiry that abstracts away from the idiosyncracies of particular individual desires and needs—it is for the community of inquirers, whatever their psychological histories and contingencies, that truth is what is best all things considered to believe. That which they would all eventually settle on (Peirce) is either a candidate or replacement for truth.

To refute this claim it is necessary to look at the context of inquiry, then. Two agents suffice for simplicity, but the games to be considered are multiplayer. Prisoner's dilemma (PD) situations show that irrationality can sometimes pay. Two rational individuals will be unable to achieve the Pareto-optimal outcome of joint cooperation that two well-meaning fools might stumble on. This is because mutual defection is the

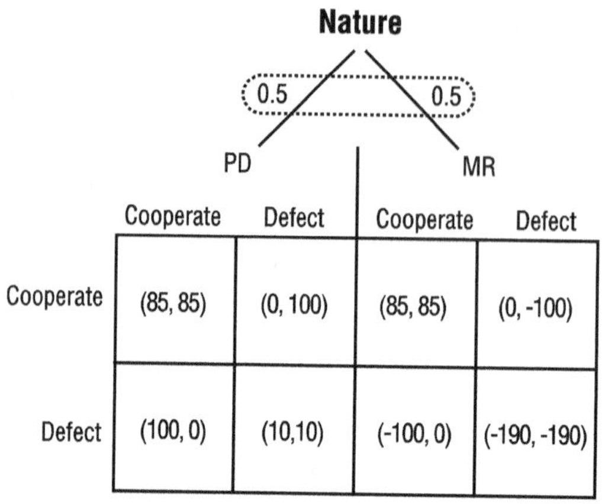

                                   Nature
                              0.5 /\ 0.5
                                  / \
                                PD   MR

                      Cooperate Defect Cooperate Defect

         Cooperate   (85, 85)   (0, 100) (85, 85) (0, -100)

         Defect   (100, 0)   (10, 10) (-100, 0) (-190, -190)

Figure 8.1

Nash equilibrium in PD situations, and Nash equilibria are standardly taken to represent necessary conditions on rationality. Yet the Nash equilibrium of (defect, defect) is Pareto-suboptimal. So consider a game in which two agents are irredeemably ignorant of their situation at the time of choice. There is a 50 percent chance they are in a PD situation and a 50 percent chance they face major reprisals (MR) if they do not cooperate with each other. Call this game U, diagrammatically represented in figure 8.1. The dotted line represents a veil of ignorance under which both players make their moves, choosing to either cooperate or defect. A and B have *incomplete information* of their situation, formally represented by the presence of Nature at the top node of the tree. Nature makes or has made her move but has done so inscrutably. A and B are unable to determine whether they are in situation I on the left-hand side of the tree or situation II on the right-hand side. The disvalue of defection is −200, accounting for the values in the relevant cells of the MR matrix. Agent A and agent B have their beliefs aligned. However, fearful of reprisals, they cooperate if they are rational, as shown in figure 8.2.

As the cell values are identical for either situation I of PD or situation II of MR, neither agent A nor agent B can determine whether they are in a PD situation or a MR situation, as the resulting matrix for the game shows in figure 8.3. So, for the game U it is impossible for A and B to know which game they were playing. That is, we can so choose the values for defect and cooperate that it is indistinguishable for them whether they are in I or in II. One could think of A and B as moral

	Agent B	
	Cooperate	Defect
Agent A Cooperate	85 × 0.5 + 85 × 0.5 85 × 0.5 + 85 × 0.5	0 × 0.5 + 0 × 0.5 100 × 0.5 + (-100) × 0.5
Defect	100 × 0.5 + (-100) × 0.5 0 × 0.5 + 0 × 0.5	10 × 0.5 + (-90) × 0.5 10 × 0.5 + (-190) × 0.5

Figure 8.2

	Cooperate	Defect
Cooperate	(85, 85)	(0, 0)
Defect	(0, 0)	(-90, -90)

Figure 8.3

skeptics (or legal skeptics) who benefit from their ignorance. Their incurable ignorance makes it rational for them to choose to cooperate, as the matrix above shows. (C, C) is the only Nash equilibrium and is the solution to our U-styled game. If they achieve their mutually beneficial payoff of (85, 85)—which they will (if they're rational) by cooperating—neither A nor B will be able to find out which situation they were in. So neither will be able to answer the question, "Am I in a PD situation or not?" In other words, it is better for each of them to choose to remain ignorant of the game they are playing just so that they can flourish. Culpable epistemic ignorance can, and sometimes does, have its instrumental rewards.

This result has an immediate bearing on the pragmatists' claim that truth is what is best, all things considered, to believe. It is not in their interests to find out the answer to the above question. To the contrary, it is in each of their interests (and to the mutual benefit of both) that they remain ignorant: The rational choice for each agent is to cooperate, and cooperation will not reveal which situation they were really in. Yet if we suppose that they were in fact in a PD situation, defection by either agent would reveal this—netting the unilateral defector a payoff of 100 and joint defectors a payoff of 10. They may in fact be tempted to defect because of insatiable curiosity about their situation. Yet it would clearly be irrational for them to indulge such an epistemic preference.

It might be thought that we can neutralize any threat to the pragmatist understanding of truth posed by this example if we but distinguish between instrumental and epistemic rationality. But this is a failure for at least two reasons. The most basic is that epistemic rationality is simply a special case of instrumental rationality (IR)—that form of IR which is activated by a preference to find out how things are. It is not a different species of rationality. Instrumental rationality is simply means–ends reasoning, and Reason, as Hume reminded us, is a slave of one's preferences. I am under no illusion that this opinion about the relation between instrumental and epistemic rationality is uncontroversial. Robert Nozick in his *Nature of Rationality* explicitly rejects it, insisting that we maximize not just utility but something over and above mere expected utility—he calls it decision value and requires that it at least includes as distinct and separable components causal, evidential, and symbolic utility. Nozick's view is widespread among philosophers. I think it rests on a mistake, a mistake about what the principle of maximization of expected utility (MEU) amounts to. A simple statement of MEU is:

Every individual acts so as to maximise their utility or satisfaction—be it in terms of wealth, health, social prestige, or whatever.

However, MEU can be given a wider and a narrower interpretation. The wider one comprises all conceivable varieties of preference, including a possibility that the individual in question cares about someone else's well-being and includes it in his own utility calculus. This wider interpretation does not, thus, exclude a possibility of altruistic preferences. Actually, it does not exclude *any* coherent pattern of the agent's preferences. This interpretation can be thought of as coinciding with the principle of optimization. The narrower one restricts the agent's utility to purely self-regarding values like *their own* wealth, health, social prestige, and so on. It is the economist's preferred interpretation, and there is often a tacit understanding among theorists that it is exactly this narrower, egoistic interpretation that should underlie any model of rational choice. But this is just a prejudice, in my view, and a clearly ideological one.

Once agents are permitted to include in their EU calculations any consideration at all that moves them, views such as Nozick's collapse— for it is then gratuitous to insist that, say, symbolic utility feature as an isolable component in what, after all, is supposed to model the deliberations of an agent. If symbolic utility is a factor that moves or should move the agent it will or should already appear in the EU calculations as a component weighted in a multidimensional aggregation of all components.

The second reason a distinction between instrumental and epistemic rationality is a failure is that even if such a distinction could be drawn it is one no pragmatist could avail herself of since for the pragmatist *all* theoretical notions must be grounded in practice. Thus, epistemic rationality would have to be explicated in instrumental terms—that is, in terms of IR.

So we have that A and B are in a PD situation. They can discover that they are if they bother to inquire. So set p = "A & B are in a PD situation in game U." We have that p is true but it is not best all things considered for A and B to believe p. If we were to extend this to the whole community of inquirers, we would similarly have that it is possible for the whole community to be in a PD situation but that it is not best for them to believe that they are—for by not believing that she is in a PD situation, each inquirer within a whole community can, in certain circumstances, maximize her EU.

The upshot is that *the pragmatist claim, that truth is what is best all things considered to believe, is flatly false.* There is a difference between what is instrumentally best even for the whole community of inquirers to believe and what is actually the case. A and B act in a PD situation; they are able to find out that they are in this situation. But it is in their best interests not to. It is in their best interests not to inquire whether there are objective moral or legal norms punishing defection and rewarding cooperation.

Let me deal with some possible pragmatist objections at this point. The first one is that there is an illicit realism being smuggled into the description of U. After all, one of the interpretations of the RH path, situation II, of the game tree was that this was a situation in which there were objective moral values. But pragmatists insist that what it is for there to be moral values differs not a whit from what it is for there to be electrons or tables or beautiful sunsets or polite conversation—it is just for our practices to warrant the assertion that these "things" exist, which they clearly do. In fact, the only sense in which objective moral values need exist is the minimalist sense above already provided for by pragmatism. Indeed, "MR" need not be interpreted in terms of *moral* sanctions at all. Perhaps there is a *legal* penalty for defection, a fine or prison term, say. Neither is there any illicit realism involved in claiming that A and B are really in a PD situation. This is something that *they themselves can find out* if they bother to inquire by defecting. There is no God's-eye view inaccessible to A and B being tacitly presupposed.

The more serious objections concern whether pragmatist attitudes to truth are in the end really being respected. The view of pragmatists who are *alethic reductionists* can be represented thus:

(PΘ_1) $Tr(p) \leftrightarrow \beta * (Bp)$

which states, less formally, that p is true if and only if it is best all things considered to believe p. A weaker "reductionist" view, perhaps the view that truth merely supervenes on what is best all things considered to believe, holds that the latter is a necessary constraint on truth only:

(PΘ_2) $Tr(p) \rightarrow \beta * (Bp)$

Let us call this view *alethic reductivism*.

I take it that U shows that both alethic reductionism and alethic reductivism cannot be sustained since it presents us with the prospect of situations, indeed, real situations that can and arguably do recur in ordinary life as I shall argue below, wherein $Tr(p) \& \neg \beta * (Bp)$.

How can any of this have an impact on pragmatists who are *alethic eliminativists*, though? Alethic eliminativists hold that the intuitive notion of truth is incoherent, ineradicably infected by the illusion of a special God-ordained correspondence between human beliefs and a reality that is completely independent of those beliefs, a correspondence that, in the very nature of the case, can never be sanctioned by our practices. Alethic eliminativists are entitled to a truth predicate of some sort—a disquotational one. But the presence of such a truth predicate is not essential; it is of use only in generalizing from specific instances of "p."

(PΘ_3) $p \leftrightarrow \beta * (Bp)$

or perhaps

(PΘ_4) $p \rightarrow \beta * (Bp)$

Yet it does not matter whether or not we use the truth predicate to describe the situation in Game U: *A and B are in a PD situation but it is not best all things considered for them to believe that they are*. Precisely the opposite. Thus we have $p \& \neg \beta * (Bp)$.

This "game" would be of little interest if it had no serious applications. In fact, I think that it has. It shows that there can be subtle pressures at work in a community actively fostering shared illusions and actively preventing inquiry into the provenance of certain unquestioned assumptions within the community. An obvious example is the reality of moral values and norms. Martin Hollis once claimed that the whole of society is an intricate device for escaping the Prisoner's dilemma. I think that it may be morality that better fits this description.

I am not promoting moral antirealism, but there is an unsettling moral that might be drawn from these examples. Suppose evolution had factored in just enough altruism to human nature that it seemed to each, or at least, the great majority, that there was at least a fifty percent chance that there are objective moral norms. We could all start off as moral skeptics. Then even in a society of perfectly rational moral skeptics, morality could take hold in the form of cooperative behavior and the emergence of a folk theory of morality that permitted the transmission of folk moral norms to novices. What better way to break out of the trap of the Prisoner's dilemma than for everyone in the society to believe, along with Kant, that not to cooperate with one's fellows is to sin against one's very nature?

If this shared illusion ever became explicit, PD considerations would suggest that agents should defect. There are two necessary conditions that must be met for me as an agent to escape the PD trap: I must have a reason to believe that you will cooperate and I must have a reason to cooperate given that you cooperate, the problem being that these reasons conflict in PD situations since any reason to believe that you will cooperate is a perfect reason for me to defect—unless, of course, it is objectively wrong to do so.

So there are two ways, then, in which a shared illusion of objective moral norms could be fostered by nature:

(I) Create agents who pretend that certain PD situations are not genuinely PD—that there is some further dimension or some undecidability (possibly they are MR situations and PD situations are in reality U-styled games).

(II) Prevent the realization of fictional status of objective moral values ever surfacing by making it seem plausible to agents that these entities are real.

The more successful strategy for nature to prosecute is surely (II).

An interesting and novel metaethical position results when one takes the "unreasonable effectiveness" of moral values in such contexts as irredeemably equivocal—either it is evidence of their being objective or alternatively of their being unrecognized fictions constructed purely to defuse PD situations. If one believes that the evidence is indeed equivocal between the moral realist and the fictionalist interpretations of moral values and norms, one arrives at a metaethical Pyrrhonism, which although conserving moral practice gives a very different vindication than that provided by moral realism. Moral practice should be conserved only if the disvalue of inquiring into the objective status of moral values and norms within PD/MR contexts is too high. I develop this view in section 8.4 both for its intrinsic interest and because it poses problems for popular analytic functionalist versions of naturalistic realism.

8.3 Internalism and the Representation Problem

I want to approach the topic of internalism's relation to the representation problem in a slightly unconventional way, by looking at Saul Kripke's recent attempt on behalf of Wittgenstein to deny the factuality of meaning. Kripke's Wittgenstein (henceforth KW) rejects the idea that there are any facts that correspond to one's meaning something by one's words or mental symbols. If such a position can be sustained, the representation problem may well be a pseudo-problem after all. KW develops an assertibilist account of meaning, an account compatible with internalism, in other words. Yet it is also advertised as a nonfactualist one. *Moreover, if the arguments Kripke puts forward against the possibility of semantic facts are sound, internalist meaning cannot be assumed to be any more secure than externalist truth-conditional meaning.*

Yet *can* one consistently deny the factuality of meaning? Some recent discussions of Kripke's famous explication of Wittgenstein's rule-following argument suggest the answer to this question is "No." If this is true, eliminative materialism is placed under threat since eliminativists deny that human agents are ever in mental states with intentional content. Moreover, since KW puts forward a uniquely powerful case for believing that there can be no facts about meaning, a demonstration that the attendant semantic eliminativism is itself incoherent would constitute a telling reason for thinking that there must be something wrong with those semantic eliminativist arguments. It would be nice to be able to dodge interpretative issues in discussing the substantive points raised by Kripke's presentation of Wittgenstein. Unfortunately this is not possible, since any answer to our question about the factuality of meaning will also be an answer to such questions as "Is there a coherent interpretation of Kripke's 'skeptical solution'?" and "Does Kripke's Wittgenstein deny that meaning attributions are ever true?" I propose to look at the interpretative issues in relation to substantive questions since, to repeat, I think that KW is unique in showing us what it would be for there to be no semantic facts, no facts that anyone ever meant anything by any word or that anyone ever believed any specific proposition. In other words, KW is unique in showing us how the world would have to be for eliminative materialism to be true. Part of my project is to clarify KW's case against semantic factualism and his own preferred alternative.

I will argue that KW is, indeed, a semantic eliminativist; that there is no inconsistency between the position put forward by KW *qua* meaning skeptic and KW *qua* proponent of a "skeptical solution" to the rule-following paradox; and that the attempt to portray KW as holding that there are meaning facts, only of some "nonsuperlative" sort, is misguided and merely highlights an inadequacy in current understandings of the notion of a fact as it features in various debates over nonfactualism, such as in ethics.[10] Finally, I will argue that there is a nontrivial threat of self-referential instability attending KW's semantic eliminativism that suggests that the a priori thesis that there can be no facts about meaning may not ultimately be defensible. All that follows from the instability of a priori semantic eliminativism, if indeed anything follows at all, is the possibility that there are meaning facts. Whether there are any is a matter for further empirical and philosophical inquiry. I begin with a review of some recent interpretations of KW.

8.3.1 Is There a Single Coherent Interpretation of Kripke's Skeptical Solution?

Scott Soames has recently argued that there is no coherent interpretation of Kripke's skeptical solution. There are in fact three partial interpretations, he surmises, none of which is completely satisfying: "Each has important virtues; each has fundamental defects.... The reason for this, I suspect, is that, like many leading works in philosophy, there is no single coherent line of argument that runs through the whole of the text. Rather, Kripke's text is a fabric through which the different threads of these three interpretations are woven together."[11] I disagree. I shall present a single coherent interpretation of KW that does justice to the text, comparing it with one of the three partial interpretations Soames offers. What initially sows the seeds of interpretative doubt for Soames is a worry about how the proponent of the skeptical paradox could be one and the same as the proponent of the skeptical solution. Why? Because the skeptic who presents the original argument for the radical thesis that there are no facts about me in virtue of which I mean addition by "+" apparently then turns around and endorses the very thesis he has just denied:

> We do not wish to doubt or deny that when people speak of themselves and others as meaning something by their words, as following rules, they do so with perfect right. We do not wish to deny the propriety of an ordinary use of the phrase "the fact that Jones meant addition by such-and-such a symbol," and indeed such expressions do have perfectly ordinary uses. We merely wish to deny the existence of the "superlative fact" that philosophers misleadingly attach to such ordinary forms of words, not the propriety of the form of words themselves.[12]

Kripke is clearly worried here by the potentially *revisionary consequences* for our linguistic practices of the skeptic's denial of the existence of meaning facts. He fully realizes that Wittgenstein was a nonrevisionist about our linguistic practices and so any interpretation of Wittgenstein's rule-following argument must respect this precept. Yet what is put forward in the skeptical solution to the skeptical paradox is not some hitherto undiscovered fact that fixes what I mean by "+." Rather, *the propriety of certain forms of words* is preserved in the skeptical solution, forms such as "Jones meant addition by '+,'" "The rule of addition determined that the correct response for Jones to give to '68 + 57?' was '125,'" even, presumably, "The infinity of cases covered by the rule of addition is somehow encoded in Jones's mind," and, indeed, crucially, "It is a fact that Jones means addition by '+,'" which KW, *qua* Kripke's representative of Wittgenstein, is concerned to preserve. After all, talk of rules, meaning, truth and facts is part and parcel of ordinary linguistic practice. Philosophical interpretations of those notions, however, are not. Thus typical philosophical questions concerning meaning, content, and rule-following would be these: "*In virtue of what* do I mean what I mean by my words?" "Do the *nonintentional* facts *metaphysically necessitate* the *intentional* facts?" These are the types of questions that are supposed to be reduced to absurdity by KW.

KW's point seems to be this: *If* one thinks that intentional facts such as my meaning addition by "+" need *metaphysical grounding* by nonintentional facts, one will be forced to conclude, absurdly, that there aren't any intentional facts. And, indeed, as far as Wittgenstein and KW are concerned, *there are no intentional facts*, in the philosopher's special sense of "fact," the metaphysical one in which questions of the supervenience of the set of intentional facts on some other more privileged set (the "superlative" facts) supposedly make sense. There are no *truth-makers* for my meaning addition by "+." That is precisely what the skeptical paradox is supposed to show.

KW is definitely a nonfactualist about meaning, to use current jargon.[13] The sense in which one can *say* things like "There are facts about what I mean" is not the sense that interests a philosopher. It is merely the sense endorsed by folk-linguistic practice involving the notions of truth and fact. KW's point is that we do not *need* metaphysical facts about intentionality to preserve the integrity of ordinary linguistic practice governing meaning attribution. To relinquish the assumption that there is some metaphysical truth-maker that determines that I mean addition by "+" and which *thereby* determines that I *ought* to say "125" rather than "5" in answer to "68 + 57?" is, to all appearances, to embrace semantic eliminativism. I shall argue that the appearances do not deceive.

8.3.2 Soames on Kripke

Let us compare this sketch of KW's views with two recent interpretations of the skeptical solution due to Scott Soames and Alex Byrne. Having done this, I will explain why I think Soames's reply to Kripke's skeptical paradox is inconclusive. Kripke says that what makes the skeptical solution a *skeptical* one is that it accepts the conclusion of the skeptical paradox, namely, that there are no such facts as the fact that I mean addition by "+." On one of Soames's "partial" interpretations, on the other hand, the skeptic and the proponent of the skeptical solution agree in denying not the existence of facts *tout court* but only the existence of facts that are, in a certain sense, epistemically transparent:[14]

(AR)   There are no nonintentional facts such that knowledge of them, would, in principle, provide me with a sufficient basis for concluding (demonstrating) that I ought to give the answer "125" to the question "68 + 57?" (and similarly for all questions of this type) provided I intend to use "+" with the same meaning as I did in the past.

What distinguishes the skeptic from the proponent of the skeptical solution, according to Soames, is not their common acceptance of (AR) but their differing attitudes to the following thesis:

(N_{PLUS})   If in the past I meant addition by "+" then there is a set of nonintentional facts such that knowledge of those facts would in principle suffice to allow me to conclude (demonstrate) that I ought to answer "125" to "68 + 57?" (and similarly for all other questions of this type) provided I intend to use "+" with the same meaning as I did in the past.

The contrast between the skeptic and the proponent of the skeptical solution is, then, this: Where the skeptic accepts *both* (N_{PLUS}) and (AR) and so concludes that I did not mean addition by "+," the proponent of the skeptical solution, while accepting (AR), *rejects* the skeptical conclusion that I did not mean addition by "+" or, more radically, that I never mean anything by any of my words, and so treats the skeptic's argument as a reductio of (N_{PLUS}).

One fundamental problem with this interpretation, and the reason Soames thinks it is at best "partial," is that (N_{PLUS}) is not a reasonable commitment to demand from one who simply holds that my meaning something by my words is a factual matter (meaning factualism): What does a priori deducibility, a strong epistemic constraint, have to do with the metaphysical thesis of meaning factualism? As Soames himself says, "a solution that rejects it hardly qualifies as even mildly surprising, let alone skeptical."[15] To the contrary, if one could show how my meaning addition rather than quaddition by "+" was by far the *most likely explanation* of why I use the symbol in the way that I do, the skeptic would have been silenced. It would be irrelevant that this fact could not be deduced a priori from the nonintentional facts.

The other problem concerns the notion of "justification" as it appears in Soames's (N_{PLUS}). It is true that the proponent of the skeptical solution thinks that my answering "125" to "68 + 57?" is, in some sense of "justified," justified. However, that sense of "justification" is not the sense that the skeptic originally contests. The sense contested by the skeptic is the sense that philosophers have in mind when they wonder how content could arise in a world of fields and forces. Hartry Field has expressed this sense nicely:

> A natural question to raise about words—or about their mental analogue, concepts—is: in virtue of what facts do they refer to whatever it is that they refer to? In virtue of what does the word "insanity" refer to insanity, the word "entropy" refer to entropy, and so forth?... it would seem that this question about words or concepts needs an answer. And the only type of answer we can take seriously is a naturalistic answer.... What if no naturalistic answer is possible?... the only conclusion to be drawn is that the assumption that "insanity" and "entropy" determinately refer to insanity and entropy is an illusion.[16]

If we call this sense of justification, metaphysical justification then both skeptic and the skeptical solution proponent *agree* that since nothing metaphysically determines that I mean addition rather than quaddition by "+," my answering "125" to "68 + 57?" is *not* metaphysically justified, justified *sub specie aeternitatas*. So instead of Soames's (N_{PLUS}), what we really require to do justice to Kripke's argument, is the following:

(N_{FACT}) For my present response of "125" to "68 + 57?" to be metaphysically justified, it is necessary that there exist some set of facts that determine that I meant addition by "+" in the past, which also determine that, provided I now intend to use "+" with the same meaning as I did in the past, I should now give the answer "125" to the question "68 + 57?"

The sense of "determine" in (N_{FACT}) is that of metaphysical necessitation rather than a priori deducibility. Correspondingly, we have an alteration in the antireductionist thesis (AR) so that it becomes the much more radical antifactualist thesis (AF):

(AF) There are no facts that determine that I meant addition by "+" in the past, and which, consequently, also determine that, provided I now intend to use "+" with the same meaning as I did in the past, I should now give the answer "125" to "68 + 57?"

Pace Soames, there are not two voices in play in Kripke's exposition— the voice of the skeptic and the voice of the proponent of the skeptical solution. Instead, there is only one voice, that of KW who presents a metaphysically skeptical argument proceeding from (N_{FACT}) to the conclusion (AF), a conclusion *accepted* in the formulation of the skeptical solution.[17] But wait. We have encountered the troublesome notion of a "fact" once more in (AF). Perhaps it would be better to recast it as the denial that there are any *truthmakers* for meaning attributions:

(ATM) There are no truthmakers that metaphysically necessitate that I meant addition by "+" in the past, and which, consequently, also necessitate that, provided I now intend to use "+" with the same meaning as I did in the past, I should now give the answer "125" to "68 + 57?"

KW as skeptic thus argues that there are no nonintentional truthmakers for my meaning one thing rather than another by "+." Nothing about me or my dispositions or indeed *any* internal state of mine, nothing about any external state of the world or relation between the world and me or between my linguistic community and me, can possibly make it the case that in the past I meant addition, not quaddition, by "+" and thus that I should now respond to the question "68 + 57?" with "125" rather than "5" or some totally arbitrary reply, if I am to remain faithful to my past intentions concerning how I meant to use "+."

This is about as clear a statement of semantic eliminativism as it is possible to formulate. What then of KW *qua* proponent of the skeptical solution? What are we to make of his claim that "We do not wish to deny the propriety of an ordinary use of the phrase 'the fact that Jones meant addition by such-and-such a symbol,' and indeed such expressions do have perfectly ordinary uses"? Isn't this just an about-face? It can easily seem that way and has done so to many philosophers. One might be tempted to think that KW's skeptical solution amounts to viewing intentionality as a primitive, naturalistically irreducible fact about human beings, for it does permit us to speak of facts concerning what I meant by "+." Perhaps, then, KW is concerned only to deny the existence of *superlative* facts of meaning addition by "+." Such a view is promoted by Alex Byrne, who insists that "Kripke's Wittgenstein cannot possibly be a non-factualist," citing as his ground p. 86 of *Wittgenstein on Rules*:

Do we not call assertions like ["Jones, like many of us, means addition by '+'"] "true" or "false"? Can we not with propriety precede such assertions with "It is a fact that" or "It is not a fact that"? Wittgenstein's way with such objections is short. Like many others, Wittgenstein accepts the "redundancy" theory of truth: to affirm that a statement is true (or presumably to precede it "It is a fact that ...") is simply to affirm the statement itself, and to say that it is not true is to deny it: ("p" is true =p).... We *call* something a proposition, and hence true or false, when in our language we apply the calculus of truth functions to it.[18]

Byrne infers from this passage that KW must be a meaning factualist: "As the above passage makes clear, [KW] holds that 'Jones means addition by '+' does (or could) state a fact, in the perfectly ordinary sense of 'fact.'"[19]

Further, KW, on Byrne's reading, believes that facts about meaning are primitive facts: "Kripke's Wittgenstein is claiming that statements like 'Jones means addition by "plus" can be 'barely true': true and reducible only to trivial variants of the statement itself."[20] I think Byrne has misunderstood Kripke's dialectic in the passage at p. 86. In this passage KW is replying to an *objection*. That objection is that it cannot be right to believe with the skeptic that there is simply no fact as to what I mean by "+" given that it is our practice to call assertions like "Jones means addition by '+'" true or false. In other words, it is precisely factualism that is being urged as an objection *against* KW. Kripke's reply, on behalf of KW, is that we *call* some statement a proposition, that is, recognize it as meaningful, when we apply the notions of truth and factuality to it. The operative word, which Kripke himself emphasizes, is "call." This is part of our practice. But we must understand what we are doing when we do call a proposition true or classify it as a fact.

Philosophers, wedded to an "Augustinian" view of language that demands a referent for every meaningful term, compulsively seek some entity in the world to which the term "fact" corresponds. But there are no such entities. The philosophers who demand them have been misled by surface grammar:

"It is a fact that *p*" simply means "*p*."

Once we appreciate the definitional eliminability of the operator "it is a fact that ...," there is no longer any need to reify facts so as to account for its meaning. So the point of KW's reply in the above passage is that one cannot buy the existence of facts if there aren't any simply by using the locution "It is a fact that...." Whatever nonfactuality or other type of indeterminacy exists in the claim "I mean addition by '+'" will just be inherited by the notational variant "It is a fact that I mean addition by '+,'" in just the same way as my borderline baldness makes it the case that there is no fact as to the truth value of "I am bald" or, equally, of "It is a fact that I am bald."

It is worthwhile pausing to see how objective indeterminacy or nonfactuality can be masked by a linguistic practice that assumes determinacy. Field has shown how a holistic indeterminacy that he calls "correlative indeterminacy" can insinuate itself even into the use of words whose meanings we take to be perfectly determinate:

> ... it is easy to use the machinery of correlative indeterminacy to tie the reference of "refers" to that of indeterminate "ground-level" concepts, such as perhaps "entropy" and "insanity." So if "entropy" partially refers to E_1 and E_2, then we can say that relative to an assignment of E_1 to "entropy," "refers" refers to a relation that holds between "entropy" and only one thing, viz. E_1; and analogously for E_2. In this way we can get the result that even if "entropy" partially refers to many things (and hence doesn't determinately refer to anything), still the sentence "'Entropy' refers to entropy and nothing else" comes out true. (Indeed, determinately true: true on every acceptable combination of the partial referents of "entropy" and "refers.") The advocate of indeterminacy can still "speak with the vulgar."[21]

The type of indeterminacy Field has in mind, which he calls radical indeterminacy, is still tame by KW's lights. KW means to deny that there is anything to which "entropy" or "+" or even "square" could refer. KW is questioning the *existence* of referents for our terms. Field is addressing the secondary issue of the *uniqueness* of any such referents. Field thinks that a KW-styled view simply could not be correct:

> Of course, it surely isn't a complete illusion (that "insanity" and "entropy" determinately refer to insanity and entropy): even if there are no naturalistic facts that fully determine the referents of these words or concepts, surely there are naturalistic facts that partially determine the referents. (Surely facts about our use of "insanity" determine that the word doesn't stand for lubricating jelly.)[22]

But for KW there could as justifiably be a rule for applying the term "insanity" to lubricating jelly as applying it to, as we think, insanity. Even if Field himself rejects it, KW's view can be approximated through Field's device of partial reference and correlative indeterminacy. There would simply be no limits on the number of acceptable referents to which any term partially refers. "'Dog' refers to dogs and to nothing else" and "'+' refers to addition and to nothing else" will still come out determinately true even in the teeth of the massive indeterminacy KW imagines. It is undeniable that KW's acquiescence in locutions such as "It is a fact that I mean addition by '+'" is confusing. So to see why KW cannot possibly be a meaning factualist committed to primitive intentional facts, we need only compare his views with those of one who was a meaning factualist—Brentano. As Field explains it:

> Many mental properties ... appear to relate people to nonlinguistic entities called propositions. So ... any materialist who admits that belief and desire are relations between people and propositions ... must show that the relations in question are not irreducibly mental. Brentano felt that this could not be done; and since he saw no alternative to viewing belief and desire as relations to propositions, he concluded that materialism is false.[23]

Brentano could certainly make sense of metaphysical questions about intentional facts. KW feigns not to be able to: They are confusions, deep confusions about the nature of our linguistic practices, according to him. To cast KW as believing in primitive facts about my meaning one thing rather than another by my words is to locate his views in the philosophical spectrum of options concerning the relation between intentional and nonintentional facts: reducibility, supervenience, primitive irreducibility. KW means to reject this whole metaphysical picture.

From the perspective of the philosopher for whom the question "*In virtue of what* do I mean addition by '+'?" makes sense, what KW is endorsing is not the existence of metaphysical truth-makers for meaning-claims like "I mean addition by '+,'" but rather *the propriety of a certain form of words*, namely, "*It is a fact that* I mean addition by '+.'" The propriety of such a form of words is secured, according to KW, as soon as we locate it within an accepted linguistic practice. "I mean addition by '+'" has a clear use in our linguistic practices involving the "+" symbol, and ordinary linguistic practice involving the notions of truth and fact endorses the transition from "*p*" to "It is true that *p*" or "It is a fact that *p*." Thus, once we have established the acceptability and utility conditions for "I mean Addition by '+,'" we thereby establish, as an immediate inferential consequence, the acceptability and utility conditions for statements like "It is a fact that I mean addition by '+,'" "There is a fact of the matter about what I mean by '+,'" "There are facts about what I mean in general my words," and so on. KW *qua* proponent of the skeptical solution is thus one and the same as KW *qua* skeptic. There has been no backtracking on the thesis (ATM) above, that of the non-existence of truth-makers for my meaning what I do by my words. Provided we use the notions of fact and truth in their ordinary ways, the ways folk who have learned to use these notions actually do use them, we can justifiably assert claims like "It is a plain fact that I mean addition not quaddition by '+.'" But philosophers beware! The requisite sense of "justification" is not the sense philosophers have in mind when they demand metaphysical justification, the sense rejected in (N_{FACT}) above.

The claim "It is a plain fact that I mean addition, not quaddition, by '+'" would have a clear use in contexts where someone from my linguistic community has questioned my understanding of addition on the grounds that I have made systematic arithmetical errors, say. It is only when we ask philosophical questions, pathological questions that cannot be grounded in actual linguistic practice, about what sort of facts meaning facts might be, how they relate to ordinary physical or biological facts, how they could ever have arisen in a purely physical world, and so on, that we are forced to deny that there either are or could be such entities as meaning-facts. That there is no metaphysical ground for our linguistic practices involving meaning-attributions, including those involving "true" and "fact," might be construed as a ground for revising them. KW demurs: When we understand ordinary use of "true" and "fact" aright, we see that the demand for facts as entities is spurious.

From the metaphysical perspective in which questions of the supervenience of semantic facts on, or their deducibility (a priori or otherwise) from, nonintentional facts do make sense, KW's position represents semantic eliminativism. We tried to locate the problematic intentional facts in relation to the unproblematic physical or natural facts, convinced that it could not just be a primitive fact about the world that it contains creatures who entertain contentful states. This would be an inexplicable philosophical mystery if it were true. KW purports to show that there can be no nonintentional facts that metaphysically ground the intentional ones. We asked for metaphysical truthmakers and were sent away empty-handed. To be assured that we can still talk in ways that suggest to philosophers that there are truthmakers provided we agree not to ask for any is cold metaphysical comfort indeed. What we got instead of the desired truthmakers was the assurance that *despite the fact that there aren't any such facts*, we could go on using *a certain form of words*, "It is fact that I mean addition by '+,'" the very form that occasioned the philosophical puzzlement in the first place. Since when did semantic eliminativism together with linguistic quietism add up to semantic factualism? And why on earth should we accept linguistic quietism in the first place, having been given a powerful argument for semantic eliminativism?

For this reason, current ways of arbitrating disputes between realists and antirealists by using notions like truth-aptness or a contrast between factualism and nonfactualism as benchmarks are fruitless. Thus in ethics it is often assumed that to assert that ethical judgments are truth-apt or, more strongly, both truth-apt and largely true, is to commit oneself to moral realism. But if KW's position is anything to go by, it would seem that moral nihilism could quite peacefully cohabit with a semantic quietism that endorses the acceptability and utility within our practices of forms of words such as "It is a fact that one ought not to boil one's own grandmother in oil" or "It is true that unrestricted commodification is morally repugnant."

On such a view, even though there are no objective values that could undergird the truth of our claims about moral obligation—nothing, that is, that *makes* it morally right for me to say or do one thing rather than another—the practice of asserting ethical judgments plays a definite and socially useful role in our lives. Thus, on quietist grounds, it should be continued.

Wittgenstein is, of course, not alone in rejecting the general demand for truth-makers for our linguistic and other practices. It is a recurrent theme of pragmatism, a theory that Wittgenstein himself did much, intentionally or not, to make plausible, that our linguistic and cognitive practices are not answerable to any standards or ideals transcending them. There is nothing beyond or behind the practice of inquiry to which that practice is responsible; standards and values governing inquiry emerge as reflective equilibria within the practice of inquiry itself. We saw in section 8.2, though, that this pragmatist attitude to *truth* cannot be sustained.

More generally still, even some who count themselves realists about theoretical entities of various sorts (contentful states included) often endorse a minimalist view of truth and facts on the grounds that the epistemological and metaphysical costs of a substantial theory of truth and factuality are simply too high to bear. Disquotationalism about truth is surely the most austere form of minimalism, and it is to that which Kripke signals Wittgenstein was committed. Yet even though disquotationalists side with Wittgenstein in seeing the question that philosophers naturally want answered—"In virtue of what do I mean addition by '+' and not some other thing?"—as misconceived, it is quite another matter whether they hold that there are semantic facts in anything like the sense that those who ask such reductive questions intend. As Hartry Field has consistently emphasized: "To view truth and reference disquotationally is to view them as not really semantic notions at all, especially in their most central applications. The most central applications of 'true' and 'refers' (according to the disquotationalist) are to our own idiolect; and in these central applications they function as logical terms."[24] What does it mean to say that "true," "refers," and so on are "logical terms"? Just this:

... "S is true" (since it is equivalent to "Some sentence of our language that is identical to S is true") is equivalent to the disjunction of all possible sentences of the form: "p" = S and p; and hence anything of the form:

"q" is true

is equivalent to the corresponding q.

Reference, both for predicates (truth of) and for singular terms, is similar; for singular terms, we have that:

Some terms of our language that are F refer to x

is, in effect, the disjunction of all formulas of our language of the form:

F("t") and t = x;

which implies as before that any formula of the form

"s" refers to x

is equivalent to the corresponding formula s = x.[25]

On my interpretation of Kripke's dialectic, KW is indeed a disquotationalist about truth and facts. "It is a fact that I mean addition by '+'" is a simple logical variant of "I mean addition by '+,'" and, despite the fact that there is nothing in the world that makes them true, these logically identical claims of mine have a definite use and utility in the linguistic practices of the community to which I belong. On those grounds, these practices ought to be preserved, according to KW, since it is the metaphysical demand for a *ground* for them that is pathological, not the practices themselves.

How is this linguistic quietism compatible with semantic eliminativism? As Field explains, disquotationalist truth is not a semantic notion at all. The only entities introduced into our ontology by KW's "facts" are sequences of vocables involving the word "fact," and these sequences of vocables are themselves eliminable in favor of others that do not even appear to quantify over facts.

8.3.3 Soames's Reply to the Skeptical Paradox

Let us turn now to Soames's reply to Kripke. Soames has an interpretation of KW's argument for the skeptical paradox that questions the univocity of a key term. According to his explication, the argument runs as follows:

(P1) If in the past it was a fact that I meant addition by "+" then either:

(i) This fact was *determined by* nonintentional facts of some sort

or

(ii) This fact was a primitive fact, that is, one not *determined by* nonintentional facts.

(P2) It is not the case that nonintentional facts of type (I) *determined* that I meant addition by "+."

(P3) It is not the case that the fact that I meant addition by "+" was a primitive fact.

(C) Therefore, in the past there was no such fact as that I meant addition by "+."

The key term that Soames believes to be equivocal is "determined" as in "determined by." Let us label the supposed meaning fact M and the nonintentional facts F. Then, according to Soames, by "determine" we might either mean that (a) M is a necessary consequence of F or that (b) M is a priori deducible from F. Thus:

(I) If we take "determine" to signal metaphysically necessary consequence, then although (P1) and (P3) are true, (P2) is false.

(II) If we take "determine" to signal a priori deducibility, then although (P1) and (P2) may well be true, (P3) is false.

Soames concludes: There is no single interpretation in which (P1), (P2), (P3) are all jointly true; nor is there a single interpretation in which they are jointly plausible. I have already hinted at why I think Soames's response to KW is inconclusive. The only sense of "determine" that the skeptical paradox requires is metaphysical determination, metaphysically necessary consequence. The epistemic sense of a priori deducibililty is palpably irrelevant *if* one takes Kripke at his word since he emphasizes from the start that the skepticism in play is a metaphysical one and has nothing at all to do with limitations on our knowledge. Still, Soames may well be right that KW's argument looks plausible only because of a tacit slide between the different sorts of "determination" in moving between (P2) and (P3). To allay that concern, one would have to show that Kripke has an argument for (P2) *qua* thesis about metaphysical determination—the fact that I meant addition and not quaddition by "+" had better not be capable of being metaphysically fixed by nonintentional facts, if KW's official argument is sound.

It lies outside the scope of this discussion to pursue this matter further. We shall have to be content with some brief observations. Establishing that there could not be a fact of the sort that everyone intuitively believes does exist is a difficult assignment. In spite of this, KW produces a powerful argument for just this conclusion.

One way of presenting KW's argument for (P2) is this: Addition is a total function, as is Kripke's deviant alternative quaddition. Why should we believe that some set of nonintentional facts F single out a total function as the referent for my symbol "+"? Why is it not just as plausible, indeed, more so, given our finite computational and recognitional capacities, to believe that a partial function agreeing with my considered and, where necessary, suitably corrected, past responses involving "+," was all that the complete set of nonintentional facts F *could* pin down? Why does it beggar belief that the complete set of such facts either about my past brain states or about my dispositions simply failed to settle back then how I would respond to a novel question involving "+," let alone how I *ought* to respond?

Think what we are asking. We are asking F, the complete set of non-intentional facts about how I was in the past, *to have made it the case back then* that there was a determinate response that I ought to give now to a problem undreamed of back then. Perhaps each new such problem really does in principle call for a new decision, just as Wittgenstein claimed. Perhaps the partial function is undefined for the particular arguments in question even though in practice the matter is handled by some module in my brain—each novel problem acting as a stimulus for me to adopt some new determination for my partial function, to define it for these new arguments in one way rather than another, *replacing* the original with a new one. I may well be so disposed as to automatically adopt a succession of partial functions $f(x, y)$ that agrees in extension with the addition function up to some specified arguments m and n for x and y but that is simply undefined for arguments greater than m and n. This seamless succession of new partial functions might conjure the illusion that there is an infinitary function, a total one, that I intended all along—the addition function—even where there is no such total function. Moreover, even if my dispositions *were* infinitary ones, or my mental states infinitely fine-grained, fine enough to handle an infinity of possible questions posed within an infinity of possible situations, couldn't it still be the case that among those infinitary dispositions were dispositions to err unwittingly or to adopt a new rule when prompted by just this stimulus under just these conditions, a rule that does not at all accord with what I meant by "+" in the past? For these reasons, I think that Soames's response to Kripke is inconclusive.

8.3.4 Is KW's Semantic Eliminativism Stable?

Are there any general considerations that might lead one to doubt the tenability of KW's skeptical conclusion that there are no facts in virtue of which I mean one thing rather than another by "+"? Crispin Wright has mentioned an obvious one: Given the intuitively unassailable thesis that the truth value of any sentence depends on the meaning of that sentence together with the state of the world, how can KW stop short of a flat rejection of the concept of truth?[26] If there is nonfactuality in one of the determinants of truth value, there is surely nonfactuality in the resultant truth value. So KW's position seems to lead from the unnerving but still credible claim, if only barely so, that there are no facts about meaning to the genuinely "incredible and self-defeating conclusion"[27] that there are no facts simpliciter.

Perhaps the seemingly unassailable intuitive thesis that the truth value of a sentence depends on what that sentence means together with how the world is can be undermined. It is difficult to see how this could be done, though. It is no good claiming that this is just a philosophical "spin" placed on virgin linguistic practice, for example. The folk surely do believe that once they've settled what someone means by their words, it is up to the world to determine whether what that person says is true or not. It is difficult to make sense of their practice otherwise. Moreover, as Wright observes, any reconstruction of the folk notion of meaning that freed it in this way from its conceptual ties to truth "looks utterly daunting and even if possible it seems that a reconstruction of the sceptical paradox is available to rob any assignment of truth-conditions to a sentence of any possible behavioural or psychological corroboration."[28] If there are no facts at all, there is no such fact as the fact that there are no facts. So, given the unassailability of the truism connecting meaning and truth, the skeptic's thesis that there are no facts as to what any individual means by his use of any linguistic expression must be false since it leads to a position that is self-refuting. Let us call this the stability problem for KW.

KW has a ready response to the stability problem: His account precisely denies that meaning attributions have any truth conditions in the first place. Such statements as "I mean addition by '+'" can be supplied only with justification and utility conditions. So far we have been content to pretend that we understand more or less what Kripke means by these notions of justification and utility. We can afford to pretend no longer. We should first note, though, that there is a problem with Kripke's own formulation of the thesis that meaning-attributions have no truth conditions. KW emphasizes throughout the development of his skeptical paradox that there is no fact about what any individual meant by an expression E in the past, nor, by way of consequence, about what he means by E now. Even granted omniscience about my past mental states and behavior I still could not produce the requisite fact. Therefore there can be no such fact. This is what makes KW's conclusion metaphysical rather than just epistemological. Yet on page 111 Kripke writes: "One must bear firmly in mind that Wittgenstein has no theory of truth-conditions—necessary and sufficient conditions—for the correctness of one response rather than another to a new addition problem." This latter claim cannot be true if the former is. If, as the skeptical conclusion alleges, no truth conditions can be assigned in principle to statements imputing one rule rather than another to an agent, then Wittgenstein does have a theory about the truth conditions of such statements, namely, that there aren't any.[29] If, on the other hand, it is still an open question whether there are truth conditions for such statements, then it is also an open question whether there is some fact about me that makes my saying "125" rather than "5" to "68 + 57?" correct. Kripke cannot have it both ways. Does he try to?

Whether or not he does try to is uncertain. I am sure that such a slide would be unintentional, but it would be very convenient to stress the nonexistence of truth conditions when attempting to establish the metaphysical thesis that there is simply no fact as to what I mean by "+" (the skeptical paradox) while playing down their nonexistence in the course of elaborating the epistemic skeptical solution. Why would the latter move be useful? Because even though there are no facts about what an individual considered by himself means by E, there might yet be facts about how a linguistic community responds to his uses of E, which, in concert with the individual's own use of E, might constitute the appropriate fact.

It is interesting to see what Kripke actually says when he addresses this issue:

> Wittgenstein holds, with the sceptic, that there is no fact as to whether I mean plus or quus. But if this is to be conceded to the sceptic, is this not the end of the matter? What can be said on behalf of our ordinary attributions of meaningful language to ourselves and others? Has not the incredible and self-defeating conclusion that all language is meaningless already been drawn?[30]

In response, after quoting with approval Michael Dummett's claim that the *Philosophical Investigations* repudiates the truth-conditional view of meaning of the *Tractatus*, Kripke replies: "Wittgenstein replaces the question 'What must be the case for this sentence to be true?' by two others: first, 'Under what conditions may this form of words be appropriately asserted (or denied)?'; second, given an answer to the first question, 'What is the role, and the utility, in our lives of our practice of asserting (or denying) the form of words under these conditions?'"[31] But the fundamental question that Kripke avoids is whether KW is *entitled* to this "replacement" after he has questioned the factuality of meaning. If folk reactions to the revelation that there is no fact to the matter as to whether I mean addition or quaddition by "+" are anything to go by, KW's skeptical conclusion is simply bizarre and a paradigmatic example of the mischief philosophical reinterpretations of clearly sound practices can cause. Wittgenstein's protestations to the contrary, the folk do not doubt that what we mean by our words is fixed somehow by nonintentional facts of some sort or other. It is the quietistic alternative that they find truly incredible. For these reasons, they resist KW's redescription strategy. Judged by folk reactions, then, the answer to the question of whether KW is entitled to the replacement above is quite definitely "No."

That the meaning of a statement is in general fixed by its acceptability conditions is in no way inconsistent with its having truth conditions to begin with. Indeed, we may be forced, on analytic grounds, to turn to such notions as justification conditions, conceptual role, narrow meaning, and so on when the facts that comprise the truth conditions are not susceptible to conceptual analysis. We might then look to the functional role the attendant concepts played within the folk theory to provide such an analysis and glean what we could of the statement's meaning by surveying the network of connections with other statements and concepts as these appear within that theory and as these are applied within the folk practice of which the theory is a theory. Perhaps this is our general plight with respect to truth-conditions. Perhaps it is only in the context of radical interpretation, say, or reflection on folk theory, that the assignment of truth conditions to statements is in any way informative of their meanings.

Suppose no informative statement of the necessary and sufficient conditions for me to mean one thing rather than another by my words can be given, no truth-theoretic analysis of intentional content beyond the bare homophonic "I mean addition by '+' is true if and only if I mean addition by '+.'" How would this show that, as we are forced to rely on justification and utility conditions (i.e., functional role) to explicate the meaning of this claim, its truth conditions thereby evaporate? KW offers no answer to this question. This is no accident. Meaning-attributions do indeed have truth conditions of a sort on his view.

The crucial problem with KW's skeptical solution is this: *It seems to duck the basic challenge issued by the skeptical paradox—namely, having denied that there is any fact as to what I mean by "+," why doesn't the matter end there? Why isn't all talk of meaning or intentional content forthwith dismissed as vacuous?* It simply will not do for KW to respond to this, Kripke's own question, by describing our actual practice involving ascriptions of the rule of addition to people, however much he seeks to correct our mentalistic misconstrual of it—for the skeptic's challenge, that is, KW's own challenge, was to show how, given that there could be no fact as to whether I mean addition or quaddition by "+," this practice could possibly be coherent. Kripke writes, on behalf of KW:

> Now if we suppose that facts, or truth-conditions, are of the essence of meaningful assertion, it will follow from the sceptical conclusion that assertions that anyone ever means anything are meaningless. On the other hand, if we apply to these assertions the tests suggested in *Philosophical Investigations*, no such conclusion follows. All that is needed to legitimize assertions that someone means something is that there be roughly specifiable circumstances under which they are legitimately assertable, and that the game of asserting them under such conditions has a role in our lives. No supposition that "facts correspond" to those assertions is needed.[32]

In the face of his own skeptical challenge, though, this is just argument by fiat. KW has not proved, and I believe, cannot prove, that the supposition that facts, in some sense of "facts," correspond is unnecessary. I take it, though, that Kripke's reply to this objection will be the Wittgensteinian one: Don't think but look. Look at the way KW develops the skeptical solution and you will see that the assumption that facts correspond to meaning-attributions is otiose, that one can be entitled to assert p even though one is not thereby asserting one believes p to be true, in a substantial sense of "true."[33] So is Kripke right? Can we make do with justification and utility conditions alone? For his part, Kripke has no difficulty at all in seeing the utility of such a "nonfactual" practice: "We say of someone else that he follows a certain rule when his responses agree with our own and deny when they do not; but what is the utility of this practice? The utility is evident...."[34] Kripke illustrates this "utility" by considering the interactions between a customer and a grocer, showing how agreement in response is crucial for the mutual achievement of ends.[35]

I confess that I find it harder than Kripke evidently does to see the utility of the practice in question. There is no difficulty, of course, in appreciating the general significance or utility of *broad agreement in response* through a community at least as this touches its members' fundamental and everyday transactions with one another—the solution to the myriad simple and complex coordination problems presented by such social interaction depends on it. What is not so obvious, to me at any rate, is how *the mutual issuing of sequences of vocables* at the point at which our actions coordinate can itself assist further transactions between the grocer and me if that sequence (or constituent vocables within it) does not (do not) correspond to anything involved in such transactions—for example, if neither my "five apples" nor the grocer's "five apples" refers to the five apples I bought from him. Kripke's example, and all other examples like it, shows the utility of the grocer's *meaning the same* as we do. What he has to show is the utility of having that *form of words* in the language. It is only because he tacitly assumes the correct interpretation of the terms "five," "apple," and so on that Kripke can think that he has "explained the utility" of the linguistic practice in question.

What of the justification conditions for attributions of rule-following and meaning? Does the absence of any fact create problems for these also? We judge that Jones means square by "square" when he applies the term as we would apply it to (what we take to be) all and only square objects, allowing for borderline cases. But, according to KW, it is not because Jones and I have identical, determinate intentions to so use "square" as to mean square that we call the objects we do "square." Rather, contrapositively, it is simply that if we didn't call square objects "square," we couldn't be said to mean square by "square." Yet it seems that, Kripke's assertions to the contrary, we *do* have a fact that corresponds to my assertion of "Jones means square by 'square'": *the fact that I have judged that Jones responds as I do to situations in which "square" is applicable.*

Following KW's prescriptions, my assertion about Jones's meaning square by "square" cannot be accepted unconditionally. It is subject to correction by other rule-followers. Granted. So the fact of my judging Jones's meaning as I do is not sufficient to make my assertion about him true. Then the requisite contrast between assertibility and truth arises as follows: *I am entitled to assert "Jones means square by 'square'" just when I judge that Jones's responses coincide with my own with respect to "square."* This is an *assertibility condition* that holds good for each speaker. But if we are to faithfully describe our actual practice of concept attribution, in accord with KW's invocation to look and not think, we need to distinguish *thinking* one is obeying a rule from *really* obeying it.

The distinction arises only in the social context. Although each speaker has assertibility conditions for uttering "Jones means square by 'square,'" it is only if their individual responses with "square" coincide that this practice can have a utility for us. So we consider the community of speakers, C, and say that:

"Jones means square by 'square'" is *true* if and only if the dispositions of the majority of C-members to use "square" coincide with Jones's dispositions to use "square."[36]

Kripke considers this theory but dismisses it:

> Wittgenstein's theory should not be confused with the theory that, for any m and n, the value of the function we mean by "plus" is (by definition) the value that (nearly all) the linguistic community would give as the answer. Such a theory would be a theory of the truth-conditions of such assertions as "By 'plus' we mean such-and-such a function." ... The theory would be a social, or community wide, version of the dispositional theory, and would be open to at least some of the criticisms as the original form.[37]

Kripke is undoubtedly right that the same problems afflicting the individual's dispositions—systematic errors, finitude, and, crucially, normativity (the foundation of a standard for correct use)—stymie the attempt to reinstate dispositions, albeit collective ones, as objective metaphysical truthmakers for "I mean addition by '+'" or "Jones means square by 'square,'" that is, facts that metaphysically necessitate that I mean addition or Jones means square and that thereby justify my now responding with "125" to "68 + 57?" But that is not the suggestion. The suggestion is that shared responses might determine in a linguistic community *what is to count as the correct answer* to "68 + 57?" in just the same way as social convention determines the correct side of the road to drive on. If my responses, or Jones's, match those of our fellows over a wide range of actual and counterfactual cases involving "+" and "square," then, in our community C, I mean addition by "+" and Jones means square by "square." This holds good even if, as would be the case, in C* I would mean quaddition by "+" and Jones would mean sqwore by "square."

So there are indeed facts, on KW's own showing, about what I mean by "+" and what Jones means by "square," albeit community-indexed facts. The responses of my fellow language-users provide the intentional frame of reference, so to speak. But a fact of any sort is all that we need to generate a stability problem for Kripke's skeptic KW. So we have as our conventionalist truth conditions:

"I mean addition by '+'" is true iff my responses agree with my fellows' with respect to "+."

Kripke discusses this proposal but rejects it along the following lines:

> If Wittgenstein had been attempting to give necessary and sufficient conditions to show that "125," not "5," is the "right" response to "68 + 57?", he might be

charged with circularity. For he might be taken to say that my response is correct if and only if it agrees with others'. But even if the sceptic and I both accept this criterion in advance, might not the sceptic maintain that just as I was wrong about what "+" meant in the past, so I was wrong about "agree"? Indeed to attempt to reduce the rule of Addition to another rule—"Respond to an Addition problem exactly as others do!"—falls foul of Wittgenstein's strictures on a "rule for interpreting a rule" just as much as any other attempted reduction. Such a rule, as Wittgenstein would emphasize, also describes what I do wrongly: I do not consult others when I add. (We wouldn't manage very well, if everyone followed a rule of the proposed form—no one would respond without waiting for everyone else.)[38]

Kripke's objection seems to me to fail entirely to engage with the conventionalist's proposal. The conventionalist is not suggesting that we need to agree about the meaning of "agree" before we can be said to agree. Nor is this any objection to his proposal. The requisite agreement is, in Wittgenstein's words, "not agreement in opinions but in form of life"[39]—that is, agreement in responses.

For the conventionalist, "*p*" is true iff most people would assent to "*p*." Collusion, either implicit or explicit, is neither necessary nor sufficient for this type of agreement, agreement in response. It is not *necessary* because we could be independently inclined to give the same answers without agreeing or even disagreeing that our responses constituted "agreement." It is not *sufficient* because we could agree on the formulation of what constituted "agreement" and find ourselves brutely disposed to react in totally different ways. Moreover, and this is the decisive point, Kripke's own preferred solution itself depends on this type of agreement. As he says:

> ... if there were no general agreement in the community responses, the game of attributing concepts to individuals—as we have described it—could not exist. In fact of course there is considerable agreement, and deviant quus-like behaviour occurs rarely.... almost all of us, after sufficient training, respond with roughly the same procedures to concrete addition problems. We respond unhesitatingly to such problems as "68 + 57?" regarding our procedures as the only comprehensible one ... and we agree in the unhesitating responses we make.[40]

Kripke thus cannot raise a skeptical problem for the conventionalist's sense of "agreement" as it features in the conventionalist truth conditions above without also raising the same problem for KW's own skeptical solution. *So the skeptical solution can be saved from incoherence only by positing communal truth conditions for attributions of rule-following.*

Seen through the eyes of the conventionalist, KW's skeptical solution does *not* establish the metaphysical conclusion that there is no fact as to whether I mean addition or quaddition by "+," but instead corrects the distorted metaphysical picture of its being a fact *about me*, in isolation from my community, that makes it true that I mean one thing rather than another by "+." The relevant fact is a social one, not a solipsistic one. *The skeptic shows us what the real fact is, not that there isn't any fact.* Must Kripke take issue with this analysis? I don't see why. To have to admit that there are facts that correspond to my meaning addition by "+" is no backdown at all if one is sufficiently deflationist about the facts in question.

The crucial point is that these facts (about the agreement of my responses with those of my fellows') are not metaphysical truth-makers for my meaning addition by "+"—that is, they are not nonintentional entities that settle what I mean in the sense of determining the response I ought to give *sub specie aeternitatas* in a novel situation. Now this is not obvious and therefore calls for comment. We have already seen that had I been a member of C* rather than C, the response I "ought" to give to "68 + 57?" would have been "5" rather than "125," since in C* they mean quaddition rather than addition by "+" in the sense that when quizzed about the result of adding addends greater than 57 they respond with "5." This by itself shows that the conventionalist truth conditions are not nonintentional facts that metaphysically necessitate that I mean addition rather than quaddition by "+." Still, my response of "125" is justified in my community. So in some sense of "ought," I ought to reply as I am inclined to do. In what sense of "ought," though? In just the same sense of "ought" as I ought to drive on the same side of the road as my fellows. Social, "conventionalist" facts can no more mandate that I answer "125" to "68 + 57?" than any other purely conventional facts can mandate that, say, I drive on the left-hand side rather than the right-hand side of the road. If I wish to stay alive, not terrify other drivers, not get busted by the cops, and so on then in my, Australian community I should choose to drive on the left. I *ought* to drive on the left in the sense that this is the instrumentally rational choice for me to make given that the coordination problem of which side to drive on has been solved in one way rather than another. Had I been in North America, though, the same considerations would have dictated that I drive on the right. Were I to be asked the question "What is the *correct* side tout court of the road to drive on *sub specie aeternitatas*?" I would be incredulous. There is no such thing as the correct side of the road to drive on *sub specie aeternitatas*. There is no metaphysical truthmaker that fixes the correctness of one side of the road rather than another as the one I ought to drive on. Similarly, there is no metaphysical truthmaker that *necessitates* my responding "125" rather than "5" or, indeed, nothing at all to "68 + 57?" from this conventionalist perspective.

We should note, though, that there is one final point of contention between this interpretation and the one Kripke endorses that requires comment. On my interpretation, the very conditions Kripke believes immune to skeptical attack—my assertibility conditions for "Jones means square by 'square'"—are the ones ultimately open to the paradox. Conversely, the very conditions that Kripke thinks are open to the skeptical argument I contend are immune—the conventionalist's disquotational truth conditions for "Jones means square by 'square.'"

I claimed these conditions were immune because they did not involve judgments about agreement at all; they only involved the one type of agreement KW cannot afford to disavow—agreement in responses. Moreover, recalling Field's point noted earlier about the nonsemantic nature of disquotational truth, we arrive at the same conclusion: No judgments of content are involved in fixing disquotational truth conditions—having settled the (conventionalist) grounds on which "p" may be asserted, the grounds for asserting that "p" is true are automatically determined. No appeal to shared judgments of agreement is necessary to fix the conventionalist truth conditions for "I mean addition by '+,'" namely:

"I mean addition by '+'" is true iff my responses involving "+" match those of my fellows'.

However, an appeal to constancy in judgments of agreement is necessary in formulating the assertibility conditions:

"Jones mean square by 'square'" is assertible by a speaker iff the speaker judges that Jones's responses match those of his own over a wide range of cases.

This ought not to be surprising. It would be obviously incorrect to state Smith's assertibility conditions for "Jones means square by 'square'" as "Jones means square by 'square'" is assertible for Smith iff Jones's responses involving 'square' match Smith's own over a wide range of cases," since Smith might be totally oblivious to any match between Jones's responses and his own. So if the skeptical paradox can be turned against any factual condition on "I mean Addition by '+,'" it can surely be turned against KW's assertibility conditions and not the conventionalist's truth conditions.

8.3.5 The Stability Problem for Kripke's Wittgenstein

Now we can return to the paradoxical status of the skeptical paradox itself. We saw before that if we were granted the truism that the truth of a statement depends jointly on the meaning of the statement and the state of the world, acceptance of the skeptic's conclusion that there are no facts about what any speaker meant by any statement logically entails acceptance of the radical conclusion that there are no facts tout court, a position that is self-refuting.

The only feasible ways to block this result are to deny the truism itself, a course not open to KW, at least, concerned as he is to conserve and not revise or even reinterpret ordinary folk practice involving the notions of meaning and truth, or to deny either that the truism or the skeptic's conclusion, or perhaps both, have truth conditions, claiming instead they have only justification and utility conditions. But it should now be clear that this latter alternative is unworkable also. It is a necessary condition for such statements to possess justification and utility conditions that they also possess at least disquotational truth conditions. We thus have good reason to suspect that KW's position is internally unstable.

8.3.6 The Feasibility of Semantic Eliminativism

Does this stability problem for KW's brand of semantic eliminativism show that eliminative materialism is internally incoherent? No. Eliminative materialists will presumably respond in just the way KW cannot afford to. They will deny that there is any coherent notion of "meaning" on which the truism that the meaning of a statement together with the state of the world fixes what's true about the world is itself true. Rather, this truism is simply part of a package of folk semantics which must be rejected *in toto*.

There does remain a problem for eliminative materialism. This concerns its communicability. Kripke's Wittgenstein is interesting not only because of his nonfactualism about meaning but also because of the semantic quietism with which this is conjoined. If our ordinary uses of the notions of truth and meaning really are perfectly in order as they stand, as Wittgenstein held, there is no difficulty at all in articulating the semantic eliminativist's theory. What happens, though, if these linguistic practices also have to be revised? Which, if any, inferences are licit, and which, if any, interpretations of the eliminativist's own theses are to be preferred? Unless every useful semantic notion can be deflated and replaced by a nonsemantic disquotational ersatz, the eliminative materialist might, ultimately, be at a loss for words.

8.4 Analytic Functionalism: A Wrong Turn for Naturalistic Realism

In his *From Metaphysics to Ethics: A Defence of Conceptual Analysis*, Frank Jackson formulates a reductionist naturalistic metaphysics according to which the manifest way things are is deemed a priori deducible from contingent a posteriori premises made true by the microphysical facts. Jackson's "location problem," the main task for "serious metaphysics," is then to find microphysical truthmakers for truths concerning the supervenient aspects of reality. Conceptual analysis—examination of concepts through possible cases—is required to explicate properly what the folk mean when they refer to certain recurrent patterns in their manifest experience of the world in such a way that not only colors but also the norms and values they appeal to in their social transactions with one another have somehow to be upwardly necessitated by the distribution of forces and fields.

Further, *that* these manifest phenomena are so necessitated will be *a priori deducible from* the microphysical facts when once we Ramsify those (analytically enhanced) platitudes the folk themselves endorse as they unwittingly record the physical basis for the various patterns they detect in manifest experience. That is, we will have *located* the elusive facts when we show how, by first Ramsifying the folk platitudes concerning them, a natural realizer can be found that fills the functional role subtended by those platitudes. If no such physical realizer can be found, the phenomenon in question will be apt for elimination instead of reduction as provided by a physical realizer.

Jackson's program is nothing if not ambitious. I wish to explain in this section why it cannot work. One initial reason for skepticism is straightforwardly Humean but none the worse for that. Our folk theories are not the product of either reason or scientific investigation but are amalgams of the usual Humean suspects: custom, habit, and unfettered imagination. Given that they were conceived in epistemic sin, what possible benefit could there be in Ramsifying them?

Suppose, though, that at least in simple and obvious matters about their manifest experience, the folk cannot *help* getting things right in the sense that they are differentially responsive to some real patterns in the descriptive way things are. Is there a reliable backward route from differential response to descriptive pattern? There is, only if we can be sure there is no room for Nature to interpose systematic errors or shared illusions somewhere along the complex chain that begins with physical detection and ends in folk conceptualization. If Jackson has an argument to show this cannot happen, he doesn't let on what it might be. To the contrary, he seems happy to accept that careful explication of what the folk really mean by their words when they describe their manifest experiences will yield at least some truths guaranteed by those very meanings (the *analytic* ones), truths that hold good irrespective of which world is actual, ones that are, in other words, a priori.

How does Jackson know that such explication of folk concepts will yield such truths? How can he know a priori that colors or moral values are not illusions? He cannot just rest with the response most naturalistic color realists would give to this question: that the best theory of colors takes them to be physical properties of some sort (e.g., reflectance properties). Some physical property R may well play the red-role in Ramsified folk color-theory, but if colors are illusions, that physical property is not redness since there isn't any property of redness. Yet for Jackson it is both analytic and a priori that R is redness. The sentence "R is redness" expresses a conceptually necessary truth; it is a sentence "that could only come false by virtue of meaning change."

So why think that there is anything that the folk at bottom *really do mean* by their words, at least as these folk meanings bear on the location problem? Is the folk concept of a table or a rock detailed enough to decide between Lewis's view that tables and rocks are mereological sums of time-slices of their constituent molecules and Quine's competing view that tables and rocks are the spatiotemporal regions they occupy? Jackson's concept of a table or of a rock no doubt is enough to decide, but this is not what we are after. We are supposed to be teasing out the implications of a preexisting folk concept when we engage in conceptual analysis, not indulging a predilection for unfettered rational reconstruction.

Yet if anything is clear about the folk concepts of tables and rocks, it is that there is simply no fact to the matter *as far as the folk are concerned* as to which metaphysics of tables and rocks is to be preferred—and this for the simple reason that the folk endorse *no* metaphysical views, not even tacitly, about tables and rocks, nor, indeed about most other things.

Recall Putnam's assessment of this matter:

> ... I am not asking us to abandon any part of the commonsense standard, of the commonsense practice (for such I take it to be) of regarding it as no real question at all whether a table is "identical with the region it occupies in space-time or with the mereological sum of time-slices of molecules that it contains." *What I am asking us to "abandon" is the idea that such a question must have a non-conventional answer.*

I said in section 5.4 that I think Putnam is right about this. As regards the manifest image, I endorse Putnam's view that there is not in general any fact of the matter as to how the items and properties of manifest experience are to be connected to the myriad physical properties on which they supervene. One can choose to identify rocks with spatio-temporal regions they occupy or with mereological sums of time-slices of their constituent molecules.

There is indeed a fact of the matter as to which account of material continuants is best, in my view. But the best account of material continuants is not implied by a folk theory of "middle-sized dry goods" that is entirely oblivious to it or any competitor account. It is implied by our best overall theory of nature. Hence, we should recognize rational reconstructions of folk theory for what they are: not explications of indefinitely detailed preexisting concepts but replacements for folk precursors that are too vague and inexplicit to discharge any serious scientific or metaphysical role. With these general observations behind us, I now want to examine the case of moral norms and values in more detail.

J. L. Mackie famously held that there is no good reason to believe there any moral values of the sort required for folk morality to be true. His main reason was that folk moral views all presupposed the existence of a property of objective "to-be-doneness" not indexed to the attitudes of any agent or agents, a property he took to be too "queer" to be reduced to any natural property. Jackson, on the other hand, is committed to ethical naturalism, even adducing an a priori "proof" that, *pace* Mackie, ethical properties *must* be reducible to natural properties. Thus, in discussing Mackie, he contends: "Any account of M (matured Folk Morality) which makes it all but impossible for any actions in the world as it is actually constituted, to be right must be mistaken. It is a constraint on interpreting our moral discourse that some actions have the moral properties our discourse putatively ascribes to them."[41] So what is it that secures the overall truth of the folk theory of morality? Why couldn't it be based on a systematic but seductive error just as Mackie argued? Isn't Jackson's claim that Mackie's moral skepticism *must* be mistaken mere dramatic overstatement? Surely Jackson does not really believe that there is no chance at all that Mackie is right, that he assigns a subjective probability of 0 to arguments that even the most fervent of Mackie's critics admit to be powerful ones?

In fact, as will emerge below, Jackson apparently has to be taken at his word. If analytic moral functionalism (AMF) is true, moral skepticism *must* indeed be false—reflective fallibilism, the very epistemic attitude naturalism urges we adopt toward all our theories, is rationally inaccessible for one who subscribes to the analytic functionalist's views on metaphysical determination and the a priori.

We can know a priori that Mackie is wrong, Jackson contends. I shall argue that if we can know this a priori then the original puzzle posed by moral obligations in a purely physical world ought to be incomprehensible to Jackson and the supporters of AMF given only the a priori deducibility of moral facts from natural facts together with the existence of a natural realizer of the folk moral platitudes.

Consider the beliefs of certain sorts of moral skeptics or moral agnostics—Pyrrhonian skeptics, let's call them. They hold *not* that there are no objective moral values and norms, as the moral nihilist holds, nor that we can have no reasonable ground for believing that there are, as Mackiean moral skeptics aver, but rather that it is undecidable in principle whether such entities exist. Like their ancient namesakes, they believe that every argument in favor of moral realism can be counterbalanced by one against. These opposing arguments are in equipollence in their view. Hence, following Pyrrho, they conclude that they have no option but to suspend judgment on the issue of whether there are objective moral values and norms.

In fact, we have already encountered individuals whose epistemic situation exactly mimicked that of these Pyrrhonians in section 8.2 when we discussed the implications of the U-style game for a pragmatist view of truth. In what follows, we shall assume that the decision matrix for U is precisely the one they believe to be in play in their ethical transactions with one another, where to "cooperate" is to act in accord with the maxims of folk morality and to "defect" is to refrain from so doing.

Our Pyrrhonians are, as it turns out, largely altruistic by nature. Their problem is that they cannot decide, and cannot see how anyone could decide, whether this natural altruism derives from an implicit recognition of an objective property of acts or wells up from within them—do they cooperate with each other and act selflessly on occasion because it is objectively right to do so, or do they merely falsely believe that it is objectively right to do so because they are internally impelled to cooperate with each other and act selflessly on occasions?

Instrumentally, the answer to this question does not matter. Society works much the better for their natural altruism, whether grounded or not in the objective way things are. They know this, everyone knows that everyone knows this, and a collection of folk platitudes about morality springs up codifying the instrumentally useful expectations of their moral community. These platitudes set out how everyone *ought* to behave in certain contexts. Provided their moral dispositions largely agree, which, aided by the platitudes, their natural altruism ensures, everyone is collectively better off. No matter that their "ought" as it appears in the platitudes they endorse is systematically ambiguous between the deontic sense and the sense of practical rationality.

Still, they remain Pyrrhonian skeptics about morality. They think there is a fifty percent chance that the world they inhabit is a world in which there are real moral norms and values, and a fifty percent chance that they inhabit a world in which evolution has played an instrumentally useful trick on them to ensure their collective survival: It has made them compulsive altruists who benefit from the illusion that they objectively ought to cooperate. In short, Pyrrhonians understand moral discourse just as the folk do to the extent that they believe that it certainly *appears* as if various acts have moral qualities. What's more, they know that everyone is better off by and large if all act on the basis of these appearances. What they don't know is whether these appearances stem from some foible of human nature or from something external to it, something objective in the world. They agree that it is *as if* there are moral values and that we should act on the basis of these appearances. That is what justifies thinking of them as *Pyrrhonian* skeptics about morality.

Moreover, they have, let us suppose, in addition to their platitudes, a sophisticated theory about what moral values *might* be. If moral values are real at all, they reason, they could only be natural properties of some sort or other. The natural property that best realizes the generalizations systematized in the folk theory of morality about moral obligation, say, is the property of maximizing overall happiness, N_u. They have developed a utilitarian moral theory as the best systematization of folk theory. Let us assume for the sake of argument that this theory really *is* the best systematization of folk morality. The question is, "What does AMF make of the Pyrrhonians' views?"

To answer this, we need to express AMF a little more accurately. According to AMF, it is a priori that the following holds with respect to the natural property that fixes the extension of "morally obligatory":

At any world w at which there is a unique property n_w that makes true some weighted quorum h of M_u's theses concerning what maximizes overall happiness, the extension of the folk moral term "morally obligatory" at w is just n_w.

$$\forall w \exists ! n_w \exists h [(h \subseteq M_u \ \& \ n_w \Vdash_w h) \rightarrow |\text{``obligatory''}|_w = n_w)]$$

On this basis, AMF might claim that it is indeed possible that there exist a world wherein moral values are merely illusory properties. If the mature theory of morality is a utilitarian one, M_u, what is a priori is not that some weighted quorum Q of M_u's moral generalizations hold in all possible worlds but rather that *if* a natural realizer N for Q exists at all in a world w, *then* that realizer N will determine the extensions of the folk moral terms *in w*. In this way the Pyrrhonians can make sense of a possible world wherein their moral beliefs turn out to be illusory, for that is just a world in which no suitable N exists to fix extensions in this way.[42]

The problem is that this misrepresents the Pyrrhonians' situation. They are agreed that *if* there is a natural realizer for "morally obligatory" at all, it is undoubtedly N_u, the realizer posited by their mature utilitarian moral theory M_u. What they regard as rationally undecidable is whether N_u's satisfying the quorum Q of M_u's theses concerning what maximizes overall happiness really *is* what being morally right consists in. We can put the Pyrrhonians' epistemic quandary about moral norms thus: Is it the case that we all agree in our judgments about what to call "morally obligatory" because we can all detect the objective obligation-making property N_u, or is it rather that we all erroneously believe of N_u that it is an objective obligation-making property simply because we all happen to agree in our judgments as to what to call "morally obligatory"?[43]

The Pyrrhonians think it is undecidable which of two possible worlds, or, better, *universes* of worlds, they inhabit, w_R or w_I.[44] In the first world or universe w_R, moral values are real objective natural properties. In the second world or universe w_I, they are not real objective natural properties; there is only a pervasive cognitive illusion that they are. Thus N_u exists in both possible universes. What differs between universes is the metaphysical status that N_u enjoys. In the one universe N_u is a *truthmaker* for our judgments of moral obligation, whereas in the other it is that which, in the presence of certain natural altruistic dispositions, fosters a pervasive illusion of moral obligation.

For both worlds there is a unique natural property, N_u, say, that makes true some weighted quorum of M_u's theses concerning what maximizes overall happiness. Yet for w_I the extension of the folk term "morally obligatory" is not N_u since *no* folk moral term has an extension among the natural properties in that world.

AMF thus seems to be committed to there being a conceptual incoherence in the description of w_I, the world wherein objective moral values are merely illusory—false reifications, that is, of the Pyrrhonians' own altruistic inclinations. In the light of the supervenience of the moral facts on natural facts, though, this means that there must be some sort of incoherence at the subvenient natural level if this appearance of conceptual incoherence at the moral level is indeed veridical. Yet *where* in the natural evolutionary tale told above might there be such an incoherence? *Which* conjectured natural facts must be rejected to restore coherence?

AMF apparently cannot allow that a world such as w_I could exist, given only the existence of a realizer N_u for the property that the best systematization M_u of folk morality posits as the mature representation of moral obligation. If AMF is right, our Pyrrhonians' epistemic quandary is itself incoherent. The Pyrrhonians can know a priori that they *could not* inhabit a world in which moral values are illusory. Metaethical Pyrrhonism is therefore unstable.

Yet how could this possibly be right? If I am a moral agnostic, what I need to be assured of, if I'm to abandon my position and commit myself to believing in objective moral norms and values, is that there really is good evidence that such entities exist. Otherwise I have no reason at all to change my mind. How can the news that the best systematization of folk morality is undoubtedly utilitarianism and that there is some natural property that secures happiness for the greatest number persuade me in the slightest that I should revise my view and start believing that there really are objective moral norms after all? This is information I may already *have*. It beggars belief that the only thing preventing me from drawing the conclusion in those circumstances that objective norms and values exist is some failure of rational acumen. *What I doubt is precisely that folk morality is (largely) true to begin with.* So far, AMF has offered me no new evidence to assuage *this* doubt.

Unless AMF proponents can somehow allow that AMF itself, although a priori true may yet be false in the circumstances in which the moral Pyrrhonists find themselves, it certainly *seems* as if it has to declare this form of moral agnosticism conceptually incoherent in those conditions. So AMF proponents will naturally want to question whether AMF really *does* entail that metaethical Pyrrhonism is epistemically unstable.

By way of comparison, consider a view we might call perceptual Pyrrhonism, a view agnostic as to the competing claims of reductive and eliminative phenomenalism. The analogue of AMF will be analytic phenomenalist functionalism, APF. If metaethical Pyrrhonism is an unstable position from the perspective of AMF, so also should perceptual Pyrrhonism be from the perspective of APF.[45]

Perceptual Pyrrhonism regards it as rationally undecidable whether there are physical objects such as the folk take there to be or whether there are simply sensory arrays that foster the ingrained cognitive illusion of physical objects. To complete the structural similarity with the moral case, we also need to assume that there is some best systematization of folk physical object theory endorsed by APF that the perceptual Pyrrhonian knows about and accepts as such and that, similarly, there is some sense-data construction $C(\Psi)$ that best realizes the functional role associated with folk physical object statements relative to this systematization. Thus, reductive phenomenalism is vindicated from the perspective of analytic perceptual functionalism.

Both reductive and eliminative phenomenalism hold that once you fix the phenomenal facts, you fix the physical object facts. The crucial question now concerns what it means for one set of facts to *fix* another set. If the notion of "fixing" is explicated in terms of *truthmaking*, and truthmaking in its turn explicated in terms of *entailment*, the same result would indeed appear to hold for perceptual as for metaethical Pyrrhonism. Given sufficient rational acumen, our Pyrrhonian would be able to deduce supervenient physical object truths a priori from the truths furnished by the subvenient phenomenal base. Therefore, he would be able to determine which of two possible worlds w_R or w_I he inhabits—w_R where the physical objects of folk theory exist as constructions out of sense data, or w_I where the folk conception of a physical object is revealed to be an illusion, a matter he previously held to be rationally undecidable.

Hence, an analytic phenomenalist functionalist, convinced of the overall truth of folk physical object theory, will hold that in the circumstances of there being a realization $C(\Psi)$ of the best systematization of the actual and possible sensory arrays that correspond to folk physical object theory, we can indeed deduce a priori from the phenomenal facts that there are physical objects of (more or less) the sort the folk believe in.

Yet isn't it clearly a defensible position for a phenomenalist to be *agnostic* about whether the phenomenal facts are sufficient to ground the (overall) truth of physical object claims or whether they instead reveal the folk notion of a physical object to be erroneous, on a par with witches and phlogiston? It seems compelling that analytic phenomenalists *can* allow that they might be mistaken about the overall truth of folk physical object statements. Why then can't analytic moral functionalists likewise hold that they might be mistaken about the overall truth of folk moral claims? If they can, then AMF can indeed countenance the conceptual coherence of metaethical Pyrrhonism.

The clearly best systematization may leave out certain features crucial to the folk conception (e.g., the mind-independence of physical objects), or else equally balanced competing explanations of these features, as in the moral Pyrrhonian's explanation of moral obligation, may be possible. The question is whether analytic phenomenalist functionalism, APF (the perceptual analogue of AMF), can allow for this. I don't believe it can. The problem does not lie in the underlying coherence of positions, perceptual Pyrrhonism and metaethical Pyrrhonism, which patently do not even appear incoherent. The problem lies in the subsidiary assumptions the APF and AMF supporter makes about how one set of facts *fixes* another set and about whether the relevant folk claims are so much as true in the first place.

Analytic functionalists think of "fixing" or "metaphysical determination" of a supervenient set of facts by a subvenient set in terms of the existence of an *entailment* relation between the two sets of facts. It is this relation that permits an a priori deduction of the supervenient facts from the subvenient ones. But this conception of supervenience is in no way obligatory. One alternative view holds that supervenience is a *metaphysically necessary* relation that is discoverable only *a posteriori*. However, *if* one thinks that metaphysical determination is a matter of entailment and *if* one is antecedently convinced of the overall truth of the folk claims that are to feature in the supervenient class, *then* one will also be committed to believing perceptual Pyrrhonism to be every bit as unstable as metaethical Pyrrhonism, provided only that there is something from the subvenient domain that fills the functional role etched out by the supervenient folk claims. So much the worse, I think, for this conception of metaphysical determination as truthmaking and truthmaking as a priori deducibility.

But perhaps it is not just analytic phenomenalist functionalism but analytic phenomenalists *in general* who cannot allow they might be mistaken about the overall truth of folk physical object claims. They had better be able to if perceptual Pyrrhonism is to be so much as defensible. In fact, they can, provided they abandon the above model of metaphysical determination, which Jackson calls "entry by entailment."[46] The key is to distinguish the very epistemic and metaphysical modalities that Jackson's view quite deliberately conflates.[47]

When reductionist (or eliminativist) analytic phenomenalists admit they might be mistaken about their analysis of folk physical object claims, what they should be taken to mean is that $\Diamond_E \Diamond_M \neg \Pi$, where $\Diamond_E$ and $\Diamond_M$ represent the modalities of epistemic possibility and metaphysical possibility respectively and Π is the claim that it is metaphysically necessary that physical objects are complex constructions out of sensory arrays.

In symbols, Π can be written as: $\Box_M \forall o[Po \rightarrow (o = C(\Psi))]$. In asserting $\Diamond_E \Diamond_M \neg \Pi$, reductionist analytic phenomenalists thus mean to be saying that it is at least epistemically possible that physical objects might not in reality be what the analysis they accept suggests they are, namely, complex constructions out of sense data.

But since, as Kripke has taught us, $\Diamond_E \Diamond_M \neg \Pi$ does not entail $\Diamond_M \neg \Pi$, reductionist analytic phenomenalist (whose views the APF proponent takes to be vindicated in the perceptual Pyrrhonian case above) can consistently hold *both* that Π is a priori *and* that it is yet reasonable to doubt it. This is just to say that a reductionist analytic phenomenalist can allow that eliminativist analytic phenomenalism is indeed *epistemically* possible, and hence so is, as required, perceptual Pyrrhonism. Here we have exactly the result AMF needs in order to make sense of metaethical Pyrrhonism. Unfortunately, no such option is open to anyone who subscribes to the APF/AMF explication of metaphysical determination as a priori entailment. *This is because such a view precisely denies that there is any difference between conceptual and metaphysical necessity.* For proponents of this view, we simply have $\Diamond \Diamond \neg \Pi$, and it seems intuitively compelling that this does indeed entail $\Diamond \neg \Pi$, at least when the notion of conceptual possibility is explicated (even if only partially) in terms of a priori deducibility—for $\Diamond \Diamond \Theta \rightarrow \Diamond \Theta$ is the reduction principle of the modal logic S4, and we know from Gödel's work that the necessity operator of S4 can be interpreted as a provability operator.

Yet it cannot be true that $\Diamond \neg \Pi$, if, as required, Π is a priori deducible, in the presence of $C(\Psi)$, from the phenomenal facts, since this a priori deduction will yield $\neg \Diamond \neg \Pi$. The result is thus the same for APF as for AMF: perceptual Pyrrhonism is every bit as epistemically unstable as metaethical Pyrrhonism in the envisaged circumstances.

What is the final upshot of our discussion? Metaethical Pyrrhonism is neither conceptually incoherent nor unstable. Yet if AMF is correct, given perfect rational acumen, moral Pyrrhonians themselves ought to be able to deduce a priori, in the presence of a best natural realizer of the folk moral claims, that moral norms are indeed real and thus rule out the possibility that they are merely beneficial illusions. AMF seeks to answer the philosopher's question about where in the world one might find moral values. The problem is not that the answer is no good, but rather that it is so good we can no longer make sense of the question.[48]

8.5 Truth and the Presence of Facts

It is implicit in the arguments against antirealism advanced in this book that truth does indeed require mind-independent links between our truthbearers and the various things in the world they represent. However, so far my strategy has been to show that the epistemic and instrumental ersatzes for truth required by antirealists simply will not do. I have until now left it undecided where I stand on the crucial issue of whether truth is itself a robust language–world relation or some merely logical property that can discharge no substantive explanatory role. My view, which I shall argue for in this section, is that truth is a robust property—truth is indeed a relation of correspondence between our beliefs and the world—but the nature of that relation and the nature of the facts that are the worldly relata has been poorly understood. Accordingly I seek to provide a better analysis of both "correspondence" and "facts."

We should note first, though, that almost everyone attaches *some* credence to the correspondence theory. Almost everyone believes in the relevant correspondences. The question has always been whether these correspondences *explain* the nature of truth. Thus, Paul Horwich: "The correspondence conception of truth involves two claims: (a) that truths correspond to reality; and (b) that such correspondence is what truth essentially is. And the minimalist response ... is to concede the first of these theses but to deny the second."[49] Truths do indeed correspond to reality for the minimalist. This is a trivial consequence of a trivial property accessible to anyone who grasps the (uncontroversial) instances of the schema "The proposition that p is true iff p," according to minimalists. By virtue of knowing our language and understanding the predicate "true" we can know a priori which bits of reality should get paired with which truths. All of this is conferred for free on anyone who grasps the meaning of the little word "true." What need, then, to posit any interesting metaphysical nature for that word to stand for?

I think the most persuasive reason for seeking an explanatory role for language–world relations is the one for which I have argued consistently throughout this book: *These relations are required to account for mental and semantic representation.* In fact, a measure of how seriously one takes the notion of mental representation, in my view, is how seriously one takes deflationism.

Consider Horwich's claim above that minimalists accept the *correspondences* while denying the *theory* of correspondence theory. Suppose we build two robots, Success and Failure, that develop their own mental representations in some language of thought. We find that whenever Success tokens some repeatable sequence of symbols, there is an object in its path that it succeeds in circumventing. By way of contrast, Failure has no repeatable sequence of symbols representing objects in its path, a disparate variety of such sequences being used, and Failure rarely, if ever, manages to avoid obstructions to its movements caused by objects whose presence it fails to detect. Surely one way of describing the manifest difference in the performances of Success and Failure is by saying that it is because its representations of spatial arrangements and objects within space are accurate that Success succeeds in negotiating its way around its environment, whereas it is because its representations are inaccurate that Failure fails. How does this differ from saying that the secret behind Success's success is the fact that its beliefs about where it is and what's in front of it are, on the whole, true?

However, although robust mind-independent language–world relations, are, in my view, needed to explain mental representation, the representation problem that dogs naturalistic attempts to theorize about the world and our place in it again looms large. There are, in my view, no credible theories of *how* our mental and linguistic symbols hook onto the right objects in the world. There are some initially attractive suggestions—teleosemantic, causal covariance—but none carries genuine conviction beyond the first round of objections. This is a serious problem for naturalistic realism, as Hartry Field has long urged. An appreciation of its difficulty has led many, including Field himself, to abandon the correspondence theory as hopeless and embrace deflationism about truth. Is the relation of correspondence just too mysterious after all? To answer this, we need to first survey some of the better-known objections to the correspondence theory of truth.

8.5.1 Doubts about the Correspondence Theory of Truth

Donald Davidson once wrote:

Nothing ... no thing, makes sentences and theories true: not experience, not surface irritations, not the world, can make a sentence true. That experience takes a certain course, that our skin is warmed or punctured, that the universe is finite, these facts (if we like to talk that way) make sentences and theories true. But the point is better put without any mention of facts. The sentence "My skin is warm" is true if and only if my skin is warm. Here there is no reference to a fact, a world, an experience or a piece of evidence.[50]

Davidson is not the only one who finds the generic idea of truthmakers suspect. As we have seen, it is a consistent theme of pragmatism that our beliefs and statements do not stand in need of any justification beyond those practices in which they are formed. Richard Rorty gives expression to the pragmatist view:

> The pragmatist tells us that it is useless to hope that objects will constrain us to believe the truth about them, if only they are approached with an unclouded mental eye, or a rigorous method, or a perspicuous language. He wants us to give up the notion that God, or evolution, or some other underwriter of our present world-picture, has programmed us as machines for accurate verbal picturing, and that philosophy brings self-knowledge by letting us read our own programs.[51]

These objections to the correspondence theory of truth all allege various epistemological failings. The correspondence theory allegedly requires a "confrontation" between our beliefs and reality, according to Davidson, a confrontation that is absurd. A system of mappings between our beliefs and "little bits of the world" cannot explain why or whether our best theories are roughly true, how we could ever know they were, or why we should even care if they are in the first place, according to Rorty and the pragmatists.

If any of these objections are right, the correspondence theory of truth is in real trouble. But are they right? We surely cannot get outside our conceptual skins to compare our beliefs with reality, but why do we need to? If the mappings between our beliefs and "little bits of the world" are theoretical posits, why should we demand any more epistemically of these posits than of other theoretical entities with respect to theory confirmation, and so on? We do not require extratheoretical confrontation between the early stages of the universe or fundamental particles and our beliefs about those things, so why demand it here? A mapping between our beliefs about electrons and electrons seems what we'd *minimally* need to explain why or whether our beliefs about electrons are roughly true, so why shouldn't this hold generally for all those beliefs we think of as true or roughly true?

Perhaps this line of thought is mistaken, however. Perhaps it is just an error to see facts as theoretical posits of a sort comparable to the theoretical posits of scientific theories. May be we are led to posit facts by analytic considerations—when we consider *what it is* for our beliefs or statements to be true.

It is not only pragmatists and antirealists who express skepticism about any such demands of analysis. Consider the following passage from Stephen Yablo's lovely article "How in the World?"[52]

> Is it just me, or do philosophers have a way of bringing *existence* in where it is not wanted? All of the most popular analyses, it seems, take notions that are not overtly existence-involving and connect them up with notions that are existence-involving up to their teeth. An inference is valid or invalid according to whether or not there *exists* a countermodel to it; the Fs are equinumerous with the Gs iff there *exists* a one-to-one function between them; it will rain iff there *exists* a future time at which it does rain; and, of course, such and such is possible iff there *exists* a world at which such and such is the case.
>
> The problem with these analyses is not just the unwelcome ontology; it is more the ontology's intuitive irrelevance to the notions being analyzed. Even someone not especially opposed to functions, to take that example, is still liable to feel uneasy about putting facts of equinumerosity at their mercy. For various awkward questions arise, of which let me mention three.
>
> How is it that I can tell that my left shoes are equal in number with my right ones just by pairing them off, while the story of how I am supposed to be able to ascertain the existence of abstract objects like functions remains to be told? Pending that story, who am I to say that the equinumerosity facts even *correlate* with facts of functional existence—much less that the correlation rises to the level of an analysis?
>
> If my left shoes' numerical equality with my right turns on the existence of functions, then in asserting this equality, I am giving hostage to existential fortune; I speak truly only if the existence facts break my way. But that is not how it feels. Am I really to suppose that God can *cancel* my shoes' equinumerosity (and so make a liar out of me) simply by training his or her death gun on the offending functions, without laying a hand on the shoes? Assuming that a one-to-one function between my left and right shoes exists at all, there are going to be lots of them. But then, rather than saying that my left and right shoes are equal in number because these various functions exist, wouldn't it be better to say that the functions exist—are *able* to exist, anyway—because my left and right shoes are equal in number? That way we explain the many facts in terms of the one, rather than the one in terms of the many.[53]

Yablo's point may be thought to gain much of its force from a judicious choice of example—the epistemological difficulties of Platonism about abstract objects like functions may be thought to comprise a rather special case; by way of contrast, we have independent nonanalytic reasons for believing in future times. Moreover, his analysis of "the number of Fs is equal to the number of Gs" in terms of equinumerosity was surely one of Frege's triumphs in the *Grundlagen*. That subsequent to this analysis dispute arises as to what functions *themselves* are need not in any way detract from its correctness.

Still, it is not obvious folly to question the need for facts or other truth-makers on either analytic or broader "synthetic" grounds. Yablo's misgivings about the relevance of ontology to the analyses of the concepts he considers in the passage above echo the pragmatists' claim that we do not need facts or other truthmakers to epistemically secure our beliefs.

So *does* truth require (truthmakers) of some sort, things in the world that make our beliefs and statements true? If the conclusions that I have drawn about the shortcomings of epistemic and pragmatist ersatzes for truth throughout this book are indeed correct, then I have at best removed one obstacle in the way of an affirmative answer: *Facts* are what make our beliefs and statements true.

I think this answer is right and I mean to defend it. But there are some conceptual difficulties about both facts and the idea of truthmaking that need to be addressed first.

Facts are supposed to be not only things in the world, but things with content—items both in and about the world. One intuition says that there is nothing in the world that makes "There are no goblins" true. Rather, it is something missing from the world that does this, namely, goblins. It is the absence of something rather than the presence of something that makes this sentence true. Yet another intuition says that there *is* something that makes it true: *the fact that there are no goblins*.

What is this thing, the fact that there are no goblins? It is not just an item in the world along with other items, if, indeed, it is any item in the world at all, since it is an item that tells us *how* the world is. But that sounds more like the task of a statement or a theory or a belief than an entry in the book entitled "What the world contains." Our goblin fact would have to assume the status of a Leibnizian monad—something *in* the world reflecting information *about* the whole world.

But is this status so mysterious? Something in the world that reflects information about the world is *a property of the world*. We live in a no-goblin type of world. That's one of the properties our world has that distinguishes it from other possible worlds otherwise identical to it. *Facts, thus construed, are just properties of the world*—our world, that is.

One who does find this type of response mysterious is Stephen Yablo. After commending Robert Stalnaker's response to Lewis's famous "paraphrase" argument for the existence of concrete alternative worlds that unlike ours do not actually exist, Yablo expresses puzzlement about

Stalnaker's own alternative. Lewis had argued that there are other ways things could have been and that "other ways things could have been" exist since things objectively could have been different from the way they actually are. To this, Stalnaker had replied, "If possible worlds are ways things might have been, then the actual world ought to be the way things are, rather than I-and-all-my-surroundings. But the way things are is a property or state of the world, not the world itself."

Yablo is puzzled by Stalnaker's positive claim that the statement "the world is the way it is" is true provided it is not read as an identity claim. He worries that it makes little sense if read as a predication either. Specifically, he worries that if you interpret it as a predication, you are going to be stuck with Lewisian concrete possible worlds.

I don't see why. It is true that we can as easily say "the way the world is is large and complicated" as say "the world is large and complicated." It is also true that in both claims the thing that is deemed large and complicated is the world, I and all my surroundings, not some property of me and all my surroundings. "The way the world is" refers to the sum total of the properties of the world, the totality of facts if these are, as I believe them to be, simply properties of the world. Contra Wittgenstein of the *Tractatus*, the world is not identical to the totality of facts unless objects generally are identical to the sums of their properties. "The world is the way it is" simply means that the world has just those properties that it has. To say that "the way that the world is is large and complicated" is simply to say that included in the properties of the world are the following: largeness and complexity. Clearly this will be true if and only if that humungous object that is the world, that is, I and all my surroundings, *is* large and complicated.

So we have the start of a defense of the thesis that facts are what make our beliefs true. Facts are properties of the world. Our beliefs and statements are "made true" by how the world is—that is, by what properties it has. A belief that a cosmic antigravity controls the expansion of the universe or that the abortion debate is not really about the rights of fetuses are, if true, made true by our world's being a cosmic-antigravity-universe-expansion-controlling world or a world wherein the existence or nonexistence of rights for fetuses does not determine the abortion debate.

Every belief or statement we make can thus be construed as a conjecture about which world we inhabit, which properties it has. It is the role of our truthbearers to specify which properties the world has, and these truthbearers will be true according to whether the world has the properties specified. The relation of "correspondence" in the correspondence theory of truth is then not a mysterious one at all, for it is just property instantiation.

Davidson, to recall, dismisses all talk of facts as explanatorily vacuous. This seems unwarranted to me. To the extent that he acknowledges that the world is thus and so, which he clearly does, that it has certain properties and not others, Davidson ought to acknowledge that there are "things" that "make" our beliefs true—namely, the world's having just those properties our beliefs impute to it.

Davidson's point might rather be that the mere existence of some special type of entity in the world cannot itself suffice to make a statement or belief true. He is not alone in this view, as we saw earlier. Many who resist the idea that truths need truthmakers do so in response to some such intuition. It cannot be the mere existence of some entity, some state of affairs that excludes goblins, they think, that by itself makes "There are no goblins true."

As I argue below, I think this intuition is absolutely correct—in opposition to the currently fashionable truth-maker theories examined below, many of our beliefs are true precisely because the world *lacks* certain entities. Yet the world's being a certain way accounts for "There are no goblins" being true. The world's instantiating the property of goblinlessness, whatever that may come to, accounts for the sentence "There are no goblins" being true. But the world's instantiating a property is not itself another entity in the world but rather a mode of configuring those entities which with their properties and relations make up the world.

The deeper source of resistance to the idea of worldly facts as the correspondents of true sentences, however, stems from the apparent insolubility of the representation problem. Plainly, no mere citation of what properties the world contains will assist in explaining why our truthbearers are true when correctly matched with the appropriate properties if there is no prior account of how those properties came to be associated with the truthbearers in the first place. This was, after all, the moral of Putnam's model-theoretic argument. The mere existence of the property of goblinlessness does not begin to explain why the sentence "There are no goblins" has the truth condition it has.

This apparent insolubility of the representation problem, I submit, is one of the genuine bases for the complaint of explanatory vacuity so often leveled at the correspondence theory of truth. *Given* that the sentence "There are no goblins" is understood in the way it is, though, pairing it with the property of goblinlessness does indeed explain why it is true. Facts by themselves, though, offer no solution to the representation problem—to invoke them in an explanation of why our beliefs are true presupposes that Nature has somehow provided such a solution.

8.5.2 Truthmaker Theory

It would be nice, then, if we didn't have to run up against the representation problem in theorizing about the relation our beliefs bear to the world. Is such a thing possible?

Indeed it is, by the lights of truthmaker theory. According to David Armstrong in his 1997 book *A World of States of Affairs*: "Anybody who is attracted to the Correspondence theory of truth should be drawn to the [idea of a] truthmaker. Correspondence demands a correspondent, and a correspondent for a truth is a truthmaker" (p. 14). Fred Kroon describes the attraction truthmaker theory exerts on correspondence theorists thus:

> ... the notion of a truthmaker is in a happy position to help out the notion of correspondence truth. The correspondence theory of truth has attracted a great deal of criticism, much of it centred on the notion of a truthmaking relation of correspondence between propositions and the world. But the modern idea of truthmaker can be spelled out without appealing to anything very problematic and without, in particular, appealing to a relation of correspondence. Officially, a truthmaker for a true proposition, judgment or statement Q is simply something whose existence entails the truth of Q. On this conception, there is thus no need for the controversial idea that to every truth there exists a unique correspondent fact. The Truthmaker Principle simply says that, necessarily, given any truth Q, there is something—perhaps more than one thing—that logically suffices for the truth of Q; that is, necessarily every truth has a truthmaker. Believers in the principle then see their main task as spelling out and defending their account of the nature of truthmakers.[54]

We need to introduce some qualifications before proceeding. Not every truthmaker theorist believes in what might be dubbed an extreme truthmaker—that for every truth there is a truthmaker. More temperate versions can and have been defended.[55]

A moderate version of the truthmaker principle holds merely that to every contingent or synthetic truth there corresponds a truthmaker. Further restrictions on the base class can be motivated so that only "atomic" contingent sentences require truthmakers. What I wish to show is that even in its weakest interesting form, truthmaker theory is indefensible. But first we need some principles governing truthmaking.

The basic axiom of truthmaker theory, the truthmaker axiom (TA) asserts that if p is true then there is some entity e that makes it true:

(TA) For all p, if p is true then there is some entity e such that $e \Vdash p$

The truthmaking relation is assumed to be a factive one. This gives rise to the following factive condition:

(FC) For all e and p, if $e \Vdash p$ then p is true

As Stephen Read points out, given (TA) and (FC), one can vindicate the correspondence intuition that the connection between the truth of a truthbearer p and its truthmaker e is an internal one:

(CI) For all p, p is true iff $\exists! e (e \Vdash p)$[56]

Left-to-right follows from (TA) whereas right-to-left follows from (FC).

Given the conventional understanding of "$\Vdash$" as a necessitation relation, truthmaking is closed under entailment as asserted in the entailment thesis:

(ET) $\forall e, p, q [(e \Vdash p \ \& \ p \Rightarrow q) \to e \Vdash q]$

In the light of this understanding of the relation between truthmakers and those sentences they make true, some truthmaker theorists simply express the truthmaker axiom as follows:

(TM) $e \Vdash p \leftrightarrow [\exists! e \ \& \ \neg \Diamond (\exists! e \ \& \ \neg p)]$

Given this understanding of truthmaking, let us proceed to some problems for the theory. The first is fashioned on Curry's paradox.

Consider the following sentence:

(χ) If (χ) has a truth-maker then pigs can fly.

We now show that we can use (χ) to prove that pigs can fly using standard logic, introduction and elimination rules for "true," and the axioms of TM theory:

(1) χ has a TM   Hypothesis
(2) "If χ has a TM then pigs can fly" has a TM   1 Df χ
(3) "If χ has a TM then pigs can fly" is true   2 by (FC)
(4) If χ has a TM then pigs can fly   3 Tr. E
(5) Pigs can fly   1, 4 $\to$ E

(6) If χ has a TM then pigs can fly   1, 5 → I
(7) "If χ has a TM then pigs can fly" is true   6 Tr. I
(8) "If χ has a TM then pigs can fly" has a TM   7 by (TA)
(9) χ has a TM   8 Df χ
(10) Pigs can fly   6, 9 → E

It may be that from the standpoint of TM theory the Curry sentence (χ) is *pathological* and this somehow invalidates the above proof. If (χ) is pathological, then perhaps the step from (7) to (8) can be questioned. Even extreme TM theorists can agree that (TA) need not apply to pathological sentences. This analysis is unconvincing, however. What is pathological about a sentence asserting of itself that if some entity can be found whose mere existence entails it then pigs can fly?[57]

The TM analogue of the Contingent Liar is even harder for the extreme theorist to account for:

(λ) The sentence written on the board in room 122 has no truthmaker

as tokened in a context where the sentence referred to is in fact (λ) itself. Let me specify one such context: You are told to go to one of two unfamiliar rooms, the numbers of which have been masked. One of these is room 122, the other room 155. You choose which room. You are to wait a couple of minutes while someone else goes to the other room and writes (π) *Pigs can fly* on its board. You are told that this is what will be written on the board in that room. You are then to write on the board in your room:

(λ) The sentence written on the board in room 122 has no truthmaker

While you write, the masks on the door numbers are removed. You then go outside and check the number of your room. A simple decision procedure can then be implemented to determine a yes/no answer to the question, "Does the sentence written on the board in room 122 have a truthmaker?"

(1) If your room number is 155, the definite description "the sentence written on the board in room 122" picks out the sentence (π) *Pigs can fly*. Since (π) is false it has no truthmaker. Thus the answer to the question is "No" and (λ) is true.

(2) If, on the other hand, the room number is 122, the definite description "the sentence written on the board in room 122" picks out (λ). Since on pain of contradiction (λ) cannot be its own nor possess any other truthmaker, (λ) has no truthmaker, and (λ) is thus true. Thus, again, the answer to the question is "No" and (λ) is true.

TM theory rules (λ) to be pathological in the circumstance where it is tokened in room 122. For suppose that it is true. Then what it says is the case. So it has no truthmaker. Thus, by (TA), it is not true. Alternatively, suppose that it is not true. Then by (FC) it has no truthmaker. But as this is what (λ) says, it is true after all.

But it is highly implausible to interpret (λ) as semantically pathological. For a start, we have no apparent difficulty in understanding its meaning—it asserts that there is no entity e whose existence necessitates that λ. Thus, in crucial contrast with the case of the Liar or the Truth-Teller, we can specify a truth condition for λ *that does not itself involve the concept of truth* (or other closely related semantic notions such as meaning). Moreover, unlike in the case of the Liar or the Truth-Teller, we can provide a principled reason for believing λ to be true: Since the supposition that any entity e is a truthmaker for λ leads to contradiction, λ's claim that there is no such entity is simply correct. There is, finally, a "revenge problem" with which those who evaluate λ as pathological must contend. If λ really is pathological then in particular it is not true. Hence by (FC) it has no truthmaker. But as this is precisely what λ says, it is true after all.

TM theorists might wish to respond by debarring sentences such as λ from the domain of sentences that do genuinely require truthmakers to be true. This might be achieved through a hierarchical approach. But for reasons Kripke made clear in his classic "Outline of a Theory of Truth" there are serious questions as to whether the levels of any such hierarchy can be consistently assigned in all contexts.

A different method for absolving the TM theorist from providing a truthmaker for λ would be to stipulate that any sentence whose truth value is a priori deducible from the facts concerning its context of utterance and relevant background facts has no need of a truthmaker. But this seems pretty hard to accept. As we saw in the previous section, if Frank Jackson is right, even the putatively necessary a posteriori bridge laws that link the manifest way things are to the fundamental way they are follow a priori from contingent a posteriori premises made true by the microphysical facts. Jackson's "location problem" is just to find microphysical truthmakers for claims about supervenient aspects of reality that are conceived of as a priori deducible from the microphysical facts.

To be sure, we may well despair of ever deducing the truth of λ from *those* types of facts, but Jackson's basic intuition is surely right: It is the *nonbasic* sentences such as λ that supervene on the basic ones that most stand in need of a truthmaker, on pain of our not being able to "locate" the facts to which they purportedly correspond among the facts about the world.

TM theory advertises itself as explaining why truths are true. So if λ is true, we want to know *how* this can be; and if TM theory promises to explain this in terms of some entity whose existence necessitates the truth of λ it had better deliver such an entity. Moreover, even if moderate TM theory can come up with a plausible explanation of why no entity is needed to make λ true, it still owes us an explanation of other anomalous cases where an appropriate truthmaker exists but fails to make a truth true.[58]

Consider the case where I write on the board the following sentence:

(ι) Someone somewhere has just penned a sentence that lacks a truthmaker.

Suppose that halfway across the world Jorge writes exactly the same sentence on a piece of paper and that his inscription and mine are, at the time, the only inscriptions produced. Then, even if we insist the truthmaking relation be irreflexive, there is no way for a TM theorist of any stripe to explain the evident fact that both inscriptions must receive the same semantic valuation, let alone the fact that if both are true, they are so only because each inscription ι_1, ι_2, which grounds the truth of the other one, lacks a truthmaker. Indeed, the TM theorist is forced to deny our intuitions of semantic parity for ι_1 and ι_2: It is incoherent to suppose, according to the TM theorist, that ι_1 and ι_2 can both be either true, false, or even pathological (neither true nor false, both true and false, unstably true or false, etc.).[59]

There must, paradoxically, be an *asymmetry* in semantic value between ι_1 and ι_2 according to the TM theorist, yet nothing *makes* it the case that this is so. But this is just the problem of "bare" semantic valuations all over again: the very problem that TM theory sets out to solve.

I think TM theory lacks the resources to explain how either λ or ι could be true. Since both λ and ι *are* simply and stably true, TM theory gets the extension of the truth predicate wrong and is thus no use as, or to, the theory of truth. What is crucial is that neither λ nor ι is a version of the Liar sentence. To the contrary, they can be interpreted as generalized versions of the Gödel sentence that asserts of itself that it is not provable. That is perhaps the most powerful reason for taking them as *non*pathological.[60]

8.5.3 Facts and Correspondence Again

Recall my proposal concerning the correspondence theory and the notion of facts: Truth consists in a correspondence between our truthbearers and the facts. Truths correspond to the facts, and facts are simply those properties of the world specified by our truthbearers. So the Spanish sentence "La tierra se mueve" specifies a property the world must have if that sentence is to be true. The property in question is that the universe contain a moving Earth. Since the universe does indeed possess this property, the Spanish sentence is true.

Thus the correspondence relation *is* a familiar one, as truthmaker theorists suspected. But it is not one of entailment. It is, instead, property instantiation. There is only one "truthmaker," namely, the world itself. But truthmaker monism of this sort trivializes truthmaker theory. There are no entities within the world whose mere existence entail any truths. There is just the world, and the relation the world bears to our truths is not one of entailment but rather one of property instantiation.

In what follows I try to respond to some of the more serious problems the proposed theory attracts.

8.5.4 Difficulties with the Theory

Commitment to properties The basic questions to be asked about my proposal concerning facts are first whether there are any properties to begin with and, second, if there are, whether the world has to be credited with any. The second question is far easier than the first. *Being approximately fourteen billion years old* is a bona fide property of the world, if properties exist at all. *Containing neither goblins nor truthmakers* is another such property, no less objective or mind-independent than the first—but that view gives rise to the next challenge.

Negative properties? How can *lacking* something be a genuine property? Being goblinless, lacking a truthmaker, and so on are negative properties, it might be alleged, and so even if there are some positive properties the world has that account for the various truths specifying those properties, the same cannot be said for negative properties—lacks, deficiencies, absences, and their ilk—for there are no negative properties.

I do not know whether there are negative properties or not. Influenced as I am by Ramsey's view, I doubt that we need believe in any logically complex properties. "*The fact that* the world lacks goblins or truthmakers" certainly sounds pleonastic—a mere nominalization of the sentence "the world lacks goblins or truthmakers."

I think we have good reasons, both metaphysical and semantic, to concede the point that logically complex sentences do not require logically complex facts. This does not mean that all talk of facts as properties of the world is pleonastic. Just as there can be extreme and moderate TM theories so there can be extreme and moderate fact theories. Extreme fact theorists demand a property of the world for every true sentence, irrespective of that sentence's logical complexity. Moderate fact theorists impressed both by truth-conditional semantics (TCS) and Ramsey's view of properties see no reason to accede to this demand and independent reason to resist it, for we need to semantically process sentences before we can properly determine which properties the world must have if they are to be true.

For the TCS theorist, this semantic processing just amounts to an identification of the sentence's truth condition, which, for a fact theorist, will ultimately provide a specification of the appropriate worldly property for the base sentences from which the complex sentence is compounded. Thus when we encounter logically complex sentences in TCS, we look to the appropriate recursion clause. In the case of "There are no goblins" the recursion clause tells us that this sentence will be true on condition that it is not the case that there are any goblins. So this yields that "There are no goblins" is true if and only if the world does not contain goblins.

In the case of negative existentials such as "There are no goblins," then, it is the world's *lacking* the property specified in their positive existential counterparts that grounds their truth. "Instantiating goblinlessness" is, if not a pleonastic property of the world, a reducible one. Even more dramatically is a universe's containing nothing, as in "Nothing exists." Talk of specific lacks, deficits, and privations is to be replaced by specification of those properties the world does not contain. Lacks and absences thus no more need direct instantiation by the world than do "nowheres" and "nobodies."

So it is the world's failure to contain goblins, not its instantiating the property of goblinlessness, that grounds the truth of "There are no goblins." I would prefer to say that the world's instantiating the property of goblinlessness semantically reduces to (via TCS) its not instantiating the property of goblinfulness. There are no negative facts for the moderate fact theorist. Hence there are no negative world-properties.

What of the empty universe? For such a case, "Nothing exists" comes out true. What property of such a "universe" could correspond to this sentence? No property. Rather, it is because the empty universe fails to instantiate the property of containing at least one thing that "Something exists" comes out false within it. Thus "Nothing exists" comes out true of it.

Vacuity Deflationists will urge that this account of facts is simply vacuous. They might put their point as follows:

Consider your claim that "'penguins are flightless' is true if and only if the world has the property of containing flightless penguins." Surely there is nothing to this claim over and above the truism that "penguins are flightless" is true if and only if penguins are flightless. More pointedly, if there is *not* something to this talk of facts as worldly properties beyond the simple platitudes to be found in the T-sentences then all such talk is pleonastic. If on the other hand there *is* some additional content then there is no guarantee that the resultant truth theory will be even extensionally correct.

I suspect some such objection has in one form or another dogged every serious attempt to develop a theory of facts. I also suspect that it contributes tacitly to the uncertainty over whether facts are to be counted as properties of the world our words describe or as (semantic) properties of the words we use to describe that world (true propositions).

I concede that the objection above can look quite formidable; given the protean state of my own explication of "property," it is indeed well taken. I think we must also acknowledge that similar objections are often driven by a genuine worry in the form of the representation problem. My view, however, is that as an a priori method for dismissing any finished version of a theory such as mine, the objection is fatally flawed. It derives all its power from conflating two distinct projects within which T-sentences such as "'penguins are flightless' is true if and only if penguins are flightless" typically appear.

The two distinct projects are:

(i) TCS, the project of specifying the meanings of the sentences of a given language by specifying their truth conditions.

(ii) The project of articulating a theory of truth.

Were the fact theorist's project to be (i) the criticism above would be quite apposite: The Spanish sentence "La tierra se mueve" does not *mean* "Our universe contains a moving Earth." It simply means that the Earth moves. To ensure they get the semantics of Spanish right, TCS theorists had better pair the Spanish sentence "La tierra se mueve" just with the English sentence "The Earth moves" as its translation in the metalanguage. Anything other than "The Earth moves" is going to be wrong semantically, relative to project (i) of TCS, that is. But the theory that treats facts as properties of the universe is a theory in metaphysics, not semantics. It is part of an attempt to articulate a theory of truth—to wit, the correspondence theory.

If the account it gives of facts is any good, of course, this account should receive independent corroboration from other theories (not just in metaphysics) that seem to require the existence of facts. Perhaps causation is a relation between facts; perhaps mental representation is possible only if there are reliable means of detecting facts; perhaps perception or knowledge likewise requires us to posit a capacity for detecting facts—and so on.

The fact theorist's project is (ii), not (i), and as Dummett, Davidson, and many others have emphasized, when interpreting T-sentences such as "'Penguins are flightless' is true if and only if penguins are flightless" one has to choose between reading them as specifications of the meanings of the OL sentences by means of an antecedently understood notion of truth or else reading them as "partial definitions," as Tarski dubbed them, of the predicate "is true." This is a forced choice between (i) and (ii).

The Spanish sentence "La tierra se mueve" does not *mean* that the universe contains a moving Earth. Nonetheless the Spanish sentence could not be true unless the Universe had this property, and it is the Universe's having just this property and no other that grounds the truth of this particular Spanish sentence—"grounds" it in the sense that it satisfies its truth condition, not in the exotic "entity-necessitation" sense given to that term by truthmaker theory.

It is the task of TCS to specify conditions the world must satisfy for our sentences to be true. It is not the task of TCS to speculate about the metaphysical nature of the satisfiers. Yet this in no way implies that the latter have no interesting underlying metaphysical nature. In like fashion, it is deemed to be a truism that true statements tell us how things are, what the world is like. Yet many frown on any attempt to give substance to these vague metaphors. Why? Is the thought that if something is a truism, there cannot be any substantive truth it tracks?

Some such thought may partially explain the appeal of deflationism, which brings me to an important respect in which the above response to the vacuity objection is unsatisfactory. I alleged that the vacuity objection to my theory of facts rested on a conflation of two distinct projects involving truth—the conflation of truth-conditional semantics with a theory of truth. But it is implausible to believe that philosophers who object to substantive accounts of facts do so *solely* because they have made some simple gaff. Rather, deflationism with respect to facts often derives from a prior allegiance to deflationism with respect to truth.

When we look at the alethic deflationist's response to my criticism of the vacuity objection, things at once look more interesting. Recall Paul Horwich: "The correspondence conception of truth involves two claims: (a) that truths correspond to reality; and (b) that such correspondence is what truth essentially is. And the minimalist response ... is to concede the first of these theses but to deny the second."[61] It is crucial to appreciate that minimalism and deflationism in general can appear plausible only if they first deny the legitimacy of truth-conditional semantics (TCS): If truth is insubstantial in any one of the ways suggested by such theories, it cannot possibly function as a theoretical primitive in a semantic theory. This at once affords us a deeper explanation of the source of the vacuity objection to any substantive theory of facts—far from conflating two distinct but equally legitimate projects involving truth, TCS and theories of the nature of truth, deflationists mean precisely to deny the legitimacy of the first of these. How plausible is this denial?

In my view, not plausible at all. Even if the *only* virtue of TCS was that it gave us the wherewithal recursively to characterize the semantics of logically complex sentences (and predicates), this would be virtue enough—virtue that rival theories invariably struggle to duplicate. The easiest thing for rival theories such as a "use" theory to do, of course, is to just ignore this problem of semantic structure—to pretend that the platitude that words mean what they do because of how we use them actually explains something about meaning.

Suppose such a theory were to be developed in an instructive way so that it tied down which particular nonsemantic aspects of our use of expressions[62] ground the semantic facts about expression meaning. This would have to be done without appealing to the expressions' semantic contribution to truth conditions, of course. How any such use theory is then supposed to explain the existence of recursive semantic structure without at that point adverting to truth conditions remains wholly mysterious to me.

Denying the legitimacy of TCS entails denying that what makes a translation between two languages correct is simply that it preserve truth conditions. Hartry Field, in many ways the most careful deflationist, defends precisely this consequence. Less sanguine than Horwich about the legitimacy of an appeal to propositions or the explanatory value of use, Field draws the solipsistic conclusion that "true" applies only to sentences of one's own idiolect, a view he calls pure disquotationalism. Yet we surely recognize that there are true utterances in languages we do not understand. How can anyone deny this?

Field does not deny this. He simply reinterprets its significance. Rather than there being some relation of interlinguistic synonymy that is preserved when Jorge utters "La tierra se mueve" and Diana reciprocates with "The Earth moves," a relation that is to be explicated in terms of sameness of truth conditions for the Spanish and English sentences uttered, Field looks elsewhere for his ersatz translation relation. Thus: "What we are doing when we conjecture whether some utterance we don't understand is true is conjecturing whether a good translation of the utterance will map it into a disquotationally true sentence we do understand."[63] But Field's ersatz relation is not even a close cousin of translation. Understanding is an epistemic issue. Translation between languages is not. Like most people I have every confidence that there are truths of, say, quantum field theory that I have no prospect of appropriating within my cognitive repertoire. That does not make them any less true. Neither does it mean that when I conjecture that there are such truths I am speculating about the expressive resources of my own limited cognitive repertoire—I already know the answer to that question: There are no sentences there that can even roughly translate (let alone faithfully represent) the relevant quantum-theoretic truths.

So, in my view, the vacuity objection rests on a conflation of two distinct projects, a conflation aided and abetted by the present naturalistic infatuation with deflationary theories of truth. These latter theories deny the legitimacy of one of these two projects, to wit truth-conditional semantics, thereby collapsing the distinction between the metaphysical and semantic projects concerning truth.

If there are good reasons for doubting that facts can most profitably be conceived as properties of the universe, these do not derive from any apriori argument about the semantics of the sentential operator "it is a fact that" or from complaints that a metaphysical theory of facts cannot discharge the functions of a semantic theory, something it does not even set out to do.

The "slingshot" argument against facts This rather notorious argument, which Davidson has done most to promote, would, if sound, undermine my proposal concerning facts and the correspondence theory. One persuasive discussion of its shortcomings is to be found in Stephen Read's "The Slingshot Argument."[64]

The slingshot argument (SA) performs two types of logical operation on complex singular terms to establish its conclusion that if a sentence corresponds to one fact it corresponds to the *great fact*, which is the sum of all other facts. The first is substitutivity of identicals (SI); the second is substitutivity of logical equivalents (SLE). Read argues that however complex singular terms are to be understood, the SA fails. If such terms are contextually defined as per Russell, SI fails. If they are understood as rigid designators, SLE fails. Finally, if they are interpreted nonrigidly, SI fails.

The defeater worry It would be folly to rest one's whole case against an interesting and influential theory largely on the strength of one problematic example without at least checking to see that the example does not undermine one's preferred alternative. And prima facie, this seems as if it may well be the case. An analogue of (λ) can indeed be constructed for my theory of facts as properties of the world:

(λ^*) The world does not possess the property specified by (λ^*).

It is simple to show that by the lights of the proposal (λ^*) is pathological. By the lights of TM theory, (λ) is pathological also. Yet I claimed that (λ) was *not* pathological and that TM theorists themselves must face up to this. Does not (λ^*) place me in exactly the same uncomfortable position of declaring a stably true sentence pathological? Have I not here succumbed to a rather extreme form of myopia?

No. There is a crucial difference between truthmaker theory and the correspondence (and indeed any other) theory of *truth*. Truthmaker theory is *not* in the first instance a theory of truth, but rather of the *ontological grounds* for truth. My left ear makes it true that there is a piece of flesh sticking out the left side of my head. It may also make it true that $2 + 2 = 4$ if indeed its making any contingent sentence true makes any necessary truth true. But it would be ludicrous to identify the property of being my left ear with that of the truth of the proposition $2 + 2 = 4$. Truthmaker theory is not an attempt to provide a property that can be identified with truth, either analytically or naturalistically; it is, instead, an attempt to provide an ontological ground for truths.[65]

Precisely because I *am* offering a theoretical identification of the property of being true with the property of being a property of the world specified by a truth-bearer, it is legitimate to regard (λ^*) as pathological on substitution of the explicans, "*The world does not possess the property specified by* . . ." by the explicandum, ". . . *is not true.*"

But there had better be independent reasons for thinking (λ^*) is pathological, reasons that do not carry over to the original truth-maker case of (λ). *Are* there? I think so. Consider the empirical counterpart of (λ^*):

(λ^*) The world lacks the property specified by the sentence written on the board in room 122.

Upon removing the mask from the door numbers you discover to your dismay that the room in which you penned these lines was none other than room 122. You reason that (λ^*) will indeed be true if the world lacks a certain property. But now you are puzzled. *Which* property is it that the world is supposed to lack according to (λ^*)? Well, it is the property specified by that very sentence itself, the sentence that says that the world lacks the property *it* specifies. But *which* property is that? We are never told.

This case stands in sharp contrast to the case where the sentence written on the board in room 122 turns out to be "Pigs can fly." Here, as in all nonpathological cases, we can say precisely which property the world either has or, in this case, lacks—namely, that of *avianporkerhood*. However, it also contrasts with the original case of (λ), where it is (λ) that is tokened in room 122. There we can say which property the world instantiates—it contains a sentence, namely (λ), for which there is no entity whose mere existence entails it. *That* is why (λ) is *true* rather than pathological.

Whereas (λ) is *not*, (λ^*) *is* indeed redolent of the Liar (L) and the Truth-Teller (TT). The Liar and the Truth-Teller are semantically anomalous in just this way—when we try to specify *interpretational* truth conditions for them, ones that do not themselves contain the concept of truth (or some related semantic notion), we are stymied: L is true if and only if L is not true; TT is true if and only if "TT is true" is true.[66]

If true sentences correspond to the facts and facts are properties of the world, we can see why this is so problematic—we are simply not told which property the world is supposed to lack if and only if it has the property specified by L, nor which property the world is supposed to possess if and only if it has the property imputed to it by TT. Their failure to specify the relevant worldly properties justifies Kripke's position that both L and TT lack a truth value.[67]

Finally, consider Curry's paradox once more, as originally expressed in terms of truth:

1	(1)	χ is true.	Hypothesis
1	(2)	"If χ is true then pigs can fly" is true.	1 Df χ
1	(3)	If χ is true then pigs can fly.	2 Tr. E
1	(4)	Pigs can fly.	1, 3 $\rightarrow$ E
	(5)	If χ is true then pigs can fly.	1, 4 $\rightarrow$ I
	(6)	χ.	5 Df χ
	(7)	χ is true.	6 Tr. I
	(8)	Pigs can fly.	5, 7 $\rightarrow$ E

Pace Kripke, the claim that χ is true is a substantive claim about the properties the world possesses—to wit, that it possesses the property specified by χ.

But in fact χ specifies *no* property at all. Hence $Tr(\chi)$ is false rather than without truth value. This invalidates the step from line 6 to line 7. The sentence at line 6, namely χ, is without truth value, whereas the sentence at line 7, "χ is true," is false, on the account I am arguing for. Thus the inference rule of truth introduction, permitting one to derive $Tr(A)$ from A, is unsound in the presence of pathological sentences to the extent that it permits one to infer a sentence less true than the sentence from which it is inferred. Since we wish to reason about pathological sentences using ordinary modes of inference, it is far more plausible in my view to locate the difficulty with Curry's paradox at the level of the valuation $Tr(A)$ receives when A is pathological. It is welcome news that we can give a principled reason for doing so.[68]

8.5.5 Correspondence Truth, Disquotational Truth, and Semantically Defective Sentences

A proper comparison of my version of the correspondence theory of truth with deflationary theories of truth lies outside the scope of this book. However, it might prove instructive to sketch some of the relevant issues if only for the purposes of fuller discussion on a future occasion.

In his recent book *Truth and the Absence of Fact*, Hartry Field has explored the resources of deflationary theories of truth to capture the notion of both semantic and factual defectiveness. Prima facie, a purely disquotational theory of truth should have a hard time accounting for sentences that are semantically indeterminate, vague, pathological, or nonfactual. How, for instance, is the disquotationalist to account for truth-value gaps invoked by popular theories of indeterminacy and vagueness and by some theories of semantically pathological sentences such as the liar and the truth-teller?

The very idea of a truth-value gap threatens to elude the expressive resources of disquotationalism, as Keith Simmons has observed.[69] Given the standard disquotationalist accounts of first truth:

Disq(Tr) p is true iff ($p =$ "s_1" and s_1) or ($p =$ "s_2" and s_2) or ...

and then falsity:

Disq(F) p is false iff ($p =$ "s_1" and $\neg s_1$) or ($p =$ "s_2" and $\neg s_2$) or ...

it is straightforward to prove that no sentence can be neither true nor false using an infinitary classical logic.

Field is unmoved by such arguments. Expressing a preference for the strong Kleene valuations, he has this to say about truth-value gaps:

> ... for anyone who wants to maintain an equivalence between "'p' is true" and "p" ... to assert a truth-value gap in a sentence "A" would be to assert "$\neg[\text{True}(`A') \vee \text{True}(`\neg A')]$," which should be equivalent to "$\neg(A \vee \neg A)$"; but no sentence of that form can ever be a legitimate assertion to an advocate of Kleene logic.... on the Kleene logic one can't assert of a "deviant" sentence either that it has a truth-value gap or that it doesn't.... Since sentences attributing truth or non-truth or falsity or non-falsity to deviant sentences are themselves deviant, this means that the advocate of Kleene logic can say nothing whatever about the truth value of deviant sentences....[70]

This sounds like a frank acknowledgment of the inability of not just the Kleene logic but deflationism in general to account for truth-value gaps. Yet, surprisingly, Field does not see this as any sort of inadequacy. He summarizes his views about the impact of the semantic paradoxes on deflationism as follows:

(1) The paradoxes do not undermine deflationism as a reconstruction of our ordinary truth-theoretic concepts; (2) they certainly don't undermine deflationism even for our improved concepts, if 'deflationism' is used in the weak sense on which a Tarskian theory is deflationist; and (3) there are several ways of maintaining even a strong form of deflationism for improved truth-theoretic concepts.[71]

Perhaps Field is right about this, but, prima facie, things do not look at all promising for the deflationist who denies any distinction in truth value between "A" and "$Tr(A)$." For one thing, such a theorist needs to explain how liar sentences differ from straightforward contradictions of the form $A \leftrightarrow \neg A$ that are normally regarded as just false, albeit necessarily so. Given the standard disquotationalist definition of falsity above, $F(A) \leftrightarrow \neg A$, liar sentences logically reduce to straightforward contradictions of the form $A \leftrightarrow \neg A$. Whence the need, then, for a three-valued logic such as Kleene's, and what could a "third" truth value mean? What is "indeterminate" about a contradiction?

As regards its expressive capacities, the Kleene logic is even more limited than one might suspect, according to Field. Not only can the Kleene logic not express the concept of a truth-value gap, it cannot even distinguish truth-value gaps from truth-value gluts.[72] Could it be Field's view that this is precisely its merit—the intuitive notions of a gap and of a glut really only make sense *relative to* a robust conception of truth, a conception the paradoxes show to be incoherent? But the semantic paradoxes do not just pose problems for robust theories; any theory of truth has to respond to them, as Tarski emphasized. The more general worry with alethic deflationism, then, is that it seems to lack the resources to say what is *paradoxical* about the liar in the first place. This consequence will be immediate and unavoidable if deflationism does indeed lack the resources to express the *concept* of paradoxicality.

This latter problem seems very likely for Field's favored version of deflationism, pure disquotationalism. Consider the reasoning that supports the strengthened liar paradox:

(1) (1) is not true.

Noting that (1) is paradoxical, we can justifiably conclude:

(2) (1) is not true.

Some theorists, such as those who advocate a contextualist approach to truth, infer from (2) and from what (1) says that:

(3) (1) is true.

Disquotationalists might wish to resist this reasoning. They would not be alone in that. But the prior and more pressing question is whether they can even make sense of the reasoning. Keith Simmons, an advocate of a contextualist approach, offers his assessment:

> It is not easy to square such contextual accounts with disquotationalism. If (1) really is semantically pathological, then it is so because it attributes lack of truth to itself: *"true" in (1) is ineliminable, and cannot be disquoted away.* And if (1) really is true (when assessed from a reflective context, or from a higher level of language) then *the disquotationalist must admit truths from which "true" cannot be disquoted.* And this compromises the disquotational conception of truth.[73]

My own view is that (3) is simply false, and that, quite generally, if (λ) is a liar sentence, "$Tr(\lambda)$" is false in *every* context of utterance and of evaluation. The problem with the "strengthened" reasoning above, in my estimation, is that it makes uncritical use of the notion of *what a liar sentence says*. To be sure, liar sentences are not meaningless—(λ) says that the world lacks the property it specifies—but in failing to specify any property, (λ) is semantically incomplete, and for *that* reason it lacks a truth value. It is not that (λ) says nothing; it simply does not say enough, irrespective of its context of utterance or evaluation, for it to be truth-evaluable. Thus, the inference from (1) and (2) to (3), which proceeds on the assumption that (1) does indeed express a truth-apt proposition within some context of evaluation, is fallacious.

However, as Field notes, disquotationalists are not able to assign different truth values to "A" and "$Tr(A)$." So for them, each of (1) to (3) and thus, presumably, the reasoning that leads from (1) to (3), is pathological. But then, as every attempt to say something about the semantic status of (λ) simply results in the production of one more semantically defective statement, the original reasoning used to conclude that the liar sentence is pathological is also pathological. What then could a deflationist possibly *mean* in declaring (λ) *pathological*?

My provisional conclusion, therefore, is that deflationists are far from offering us a plausible account of how semantic pathology is possible given their understanding of truth. The difficulties involved in providing such an account provide further reason to believe the robust account of truth proferred here.

Notes

Introduction

1. For a fuller treatment of the issues discussed under this heading please see my "Semantic Challenges to Realism," S*tanford Encyclopedia of Philosophy*, Edward N. Zalta (ed.), 2001, ⟨http://plato.Stanford.edu/entries/realism⟩.

Chapter 1

1. W. D. Hart's claim.

2. I mean it is problematic whether Davidson *really is* a pragmatist of any sort.

3. At least an earlier stage of Putnam held this view. It is renunciated in his *Dewey Lectures*. See his "Sense, Nonsense, and the Senses: An Inquiry into the Powers of the Human Mind," *Journal of Philosophy* 91, no. 9, pp. 445–515.

4. This does not mean, of course, that *specific* antirealist arguments cannot be undermined if truth is minimalist. I argue that some of Putnam's arguments can be undermined in precisely this way. The point is just that the Hume–Kant challenge that Dummett and Putnam present cannot be so undermined.

5. My claim that it makes no difference to the antirealist's challenge to realism whether truth is deflationary or substantial might seem to founder on the following obvious point: As Dummett characterizes the realist, she is one who believes that truth is the central explanatory concept in the theory of meaning. If truth is *not* a substantial property, however, this characterization is effectively undermined, as it casts *deflationists* as antirealists simpliciter rather than antirealists *about truth*. Since this is clearly incorrect, it will be held, a demonstration that truth is deflationary would indeed reveal Dummett's and Putnam's attacks on what they *call* realism to be misguided.

This argument, however, simply accepts uncritically Dummett's characterization of realism and makes no attempt to dissociate this characterization from his challenge to realism. If metaphysical disputes really are meaning-theoretic ones at bottom as Dummett believes then the suggested conclusion might follow; but one might take this consequence of Dummett's view, if such it be, as prima facie evidence against its plausibility. In that case, meaning-theoretic issues would not play the deciding role in metaphysical disputes that Dummett believes they already tacitly play, and there would be no direct way of inferring from premises about semantic competence to conclusions about meaning let alone conclusions about the nature of reality if the Dummettian thesis were to be rejected.

However, as explained above, the Dummett–Putnam accusation of metaphysical credulism against the realist is a version of the Hume–Kant gambit, and that challenge still stands even if both Dummett and Putnam are quite mistaken about the relation between meaning (reference, for Putnam) and metaphysics.

The most that a demonstration that truth is deflationary could hope to show, then, would be that truth cannot explain semantic competence or linguistic understanding since truth is not an explanatory property at all but a device for a certain type of generalization—an alternative to substitutional quantification, say.

Since it is not necessary to appeal to truth at all, even in its role as a generalization device, to formulate the Hume–Kant challenge to metaphysical credulism, it is not necessary to do so for the Dummett–Putnam version either.

6. Michael Devitt, *Realism and Truth*, second edition, Oxford: Blackwell, 1991.

7. Crispin Wright, *Truth and Objectivity*, Cambridge, Mass.: Harvard University Press, 1994, p. 21.

8. A "Dutch book" is a bet that ensures the bettor loses come what may. A Dutch book argument purports to demonstrate that a rational agent's degrees of belief must conform to the axioms of the probability calculus on pain of the agent's being open to a Dutch book.

9. See Devitt's *Realism and Truth*.

10. William P. Alston, *A Realist Conception of Truth*, Ithaca, N.Y.: Cornell University Press, 1996.

11. Ibid., p. 111.

12. Ibid.

13. See his "What Is a Theory of Meaning? (II)" in G. Evans and J. McDowell (eds.), *Truth and Meaning: Essays in Semantics*, Oxford: Clarendon Press, 1976, and "The Justification of Deduction" in his *Truth and Other Enigmas*, London: Duckworth, 1978, pp. 290–318.

14. Alston, *A Realist Conception of Truth*, p. 114.

15. Ibid., p. 113.

16. Ibid., p. 115.

17. Paul Horwich, *Truth*, Oxford: Oxford University Press, 1990, p. 124.

18. Alston, *A Realist Conception of Truth*, p. 124.

19. Ibid.

20. Ibid.

21. Ibid.

Chapter 2

1. "Aufzeichnungen fur Ludwig Darmstaedter," in his *Posthumous Writings*, H. Hermes, F. Kambartel, and F. Kaulbach (eds.), Oxford: Blackwell, 1979, p. 273.

2. Dummett, *Frege: Philosophy of Language*, London: Duckworth, 1973, p. 4.

3. Ibid., pp. 378–379.

4. Ibid., p. 157.

5. Ibid., p. 92.

6. Ibid., p. 413.

7. Ibid., p. 415.

8. Ibid., pp. 416–417.

9. Ibid., p. 381.

10. Ibid.

11. Ibid.

12. "What Is a Theory of Meaning? (II)," pp. 69–70, emphasis mine.

13. Ibid., p. 74, emphasis mine.

14. Because of this, Dummett is skeptical of Chomsky's views. See his review of Chomsky in "Objections to Chomsky," *London Review of Books* (September 1981), pp. 5–6.

15. This is the task of section 2.3.

16. "What Is a Theory of Meaning? (II)," p. 111, emphasis mine.

17. Even more so when the preferred model is an assertibility-conditional theory rather than a truth-conditional theory, for such a theory might well construe "knowledge of assertibility conditions" for a sentence p to be nothing more than knowing when one can assert p, which need involve no propositional knowledge (knowing that) at all. Michael Devitt takes Dummett to task over his "propositional assumption" in his *Realism and Truth*.

18. A lecture Dummett gave at the Swedish Academy in 1979, reprinted as chapter 3 of his *The Seas of Language*, Oxford University Press, 1993.

19. Ibid., p. 2.

20. Ibid., p. 1.

21. Ibid., p. 4.

22. Ibid., p. 3.

23. Ibid., pp. 9–10.

24. Donald Davidson, "Radical Interpretation," in his *Inquiries into Truth and Interpretation*, Oxford: Clarendon, 1984, p. 125.

25. Michael Dummett, "Realism," *Synthese* 52 (1982), pp. 55–112, here pp. 108–109.

26. Crispin Wright, "Truth Conditions and Criteria" in *Proceedings of the Aristotelian Society*, supplementary vol. 50, 1976, p. 224.

27. For example, we know what it would be to come across the hitherto undiscovered diaries of the famous monist's mother in which this fact was mentioned.

28. It is thus unfair to saddle Dummett with a positivist epistemology, as Michael Devitt does in his *Realism and Truth*.

29. Dummett makes this claim in "What Is a Theory of Meaning? (II)," p. 115, and argues for the primacy of semantic over syntactic characterizations of deducibility in "The Justification of Deduction," in *Truth and Other Enigmas*, pp. 290–318, and elsewhere. This is not to say that the best way to characterize the meanings of the logical constants may not be in proof-theoretic terms—see sections 4.3, 4.4.

30. "What Is a Theory of Meaning? (II)," pp. 112–113.

31. Wright, "Truth Conditions and Criteria," p. 235.

32. Dummett is well aware of his obligation to provide such an account and acknowledges in "What Is a Theory of Meaning? (II)," p. 116, that "It is far from being a trivial matter how the notion of truth, within a theory of meaning in terms of verification, should be explained."

33. Recall that for Dummett truth will still play a crucial role in any plausible antirealist alternative to realist semantic theory but that it will no longer be the primitive explanatory concept in that theory, being defined instead in terms of some alternative notion such as verification or falsification that does not transcend our recognitional capacities.

34. "What Is a Theory of Meaning? (II)," p. 82.

35. John McDowell has consistently urged this line of response to Dummett. See his "On the Sense and Reference of a Proper Name," in *Reference, Truth, and Reality: Essays on the Philosophy of Language*, M. Platts (ed.), London: Routledge

and Kegan Paul, 1980, pp. 141–166, and "Truth-Conditions, Bivalence, and Verificationism," in *Truth and Meaning*, Evans and McDowell (eds.), pp. 42–66.

36. See, e.g., Colin McGinn's "Truth and Use," in *Reference, Truth, and Reality*, Platts (ed.), pp. 19–40.

37. "What Is a Theory of Meaning? (II)," p. 97.

38. Ibid., p. 101.

39. See Dummett, "Can Truth Be Defined?" in *Frege*.

40. See also Davidson's remark in "In Defence of Convention T," in *Inquiries into Truth and Interpretation*:

> The original question is not confused, only vague. It is: what is it for a sentence (or utterance or statement) to be true? Confusion threatens when this question is reformulated as, what makes a sentence true? The real trouble comes when this in turn is taken to suggest that truth must be explained in terms of a relation between a sentence as a whole and some entity, perhaps a fact, or state of affairs. Convention T shows how to ask the original question without inviting these subsequent formulations. The form of T-sentences already hints that a theory can characterise the property of truth without having to find entities to which sentences that have the property differentially correspond. (p. 70)

41. "On the Very Idea of a Conceptual Scheme," in his *Inquiries into Truth and Interpretation*, p. 194. I am not suggesting that Davidson is a minimalist about truth. He is not. See his discussion of minimalism in "The Structure and Content of Truth," *Journal of Philosophy* 88, 1990, pp. 279–328.

42. "What Is a Theory of Meaning? (II)," p. 95.

43. Ibid.

44. J. Fodor and E. Lepore, *Holism: A Shopper's Guide*, Oxford: Blackwell, 1994, and M. Devitt, *Coming to Our Senses: A Naturalistic Program for Semantic Localism*, Cambridge: Cambridge University Press, 1996.

45. "What Is a Theory of Meaning? (II)," p. 132. Dummett would thus rule out as unacceptable not only a "conceptual-role semantics" in which a speaker's understanding of all sentences was determined by his grasp of their evidential and inferential connections rather than their truth conditions, but also such a semantics for the non-ED part of a language.

46. Compare: "What we are concerned with is what determines that something is evidence of a certain strength for the truth of a given sentence, not with whether the existence of evidence of a particular strength is sufficient reason for accepting the sentence as true" (ibid.). This is a point on which Dummett and Wright disagree. Wright has the antirealist respond by asking why the realist should seek an explanation of our evidential or inferential abilities, claiming

that we just do have the practical ability to discriminate states of information justifying the assertion of p from states of information not justifying its assertion. Because he believes that the ascription of implicit semantic knowledge is of genuinely explanatory value, Dummett demurs from this—these abilities are precisely ones that require explanation, though not in the terms envisaged by the realist.

Chapter 3

1. Dummett, *Frege*, p. 300.

2. Ibid., p. 302.

3. Ibid., p. 303.

4. Ibid., p. 318.

5. Ibid., p. 313.

6. Ibid., p. 314.

7. Ibid., p. 312, emphasis mine.

8. Ibid., p. 362.

9. Ibid.

10. As developed in David Lewis, *Convention: A Philosophical Study*, Cambridge, Mass.: Harvard University Press, 1969.

11. Dummett, *Frege*, p. 347.

12. Ibid., p. 345.

13. Ibid., p. 347.

14. Ibid.

15. Ibid., p. 451, emphasis mine.

16. Ibid., p. 450.

17. "Truth and Assertibility," *Journal of Philosophy* 73, 1976, pp. 137–149. Examples of such TISCs are constructions involving "believes that," "it is possible that," "It will be the case that," "were it the case that ... then." If we start with two sentences p and q with the same assertibility conditions, then a TISC will generate two compound sentences that differ in their assertibility conditions.

18. Brandom's view is more moderate. He points out that for the purposes of the theory, truth is whatever auxiliary concept is necessary to explicate the TISCs, and this clearly underdetermines the actual truth conditions, and hence the truth concept, that will be assigned the resultant compound sentence.

19. Dummett, *Frege*, p. 393.

20. Ibid., p. 394.

21. Ibid., p. 450.

22. W. V. O. Quine, "Ontological Relativity," in *Ontological Relativity and Other Essays*, New York: Columbia University Press, 1969, p. 26. Cf.: "Semantics is vitiated by a pernicious mentalism as long as we regard a man's semantics as somehow determinate in his mind beyond what might be implicit in his dispositions to overt behaviour" (p. 27) and "... there are no meanings nor distinctions of meaning, beyond what are implicit in people's dispositions to overt behaviour" (pp. 28–29).

23. W. V. O. Quine, "The Nature of Natural Knowledge," in *Mind and Language*, S. Guttenplan (ed.), Oxford: Clarendon Press, 1975, pp. 67–81.

24. W. V. O. Quine, "Epistemology Naturalised," in *Ontological Relativity and Other Essays*, pp. 69–90, here p. 75.

25. W. V. O. Quine, *The Roots of Reference*, La Salle: Open Court, 1974, p. 138.

26. W. V. O. Quine, "Facts of the Matter," in *American Philosophy from Edwards to Quine*, R. W. Shahan and K. R. Merrill (eds.), Norman: University of Oklahama Press, 1977, pp. 176–196, here p. 177.

27. Ibid., p. 178.

28. Ibid.

29. W. V. O. Quine, "Replies," in *Words and Objections: Essays on the Work of W. V. Quine*, Synthese Library vol. 21, D. Davidson and J. Hintikka (eds.), Dodrecht: D. Reidel, 1975, p. 309.

30. Quine, *The Roots of Reference*, p. 38.

31. Quine, "Epistemology Naturalised," pp. 78–79.

32. Dummett, "What Is a Theory of Meaning? (II)," p. 79.

33. Dummett, *Frege*, p. 597.

34. Ibid.

35. Dummett, "Frege's Distinction between Sense and Reference," in *Truth and Other Enigmas*, pp. 116–144, here p. 136.

36. Dummett, "The Justification of Deduction," in *Truth and Other Enigmas*, p. 309.

37. Quine, "The Nature of Natural Knowledge," p. 77.

38. Compare the account of the acquisition of the relative clause in "The Nature of Natural Knowledge," pp. 76–77.

39. "[A]ll traits of reality worthy of the name can be set down in an idiom of this austere form if in any idiom." W. V. O. Quine, *Word and Object*, Cambridge, Mass.: MIT Press, 1964, p. 228.

40. "[T]he paths of language learning, which lead from observation sentences to theoretical sentences, are the only connection there is between observation and theory." Quine, "The Nature of Natural Knowledge," p. 79.

41. Donald Davidson, "A Coherence Theory of Truth and Knowledge," in *Truth and Interpretation: Perspectives on The Philosophy of Donald Davidson*, E. Lepore (ed.), Oxford: Blackwell, 1986, pp. 307–319.

42. Ibid., p. 312.

43. Davidson, "On the Very Idea of a Conceptual Scheme," p. 187.

44. Dummett, "Frege's Distinction between Sense and Reference," in *Truth and Other Enigmas*, p. 134.

45. "What Is a Theory of Meaning?" in *Mind and Language*, S. Guttenplan (ed.), Oxford: Oxford University Press, p. 127.

46. Ibid., p. 133.

47. It seems very doubtful that a theory in which "Maximize the number of held true sentences" is an inviolable canon could do the most fundamental thing an adequate theory of interpretation must do, namely, rationalize the actions of the native. A "preferred assignment" might attribute bizarre reasons for actions to the native consistently with that maxim; this could not be what Davidson's holism consists in.

48. Dummett, "The Philosophical Basis of Intuitionistic Logic," in *Truth and Other Enigmas*, p. 218.

49. Dummett, *Frege*, pp. 596–597.

50. Dummett, "What Is a Theory of Meaning?" pp. 116, 121, and "Frege's Distinction between Sense and Reference," p. 136.

51. Dummett, "What Is a Theory of Meaning?" pp. 116–119.

52. Dummett, "The Justification of Deduction," in *Truth and Other Enigmas*, pp. 300–304, and "What Is a Theory of Meaning? (II)," p. 105.

53. Dummett, *Frege*, p. 599, p. 622; "Wittgenstein's Philosophy of Mathematics," in *Truth and Other Enigmas*, p. 177; and "What Is a Theory of Meaning?" p. 137, among others.

54. If a speaker's use of an expression is intentional at all, it must be possible for the speaker to fail in his intention to use the expression correctly; a theory of meaning should, accordingly, give some account of how such errors are possible.

55. Dummett argues: "if a member of the linguistic community holds a divergent theory of truth for the language, he will tend to diverge more in his judgements than most speakers do from the majority. But, since no finite set of such divergences will, in itself, reveal his reliance on a non-standard theory of truth, it is hard to see how either he or the other speakers or we as observers could ever detect this, or how, once discovered, it could be corrected" ("What Is a Theory of Meaning?" p. 117). If Davidson just acquiesces in this result, it becomes very doubtful how he can avoid Dummett's charge at p. 118 that his theory of meaning is of necessity solipsistic. Davidson seems to have drawn this conclusion (or something very like it) in "A Nice Derangement of Epitaphs," in *Philosophical Grounds of Rationality: Intentions, Categories, Ends*, R. Grandy and R. Warner (eds.), Oxford: Clarendon Press, 1986, pp. 157–174, but it seems to me that in that article Davidson has misconstrued the significance contextual factors play in interpretation.

56. Davidson, "Replies to Essays X–XII," in *Essays on Davidson: Actions and Events*, M. Hintikka and B. Vermazen (eds.), Oxford: Oxford University Press, 1985, p. 252. I should quote the surrounding context of this remark. Davidson is considering Patrick Suppes's Dummett-styled objection that a child could never learn his native tongue at all if he (Davidson) is correct about the inextricability of belief and meaning. Thus he says: "I do not really think I must produce 'the details of an actual theory of language acquisition and cognitive development' in order to answer this question [i.e., how language learning is possible in the light of inextricability] for there is no reason a child cannot slowly master a complex system without it ever being accurate to say he has mastered part of it first. The trouble with this answer is that it leaves us not knowing how to describe the early stages, just as the general thesis that animals don't have beliefs leaves us without our usual way of explaining and describing their behaviour." I agree with Suppes and Dummett against Davidson that inextricability construed in Davidson's way as a substantive metaphysical thesis about the nature of belief and meaning does make it extremely hard to see how anyone, let alone a child, could come to grasp a language. But I disagree with Dummett that the solution to this is to abandon holism about meaning. I think the solution is to retain the aforesaid holism but balance it with a more realistic appraisal of the mental so that inextricability simply records the fact that the mental is itself holistic. Moreover, I think that Davidson concedes too much to the opponent of holism by claiming that semantic holism "leaves us not knowing how to describe the early stages"—we describe them as in the text above.

57. Strawson, "On Scruton and Wright on Anti-Realism etc." *Proceedings of the Aristotelian Society* 77 (1976–1977), pp. 15–21.

58. Dummett, *Truth and Other Enigmas*, preface, pp. xxxii–xxxviii; Wright, "Strawson on Anti-Realism," in his *Realism, Meaning, and Truth*.

59. See essays 19, 20, 21 in *Truth and Other Enigmas*. Dummett thinks that statements about the past present far more of a challenge to antirealism than statements about other minds (*Truth and Other Enigmas*, p. xxxviii). He criticizes

Strawson for believing that we know what it is for another to be in pain because we have given ourselves a private ostensive definition (ibid., p. xxxii) and records his conviction that Wittgenstein's polemic against the possibility of such a procedure is "incontrovertible." I am not convinced that a realist about other minds such as Strawson need believe in "private" ostensive definitions, so I am not sure that Dummett's reply is to the point. Be that as it may, Dummett reveals that he has not seen the real worry for the antirealist's position, for he takes it to be about grasping the truth conditions of statements like "John is in pain" (cf.: "To understand statements like 'John is in pain,' we must know how they are used" [ibid., p. xxxv]). I hope to show that these are not the statements that are particularly problematic for the antirealist.

60. See the essays in *Realism, Meaning, and Truth*: "Strawson on Anti-Realism"; "Realism, Truth-Value Links, Other Minds, and the Past"; "Anti-Realist Semantics: The Role of Criteria."

61. Strawson, "On Scruton and Wright on Anti-Realism etc."

62. "Strawson on Anti-Realism," pp. 289–290. Wright then comments: "naturally, this is only the sketch of an approach, and I cannot claim to know that it would prove satisfactory in detail." What would prevent such a conventionalist account from succeeding? Whatever facts about sensations are produced, the conventionalist will simply "account" for them as unremarkable facts about the language game of sensation.

63. Strawson, "On Scruton and Wright on Anti-Realism etc.," pp. xxiiff.

64. "Strawson on Anti-Realism," pp. 288–289.

65. *Philosophical Investigations*, Oxford: Blackwell, 1958, §302.

66. I am making no presumption that the internal MOP is incorrigible, only that it is available to the subject of experience alone.

67. It is a little hard to know whether to put this point in terms of sameness of meaning, given that the antirealist need not be committed to propositions. Still, we can formulate the point in terms of reporting the same state of affairs or event.

68. Can the antirealist accept sincere avowals about conscious experiences not only as a criterion that the subject has those experiences but as the ultimately decisive criterion? This seems to me to place too much faith in the understanding that the agent has of his language, particularly if the view propounded is a Wittgensteinian one in which "pain" does not refer to the sensation of pain.

69. Dummett clearly rejects it: "It is obviously correct, independently of any philosophical position, to say that 'John is in pain' is true when and only when it is with John as it is with me when I am in pain." *Truth and Other Enigmas*, p. xxxiv.

70. Ibid., pp. xxxiii–xxxv.

71. "Realism," pp. 64–65.

72. *Truth and Other Enigmas*, p. xxxv.

73. In humans, pain is most certainly not to be identified with the firing of C-fibers.

74. Dummett will most probably object that an illicit realism has been appealed to in the description of the case, but it is not clear to me that there need be any conceptual incoherence from the antirealist's point of view in the possibility that a creature could always inhibit certain of its natural behavioral dispositions if it had enough motivational strength. Perhaps the super-Spartan thinks he will be struck dead by Zeus and eternally damned if he so much as murmurs when he loses a limb. That he should believe this seems to present us with a recognizable possibility.

75. Dummett apparently does think that the realist, in this instance at least, must deny that a grasp of the assertibility conditions of "John is in pain" plays any part in understanding the statement, for he says at p. xxxii of the preface to *Truth and Other Enigmas* that on the realist view "the sense of the sentence is not given in terms of the evidence that I can have for its truth or falsity: such evidence is necessarily indirect and often inconclusive; but my knowledge of what the sentence means is independent of my knowledge of what constitutes such evidence." But perhaps Dummett means to be making a slightly different point: that the realist holds that grasp of the assertibility conditions of the sentence is somehow contingent on a prior grasp of its truth conditions. This certainly does present the naive realist, who believes that we understand the sentence by pairing it off with a verification-transcendent state of affairs, with a severe difficulty.

76. Or, for that matter what those of "I_i am in pain" are for any i.

77. This raises the question of whether Jones's external MOP is the same as the external MOP available to others. The claim that it is seems congenial to Cartesianism.

78. See Paul Churchland, *Scientific Realism and the Plasticity of Mind*, Cambridge: Cambridge University Press, 1979, ch. 1.

79. Whether antirealism is compatible with eliminative materialism is a question I shall not pursue.

80. To avoid it, the antirealist must deny that Jones's utterance of "I am in pain" has as its canonical assertibility condition that Jones experience, or believe himself to be experiencing, a pain.

81. Colin McGinn, "Truth and Use," in *Reference, Truth, and Reality*, M. Platts (ed.), p. 28.

82. Ibid., p. 30.

83. It is no use to appeal against this to the logical possibility of their sentences having the same meanings as ours since the antirealist holds that the notion of logical possibility is grounded in meaning; indeed, his whole position rests on the belief that logical laws such as bivalence or double negation elimination can be criticized on meaning-theoretic grounds. As the example does not present us with a possibility constructible in terms of our conceptual resources, it is incoherent. We should note, however, that the antirealist is committed to conceptual relativism, as his grounds for rejecting the intelligibility of McGinn's example reveal.

84. See Crispin Wright, "Truth Conditions and Criteria."

85. Dummett, "The Justification of Deduction," in *Truth and Other Enigmas*, pp. 317–318.

86. Dummett, *Elements of Intuitionism*, Oxford: Clarendon Press, 1977, pp. 376–377.

87. Dummett, "The Philosophical Basis of Intuitionistic Logic," p. 217.

88. Steven Pinker, *The Language Instinct: How the Mind Creates Language*, New York: Harper Collins, 1994, p. 33.

89. Ibid.

Chapter 4

1. My presentation of intuitionism follows that found in Dana Scott, Graeme Forbes, Martin Davies, Göran Sundholm, and Daniel Isaacson, *Oxford Notes towards the Formalization of Logic, Parts III & IV*, Oxford, 1983 (unpublished).

2. L. E. J. Brouwer, "Intuitionism and Formalism," in *Philosophy of Mathematics*, second edition, Paul Benaceraff and Hilary Putnam (eds.), pp. 77–89, here p. 80, Cambridge: Cambridge University Press, 1983.

3. Charles McCarty, "Intuitionism: An Introduction to a Seminar," *Journal of Philosophical Logic* 12, 1983, pp. 105–149, here pp. 108–109.

4. Ibid., p. 110.

5. The example is McCarty's. Ibid., p. 109.

6. The limit on the right-hand side exists and is approximately 0.5772.

7. Crispin Wright, "About 'The Philosophical Significance of Gödel's Theorem': Some Issues," in *The Philosophy of Michael Dummett*, Synthese Library vol. 239, B. McGuiness and G. Oliveri (eds.), Dordrecht: Kluwer, 1994, pp. 167–204, here p. 172.

8. I italicize the term to signal the fact that I use "reject" throughout in contrast to "refute." Rejection of a notion or principle follows a demonstration that the notion is not constructive or that the principle not intuitionistically demonstra-

ble. Refutation on the other hand is a demonstration that the principle is false, i.e., that its negation is true.

9. "No account of the Intuitionistic rejection of LEM is adequate unless it is based on the Intuitionistic rejection of the Platonistic concept of mathematical truth as obtaining independently of our capacity to give a proof," *Elements of Intuitionism* (henceforth *Elements*), p. 18.

10. See *Elements*, p. 19.

11. *Elements*, p. 22.

12. Hence, the fact that reals are extensional does not entail that we can recognize them independently of their generators: By grasping the rule in accord with which the construction of a real number is determined, we might be able to recognize that two real number generators determine the same number.

13. Or, more weakly, an effective method for proving it.

14. In *Elements*, p. 21.

15. If we were to reinterpret the universal quantifier, $\forall$, so that it could be defined in terms of $\exists$, this will still hold, since if "$\neg\forall x.\neg Fx$" meant the same as, say, "$\neg\neg\exists x\neg Fx$," it would claim that it is not the case that we will not be able to actually produce any natural number that has F, which, given that each natural number in the classically completed totality determinately is either F or not F, classically does entail that if we run through that totality, we will eventually find one that is F. See *Elements*, p. 18.

16. Compare the S4 modal translation of "$\neg$," "$\emptyset$," and "$\forall$" discussed further on.

17. The clause for the atomic case will depend on the theory under discussion—for the case at hand, there is no problem because the closed atomic wffs are all decidable arithmetical equalities.

18. *Elements*, p. 389.

19. Ibid., p. 390.

20. The alternative proposal—that we so modify the intuitive explanations that we permit C to be a proof of A $\vee$ B, for example, if it provides an EM for finding a proof of either disjunct—seems less attractive once we examine the informal explications of the meanings of "$\forall$," "$\emptyset$," and "$\neg$."

21. Geoffrey Hellman, "Never Say 'Never'! On the Communication Problem between Intuitionism and Classicism," *Philosophical Topics* 17, no. 2, 1989, pp. 47–67, here p. 52.

22. Geoffrey Hellman, "The Boxer and His Fists: The Constructivist in the Arena of Quantum Physics," *Proceedings of the Aristotelian Society*, supplementary vol. 66, 1992, pp. 61–77, here p. 61.

23. Ibid.

24. Keith Hossack, "Constructive Mathematics, Quantum Physics, and Quantifiers (II)," *Proceedings of the Aristotelian Society*, supplementary vol. 66, 1992, pp. 79–97.

25. Ibid.

26. Steven Weinberg, *Dreams of a Final Theory*, New York: Vintage, 1993, pp. 17–19.

27. Ibid., pp. 24–25.

28. Although both start from the same model, they develop it in very different ways.

29. Cf. the "Philosophical Basis of Intuitionistic Logic," p. 222: "It will always be legitimate to demand, of any expression or form of sentence belonging to the language, that its addition to the language should yield a conservative extension; but, in order to make the notion of a conservative extension precise, we need to appeal to some concept such as that of truth or that of being assertible or capable in principle of being established, or the like; *and just which concept is to be selected, and how it is to be explained, will depend upon the theory of meaning that is adopted*" (emphasis mine).

30. *Collected Papers of Gerhard Gentzen*, M. E. Szabo (trans. and ed.), Amsterdam: North Holland, 1969, p. 80.

31. See Arthur Prior, "The Runabout Inference Ticket," in *Contemporary Philosophical Logic*, Irving Copi and James A. Gould (eds.), New York: St. Martin's Press, 1978, pp. 37–38.

32. Nuel Belnap, "Tonk, Plonk, and Plink," *Analysis* 22, no. 6 (1962), reprinted in *Contemporary Philosophical Logic*, pp. 44–48.

33. Dag Prawitz, "Philosophical Aspects of Proof Theory" (henceforth "Philosophical Aspects"), in *Contemporary Philosophy: A New Survey*, vol. 1, G. Floistad (ed.), The Hague: Martinus Nijhoff, 1981, pp. 235–277, here p. 242.

34. Prawitz, "Ideas and Results in Proof Theory," in *Proceedings of the Second Scandinavian Logic Symposium*, J.-E. Fenstad (ed.), Amsterdam: North Holland, 1971, pp. 235–308, here pp. 246–247.

35. An important corollary of the normal form of a derivation is the Subformula Property: In a normal derivation of $\Delta \vdash \emptyset$, only subformulas of Δ and $\emptyset$ can occur in the derivation. This result is important because it then follows directly that intuitionistic predicate logic (IPL) is a conservative extension of intuitionistic sentential logic (ISL). If we let $\emptyset$ be a proposition that is a theorem of ISL ($\vdash \emptyset$), and consider a normal derivation $D\emptyset$ of $\emptyset$ in IPL, we know from the subformula property that only propositional connectives can occur in this deri-

vation. Hence, we have a derivation of $\emptyset$ using only propositional rules, and thus IPL is a conservative extension of ISL.

36. Reported in Prawitz's "Philosophical Aspects," p. 245.

37. "Comments on Prawitz," in *Logic and Philosophy*, G. H. von Wright (ed.), The Hague: Martinus Nijhoff, 1980, here p. 17. Dummett goes on to say that this might not prove an insuperable obstacle, but he gives no indication as to how it might be overcome. Prawitz, on the other hand, *does* seem to identify Dummett's "consequences" with logical consequences.

38. Of course this is only one hypothesis among a plethora of others.

39. Neil Tennant, "Justifying the Law of Excluded Middle," paper read to the Philosophy Society, Australian National University, 1987 (unpublished). See also his *Anti-Realism and Logic*, Oxford: Clarendon Press, 1987.

40. This is Tennant's response to the classicist.

41. Arnold Koslow, *A Structuralist Theory of Logic*, Cambridge: Cambridge University Press, 1992, p. 3.

42. Ibid.

43. Vann McGee, "Review of Arnold Koslow's *A Structuralist Theory of Logic*," *Journal of Philosophy* 90, no. 5, 1993, pp. 271–274, here p. 273.

44. Dummett discusses Prawitz's circularity charge in his *The Logical Basis of Metaphysics*, London: Duckworth, 1991, pp. 200–201.

45. See John Etchemendy, *The Concept of Logical Consequence*, Cambridge, Mass.: Harvard University Press, 1990.

46. Throughout, "$\Gamma \vdash_s \theta$" will mean: "θ is derivable from Γ in the formal system S."

47. I use this term rather than "syntactic" because if one thinks of Belnap's program as an attempt to characterize the connectives purely syntactically, one might be led to believe that he is a conventionalist about the meanings of the logical constants. This is precisely how Prior interpreted him, mistakenly in my view. Belnap's program is the very same one as Koslow's.

48. Belnap, "Tonk, Plonk, and Plink," pp. 46–47.

49. "We may now state the demand for the consistency of the definition of the new connective, *plonk*, as follows: the extension must be *conservative*; i.e. although the extension may well have new deducibility-statements, these new statements will all involve *plonk*. The extension will not have any new deducibility-statements which do not involve *plonk* itself. It will not lead to any deducibility-statements ... not containing *plonk*, unless that statement is already provable in the absence of the *plonk*-axioms and *plonk*-rules." Ibid.

50. "In short, it seems that either an 'inferential definition' is a piece of informal pedagogy, in which case it is legitimate enough, but it may work or may not; or it is a muddle—essentially a muddle about what you can do with a symbolic game where the conveying of information isn't in question. It is a muddle when its advocates say: 'Being able to do the tricks just is knowing the meaning.' In a symbolic game, this is in a way true, but vacuously, because there is no meaning to know. There, we can just *decree* that a couple of wffs with a sign between them is another wff, and lay down what rules we please for this newcomer; and after that there are no more questions to ask. But no one can make an expression consisting of two significant sentences joined by 'and' or 'or' or 'tonk' into a significant sentence just by (a) saying it is one, and (b) giving us 'permission' to utter certain other sentences before or after it and insert a few 'therefores.'" Prior, "Conjunction and Contonktion Revisited," pp. 49–53 in *Contemporary Philosophical Logic*. To be sure, nothing in Belnap's reply to Prior seems to necessitate reading "⊢" as a *derivability* operator: for all that Belnap says, we *could* read "⊢" as a license to write down further wffs in a symbolic game (a "runabout inference ticket")—TONK is then ruled out because it is not a permissible transformation relative to the total specification of permissible transformations. It *is* hard to see, therefore, how the notion of a conservative extension has any intrinsic connection with meaning. But one who like Belnap or Koslow takes the notion of implication between sentences as a specification of a more general structural notion of implication can readily admit Prior's point about the importance of the informal meanings of the operators—we have a grasp of a primitive notion of one sentence following from another that guides the encapsulation of those intuitions in the structural rules devised by Gentzen. The reason these rules are not intrinsically connected with sentence meanings and implication relations between sentences is just that they have a far more *general* application than that specific one.

For his part, Dummett has consistently argued against conventionalist approaches to the meanings of the constants, which he thinks can be motivated only by holism. He sees the conventionalist claiming that we are free to stipulate the meanings of the constants by adopting whatever set of logical laws we choose. To Dummett this is a holistic thesis because once we decide to adopt or reject even one logical law this will ramify through the whole language as logical laws in general allow us to infer the truth of statements not containing the constants those laws govern. See *Elements* and *Logical Basis of Metaphysics* (henceforth *LBM*) (particularly pp. 227–230) for his views.

51. Dummett, however, does not agree that the elimination rules are consequences in any sense of the introduction rules. See *LBM*, p. 252: "It is confusing to speak of the elimination rules as consequences of the introduction rules: it is better to speak of them as being justified by reference to them."

52. Dummett gives a similar argument for a restricted type of proof being used in the explanation of the meaning of "∀" at pp. 393–394. Again, we cannot allow $\forall x.Fx$ as the major premise of an application of universal instantiation if we're to avoid circularity.

53. Prawitz, "Ideas and Results in Proof Theory," pp. 242–243 (henceforth "Ideas").

54. *Pari passu* for "∀."

55. Again the same result holds for (∀I) and (∀E).

56. See "Ideas," appendix A, pp. 284–290.

57. Prawitz, "Remarks on Some Approaches to the Concept of Logical Consequence," *Synthese* 62, 1985, pp. 153–171. Henceforth "Approaches."

58. In his "Approaches" and "Proofs and the Meaning and Completeness of the Logical Constants," in *Essays on Mathematical and Philosophical Logic*, J. Hintikka, I. Niiniluoto, and E. Saarinen (eds.), Dordrecht: D. Reidel, 1978, pp. 25–40 (henceforth "Proofs").

59. More precisely, an argument can be defined as a tree of wffs with a specification of (i) which wffs are assumptions; (ii) at what places the assumptions are bound (if bound at all); (iii) at what places the parameters are bound (if bound at all), a bound parameter being debarred from appearing in a free assumption. See "Approaches," p. 6.

60. In the case of mathematics, a closed valid argument just will be a proof.

61. See "Approaches," p. 8, n. 12.

62. "Immediate subarguments" are simply arguments for the premises of the last inference of the argument.

63. "Approaches," p. 166.

64. In *LBM*, Dummett uses this example to question what he calls the "Fundamental Assumption" of proof-theoretic approaches to justifying inferential rules. This states that "if we have a valid argument for the premises of a proposed application of [a rule], we already have a valid argument, not appealing to that rule, for the conclusion" (p. 254).

65. Prior, "Conjunction and Contonktion Revisited," p. 49.

66. Ibid.

67. "Approaches," p. 163.

68. Prawitz, "Towards a Foundation of a General Proof Theory" (henceforth "General Proof Theory"), in *Logic, Methodology, and Philosophy of Science IV*, P. Suppes et al. (eds.), Amsterdam: North Holland, 1973, pp. 225–250. Prawitz tries to show by means of a concrete example why the Tarskian account is inadequate: "Whether $\exists x.\neg P(x)$ follows logically from $\neg \forall x.P(x)$ depends, according to Tarski's definition, on whether $\exists x.\neg P(x)$ is true in each model (D, S) in which $\neg \forall x.P(x)$ is true ... whether there is an element e in domain D that does not belong to S whenever it is not the case that every e in D belongs to S—i.e. we are essentially back to the question of whether $\exists x.\neg P(x)$ follows from $\neg \forall x.P(x)$."

A typical model-theoretic explanation of the (classical) validity of $\neg\forall x.P(x) \vDash \exists x.\neg P(x)$ seems to me to be a little more informative than Prawitz allows. One would normally argue for the validity of the inference as follows:

In any model, $\exists x.\neg P(x)$ is either true or not true.

(a) Consider when it is true: choose $e \in S$. Since $\neg P(x)$ is true of e, $P(x)$ is not true of every $d \in D$. Hence, $\neg\forall x.P(x)$ is true and thus $\neg\forall x.P(x) \vDash \exists x.\neg P(x)$ must be true.

(b) Consider when it is not true: since $\neg P(x)$ is false of every $d \in D$, $P(x)$ is true of every $d \in D$. Hence, $\neg\forall x.P(x)$ is false and thus $\neg\forall x.P(x) \vDash \exists x.\neg P(x)$ must be true.

This is a noncircular argument in the semantic metalanguage for the validity of a wff (or an inference). Prawitz will reply that all such a model-theoretic argument really establishes is that inferences and laws such as the above hold only on the assumption that *other* laws such as bivalence hold, and wherever *that* can be demonstrated, we can show that law or inference to be derivable from those others without any appeal to (Tarskian) semantic considerations. This may well be so, but it clearly needs further argument to establish that it is.

69. Witness his remark at *LBM* 270: "Proof-theoretic justifications form an interesting alternative to justifications in terms of semantic theories. Neither is autonomous, however: both depend on the defensibility of the meaning-theory within which each finds its proper habitat."

This ought also to be Prawitz's attitude, and I think would be but for his low view of Tarski. Prawitz must think that a Tarskian model-theoretic approach to validity simply generates a programmatic conception of validity (in Dummett's sense of that phrase). It is understandable that an antirealist should think this, given his doubts about realist truth, but the point is that if a realist theory of meaning is so much as defensible, and the semantic value of a sentence is a truth value that the sentence possesses independently of our capacity to establish that it does, Tarski's account of validity and of logical consequence may be both illuminating and correct. A Prawitz-styled attack on that account will therefore always be open to effective realist rejoinder while the underlying realist theory of meaning has not been challenged.

70. Since the introduction and elimination rules are required to be in harmony, it is possible to choose either sort as explicating the meanings of the constants—which one chooses will probably depend on whether one takes the conditions for asserting a sentence or the consequences of asserting it as the central concept in one's theory of meaning. Of course, one could choose both.

71. *LBM*, p. 256.

72. Ibid., p. 257.

73. Ibid., p. 258.

74. Ibid., pp. 254–255.

75. Any sentence, closed or open, in an argument A determines a subargument of which it is the final conclusion. The initial premises of this subargument are just the hypotheses on which that sentence depends.

76. Despite what one might naively have thought, the simultaneous definition of validity for arbitrary and for canonical arguments can be shown to not be circular. If we understand the *degree* of an argument to be the maximum number of logical constants occurring in any of its initial premises or final conclusion, then we can, Dummett observes, judge the validity of canonical arguments of degree n by assessing the validity of arbitrary arguments of degree *less than n*. To judge the validity of arbitrary arguments of degree n, on the other hand, we need only to be able to recognize the validity of canonical arguments of degree *less than or equal to n*.

77. This point highlights an important question that has not received the attention it deserves, viz. what types of behavior on the part of speakers from the antirealist's standpoint manifest their semantic knowledge? It is quite inadequate, since merely programmatic to reply: "The activities of criticizing and justifying assertions." Not all such criticisms manifest one's understanding—only criticisms directed at the content of the assertion; and what behavioral markers indicate that a criticism is so directed? Prawitz's proposal has the great merit of making this programmatic response contentful.

78. We can similarly define stability for a set of introduction rules.

79. See *LBM*, pp. 280–300, and especially pp. 320–321.

80. At least one writer, Timothy Williamson in "Intuitionism Disproved?" *Analysis* 42, no. 4, 1982, pp. 203–208, has seen this as a satisfactory intuitionistic reply to Fitch's argument, provoking the following volley from Roy Sorensen: "... even if Williamson is correct, the argument remains significant. For if it really shows that anti-realists must be intuitionists, it shows that anti-realists must adopt a logic that almost no one accepts. The intuitionist is only of philosophical interest in the same way that the solipsist, the anarchist, and the pacifist are of philosophical interest. Almost no one considers it a live option." *Blindspots*, Oxford: Clarendon, 1988, p. 129.

81. Dummett, "Victor's Error," *Analysis* 61, no. 1, 2001, pp. 1–2.

82. Berit Brogard and Joe Salerno, "Clues to the Paradox of Knowability: Replies to Dummett and Tennant," *Analysis* 62, no. 2, 2002, pp. 143–151.

83. As developed in Tennant, *The Taming of the True*, Oxford: Clarendon, 1997, and defended more recently in "Victor Vanquished," *Analysis* 62, no. 2, 2002, pp. 135–142.

84. Brogard and Salerno, "Clues to the Paradox of Knowability," p. 147.

85. Ibid.

86. In fact, this leads to a certain modal blindness that accounts for some of the expressive inadequacies of intuitionistic languages we'll encounter later.

87. Recall Markov's principle is $[\forall x(Fx \vee \neg Fx) \,\&\, \neg\forall x \neg Fx] \rightarrow \exists x.Fx$.

88. Recall Hellman's comment: "*everyone* can see that the intuitionistic 'law of the excluded middle' (LEMi) is not generally correct for arbitrary propositions *p*. If *p* is a problematic statement (say, the Goldbach conjecture) for which we possess neither a constructive proof nor a constructive refutation (nor any method of finding either), then *no one* would want to assert *this* instance of (LEMi). And, of course, this is entirely irrelevant to the corresponding instance of (LEMc), which makes no claim whatsoever about anyone having constructive proofs." "Never Say 'Never'!" p. 52.

89. Dummett, *Elements*, p. 45.

90. Hellman, "Never Say 'Never'!" p. 62.

91. Dummett, *Elements*, p. 13.

92. Hand, "Radical Antirealism and Neutral States of Information," *Philosophical Topics*, 24, no. 1, 1996, pp. 35–51.

Chapter 5

1. Michael Devitt, "Review of *Reason, Truth, and History*," *Philosophical Review* 93, 1984, p. 277.

2. Ibid.

3. Putnam, "Reply to Miller," *Philosophical Topics*, 20: *The Philosophy of Hilary Putnam* (Christopher Hill, issue ed.), no. 1, 1992, p. 373: "It was the hope that this ultimate circularity (of defining epistemic luck in terms of the concept of truth) might be avoided, and that truth might actually be reduced to notions of 'rational acceptability' and 'better and worse epistemic situation' that did not themselves presuppose the notion of truth that was responsible for the residue of idealism in *Reason, Truth and History*. As Miller notes, the residue has now been repudiated."

4. "Reply to Gary Ebbs," pp. 347–358, and "Reply to David Anderson," pp. 361–369, both in *Philosophical Topics* 20: *The Philosophy of Hilary Putnam*, no. 1, 1992.

5. "Reply to Gary Ebbs," p. 357.

6. Ibid., pp. 357–358.

7. *Reason, Truth, and History*, p. 55.

8. Ibid.

9. "Reply to Gary Ebbs," p. 353.

10. Ibid., pp. 352–353.

11. Ibid., p. 354.

12. *Realism and Reason*, p. viii.

13. Resnick, "Putnam's Objections to Metaphysical Realism" (unpublished ms.), p. 3.

14. Daniel Dennett, *Consciousness Explained*, Boston: Little, Brown, 1991, p. 5.

15. Ibid.

16. Indeed, the response to the imagined BIVA supporter's retort was deliberately Putnamesque.

17. Brueckner, "If I'm a Brain in a Vat then I'm not a Brain in a Vat," *Mind* 101, no. 401, 1992, pp. 123–128.

18. Leeds, "Brains in Vats Revisited," *Pacific Philosophical Quarterly* 77, no. 2, 1996, pp. 108–131.

19. Putnam, "Equivalence," reprinted in his *Realism and Reason: Philosophical Papers*, volume 3, Cambridge: Cambridge University Press, 1983, chapter 2, pp. 26–45.

20. Ibid., p. 39.

21. Ibid., p. 35.

22. It is not that Putnam does not acknowledge this. He does, for he writes: "That there is a hidden relativity to ascriptions of simultaneity—that which events will turn out to be 'simultaneous' if we rely on, e.g. clocks which are transported to a distance to remain 'synchronized' will depend on whether the clocks are transported with the same velocity relative to the rest system—is a matter of hitherto unknown empirical fact. Equivalence is of philosophical importance precisely in such cases as these, cases in which it does not seem that anyone has altered the ordinary meaning of any expression and yet, for factual reasons, apparently incompatible bodies of theory turn out to be equivalent in the sense we have been discussing" (ibid., p. 41). The point is that he confounds the issue with an adequate characterization of cognitive significance, so that the net effect is comparable to claiming that since the phenomenon of token-reflexivity really supports a disturbing epistemic relativity when sentences containing these devices are construed "literally," an adequate theory of meaning for indexicals should reveal just how it is that one theory adequate for the explanation of a given class of phenomena can make "I am Australian" true while a cognitively equivalent theory can make the very same claim false. If he is not confounding the issues in something like this manner, it is mysterious why, having recorded Reichenbach's resolution of the conflict between simultaneity claims in just these token-reflexive terms, he does not acknowledge that what Reichenbach said was true.

23. Ibid., p. 44.

24. In Mormann, "Incompatible Empirically Equivalent Theories—A Structural Explication," *Synthese* 103, 1995, pp. 203–249. I am indebted to Professor Mormann for bringing this paper to my attention and for his written response to this section on which my description of his work is based.

25. Ernest Sosa, "Putnam's Pragmatic Realism," *Journal of Philosophy* 90, 1993, pp. 606–626.

26. Ibid., pp. 624–625.

27. Michael Lynch, *Truth in Context*, Cambridge, Mass.: MIT Press/Bradford Books, 1998, pp. 77–78.

28. Ibid., p. 93.

29. Hilary Putnam, "Reply to Blackburn," in *Reading Putnam*, Peter Clark and Bob Hale (eds.), Oxford: Blackwell, 1994, pp. 250–251.

30. Ibid., p. 251.

31. Ibid.

32. Reprinted as chapter 7 of *Truth and the Absence of Fact*, Oxford: Clarendon Press, 2001.

33. Michael Dummett, "Wittgenstein on Necessity: Some Reflections," in *Reading Putnam*, Clark and Hale (eds.), pp. 49–65, here pp. 60–61, emphasis mine.

34. Field, "Physicalism," in *Inference, Explanations, and Other Frustrations: Essays in the Philosophy of Science*, John Earman (ed.), Berkeley, Calif.: University of California Press, 1992, pp. 271–291.

Chapter 6

1. Wagner, "Why Realism Can't Be Naturalized," in *Naturalism: A Critical Appraisal*, Steven J. Wagner and Richard Warner (eds.), Notre Dame: University of Notre Dame Press, 1993, pp. 211–253.

2. By a "representationalist theory of mind" I mean any model of mind that posits physically realized mental representations as intermediaries between the cognizing/perceiving subject and the world. These mental representations need not be linguistic entities; they could be maplike. I will not try to substantiate my claim through close exegesis of Putnam's writings. Its vindication will be implicit—if this *were* Putnam's goal then his replies to realist criticisms and the subsequent development of his own philosophical views would be more readily explicable. However, Putnam's *Dewey Lectures* do strongly support this interpretation. Putnam explains there that the computational conception of mind brings in its train a "Cartesian *cum* materialist" epistemology and explains that at the

time of writing "Models and Reality" and "Realism and Reason" (and, indeed, well beyond): "my picture of our mental functioning was just the 'Cartesian *cum* materialist' picture, a picture on which it has to seem magical that we can have access to anything outside our 'inputs.'" The alternative he now favors, following John McDowell, "involves, instead, insisting that 'external' things, cabbages and kings, can be experienced. (And not just in the Pickwickian sense of causing 'experiences,' conceived of as affectations of our subjectivity, which is what 'qualia' are conceived to be)" (*Dewey Lectures*, p. 464). To forestall confusion on this point, Putnam's "qualia" are simply the inputs to the cerebral computer; they are not "raw feels" or monadic properties of sensations or anything qualiaophiles normally cite as referents for the term "qualia." Although my interpretation of Putnam has affinities with Steven Wagner's in "Why Realism Can't Be Naturalized," I dissent from Wagner's assessment of what the right target is and his conclusion that "Properly—albeit radically—recast, however, it [the MTA] refutes the position they [realists] actually hold."

Wagner thinks the MTA's proper target is a version of naturalism, "soft naturalism" he calls it, which requires semantics to be legitmated by "naturalizing definitions" that "reduce semantic terms to natural-scientific ones." If this is meant to include semantic minimalists who view truth, reference, etc. as logical properties rather than dyadic language–world relations, I cannot see how the MTA refutes their position at all. Whether the MTAs foreclose on realists who believe in a more robust semantics is one of the questions examined here. As will emerge, I think that Putnam's assumptions cannot be justified if the MTA is taken to apply to all soft naturalists in Wagner's sense. The crucial question is whether those "soft naturalists" adhere to the RTM.

3. It is not just the referent of "set" that Skolem and his followers questioned. There are, in addition to other set-theoretic notions such as cardinality, uncountability, finiteness, etc. infected by the "relativity to model," properties that affect the interpretation of "set" as it occurs in axiomatic set theories according to them. Crucially, the existence of an uncountable model for the ZF axioms is held to be "relative to a model."

4. In the strict sense of "paradox," there is no paradox here. That is, one cannot prove *within the theory* ZF that a certain set both is and is not denumerable. This contrasts with the set-theoretic paradox where one can indeed prove *within naive set theory* that a certain set both does and does not contain itself as a member. However, there *is* a dramatic discrepancy between what one can prove in the theory and what can be verified by the models of the theory.

5. Chapter 1 of Putnam's *Realism and Reason: Philosophical Papers*, vol. 3, Cambridge: Cambridge University Press, 1983.

6. By a "minimalist" theory of truth and reference I mean any such theory that denies that truth and reference are to be explained as language–world relations and asserts that they are logical properties in some sense of "logical."

7. As we know from the various forms of the completeness proof.

8. Compare Quine's assessment of the numerical model version of LST: "We're told that truths about the real numbers can via re-interpretation be carried over into truths about the natural numbers. This can appear paradoxical in the light of Cantor's proof that the reals cannot be exhaustively correlated with the natural numbers. But the air of paradox can be dispelled once we realize that whatever disparities between the reals and natural numbers may be guaranteed in those original truths about the reals, the guarantees themselves are *revised* in the re-interpretation" (*Methods of Logic*, third ed., New York: Holt, Rinehart and Winston, 1972, p. 178). Quine's comments, it is widely believed, do not apply to the transitive submodel version of the theorem.

To Putnam's claim that M^* satisfies all operational and theoretical constraints, realists have responded à la Quine: *If* it is the case that M^* satisfies all these constraints, this can be only because the constraints have themselves been revised in the reinterpretation. To which Putnam retorts, "In this context, such a reply is simply question-begging!"—but that dispute is for later.

9. Michael D. Resnick, "You Can't Trust an Ideal Theory to Tell the Truth," *Philosophical Studies* 52, 1987, pp. 151–160.

10. According to Barry Taylor in "Just More Theory?" *Australasian Journal of Philosophy* 69, no. 2, 1991, pp. 152–166, this lemma plays no part in Putnam's GCA. As he reads him, on p. 152: "[Putnam] reckons a simple but neat argument can be deployed to reject metaphysical realism ... at least if we assume that first-order resources suffice to frame the language LI in which TI is written...." *What might this "simple but neat" argument be?* Just this: "... since TI is ideal, it is at least consistent; since consistent and first-order, by the Gödel Completeness Theorem it has a model M*; so TI *must* be true, in one clear sense of 'true'—all of its theses must be true-on-M*." (Emphasis Taylor's.)

This is puzzling as GCT of itself furnishes no argument at all against realism. If GCT provided the ammunition for any such argument the argument would have to be that *any* consistent first-order theory is true in one clear sense of "true." The ideality of *TI*, as Taylor himself indicates, ensures only the syntactic consistency of *TI*. The fact of the matter is that true-on-M^* is not a clear sense of "true" at all—at least, it is not a clear sense of "true simpliciter." The realist has no quibble at all with the claim that *TI* is true-in-M^*, which is, after all, just what GCT gives us. The realist's claim is that *TI* might be false simpliciter. Nothing in the "simple but neat" argument adduced by Taylor above even remotely bears on *this* claim.

Hence, when Taylor continues, "For the realist to rebut this argument it will suffice to show that truth-on-M^* falls short of truth full-fledged," the realist can be forgiven for responding, with bemusement, "*What* argument?" If the "argument" envisaged is just GCT, there can be no rebuttal; but the realist (thankfully) needs none, for this has no bearing at all on metaphysical realism.

What is clearly missing from Taylor's argument is the premise that *M* is an intended model.* Only then will it be even plausible to claim that *TI* is true in *any* clear sense. Why doesn't he include this premise, then? The fuller version of the quotation above gives the game away—"For the realist to rebut this argument it will suffice to show that truth-on-M^* falls short of truth full-fledged. Since it is commonplace that truth full-fledged can be equated with truth on a model which is 'real' or 'intended,' this in turn can be accomplished by specifying some condition which an intended model must satisfy, and which M^* either demonstrably does not satisfy, or at least does not satisfy demonstrably." Taylor's strategy is thus to shift the burden of proof onto the realist to "specify some condition which an intended model must satisfy, and which M^* either demonstrably does not satisfy, or at least does not satisfy demonstrably." If we already *had* some evidence that M^* was an intended model, that challenge to the realist would be apposite. In lieu of that, the argument that the realist has to rebut is simply one for the conclusion that *if* M^* is an intended model *then* TI is true. But this is utterly uncontentious, for GCT together with the identification of truth simpliciter with truth-in-an-intended-model already secures this conclusion for us, and neither the completeness theorem nor the latter identification—nor of course their conjunction—poses any sort of threat to realism at all.

The same assessment applies to Catherine Z. Elgin's defense of the MTA— "Unnatural Science," *Journal of Philosophy* 92, no. 6, 1995, pp. 289–302. She cites Putnam's early "Realism and Reason" formulation. But it is clear that Putnam himself regards this formulation as too crude as it does not even attempt to justify the thesis that M^* is an intended model and all his subsequent formulations, under realist criticism presumably, have.

11. I shall discuss this question in more detail when we come to examine the LSA version of the MTA.

12. They could be regarded as limitative results on the expressive powers of partially interpreted theories.

13. David Lewis, "Putnam's Paradox," *Australasian Journal of Philosophy* 62, 1984, pp. 221–236.

14. Ibid.

15. Taylor, "Just More Theory?" p. 166, emphasis mine.

16. This is what he means when he calls metaphysical realism "incoherent," "devoid of content," etc. and also when he claims that it is impossible to express what the metaphysical realist wants to express.

17. To merely invoke this distinction with earnest avowals of the importance of distinguishing epistemic from ontological questions will obviously cut no ice with an antirealist.

18. Resnick, "You Can't Trust an Ideal Theory to Tell the Truth," p. 154.

19. Ibid., pp. 156–157. This is a more precise version of the distinction Lewis urged on Putnam above. The difference is that Resnick provides the Skolemite with convincing reasons to accept it.

20. Resnick thinks that Putnam's entire case against metaphysical realism fails because of this: "... that a given model verifies a theory which contains theorems

to the effect that certain conditions are met—making all its theses come out true—even the ones asserting that the aforementioned conditions are met, does not imply that the model itself meets those conditions. So Putnam's argument that TRUE meets all the constraints on intended models fails." Ibid.

21. Resnick has Putnam accepting the bait and claiming that it is simply question-begging to assume that there are independent concepts of identity, uncountability, simplicity, etc., which the inner models miss.

22. Likewise, *relative to the standard interpretation of ZF* we can explain, the Skolemite will contend, why it is that denumerable models allow us to verify the theorem that there are uncountable infinities of objects: We show that *within the model* there is no function f correlating N with P(N), and then we go on to prove that there is nonetheless such a mapping, thereby explaining the denumerability of the model.

23. In the former case but not the latter we can, she will claim, avail ourselves of notions such as "standard interpretation" and "intended model" without begging any questions. The antirealist herself can make unproblematic appeals to such notions in those local cases in order to explain from within total theory the types of mismatches between theories and their models that Skolem's paradox first brought to light.

24. Wagner, "Why Realism Can't Be Naturalized."

25. I think Putnam has himself come to concede this since he admits in his *Dewey Lectures* that the same problem (of selecting the intended interpretation of our ideal language) arises when we ask what it is for the epistemically ideal circumstances whose obtaining makes a sentence antirealistically true to obtain.

26. It is tempting for the realist to follow Paul Benaceraff's lead in dealing with Skolem's paradox in his "Skolem and the Skeptic," *Proceedings of the Aristotelian Society*, supplementary vol. 59, 1985, pp. 85–115. Benaceraff considers the interpretation of a sentence σ that in the standard model expresses the nondenumerability of the power set of the set of natural numbers, and he says, on p. 103:

> That P(N) is nondenumerable is, in other words, a proposition which is *not* invariantly expressed by σ over *all* transitive submodels of a given model *even if* that model starts out as somehow standard—i.e. as the (a) '*intended*' model.... The conclusion is obvious; whether σ *says* that a set is *nondenumerable* depends on more than whether:—
> (1) The interpretation is over a domain of sets;
> (2) "∈" in the interpretation coincides with membership among those sets.
> (3) Every element of any set is also in the model.
>
> The universal quantifier has to mean all or, at least, all sets or must, at the very least, range over a domain wide enough to include "enough" of the subsets of N.

The realist might then construct a parallel argument for one of the designated theoretical constraints, simplicity, for example, to demonstrate that we have no guarantee that the correct interpretation of the sentence standardly used to express the simplicity of M^* can be assumed to do so in M^*: Let $\sigma 0$ be the sentence "M^* is simple" and consider the truth condition in M^*+, the extended model that semantically explicates M^* in Taylor's sense, of the given sentence $\sigma 0$. We have:

(α) $\sigma 0$ is true-in-M^*+ iff M^* is simple....

as our target truth-condition for $\sigma 0$.

Now what evidence is there that the model M^* hits its target, that, to echo Benaceraff, the interpretation of $\sigma 0$ in M^* suffices to guarantee that $\sigma 0$ says on that interpretation that M^* is simple?

Taylor's argument establishes that $(simple)M^* = (simple)M^*+$, but *that* argument cannot possibly secure the desired conclusion that the interpretation of "simple" in either M^* or its expansion M^*+ is *simple*. As we saw, it simply assumed from the outset that M^* *was*, by the lights of the nonsemantic constraints at least, an intended model in order to test whether a semantic constraint in the form of the (RRC) could filter it out as nonstandard. So there is no plausible way for Putnam to convince us that the truth condition in M^*+ is that M^* is simple.

The problem with this argument is that it makes use of the standard interpretation of "simple" just as Benaceraff's argument makes use of the standard interpretation of "nondenumerable" and thus fails to convince anyone who is skeptical that there is such a thing as the standard interpretation.

27. "Indeed," they will go on, "the total distribution of truth values across all possible worlds does not suffice to fix the reference of the terms of a language." Thus in their minds is the PA undercut in addition to the LSA. Compare James van Cleve, "Semantic Supervenience and Referential Indeterminacy," *Journal of Philosophy* 89, 1992, pp. 344–361: "... how plausible is it anyway to suppose that reference supervenes on nothing but the distribution of truth values (in all possible worlds) over the sentences of a language? To my mind, that supposition is every bit as arbitrary as the following one: reference supervenes on nothing but the *ratio* of true sentences to false ones. If two schemes of reference for a language L both make half of its sentences true and half false (and there are few that do not do this!) then they are equally correct."

28. Michael Hallett, "Putnam and the Skolem Paradox," in *Reading Putnam*, Clark and Hale (eds.), chapter 4, pp. 66–97.

29. Furthermore, in the absence of some convincing account of how content is determined within a minimalist framework for truth and reference, it ought to give the minimalist committed to RTM some pause as well.

30. This case has been forcefully argued by Stewart Shapiro. For its fullest defense see his *Foundations without Foundationalism*, Oxford: Clarendon Press, 1991. For a defense of schematic second-order logic, see Shaughan Lavine's

Understanding the Infinite, Cambridge, Mass.: Harvard University Press, 1994. On p. 233 Lavine presents a succinct argument for second-order logic:

> The commitments of present-day physical science go beyond those of the first-order framework that Shapiro argued is *de facto* equivalent to full schematic second-order set theory: It is part of physics that many physical variables take on real-number values. The appropriate real-number values are the least upper bounds of collections of rational numbers specified in relation to some state of affairs in the physical world. First-order set theory cannot guarantee that the relevant collections of rational numbers are sets—there is no reason why such collections should be first-order definable. It therefore does not guarantee that they have least upper bounds, which is required to ensure that there are enough real numbers for the purposes of physics. Contrary to the usual conclusion, first-order set theory does not suffice to formulate the mathematics used for physics!

For a powerful defense of first-order logic against such arguments, see Steven Wagner's "The Rationalist Conception of Logic," *Notre Dame Journal of Formal Logic* 28, 1987, pp. 3–35.

31. In *Reflections on Chomsky*, A. George (ed.), Blackwell, 1989, chapter 11, pp. 213–232.

Chapter 7

1. Barry Taylor, "Common Sense, Realism and 'Common Sense Realism,'" University of Melbourne Department of Philosophy Preprint Series, 1996.

2. See Wittgenstein's discussion of rule-following and private language in his *Philosophical Investigations*.

3. John McDowell, *Mind and World*, Cambridge, Mass.: Harvard University Press, 1994, p. 9.

4. Ibid., p. 27.

5. Taylor, "Common Sense, Realism, and 'Common Sense Realism.'"

6. McDowell, *Mind and World*, p. 27.

7. Michael Friedman, "Exorcising the Philosophical Tradition: Comments on John McDowell's *Mind and World*," *Philosophical Review* 105, no. 4, 1996, pp. 427–467.

8. Ibid.

9. Ibid., p. 22n.

10. Jerry Fodor, "Review of McDowell's *Mind and World*," chapter 1 of *In Critical Condition: Polemical Essays on Cognitive Science and the Philosophy of Mind*, 1999, Cambridge, Mass.: MIT Press/Bradford Books, p. 5.

11. McDowell, *Mind and World*, p. 13.

12. Fodor, "Review of *Mind and World*," pp. 6–7.

13. Ibid., p. 8.

14. Crispin Wright, "Truth as Sort of Epistemic: Putnam's Peregrinations," *Journal of Philosophy* 97, no. 6, 2000, pp. 335–364, here p. 362.

15. Ibid., p. 361.

16. Ibid., p. 360.

17. Ibid.

18. Michael Dummett, "Truth," *Truth and Other Enigmas*, p. 24.

19. Christopher Menzel, "Actualism," in *The Stanford Encyclopedia of Philosophy*, Edward N. Zalta (ed.), 2001, ⟨http://plato.stanford.edu/entries/actualism/⟩.

20. Menzel, "Problems for New Actualism," supplement to "Actualism" in *The Stanford Encyclopedia of Philosophy*.

21. Crispin Wright, "Response to Commentators," p. 924 of *Philosophy and Phenomenological Research* 56, no. 4, Book Symposium on *Truth and Objectivity*, pp. 911–941.

22. That is, assertibility undefeated by any new evidence. Wright calls this property "superassertibility," and it is the subject of discussion in sections 7.3.2 and 7.3.3.

23. Of course, not every version of ethical naturalism entails that t is deducible from natural facts.

24. Crispin Wright, "Truth in Ethics," *Ratio* 8, no. 3, 1995, pp. 209–218, here p. 218.

25. Wright, *Truth and Objectivity*, Cambridge, Mass.: Harvard University Press, 1992, p. 48. For evidence of his view that superassertibility is a generalization of provabililty, witness "... it would be forgiveable to suppose that there is no worthwhile generalization ... of provability in mathematics. Forgiveable but, I think, wrong"; and "Interpreting the orthodox recursions for the other connectives in terms of superassertibility poses no special problems. Each connective takes on a content which is a natural generalization of its sense in intuitionistic mathematics." Both quotes can be found in Wright's essay "Can a Davidsonian Meaning-Theory Be Constructed in Terms of Assertibility?" in his *Realism, Meaning, and Truth*, New York: Blackwell, 1986.

26. This formulation comes from Jim Edwards's "Is Tennant Selling Truth Short?" *Analysis* 57, no. 2, 1997, pp. 152–158.

27. Cf. the following quotation from pp. 298–299 of "Can a Davidsonian Meaning-theory Be Construed in Terms of Assertibility?" where Wright is dis-

cussing a body of beliefs $\{B_1,\ldots,B_n\}$, each element of which is warranted as an item of knowledge, which survives arbitrarily close and extensive investigation: "More specifically, 'P' is superassertible just in case the world will, in sufficiently favourable circumstances, permit the generation in an investigating subject S of a set of beliefs, $\{B_1,\ldots,B_n\}$ (such that) ... The case provided by $\{B_1,\ldots,B_n\}$ for 'P' is not, in fact, defeasible; i.e. no $\{B_1,\ldots,B_n,\ldots B_z\}$ containing $\{B_1,\ldots,B_n\}$ ... yet failing to warrant 'P,' can be achieved in this world, no matter how favourable the circumstances for the attempt."

28. Cf. Wright's discussion in "Can a Davidsonian Meaning-theory Be Construed in Terms of Assertibility?"

29. Wright, *Truth and Objectivity*, pp. 48–70.

30. Ibid., pp. 48–70.

31. See Wright, "Can a Davidsonian Meaning-theory Be Construed in Terms of Assertibility?" p. 294.

32. It is puzzling that Wright thinks that his assertibility theorist *ought* to accept that "... both 'Not P' and 'Not Not P' are assertible in a neutral state of information" on pain of lacking any means of expressing such neutrality. Even without a superassertibility predicate, surely the natural expression of neutrality is just $\neg W \neg P \& \neg W \neg \neg P$. Wright's formulation suggests it should rather be $W \neg P \& W \neg \neg P$.

33. The proof makes use of the Heyting definition of "&" and "$\neg$." For the latter, this holds that $\nabla \neg \Theta \leftrightarrow \nabla \neg \nabla \Theta$.

34. This is a medical fact, not a metaphysical one. Metaphysical facts enter into the picture only when one is deluded into thinking these medical facts have no bearing on the case at hand. Any good metaphysician can treat such delusions.

35. Note that Wright cannot follow Dummett's (in my view) dubious lead in denying determinacy of truth value to j given that he is trying to formulate a notion of truth acceptable to both realists and antirealists. The claim that j is indeterminate in truth value is wholly *unacceptable* to realists.

36. Chapter 30 of *Logic, Logic, and Logic*, Cambridge, Mass.: Harvard University Press, 1998.

37. *Anti-Realism and Logic*, Clarendon Press, Oxford, 1997, pp. 205–206.

38. The italicized statement is a principle that *no one*, whether "realist" or "antirealist," should contest. So how do we obtain a distinctive antirealist reading? The argument to be advanced here is that we can't. "Assertibility condition semantics" tacitly presupposes a truth-conditional semantics.

39. Dummett, "The Philosophical Significance of Gödel's Theorem," in *Truth and Other Enigmas*, p. 200.

Chapter 8

1. Rorty, "Response to Hilary Putnam," in *Rorty and His Critics*, Robert Brandom (ed.), Oxford: Blackwell, 2001, p. 89.

2. Alston, *A Realist Conception of Truth*, p. 147.

3. Ibid., p. 148.

4. Ibid.

5. Lewis, "Putnam's Paradox," p. 236.

6. Richard Rorty, *Consequences of Pragmatism*, Minneapolis, Minn.: University of Minnesota Press, 1982, pp. 165–166.

7. Ibid., pp. 162–163.

8. Putnam, "Objectivity and the Science/Ethics Distinction," chapter 11 in *Realism with a Human Face*, Cambridge, Mass.: Harvard University Press, 1990, here pp. 172–173.

9. I am indebted to my colleague Arcady Blinov for making me aware of this phenomenon and for help in formulating the example in the text.

10. It must be admitted, though, that Kripke's Wittgenstein is in no small part responsible for some of this confusion concerning facts and "Factualism."

11. Scott Soames, "Facts, Truth Conditions, and the Skeptical Solution to the Rule-Following Paradox," *Philosophical Perspectives* 12: *Language, Mind, and Ontology*, 1998, pp. 313–348.

12. Saul Kripke, *Wittgenstein on Rules and Private Language: An Elementary Exposition*, Oxford: Blackwell, 1982, p. 69.

13. I think the term "nonfactualist" (or "noncognitivist") is both overworked and poorly understood. I shall later explain why I think it cannot do the work that philosophers have tried to use it for.

14. Soames, "Facts, Truth Conditions, and the Skeptical Solution to the Rule-Following Paradox."

15. Ibid., p. 341.

16. Hartry Field, "Some Thoughts on Radical Indeterminacy," *Monist* 81, no. 2, 1998, pp. 253–273.

17. "Metaphysically skeptical" in that the skepticism is not of the usual epistemic sort. KW allows our cognitive powers to be godlike for the purposes of discovering the elusive fact which determines what I ought to say now in response to "$68 + 57$?" KW's claim is that even given omniscience about my past actions and intentions, no fact establishing that I meant Addition rather than

Quaddition by "+" can be uncovered. Hence, there can *be* no fact. See Kripke, *Wittgenstein on Rules*, p. 21.

18. Alex Byrne, "On Misinterpreting Kripke's Wittgenstein," *Philosophy and Phenomenological Research* 56, no. 2, 1996, pp. 339–343, here p. 341.

19. Ibid., pp. 341–342.

20. Ibid., p. 343n14.

21. Field, "Some Thoughts on Radical Indeterminacy," p. 254.

22. Ibid., p. 253.

23. Hartry Field, "Mental Representation," *Erkenntnis* 13, 1978, pp. 9–61.

24. Field, "Some Thoughts on Radical Indeterminacy," pp. 253–273.

25. Ibid.

26. Crispin Wright, "Kripke's Account of the Argument against Private Language," *Journal of Philosophy* 81, no. 12, 1984, pp. 759–778.

27. Here I appropriate Kripke's own words in response to KW's conclusion, viz.: "Has not the incredible and self-defeating conclusion that all language is meaningless already been drawn?" *Wittgenstein on Rules*, p. 71. Wright seems to misunderstand the dialectic here in the aforementioned article. This is Kripke speaking, not KW. If it were an attempt to "formulate the conclusion of the sceptical argument," as Wright claims (p. 767), then it would be apposite to note that "If you wish to reject the suitability of a given set of concepts to figure in statements apt to be genuinely true or false, this rejection cannot take the form of a denial of statements in which those concepts figure."

28. Wright, "Kripke's Account," p. 768.

29. Kripke does seem to shift around on this question in a way that lends some plausibility to Soames's view that there is no single coherent interpretation of the skeptical solution. Witness: "... we are not looking for necessary and sufficient conditions (truth-conditions) for following a rule, or an analysis of what such rule-following 'consists in.' Indeed such conditions would constitute a 'straight' solution to the sceptical problem and have been rejected." Kripke, *Wittgenstein on Rules*, p. 87. This doesn't seem to definitively rule out the possibility that there are such necessary and sufficient conditions. One can reject the truth-conditional model of meaning without denying that there are any truth conditions at all.

30. Ibid., pp. 70–71.

31. Ibid., p. 73.

32. Ibid., pp. 77–78. Kripke realizes the awkwardness for KW's position occasioned by the denial of the factuality of meaning, for he later writes: "the picture

of correspondence-to-facts must be cleared away before we can begin with the sceptical problem." Indeed it must.

33. Witness his claim on pp. 86–87: "Following Wittgenstein's exhortation not to think but look, we will not reason apriori about the role such statements ought to play; rather we will find out what circumstances *actually* license such assertions and what role this licence *actually* plays."

34. Ibid., p. 92.

35. Ibid.

36. Naturally, C* members might judge that Jones means sqwore by "square" where x is sqwore iff it is square if observed at any time up until but excluding the present and red and wooden if observed now and henceforth. But, to transpose a remark of Michael Dummett's, if C* members react to our evaluations of Jones's use of "square" with: "Here we have a hitherto unknown kind of madness," we can go away content in the knowledge that we have our own criteria of insanity too.

37. Kripke, *Wittgenstein on Rules*, p. 111. It is in the context of this remark that Kripke claims that KW has no theory of truth conditions.

38. Ibid., p. 146, n. 87.

39. *Philosophical Investigations*, §241. Cf. §242: "If language is to be a means of communication, there must be agreement not only in definitions, but also (queer as this may sound) in judgment."

40. Kripke, *Wittgenstein on Rules*, p. 96.

41. Frank Jackson, "Review of Hurley, S. L., *Natural Reasons: Personality and Polity*," *Australian Journal of Philosophy* 70, no. 4, 1992, pp. 475–488.

42. I am indebted to Michaelis Michael here.

43. This is to put the point in terms made familiar from Kripke's discussion of Wittgenstein's rule-following paradox in his *Wittgenstein on Rules*.

44. I put the point in terms of universes of worlds since it is normally assumed that if moral values exist at all at any world then they exist at all worlds. The Pyrrhonians are thus in doubt as to which moral universe they inhabit—one wherein moral values are real, or one wherein they are fictions.

45. This example was suggested to me by Andre Gallois. Phenomenalists classically sought to reduce physical objects to sensory arrays, not eliminate them in favour of them. However, eliminativist versions of phenomenalism are indeed possible—some of Berkeley's arguments against the folk notion of enduring physical objects can be interpreted as arguments from queerness.

46. See Jackson's John Locke lectures, *From Metaphysics to Ethics: A Defence of Conceptual Analysis*, Oxford: Clarendon Press, 1998.

47. Jackson insists in his *From Metaphysics to Ethics* that Kripke did *not* explicate a new kind of necessity over and above conceptual necessity.

48. I am indebted to conversations with Michaelis Michael, Arcady Blinov, Tony Lynch, and Peter Forrest.

49. Horwich, *Truth,* Oxford: Oxford University Press, 1990, p. 124.

50. Donald Davidson, *Inquiries into Truth and Interpretation,* p. 194.

51. Richard Rorty, *Consequences of Pragmatism,* pp. 165–166.

52. Stephen Yablo, "How in the World?" *Philosophical Topics* 24, no. 1, 1996, pp. 255–286.

53. Ibid., pp. 255–256.

54. Fred Kroon, "Truthmaking and Fiction," *Logique et Analyse* 169/170, special issue on truthmakers, Drew Khlentzos and Peter Forrest (eds.), 2000, pp. 32–47.

55. For a recent sample see the articles in *Logique et Analyse* (2000), issue on Truthmakers.

56. Stephen Read, "Truthmakers and the Disjunction Thesis," *Mind* 109, no. 433, 2000, pp. 67–79.

57. For this strategy to succeed, the TM theorist must first show *how* (χ) is pathological and then more significantly *why* its pathological nature should invalidate the use of (TA) at line (8) above—why the (contrary to fact) hypothesis that (χ) is true should invalidate the conclusion that it has a truthmaker. Neither task is trivial but the latter is the more urgent: Even if, as is being mooted, (χ) is pathological it is hardly *obvious* that the claim at line (7) above that (χ) is true is *also* pathological. Why is this claim not simply false? Why is it then not a straightforward logical consequence of this (false) claim that (χ) has a truthmaker, as prescribed by TM theory?

58. There are in addition the related problems of entailment-defeaters, entanglement of truthmakers, and unintended truthmakers, discussed by John Heil, Peter Forrest, and Fred Kroon respectively in *Logique et Analyse* (2000) edition.

59. There are three cases for the moderate theorist to consider:

(a) t_1 and t_2 are both true. This they cannot be unless both lack truthmakers, as each token must be grounded by at least one sentence that lacks a truthmaker (and neither inscription can ground itself). Suppose this is so. Then t_1 makes t_2 true because it lacks a truthmaker and t_2 makes t_1 true because it lacks a truthmaker. So both t_1 and t_2 have truthmakers after all. Thus t_1 and t_2 cannot both be true.

(b) t_1 and t_2 are both false. This means that both have truthmakers. But then by (FC), both are true not false. Thus t_1 and t_2 cannot both be false.

(c) t_1 and t_2 are both pathological. But then both lack truthmakers. So then t_1 makes t_2 true and t_2 makes t_1 true. This means t_1 and t_2 are both true. Thus t_1 and t_2 cannot both be pathological.

60. This is, of course, injudicious as it stands. The requisite notion of provability for Gödel's result is provability within a formal system—one, that is, for which the vague intuitive notion of "provability" has been replaced by a clearly defined one. The difference is dramatic. The sentence "This sentence is not provable" is, arguably, either paradoxical or else semantically ill defined to the extent that it uses an unrestricted notion of proof, whereas Gödel's sentence "This sentence is unprovable within system S" is (provably) true. But the point is that the well-defined notion of provability within a system *does* specify an appropriate truthmaker for the Gödel sentence. So we can make sense of a sentence that says of itself that it has no truthmaker. Not only that, we can come to know that it is true.

61. Horwich, *Truth*, p. 124.

62. Using "penguin" to refer to penguins is not an aspect of use a minimalist or deflationist can avail himself of—especially so if reference is to likewise be deflated.

63. Hartry Field, "Deflationary Theories of Meaning and Content," *Mind* 103, 1994, pp. 249–285, here p. 273.

64. Stephen Read, "The Slingshot Argument," *Logique et Analyse* 143/144, 1993, pp. 195–218.

65. This is not to say that truthmaker theory cannot be developed into a theory of truth. A theory of truth could be developed in which p's being true consisted in its *having some truthmaker or other* (by analogy with functionalist approaches to the reduction of mind). Then my left ear would be an occupier of the functional role "being a truthmaker for '2 + 2 = 4.'" A promising theory of truth? I don't think so. On any believable TM theory, the existence of a mathematical proof will be a truthmaker for the sentence it proves. So take our old friend f, $2 + 2 = 5$. We have a truthmaker for $\neg f$ in the form of its proof. So $Tr(\neg f)$. But on this functionalist TM theory, the claim that $\neg Tr(f)$, entailed by $Tr(\neg f)$, amounts to the assertion that there is no truthmaker for f. Hence, as proofs are truthmakers, by proving $\neg f$ we have just proved there is no proof of f, Gödel au contraire. This raises a more general worry about TM theory. Suppose you show that some claim $\emptyset$ is true by producing a truthmaker for it. How do you know that the world does not harbor some truthmaker for $\neg\emptyset$ also? Something like an assumption about the consistency of the world seems required to connect up the entailments between truthmakers and truthbearers with the notion of truth.

66. By way of contrast, to repeat, (λ) is simply a more general version of the Gödel sentence that says of itself that there is no proof that makes it true. This latter is patently *not* a semantically anomalous claim.

67. Here I mean only to express a view about the source of (this type of) semantic pathology. My remarks are not put forward as any sort of solution to the paradoxes.

68. The use of the rule ($\rightarrow$I) in the above derivation is inessential. It can be replaced by the *Rule of Absorption*: From $\theta \rightarrow (\theta \rightarrow \psi)$ infer $\theta \rightarrow \psi$. A shorter derivation is, then:

(1) $T(\chi) \rightarrow \chi$ Tr. Identity.
(2) $T(\chi) \rightarrow (T(\chi) \rightarrow \pi)$ 1 Df χ.
(3) $T(\chi) \rightarrow \pi$ 2 Absorption.
(4) χ 3 Df χ.
(5) $T(\chi)$ 4 Tr. I.
(6) π 3, 5 $\rightarrow$ E.

Thus any logic licensing *absorption* and *modus ponens* for a language in which the identity properties of truth hold will be unsound in the presence of pathological sentences such as χ. Restrictions on either *absorption* or *modus ponens* lack any compelling philosophical justification, in my view. Not so a restriction on the introduction rule for "true": infer $T(\theta)$ from θ.

69. Keith Simmons, "Introduction," in *Truth*, Oxford Readings in Philosophy, S. Blackburn and K. Simmons (eds.), Oxford: Oxford University Press, 2000, pp. 23–24.

70. Hartry Field, "Postscript: Deflationism," in his *Truth and the Absence of Fact*, Oxford: Clarendon Press, 2001, pp. 145–146.

71. Ibid., p. 146.

72. Ibid.

73. Simmons, "Introduction," p. 26.

References

Alston, W. *A Realist Conception of Truth.* Ithaca, N.Y.: Cornell University Press, 1996.

Belnap, N. "Tonk, Plonk, and Plink." *Analysis* 23 (1962): 130–139. Reprinted in *Contemporary Philosophical Logic*, I. Copi and J. A. Gould (eds.), pp. 44–48. New York: St. Martin's Press, 1978.

Benacerraf, P. "Skolem and the Skeptic." *Proceedings of the Aristotelian Society,* supplementary vol. 59 (1985): 85–115.

Benacerraf, P., and Putnam, H. (eds.). *Philosophy of Mathematics,* second edition. Cambridge: Cambridge University Press, 1983.

Bernays, P. "Platonism in Mathematics." In *Philosophy of Mathematics,* second edition, P. Benacerraf and H. Putnam (eds.), pp. 258–271. Cambridge: Cambridge University Press, 1983.

Bishop, E., and Bridges, D. *Constructive Analysis.* New York: Springer-Verlag, 1985.

Blackburn, S. *Spreading the Word.* Oxford: Oxford University Press, 1984.

Blackburn, S., and Simmons, K. (eds.). *Truth.* Oxford: Oxford University Press, 2000.

Boghossian, P. "The Rule-Following Considerations." *Mind* 98 (1989): 507–549.

Boolos, G. "On Second Order Logic." *Journal of Philosophy* 72 (1975): 509–527.

——. *Logic, Logic, and Logic.* Cambridge, Mass.: Harvard University Press, 1999.

—— (ed.). *Meaning and Method: Essays in Honor of Hilary Putnam.* Cambridge: Cambridge University Press, 1990.

Boolos, G., and Jeffrey, R. *Computability and Logic,* third edition. Cambridge: Cambridge University Press, 1989.

Brandom, R. "Truth and Assertibility." *Journal of Philosophy* 73 (1976): 137–149.

Brogard, B., and Salerno, J. "Clues to the Paradox of Knowability: Replies to Dummett and Tennant." *Analysis* 62, no. 2 (2002): 143–151.

Brandom, R. (ed.). *Rorty and His Critics.* Oxford: Blackwell, 2000.

Brueckner. "If I'm a Brain in a Vat Then I'm Not a Brain in a Vat." *Mind* 101, no. 401 (1992): 123–128.

Byrne, A. "On Misinterpreting Kripke's Wittgenstein." *Philosophy and Phenomenological Research* 56, no. 2 (1996): 339–343.

Carnap, Rudolf. *Logical Structure of the World.* Berkeley, Calif.: University of California Press, 1983 (reprint).

Churchland, P. *Scientific Realism and the Plasticity of Mind.* Cambridge: Cambridge University Press, 1979.

Clark, P., and Hale, R. (eds.). *Reading Putnam.* Oxford: Blackwell, 1994.

Copi, I., and Gould, J. A. (eds.). *Contemporary Philosophical Logic.* New York: St. Martin's Press, 1978.

Corcoran, J. "Categoricity." *History and Philosophy of Logic* 1 (1980): 187–207.

Cortens, A. *Global Anti-Realism: A Metaphilosophical Inquiry.* Boulder, Colo.: Westview, 2000.

Davidson, D. *Inquiries into Truth and Interpretation.* Oxford: Oxford University Press, 1984.

———. "Replies to Essays X–XXI." In *Essays on Davidson: Actions and Events*, M. Hintikka and B. Vermazen (eds.). Oxford: Oxford University Press, 1985.

———. "A Coherence Theory of Truth and Knowledge." In *Truth and Interpretation: Perspectives on the Philosophy of Donald Davidson*, E. Lepore (ed.), pp. 433–446. Oxford: Blackwell, 1986.

———. "A Nice Derangement of Epitaphs." In *Philosophical Grounds of Rationality: Intentions, Categories, Ends*, R. Grandy and R. Warner (eds.), pp. 157–174. Oxford: Clarendon Press, 1986.

———. "The Structure and Content of Truth." *Journal of Philosophy* 88 (1990): 279–328.

Dennett, D. *Consciousness Explained.* Boston: Little, Brown, 1991.

Devitt, M. *Coming to Our Senses: A Naturalistic Program for Semantic Localism.* Cambridge: Cambridge University Press, 1996.

Devitt, M. *Realism and Truth*, second edition. Oxford: Blackwell, 1991.

———. "Review of *Reason, Truth, and History*." *Philosophical Review* 93 (1984): 277.

Dummett, M. A. E. "Wittgenstein's Philosophy of Mathematics." 1959. Reprinted in his *Truth and Other Enigmas*, pp. 186–201. London: Duckworth, 1978.

———. "Realism." 1963. Reprinted in his *Truth and Other Enigmas*, pp. 145–165. London: Duckworth, 1963.

———. "The Philosophical Significance of Gödel's Theorem." 1963. Reprinted in his *Truth and Other Enigmas*, pp. 186–201. London: Duckworth, 1978.

———. "Bringing about the Past." 1964. Reprinted his *Truth and Other Enigmas*, pp. 333–350. London: Duckworth, 1978.

———. *Frege: Philosophy of Language*. London: Duckworth, 1973.

———. "The Justification of Deduction." 1973. Reprinted his *Truth and Other Enigmas*, pp. 290–318. London: Duckworth, 1978.

———. "The Philosophical Basis of Intuitionistic Logic." 1973. Reprinted in his *Truth and Other Enigmas*, pp. 215–247. London: Duckworth, 1978.

———. "What Is a Theory of Meaning? (II)." In *Truth and Meaning*, G. Evans and J. McDowell (eds.). Oxford: Oxford University Press, 1976.

———. "What Is a Theory of Meaning?" In *Mind and Language*, S. Guttenplan (ed.). Oxford: Oxford University Press, 1977.

———. *Elements of Intuitionism*. Oxford: Clarendon, 1977.

———. *Truth and Other Enigmas*. London: Duckworth, 1978.

———. "Objections to Chomsky." *London Review of Books* (September 1981): 5–6.

———. *Frege and Other Philosophers*. Oxford: Clarendon, 1991.

———. *The Logical Basis of Metaphysics*. London: Duckworth, 1991.

———. *The Seas of Language*. Oxford: Clarendon, 1993.

———. *Origins of Analytic Philosophy*. Cambridge, Mass.: Harvard University Press, 1994.

———. "Victor's Error." *Analysis* 62, no. 2 (2002): 1–2.

Edwards, J. "Is Tennant Selling Truth Short?" *Analysis* 57, no. 2 (1997): 152–158.

Elgin, C. Z. "Unnatural Science." *Journal of Philosophy* 92, no. 6 (1995): 298–302.

Etchemendy, J. *The Concept of Logical Consequence*. Cambridge, Mass: Harvard University Press, 1990.

Evans, G. *The Varieties of Reference*. Oxford: Oxford University Press, 1983.

Evans, G., and McDowell, J. (eds.). *Truth and Meaning.* Oxford: Clarendon, 1976.

Field, H. "Mental Representation." *Erkenntnis* 13 (1978): 9–61.

———. "Physicalism." In *Inference, Explanations, and Other Frustrations: Essays In the Philosophy of Science*, J. Earman (ed.). Berkeley, Calif.: University of California Press, 1992.

———. "Deflationary Theories of Meaning and Content." *Mind* 103 (1994): 249–285.

———. "Some Thoughts on Radical Indeterminacy." *Monist* 81, no. 2 (1998): 253–273.

———. *Truth and the Absence of Fact.* Oxford: Clarendon, 2001.

Fodor, J. "Review of McDowell's *Mind and World.*" Chapter 1 of *In Critical Condition: Polemical Essays on Cognitive Science and the Philosophy of Mind*, Cambridge, Mass.: MIT Press/Bradford Books, 1999.

Fodor, J., and E. Lepore, *Holism: A Shopper's Guide.* Oxford: Blackwell, 1994.

Frege, G. *The Foundations of Arithmetic.* J. L. Austin (trans.). Oxford: Basil Blackwell, 1950.

———. *Posthumous Writings.* Oxford: Blackwell, 1979.

Friedman, M. "Exorcising the Philosophical Tradition: Comments on John McDowell's *Mind and World.*" *Philosophical Review* 105, no. 4 (1996): 427–467.

Gabbay, D., and Guenthner, F. (eds.). *Handbook of Philosophical Logic*, vol. III. Dordrecht: Reidel, 1987.

George, A. (ed.). *Reflections on Chomsky.* Oxford: Blackwell, 1989.

Gödel, K. *Collected Works*, vol. I. S. Feferman and J. Dawson (eds.). Oxford: Oxford University Press, 1993.

Haldane, J., and Wright, C. (eds.). *Reality, Representation, and Projection.* Oxford: Oxford University Press, 1993.

Hand. "Radical Antirealism and Neutral States of Information," *Philosophical Topics*, 24, no. 1 (1996): 35–51.

Hellman, G. "Never Say 'Never'! On the Communication Problem between Intuitionism and Classicism." *Philosophical Topics* 17, no. 2 (1989): 47–67.

———. "The Boxer and His Fists: The Constructivist in the Arena of Quantum Physics." *Proceedings of the Aristotelian Society*, supplementary vol. 66 (1992): 61–77.

Heyting, A. *Intuitionism*, third edition. Amsterdam: North-Holland, 1971.

Horwich, P. *Truth.* Oxford: Oxford University Press, 1990.

———. *Meaning*. Oxford: Clarendon, 1999.

Hossack, K. "Constructive Mathematics, Quantum Physics, and Quantifiers (II)." *Proceedings of the Aristotelian Society*, supplementary vol. 66 (1992): 79–97.

Jackson, F. *From Metaphysics to Ethics: A Defence of Conceptual Analysis*, Oxford: Clarendon Press, 1998.

———. "Review of Hurley, S. L., *Natural Reasons: Personality and Polity*." *Australian Journal of Philosophy* 70, no. 4 (1992): 475–488.

Khlentzos, D. "Anti-Realism under Mind?" *Dialectica* 43, no. 4 (1989): 315–328.

———. "On Putting the Semantic Cart before the Metaphysical Horse: A Realistic Appraisal of Anti-Realist Semantics." *Australasian Journal of Philosophy* 70, no. 3 (1991): 415–437.

———. "Semantic Challenges to Realism." In *The Stanford Encyclopedia of Philosophy*, E. Zalta (ed.). 2001. ⟨http://plato.Stanford.edu/entries/realism/⟩.

Koslow, A. *A Structuralist Theory of Logic*. Cambridge: Cambridge University Press, 1992.

Kripke, S. *Wittgenstein on Rules and Private Language*. Oxford: Oxford University Press, 1982.

Kroon, F. "Truthmaking and Fiction." *Logique et Analyse* (special issue, *Truth Maker and Its Variants*, P. Forrest and D. Khlentzos, eds.) 43, nos. 169–170 (2000): 195–210.

Lavine, S. *Understanding the Infinite*. Cambridge, Mass.: Harvard University Press, 1994.

Leeds. "Brains in Vats Revisited." *Pacific Philosophical Quarterly* 77, no. 2 (1996): 108–131.

Lewis, D. *Convention: A Philosophical Study*. Cambridge, Mass.: Harvard University Press, 1969.

———. "Putnam's Paradox." *Australasian Journal of Philosophy* 62 (1984): 221–236.

Lynch, M. *Truth in Context*. Cambridge, Mass.: MIT Press/A Bradford Book, 2001.

McCarty, C. "Intuitionism: An Introduction to a Seminar." *Journal of Philosophical Logic*, 12 (1983): 105–149.

McDowell, J. "On the Sense and Reference of a Proper Name." In *Reference, Truth, and Reality: Essays on the Philosophy of Language*, M. Platts (ed.), pp. 141–146. London: Routledge and Kegan Paul, 1980.

———. *Mind and World*. Cambridge, Mass.: Harvard University Press, 1994.

McGee, V. "Review of Arnold Koslow's *A Structuralist Theory of Logic*." *Journal of Philosophy* 90, no. 5 (1993): 271–274.

McGinn, C. "Truth and Use." In *Reference, Truth, and Reality*, M. Platts (ed.). London: Routledge and Kegan Paul, 1980.

Menzel, C. "Actualism." In *The Stanford Encyclopedia of Philosophy*, E. Zalta (ed.). 2001. ⟨http://plato.Stanford.edu/entries/actualism⟩.

Mormann, T. "Incompatible Empirically Equivalent Theories—A Structural Explication." *Synthese* 103 (1995): 203–249.

Nozick, R. *The Nature of Rationality*. Princeton, N.J.: Princeton University Press, 1994.

Peacocke, C. "Proof and Truth." In *Reflections on Chomsky*, A. George (ed.), pp. 165–190. Oxford: Blackwell, 1989.

Pinker, S. *The Language Instinct: How the Mind Creates Language*. New York: Harper Collins, 1994.

Prawitz, D. "Ideas and Results in Proof Theory." In *Proceedings of the Second Scandinavian Logic Symposium*, J.-E. Fenstad (ed.), pp. 235–308. Amsterdam: North Holland, 1971.

———. "Philosophical Aspects of Proof Theory." In *Contemporary Philosophy: A New Survey*, vol. 1, G. Floistad (ed.), pp. 235–277. The Hague: Martinus Nijhoff, 1981.

———. "Towards a Foundation of a General Proof Theory." In *Logic, Methodology, and Philosophy of Science IV*, P. Suppes et al. (eds.), pp. 225–250. Amsterdam: North Holland, 1973.

———. "Meaning and Proofs: On the Conflict between Classical and Intuitionistic Logic." *Theoria* 48 (1977): 2–40.

———. "Proofs and the Meaning and Completeness of the Logical Constants." In *Essays on Mathematical and Philosophical Logic*, J. Hintikka, I. Niiniluoto, and E. Saarinen (eds.). Dordrecht: D. Reidel, 1978.

———. "Remarks on Some Approaches to the Concept of Logical Consequence." *Synthese* 62 (1985): 153–171.

Prior, A. "Conjunction and Contonktion Revisited." In *Contemporary Philosophical Logic*, I. Copi and J. A. Gould (eds.), pp. 49–53. New York: St. Martin's Press, 1978.

———. "The Runabout Inference Ticket." In *Contemporary Philosophical Logic*, I. Copi and J. A. Gould (eds.), pp. 44–48. New York: St. Martin's Press, 1978.

Putnam, H. *Philosophy of Logic*. London: Allen and Unwin, 1972.

———. *Mind, Language, and Reality*. Cambridge: Cambridge University Press, 1975.

———. *Meaning and the Moral Sciences*. New York: Routledge, 1978.

———. *Mathematics, Matter, and Method*. Cambridge: Cambridge University Press, 1979.

———. "Models and Reality." *Journal of Symbolic Logic* 45 (1980): 464–482.

———. *Reason, Truth, and History*. Cambridge: Cambridge University Press, 1981.

———. *Realism and Reason*. Cambridge: Cambridge University Press, 1983.

———. *The Many Faces of Realism*. LaSalle, Ill.: Open Court, 1987.

———. *Representation and Reality*. Cambridge, Mass.: MIT Press, 1988.

———. *Realism with a Human Face*. Cambridge, Mass.: Harvard University Press, 1990.

———. *Renewing Philosophy*. Cambridge, Mass.: Harvard University Press, 1992.

———. "Reply to Miller." *Philosophical Topics* 20: *The Philosophy of Hilary Putnam* (C. Hill, issue ed.), no. 1 (1992).

———. "The Quality of Life and the Science/Ethics Distinction." In *The Quality of Life*, M. Nussbaum and A. Sen (eds.). Oxford: Clarendon, 1993.

———. *Words and Life*. Cambridge, Mass.: Harvard University Press, 1994.

Quine, W. V. O. *Word and Object*. Cambridge, Mass.: MIT Press, 1964.

———. "Epistemology Naturalised." In his *Ontological Relativity and Other Essays*, pp. 69–90. New York: Columbia University Press, 1969.

———. "Ontological Relativity." In his *Ontological Relativity and Other Essays*, New York: Columbia University Press, 1969.

———. *Methods of Logic*, third edition. New York: Holt, Rinehart and Winston, 1972.

———. *The Roots of Reference*. La Salle: Open Court, 1974.

———. "The Nature of Natural Knowledge." In *Mind and Language*, S. Guttenplan (ed.), pp. 67–81. Oxford: Clarendon, 1975.

———. "Replies." In *Words and Objections: Essays on the Work of W. V. Quine*, Synthese Library vol. 21, D. Davidson and J. Hintikka (eds.). Dodrecht: D. Reidel, 1975.

———. "Facts of the Matter." In *American Philosophy from Edwards to Quine*, R. W. Shahan and K. R. Merrill (eds.), pp. 176–196. Norman: University of Okalahoma Press, 1977.

Read, S. "The Slingshot Argument." *Logique et Analyse* 143/144 (1993): 195–218.

———. "Truthmakers and the Disjunction Thesis." *Mind* 109, no. 433 (2000): 67–79.

Resnick, M. D. "You Can't Trust an Ideal Theory to Tell the Truth." *Philosophical Studies* 52 (1987): 151–160.

Rorty, R. *Consequences of Pragmatism.* Minneapolis, Minn.: University of Minnesota Press, 1982.

Scott, D., G. Forbes, M. Davies, G. Sundholm, and D. Isaacson. *Oxford Notes towards the Formalization of Logic, Parts III & IV.* Oxford, 1983. Unpublished.

Shapiro, S. *Foundations without Foundationalism.* Oxford: Clarendon, 1991.

Soames, S. "Facts, Truth Conditions, and the Skeptical Solution to the Rule-Following Paradox." *Philosophical Perspectives* 12: *Language, Mind, and Ontology* (1998): 313–348.

Sosa, E. "Putnam's Pragmatic Realism." *Journal of Philosophy* 90 (1993): 606–626.

Strawson, "Scruton and Wright on Anti-Realism etc." *Proceedings of the Aristotelian Society* 77 (1976–1977): 15–21.

Szabo, M. E. (trans. and ed.). *Collected Papers of Gentzen.* Amsterdam: North Holland, 1969.

Taylor, B. "Just More Theory?" *Australasian Journal of Philosophy* 69, no. 2 (1991): 152–166.

Tennant, N. *Anti-Realism and Logic.* Oxford: Clarendon, 1987.

———. *The Taming of the True.* Oxford: Clarendon, 1997.

———. "Victor Vanquished." *Analysis* 62, no. 2 (2002): 135–142.

van Cleve, J. "Semantic Supervenience and Referential Indeterminacy." *Journal of Philosophy* 89 (1992): 341–361.

von Wright, G. H. (ed.). *Logic and Philosophy.* The Hague: Martinus Nijhoff, 1980.

Wagner, S. "The Rationalist Conception of Logic." *Notre Dame Journal of Formal Logic* 28 (1987): 3–35.

Wagner. "Why Realism Can't Be Naturalized." In *Naturalism: A Critical Appraisal,* S. J. Wagner and R. Warner (eds.). Notre Dame: University of Notre Dame Press, 1993.

Weinberg, S. *Dreams of a Final Theory.* New York: Vintage, 1993.

Williamson, T. "Intuitionism Disproved?" *Analysis* 42, no. 4 (1982): 203–208.

———. *Blindspots.* Oxford: Clarendon, 1988.

Wittgenstein, L. *Tractatus Logico-Philosophicus*. New York: Harcourt, Brace, 1922.

———. *Philosophical Investigations*. Oxford: Blackwell, 1958.

Wright, C. "About 'The Philosophical Significance of Gödel's Theorem': Some Issues." In *The Philosophy of Michael Dummett*, Synthese Library vol. 239, B. McGuiness and G. Oliveri (eds.), pp. 167–204. Dordrecht: Kluwer, 1994.

Wright, C. "Truth Conditions and Criteria." *Proceedings of the Aristotelian Society*, supplementary vol. 50 (1976): 224.

———. *Realism, Meaning, and Truth*, second edition. Oxford: Blackwell, 1993.

———. *Truth and Objectivity*. Cambridge, Mass.: Harvard University Press, 1994.

———. "Truth as Sort of Epistemic: Putnam's Peregrinations." *Journal of Philosophy* 97, no. 6 (2000): 335–364.

Yablo, S. "How in the World?" *Philosophical Topics* 24, no. 1 (1996): 255–286.

Index

Alston, W.
  and correspondence theories of truth, 38–40
  on Dummett's antirealism, 35–38, 40–42
  and minimalist correspondence theories of truth, 38–39
  on Putnam's model-theoretic argument, 283–285
  on realist–antirealist debate, 18
  on the representation problem, 283–286
Analytic functionalism, 321–331
  and a priori deducibility, 321
  and metaethical Pyrrhonism, 324–331
  and morals, 323–324
  and naturalistic realism, 321–322
Anderson, D., 190
Antirealism, 274, 276, 295
  Alston on, 35–38
  antirealist challenge to metaphysical realism, 4–5, 15, 62
  characterization of, 62–63
  and compositionality, 48
  Davidson and Rorty on, 17–18
  Devitt on, 30–35, 190
  Dummett's characterization of, 13–15, 62
  Lewis on, 286–287
  and the manifestation constraint, 56–57
  misunderstandings of its nature, 25–43
  and problem of other minds, 98–104
  and proof theory, 144–157
  and undecidability, 58–61
Aristotle, 36, 37
Armstrong, D., 338
Assertibility, 26–29, 119, 120–121, 154–155, 162, 173, 184. *See also* Superassertibility
  conditions for, 60, 73, 84, 145, 146, 153, 173, 184, 247, 315, 316, 319, 320
  intuitionistic, 119, 120–123, 141
  recursive definition of, 138–139
  and *tertium non datur*, 79–80
  and truth, 26–28, 61, 75–87, 119, 181, 315, 319, 320
Assertion
  characterization of, 77–79
  Dummett on, 75–77

Belnap, N., 156, 167
Belnap–Prior debate, 149–150, 156, 158–159
Blackburn, S., 216, 217
Boyd, R., 193
Brains in a vat hypothesis, 15, 24, 196–206
  Brueckner's formulation of Putnam's argument, 199–200
  Putnam on, 196–206
Brandom, R., 23, 83
  and pragmatism, 287
  on truth and assertibility, 83
Brentano, F., 304
Brogaard, B., 176–180
Brouwer, L. E. J., 117, 127

Brueckner, A., on brains in a vat, 199, 200, 202
Byrne, A., 299, 302

Canonical proof, 159–162, 273, 275, 276, 277
 and canonical argument, 164–165
Carnap, R., 212, 217
Chomsky, N., 53, 64, 112, 114, 115
Classical logic, 72, 119, 120, 131, 133, 134, 154–155
 and intuitionistic logic, 119, 120, 131, 133, 134, 154–155
 and truth-conditional semantics, 72, 184
Compositionality, 48
Conceptual relativity, 15, 206–224
Conservative extension, 150
Constructive reasoning, 118–119
Curry's paradox, 339–340, 351

Davidson, D., 17, 31, 34, 50, 53, 55, 78
 on action, 78
 alethic primitivism of, 34, 68, 332–333, 337
 holism of, 88, 91, 93–94
 on radical interpretation, 50, 55, 88, 249
 on realism and antirealism, 42–43
 and the slingshot argument, 349
Dennett, D., 198–199
Denying the doctrine or changing the subject, 140–141
Devitt, M., 18, 26, 30–35, 62, 71, 190
 on antirealism and realism, 30–33, 190
 on Dummett, 31–35
 on Putnam's internal realism, 190
 on Putnam's model-theoretic argument, 232
Dummett, M., 2, 5, 13–24, 31–42, 187, 189, 190, 192, 194, 277, 284, 312, 346
 on assertibility and truth, 75–87, 155
 and bare truths, 68–70
 on Davidson's theory of meaning, 50–51
 on decidability and truth, 58–61
 Elements of Intuitionism, 111–112, 159, 162
 and error-theoretic accounts of realist truth, 75, 85–87, 82–83
 on Fregean internalism and metaphysical realism, 222
 Frege: Philosophy of Language, 51, 75, 83, 91
 on Frege's theory of meaning, 47–50
 on holism, 53, 71–72, 87–88, 90–93, 94–97
 and intuitionism, 59, 60–61, 127–128, 277
 on language acquisition, 6, 145, 146
 Logical Basis of Metaphysics, The, 159, 168, 173, 174–175
 manifestation argument of, 5–6, 61–68
 on metaphysical determinacy and metaphysical realism, 13–15
 proof-theoretic and semantic characterizations of the logical constants, 136–138, 155, 159, 167–175
 on quantifiers, 134–135
 on realism and antirealism, 13–15, 20–23, 255, 256, 258
 on semantic competence, 47–58
 semantic content and truth-conditions, 40–42
 on semantic holism, 90–93, 94, 96–97
 on time and tense, 83–86

Ebbs, G., 190, 191
Einstein, A., 209
Eliminativism, 213
 alethic eliminativism
  and Fitch's Paradox, 175–184
  and intuitionism, 175–184
  and pragmatism, 294
 semantic eliminativism, 296–320
Empirically equivalent descriptions
 logically incompatible, and realism, 206–219
 of points with regions, 209–212
 and relativity theory, 208–209

Etchemendy, J., 157
Euclid's algorithm, 129
Euler's constant, 129, 130
Externalism, 187, 189, 192, 196, 197, 200, 201, 202, 203, 205, 258, 262
  and the God's-eye view of reality, 194
  and internalism, 194, 258, 262

Facts, 38–40, 251
  as contents of judgments, 251
  and correspondence theories of truth, 38–40, 287, 288, 296, 298, 331–351
  and minimalist theories of truth, 38
  as properties of the world, 331–351
  and semantic paradox, 352–354
  as true propositions, 38, 303
  as truthmakers, 40, 287, 288, 289, 296, 300, 301, 305–308, 309–311
Factualism, 296–299, 300, 302, 303, 305–308, 313–320
  and nonfactualism, 296–299, 300, 302, 303, 305–308, 313–320
  and realism, 3, 306
  and truth-aptness, 306, 311–313
Feferman, S., 238
Fermat's last theorem, 147–148
Field, H., 39, 62, 219–221, 222
  on deflationary theories of truth, 307–308, 319, 332, 348, 352–354
  on ethics and norms, 219–221
  on mental representation, 300, 304
  on physicalism, 223
  on semantically defective discourse and nonfactualism, 303–304
  on semantic paradoxes, 352–354
Fitch, F., 175
  Fitch's paradox of knowability, 175–187
Fodor, J., 53, 62, 71, 252, 253
Folk theories, 321–323
  and conceptual analysis, 321
  Jackson on, 321–322
  and scientific theories, 323
Frege, G., 21, 40, 47–48, 77, 112, 135, 222, 223, 334
  context principle of, 48
  Dummett on, 47–48
  sense–force distinction, 50
  and truth-conditional theory of sense, 48
Friedman, M., 251, 253

Game theory, 289–296
  and evolution of morality, 295–296
  and instrumental rationality, 292–293
  and pragmatist theories of truth, 289–296
Gentzen, G., 149, 150, 156, 158, 167, 169
Gibbard, A., 219, 220, 222
Gödel, K., 229, 230, 238, 272–277, 330, 343
  and second incompleteness theorem, 272–275
Goodman, N. D., 138, 159

Hallett, M., 240
Hand, M., 183–184
Hellman, G.
  on intuitionism, 141, 182–183
  on intuitionism and quantum theory, 142
  on intuitionistic and classical logic, alleged conflict between, 141
  on the meaning of the intuitionistic constants, 141, 183
Heyting, A., 138, 145, 164
Heyting Arithmetic, 274
Heyting clauses, 138–139, 159, 160, 161, 180
  and intuitionism, 138
Holism, 14, 21, 35, 53, 63, 64, 87–98, 111–112, 227, 245
  and bare truths, 71–72
  confirmational, 14
  Davidson's, 93–97
  moderate and immoderate, 97–98
  Quine's, 87–93
  semantic, 64
Holistic theories of meaning, 63, 64, 88–90, 93–94, 145
  Dummett's objections to, 90–93, 94, 145

Horwich, P., 23, 28, 38, 39, 40, 331, 332
 on correspondence theory of truth, 39, 331
 on minimalist theory of truth, 38, 331, 332
Hossack, K., on intuitionism and quantum theory, 142–143
Hume, D., 2, 19–20, 22, 62, 244, 245, 287, 292, 321
 Hume–Kant gambit, 20, 22
 objection to miracles, 19, 287

Internalism
 moderate, 9, 254–257
 new, 253–263
 Peircean, 254
 Putnam's, 190–196, 248, 254
 radical, 255
Internal realism, 190–196
Intuitionism, 271, 274
 and alethic eliminativism, 175–181
 and antirealism, 127–144
 Dummett's advocacy of, 127–128
 and quantum theory, 141–144
Intuitionistic logic, 59, 61, 270, 274
 Heyting's informal semantics for, 120–121, 138–139
 and Kripke trees semantics, 123–127, 267–268
 and method of weak counterexamples, 130–131
 natural deduction formulation of, 121–123
 quantification in, 133–136
 semantics for, 123–127
 and truth-conditional semantics, 181–184
Inversion principle, 150–151

Jackson, F., 216, 219
 on analytic functionalism, 216, 217, 321–324
 and a priori deducibility of all facts from microphysical facts, 216, 321
 on folk theories, 321–323
 on physicalism, 321
 on supervenience, 321, 329, 341–342

Kant, I., 7, 19, 20, 22, 117, 195
 objection to metaphysical realism, 20
Kim, J., 264
Kosslow, A., 156–157
Kreisel, G., 138
Kripke, S., 10
 on epistemic and metaphysical possibility, 330
 Kripke trees and intuitionistic semantics, 267–268
 on semantic eliminativism and Wittgenstein, 248, 249, 296–320
Kroon, F., 338

Leeds, S., 202, 203, 205
Lewis, D., 29, 216, 219, 232, 233, 234, 236, 243, 256, 286–287, 322, 335
Logical constants, 91–92, 231
 classical constructive, 136–138
 classical expressibility of intuitionistic, 136–138, 140–141
 classical understanding of, 133–136
 Dummett on, 136–138
 intuitionistic understanding of, 120–121, 133–136
 Kosslow on, 156–157
 meaning of, 91–92, 139–140, 149–152
 Prawitz on, 163–167, 149–150
 proof-theoretic characterizations of, 131–132, 149–154, 164–167, 168–175
 semantic characterizations of, 157, 163–164, 167–168
Logical consequence, 157–158
Löwenheim–Skolem argument, 239–240
Lynch, M., 214, 215, 216

Mackie, J. L., 323–324
Martin-Löf, P., 152
McDowell, J., 248, 250, 251, 252, 253, 260

antirepresentationalism of, 248, 250, 251, 252, 253
Putnam and, 248, 250, 251, 252, 253
McGinn, C., 105–106
    arguments against Dummett's antirealism, 105–106
Metaethical Pyrrhonism, 296
    and analytic moral functionalism, 324–331
Metaphysical pluralism
    Lynch on, 214, 215, 216
    Putnam's, 214, 217–224
    Sosa's discussion of, 212–214
Model-theoretic arguments, 15, 16, 18, 225–246
    Alston's evaluation of, 283–285
    formulation of, 228–230
    "just more theory" objection to, 232–239
    Lewis's evaluation of, 232
    objections to, 231
    as refutations of realism, 225–226
    as refutations of representationalism, 225–226, 235, 244–246
Mormann, T., 212

Nagel, T., 194
Nominalism, and intuitionism, 142–143
Normal form, 152
Normalization, 152
Nozick, R., 292
Numbers, 30, 31, 107, 117, 118
    intuitionistic conception of, 117–118
    natural, 107, 117, 118
    quantification over sets of, 107
    real, 117, 135, 226, 230

Permutation, 240–244
    and counterparts, 243–244
    and identity, 240–244
    and rigid designators, 241–244
Physicalism, 223–224
Points, and regions, 209–212
Pragmatism
    game theory and, 289–296
    Putnam's, 288
    Rorty's, 281–283, 287–288
Pragmatist theory of truth, 9, 287–296
Prawitz, D., 149, 150, 157, 160, 161, 162, 163–167
Principle of harmony, 152–154
Prior, A., 149–150
Problem of other minds, 98
    as a problem for global antirealism, 98–104
Putnam, H., 1, 6, 15–19, 20, 21, 23, 24, 32, 33
    and brains in a vat argument against realism, 6–7, 196–206
    and the Cartesian conception of mind, 250
    common sense realism, 247–253
    on conceptual norms, 218–224
    on conceptual relativity, 7, 214, 217, 218–224
    Dewey Lectures, 235, 245, 250
    on incoherence of metaphysical realism, 192, 194, 195–196
    internalism and externalism, 189–196, 197
    internal realism, 190, 193, 194, 195, 284
    on logically incompatible equivalent descriptions and realism, 7, 206–224
    on the manifest image, 217, 218, 322
    Meaning and the Moral Sciences, 193
    and the model-theoretic arguments against realism, 1, 7–9, 225–246, 283, 284, 286, 287, 337
    Philosophical Papers, vol. 3: *Realism and Reason*, 195
    Reason, Truth, and History, 191, 194, 195
    against representationalism, 281
    and the representation problem, 195–196, 284, 286
    on truth as correspondence, 192, 195
    on truth and rational acceptability, 190, 191, 195

Quantifiers, 133–136
  classical understanding of, 133, 134
  decidable and undecidable domains for, 133–134
  inhabited domains, 13
  intuitionistic understanding of, 133–136
  Platonism and, 135
Quine, W. V. O., 49, 71, 88–93, 145, 193, 207, 208, 223, 227, 242, 244, 245, 263, 322
  on empirical content, 89–91
  on holism, 88–89, 92
  psychologistic theory of meaning of, 92

Ramsey, F. P., on properties, 264, 344
Read, S., 339, 349
Realism
  constructive empiricism and, 194
  metaphysical realism, 2, 192, 195, 206, 207, 216, 218
    and antirealism, 2, 13–20, 256
    and the antirealist challenge, 15, 17–18
    characterization of, 2–3, 24–25, 59, 194–195
    Dummett's objections to, 19–23, 60, 63–69
    and internalism, 187–189, 192, 195, 222, 255, 257, 258, 259, 260, 262, 263
    and metaphysical determinacy, 14, 59, 187, 194
    naturalistic versions of, 15, 16, 17, 18, 19, 20, 24
    Putnam's objections to, 15–19
  naturalistic realism, 2, 9–10, 17, 18, 88, 93, 187, 188, 189, 197, 199, 222, 224, 260–261, 284, 285, 286–287
    and analytic functionalism, 321–331
    antirealist challenge to, 15
    and representation problem, 15
    and semantic deflationism, 62–63, 245
    and representational theory of mind, 225–226, 235, 244–246
  scientific realism, 3, 31, 193
    distinct from metaphysical realism, 193
    naturalistic realism and, 193
    Putnam's internalism and, 193–194
Recognitional capacities, 17, 38, 40, 57, 106, 110–111, 254, 258
  as determinants of meaning, 38, 40, 106
Reductionism, 98, 266, 294. *See also* Supervenience; Truthmakers
  and analytic functionalism, 321
Reichenbach, H., 207, 208
Representation problem, 4–5, 7–8, 15, 195–196, 245, 253, 281–287
  common sense realism and, 253
  for deflationists, 300
  for internalism, 296–320
  for naturalistic realists, 4–5, 9, 195–196, 260–261, 281–287
  Rorty on, 281–283, 287
Resnick, M., 230, 236, 237, 238, 239
Rorty, R., 17, 31, 42–43
  on antirealism and realism, 17
  antirepresentationalism, 281–283, 333

Salerno, J., 176–180
Semantic competence, 47–58
Semantic minimalism, 227, 228, 230, 245
Semantic paradox, 10, 81, 104, 352–354
Semantics, 117, 121, 131, 158, 245
  intuitionistic, 123–127, 129, 133, 139, 159, 174, 180
  model-theoretic, 231, 232–234
  truth-conditional, 9–10, 181–184, 232–234, 344, 345, 346–348
Simmons, K., 352, 354
Skolem's paradox, 226–227
Soames, S., 297, 299–310
Sosa, E., 212–214
Stalnaker, R., 335
Superassertibility
  and alethic pluralism, 263–266

and intuitionistic assertibility, 267–268
and neutral states of information, 269
and states of perpetual ignorance, 269–272
and states of persistent ignorance, 270
and truth, 266–275
Supervenience, 98, 106–107, 223–224, 299, 304, 305
and reduction, 107, 304
and truthmakers, 326, 327, 329

Tarski, A., 157, 163, 164, 167, 229, 346, 353
Taylor, B., 232–235, 247, 250, 251
Tennant, N., 154, 177
argument for revisionism, 154–155
on Fitch's paradox of knowability, 177
Theory of meaning, 248
atomic, 63, 64
holistic, 53, 63, 64
molecular, 52, 63, 64
and sense, 49
as theoretical representation of a practical ability, 51–52
truth-conditional, 181–184
and use, 49
Truth
alethic eliminativism, 294
and bivalence, 83
classical, 145, 146, 149, 155, 174, 181–184
correspondence theory of truth, 9, 16, 17, 33, 39, 40, 67, 244
and facts, 40, 288
and minimalist theory of truth, 38–41, 245
and semantic paradox, 352–354
and truth-conditions, 16–24, 245, 248, 250, 256, 257
and truthmakers, 17, 67, 288
deflationism about truth, 9,10, 281, 302, 333, 352–354
disquotationalist theory, 307–308
epistemic theories of truth, 253, 254
error theory of realist truth, 75, 85–87, 282, 283
evidence-transcendent truth, 5–6, 33–34, 38, 104–105, 109, 110, 149, 255 (*see also* Undecidability; Recognitional capacities)
and facts, 331–338, 343–351
genesis of realist truth, 82–83
intuitionistic, 117, 133, 145, 148, 149, 154–155, 174
on an intended interpretation, 232–235, 286
many-valued truth-tables, 123, 124, 125
at a node, 83–85, 127
pluralism about, 263–266
pragmatist theory of truth, 286–296, 333
and quantification, 135–136
and semantic paradox, 352–354
Tarskian, 163, 229, 236, 237
and tense, 83–86
and validity, 119–120, 157
Truthmakers, 13, 17, 40, 67, 68, 216, 281, 306, 307, 318, 326
and the correspondence theory of truth, 287, 288, 299, 301, 305, 333, 335
and physicalism, 223
truthmaker theory, 40, 338–343
truthmaking and entailment, 321, 328, 329

Undecidability, 14, 59, 60, 179, 255, 256
examples, 13, 59
formulation of Dummett's notion of, 14, 59–60

van Fraassen, B., 193
Verificationism, 35–37, 38, 41, 90, 175, 176
Dummett's model of, 35

Wagner, S., 225, 238
Weinberg, S., 143–144
Whitehead, A. N., 210

Wiles, A., 147–148
Williams, B., 194, 223, 288
Wittgenstein, L., 10, 50, 76, 77, 99, 100, 101, 102, 127, 221, 222, 247, 296, 298
  internalism and, 296–320
  Kripke's interpretation of, 10, 248, 249, 296–320
  semantic eliminativism and, 248, 249, 296–320
Wright, C., 26–29, 58, 98–99, 129, 191, 253–275, 310, 311

Yablo, S., 334, 335

www.ingramcontent.com/pod-product-compliance
Lightning Source LLC
Chambersburg PA
CBHW070747230426

43665CB00017B/2282